Alliance and Conflict

Alliance and Conflict

The World System of the Iñupiaq Eskimos

ERNEST S. BURCH JR.

UNIVERSITY OF NEBRASKA PRESS
LINCOLN & LONDON

∞

Library of Congress
Control Number: 2005925768
ISBN 0-8032-1346-8 (cl. : alk. paper)
ISBN 0-8032-6238-8 (pbk. : alk. paper)

Set in Quadraat by
Keystone Typesetting, Inc.
Designed by R. W. Boeche.
Printed by Edwards Brothers, Inc.

This book is dedicated to the memory of
Bob Tuvaaqsraq Hawley,
one of the best friends I ever had.

Contents

Illustrations

Figures

Maps

Plates

Tables

Preface

This volume draws on research I have carried out from time to time since the autumn of 1960 and, more particularly, on research undertaken since the fall of 1969. It has involved a total of more than three years of fieldwork and too many weeks in archives and libraries to count. Some of the subjects discussed here have been dealt with in previous publications, all of which should be considered out of date as of the moment of this book's appearance. Specifically included in the outdated category are the following: Burch 1970a, 1974, 1975b, 1976, 1979, and 1998c and Burch and Correll 1972.

Over the more than four decades I have been involved in this project I have been aided by a great many individuals and organizations. While I can never adequately acknowledge or repay their help, I can at least record it here.

First, I wish to thank the Native historians who taught me most of what I know about the subject matter of this volume. Most are Iñupiaq Eskimos, a few are Koyukon Athapaskans. The following list includes both their English names and their names in their own language. The dates in parentheses are the years in which they are known or thought to have been born: David Iñuqtaq Adams (1907), Effie Taapsuk Atoruk (1902), Peter Aaquuraq Atoruk (1903), Catherine Nodoyedee'onh Attla (1927), Steven Denaa'ek'oogheełtune' Attla (1924), Walter Mannik Ballott (1900), Emily Qimmikpiauraq Barr (1889), Mark Uluatchiaq Cleveland (1911), Robert Nasruk Cleveland (1884), Isaak Irauraq Coffin (1884), Mary Aullaqsruaq Curtis (1889), Samuel Pulaġun Dives (1912), Tommy Paaniikaliaq Douglas (1905), John Ivaak Evok (1910), Daniel Kunaŋnaaluk Foster (1881), Johnnie Tuuyuq Foster (1903), David Umigluk Frankson (1903), Lester Qaluraq Gallahorn (1890?), Frank Kutvak Glover (1886), Amos Apuġiña Hawley (1913), Edna Iragauraq Hunnicutt (1880), Elwood Uyaana Hunnicutt (1904), Charlie Saġġaaluraq Jensen (1893), Lucy Ayagiaq Jensen (1897), Eliza Neełteloyeenełno Jones (1938), Mamie Ataŋan Karmun (1914), Della Puyuk Keats (1907), Walter Sigliuna Kowunna (1910), Charlie Qiñugana Lee (1901), Albert Nalikkałuk McClellan (1901), Kenneth Aqukkasuk Mills (1908), Levi Alasuk Mills Sr. (1903), Thomas Uqsruġaaluk Mitchell (1904), Thomas Aniqsuaq Morris (1904), Simon Panniaq Paneak

(1900), James Putuuqti Savok Sr. (1911), Charlie Nalikkałuk Smith (1898), John Pamiiqtaq Stalker (1910), Joe Immałuuraq Sun (1900), Martha Nunamiu Swan (1907), Milton Niaqualuk Swan (1904), Herman Aumaałuuraq Tickett (1901), Leonard Putuuraq Vestal (1892), Susie Helohoołtunh Williams (1905), and John Qaniqsiruaq Wright (1885). I am enormously grateful to these people, almost all of whom are now deceased, for their help.

Not all of the people in the above list are specifically cited in this book, but most of them are. Citing individual informants at all departs from the usual anthropological approach, which is merely to make a general reference to one's field notes or to make some other similarly vague attribution. I have adopted a different procedure for three reasons. First, it is just as customary among Iñupiaq historians as it is among Western academics to acknowledge explicitly the sources of their information, so in citing individual sources I am following their custom as well as ours. Second, knowing that the above individuals were my sources should help establish my credentials at least in Alaska Native eyes as a person qualified to write this book. Third, by noting not only the names of my sources but the dates and places of the interviews I hope to assist researchers who may examine my field notes at some future date.

Most of my interviews with Native historians were tape-recorded. Both the tapes and the transcripts thereof are preserved in my personal papers and eventually will be deposited in an archive to which the general public will have access.

Most of my sources were compensated in cash or in kind for the time they gave to my education. I did not request releases from them because, at the time I conducted most of the interviews, it was not customary to do so, and, under the circumstances, I did not think it was necessary. Given the context in which my sources provided information, there could have been no doubt in their minds that I would someday share the information with others, possibly for a consideration. Indeed, some of them asked how much money I expected to make from publishing their stories. When I told them, they expressed disbelief; who would do so much work for such a small return?

Different segments of the research were supported financially by the Department of Anthropology, University of Chicago; the Department of Biological Sciences, University of Alaska; the Alaska Historical Commission; NANA Museum of the Arctic; the U.S. National Park Service; the U.S. Minerals Management Service; the Division of Subsistence of the Alaska Department of Fish and Game; and the Canada Council (now the Social Sciences and Humanities Research Council of Canada). I am grateful to NANA Museum of the Arctic and the U.S. National Park Service for help in covering the cost of preparing the material for publication.

Practical support in the field was provided by Mamie Beaver and Dave and Mabel Johnson in Kotzebue; Arthur Douglas Sr. in Ambler; Jessie and Paul Hadley and Annie and James Savok Sr. in Buckland; Louise and Amos Hawley Sr. and Sarah and Bob Hawley Sr. in Kivalina; Elsie Hunnicutt in Kiana; Marie and Chris Jones and Frank Kialook in Deering; Emma and Ralph Ramoth in Selawik; Joe Sampson in Noorvik; and Clara and John Stalker in both Shungnak and Noatak. Douglas Anderson and John Bockstoce provided me with information and contacts that helped make my fieldwork much more productive than it otherwise might have been.

Help in acquiring financial and other support was provided by Tim Cochrane, Charlie Curtis, Linda Ellanna, Suzy Erlich, Robert Gal, Sophie Johnson, Sharon Moore, John Schaeffer, Phyllis Short, Kevin Waring, Robert Weiser, Kari Westlund, and Martha Whiting.

In the preparation of this volume for publication I received assistance of various kinds from Katherine Arndt, Knut Bergsland, Robert Drozda, Matthew Ganley, Eliza Jones, Igor Krupnik, Gretchen Lake, David Libbey, Hannah Loon, James Nageak, Kenneth Pratt, Adeline Peter Raboff, Jonas Ramoth, Ruthie Ramoth-Sampson, Robyn Russell, Grant Spearman, Marietta Spencer, Rose Speranza, Nikolay Vakhtin, and Katerina Soloviova Wessels. Thomas C. Correll helped stimulate my early thinking on many of the subjects discussed here, and Lawrence Kaplan kept me from going astray in my rendition of many Native terms. I am also grateful to Terje Birkedal, John Bockstoce, Tim Cochrane, Leland Donald, Richard Erlich, Ann Fienup-Riordan, Robert Gal, Thomas Hall, Nick Jans, Deanna Kingston, Steve Klingler, Igor Krupnik, Charles Lucier, Peter Schweitzer, and Joseph Sonnenfeld for helpful comments on earlier versions of the book. Lucier's set of comments contained so much new information, based on his own extensive research in Northwest Alaska, that it is cited here as a separate source (Lucier 1997); it is included in my personal papers. The maps were prepared by Robert McLaughlin. Lois Myers provided enormous help over many years with research assistance, editing, and many other aspects of researching and writing this book.

Iñupiaq Eskimo Orthography, Malimiut Dialect

This is the standard writing system used by Alaskan Iñupiat and by the Alaska Native Language Center (ANLC), University of Alaska, Fairbanks. All Native terms appearing in this volume are written either in this orthography or in the ANLC orthographies for Yup'ik (Eskimo) or Koyukon (Athapaskan).

Consonants

	Labials	Alveolars	Palatals	Velars	Uvulars	Glottals
Stops	p	t	ch	k	q	'
Voiceless fricatives		s		kh	qh	h
Voiced fricatives	v		y	g	ġ	
Voiceless laterals		ł	ł̣			
Voiced laterals		l	ḷ			
Nasals	m	n	ñ	ŋ		
Voiceless retroflex		sr				
Voiced retroflex		r				

Vowels

	Front	Back
High	i	u
Low	a	

1. Introduction

The rise of what is known as "world system" (or "world-system") theory has been one of the most interesting developments in the social sciences over the past generation. The process began in the 1970s as a socialist critique of modern capitalism (Wallerstein 1974a) but soon expanded into an effort to understand how and why industrialized societies came into being in the first place (Wallerstein 1974b). Since then, world historians and world system theorists have extended their investigations back through time to the beginnings of agriculture (Frank and Gills 1993, 2000). In the process they have achieved new insights into how the world worked during a number of specific time periods and also of how it evolved to its present condition. One result of all this scholarship is that "there are so many variations in world systems analysis, that it is no longer appropriate to refer to it as a theory. It is better called a perspective" (Hall 1999:2; see also Goldfrank 2000:152; Peregrine 1996:1–2; Shannon 1996).

The world system perspective involves the study of international affairs on extremely broad geographic and temporal levels. It should provide us with the comparative and evolutionary frameworks needed to understand international affairs at continental and worldwide scales during different eras and over extended periods of time. In fact, world system analysis has fallen short of this goal. I am invariably impressed by the erudition exhibited in the work of world historians and world systems scholars, but I am usually also appalled by their ethnocentrism. (There are a few exceptions, however; see, e.g., Chase-Dunn and Hall 1997; Chase-Dunn and Mann 1998.) Any nation to which the label "great civilization" cannot reasonably be applied seems to be unworthy of their attention.

Nations that were not part of "great civilizations" have also been involved in the world system, and not always on the periphery of a dominant power. Human societies have rarely, if ever, existed in complete isolation from one another (see Headland and Reid 1989; Lesser 1961; McNeil 1993:xii; Terrell 1998). Those that did become isolated had to reconnect before more than a few generations passed or they became extinct. Even when the world was occupied entirely by hunter-gatherers, the members of the overwhelming majority of societies had neighbors with whom they had to deal in one way or another. In poor environments, where the human population was sparse, intersocietal contacts may have been infrequent and ad hoc in character, but they still took place. In most parts of the world, most of the time, intersocietal contacts had to have been both regular in occurrence and structured in conduct, whether or not they were peaceful.[1]

The members of each small-scale society had relations with their immediate neighbors. The neighbors, in turn, had contacts with their neighbors, who had to deal with their neighbors, and so on—all the way around the inhabited world (Lenski, Lenski, and Nolan 1991:44). In this sense, which admittedly is much broader than the originator of the phrase had in mind, there has been a world (social) system ever since humans first appeared on the face of the earth.[2] Most of the so-called world systems written about by others are or have been subsystems of this larger, world-encompassing network of international relations (about which more in Chapter 4). In order that we not lose sight of this fact—indeed, in order that we *emphasize* this fact—I believe it is this larger unit to which the label "world system" should be applied.[3]

What is different about the world system today is that it is vastly more *centralized* than it ever was before. Never before have events in one part of the world had as much impact on affairs in so many other parts of the world as they do now.[4] But the processes through which this situation developed—confrontation, negotiation, domination, alliance formation, intimidation, rivalry, intrigue, exploitation, trade, physical violence—have characterized international affairs at least since Middle Paleolithic times.

What was the world system like when populated entirely by hunter-gatherers? With only one exception that I am aware of (about which more in Chapter 4), world system theorists have failed to address this question. But it is also true that they would have had rather little evidence to work with if they had attempted to do so. Archaeological data are of some help, but ethnographic information is essential so that archaeologists have empirically grounded models to work with. Unfortunately, by the time they were first described, most of the small-scale societies in the ethnographic record were so disrupted by Western influence as to be all but useless for this type of investigation. Fortunately, there are some exceptions. I describe one of them in this book.

The region to be dealt with here is Northwest Alaska, where a number of very small scale societies of Eskimo-speaking hunter-gatherers continued to function along precontact lines for several generations after the first Westerners arrived in the area. Thanks to a number of fortunate circumstances attending contact, it has been possible to ascertain through a combination of documentary and oral sources at least the general outlines of how international affairs were conducted in this still-decentralized sector of the early-19th-century world system.

The emphasis in most of the book is descriptive. This chapter discusses some conceptual and methodological issues, but most of it is devoted to the presentation of an overview of the study region and the nations operating within and near it during the period of interest. In the second and third chapters I describe in some detail the kinds of hostile and friendly relations, respectively, that existed between and among those nations. In the final chapter, after reviewing the material discussed in Chapters 1 through 3, I return to the concept of world system. I suggest that the sector of it that I have described probably approximates in a number of respects the type of system that existed over much of the world in ancient times. Using that conclusion as an assumption, I then present a series of hypotheses concerning what the world system was like when it consisted entirely of hunter-gatherer societies and of how it evolved into a more complex system with the advent of chiefdoms.

The Iñupiaq Eskimos

The people of primary concern in this volume are the Iñupiaq Eskimos living in the sector of northwestern Alaska bordering Kotzebue Sound (see Map 1). These people spoke one or another form of Iñupiatun, a group of dialects in the Inuit Eskimo language. The particular period of interest is the early 19th century, around the time of the first Western contact. (At that time there were at least six Eskimo languages, one of which was Inuit.) During that era the Iñupiat (pl.) were organized into socioterritorial units of the type that have been variously referred to in the anthropological literature as "tribes" (Ray 1967, 1975b), "regional groups" (Burch and Correll 1972), "band nexuses" (Cashdan 1983:53; Heinz 1972, 1979; Wiessner 1983:255), "band clusters" (Barnard 1992:65–67, 138–139), and "societies" (Burch 1975a, 1980). I think that "society," at least as defined by Levy (1966:20–21 n. 10), is the most useful of these concepts for comparative purposes. However, the Iñupiaq elders who taught me about the system in which their grandparents were raised referred to a society as *nunaqatigiitch* in their own language and as a "nation" in English. Accordingly, "nation" and "society" are employed as equivalent concepts in the present study (see Burch 1998a).

"Nation" is an appropriate word to characterize these units because they were analogous to most countries, or nations, in the modern world. Like most modern nations, those of early-19th-century northern Alaska held dominion over separate territories, their citizens thought of themselves as being separate peoples, and they engaged one another in war and in trade. However, they

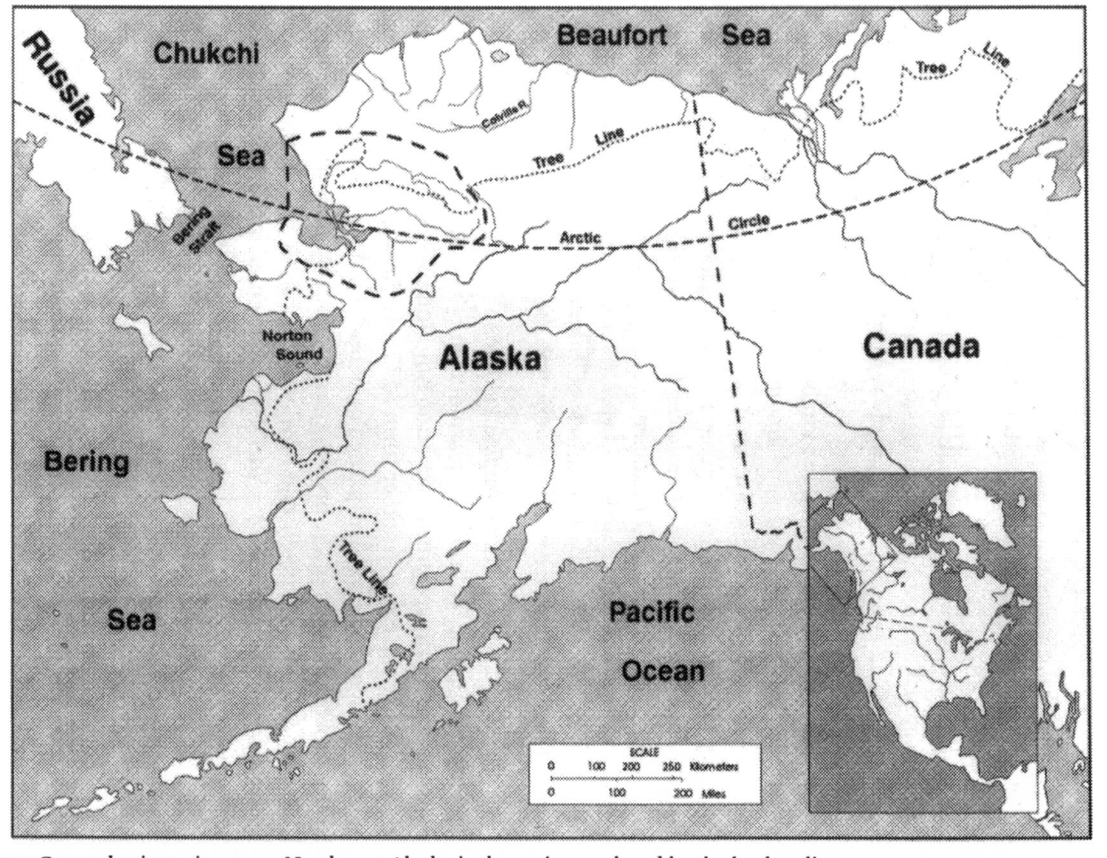

1. General orientation map. Northwest Alaska is the region enclosed by the broken line.

were tiny in comparison to modern nations, rarely involving more than a few hundred people. They were comprised of closely interrelated but otherwise highly self-sufficient families, and they lacked governments and most of the other organizational trappings of nations as most of us have come to understand them.

Relations between and among the nations of early contact northwestern Alaska were interesting and complex. On the one hand, there were hostile relations that, in their most extreme form, exhibited the most appalling brutality. On the other hand, there were friendly relations that, in their most extreme form, rivaled in peacefulness and stability the most successful international alliances known to us today.

Nations

The Iñupiat inhabiting Northwest Alaska were organized in terms of ten nations at the beginning and during most of the first half of the 19th century.[5] They are listed in Table 1, and their borders are shown on Map 2 as they seem to have been around AD 1800.

The Iñupiaq nations of Northwest Alaska were hunter-gatherer societies of intermediate complexity. They were more complex than the "immediate return" societies that have been the focus of much anthropological attention since the mid-1960s (e.g., Testart 1982; Woodburn 1980:99ff., 1982) but less complex than most of the hunter-gatherer nations whose territories were distributed around the North Pacific rim (Fitzhugh and Chaussonnet 1994; Koyama and Thomas 1981; Price and Brown 1985).

Iñupiaq nations were segmental in structure. "Segmental" nations were defined by Service as being those "composed of equal and similar component groups (normally kin groups like clans or lineages)" (1975:70; see also Sahlins 1963:287). In this case the segments were units of the sort that have been labeled "hordes" by Howitt and Fison (1885), "local bands" by Helm (1965, 1968), "hunting groups" by Rogers (1965:266, 1969:46), and "camps" by Lee (1972a:350–356). Such a unit is a spatial grouping of kinsmen, characteristically structured around a core of adult brothers and/or sisters, their spouses, and their children (Helm 1968:121).

The "segments" comprising a traditional Iñupiaq nation met the criteria of most cross-cultural definitions of "family." I think it is more useful for comparative purposes to think of them as a type of family than as a type of band or as a local group. In another book I called them "local families" because of the characteristic geographic distribution of their members (Burch 1975a:237; for examples see Burch 1975a:254–274), and that is the label I use for them here.[6] In the study region local families normally ranged in size between about 6 and 40 members.

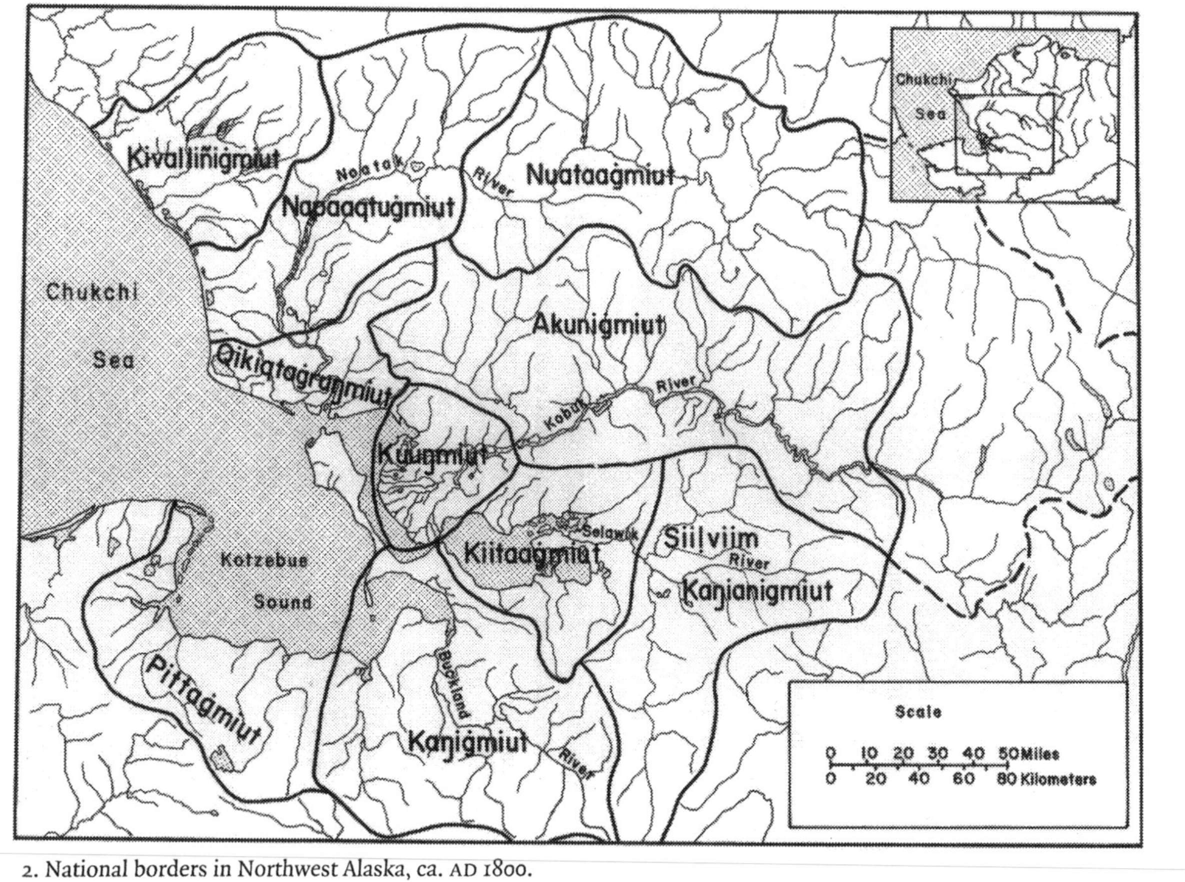

2. National borders in Northwest Alaska, ca. AD 1800.

Table 1. The Iñupiaq Nations of Northwest Alaska, ca. 1800

Nation	District	Estimated population	Estimated estate
Akuniġmiut	Central Kobuk	700	5,900 sq. mi. (15,340 sq km)
Kaŋiġmiut	Buckland River	300	4,680 sq. mi. (12,170 sq km)
Kiitaaġmiut	Lower Selawik	700	1,860 sq. mi. (4,835 sq km)
Kivalliñiġmiut	Kivalina	365	2,180 sq. mi. (5,670 sq km)
Kuuŋmiut	Kobuk River delta	415	840 sq. mi. (2,185 sq km)
Napaaqtuġmiut	Lower Noatak	300	4,015 sq. mi. (10,440 sq km)
Nuataaġmiut	Upper Noatak	535	5,720 sq. mi. (14,870 sq km)
Pittaġmiut	Goodhope	430	2,725 sq. mi. (7,085 sq km)
Qikiqtaġruŋmiut	Kotzebue	390	2,000 sq. mi. (5,200 sq km)
Siiḷviim Kaŋianig.miut	Upper Selawik	570	3,175 sq. mi. (8,225 sq km)

Source: Burch 1998a.

Most settlements were occupied by the members of just a single local family. Larger settlements were occupied by two or more such families. Dorothy Jean Ray has challenged the notion that "the local group [i.e., settlement or village] was a kinship group, pure and simple" (1967:374). My response to that is, if a family is a type of kinship group, which in my usage it is, then the great majority of settlements in the study region were indeed inhabited by members of kinship groups, pure and simple. This was not strictly true in the largest settlements, but even they were little more than aggregations of several kinship units, that is, local families. Socially, in the larger village context the members of each local family tended to form a faction, while spatially their houses usually constituted a neighborhood.

The several local families constituting the basic segments of an Iñupiaq nation were connected to one another primarily by the same array of kinship ties as those linking individuals within them. The difference is that the kinship ties linking individuals in different settlements were weaker than those existing within the same settlement. At the national level kinship ties were augmented by namesake relationships, friendships, and other connections that need not be elaborated on here. At the most general level the members of a nation were united by the dominion they exercised collectively over a particular district and by their sense of national cohesiveness and pride.

The Setting

"Northwest Alaska," as opposed to "northwestern Alaska," is defined as the region encompassing the coastline of Alaska between Cape Thompson on the north and Cape Espenberg on the south and the inland districts drained by rivers reaching the sea between those two points. It also includes the waters and floors of Kotzebue Sound and the Chukchi Sea east of a line drawn

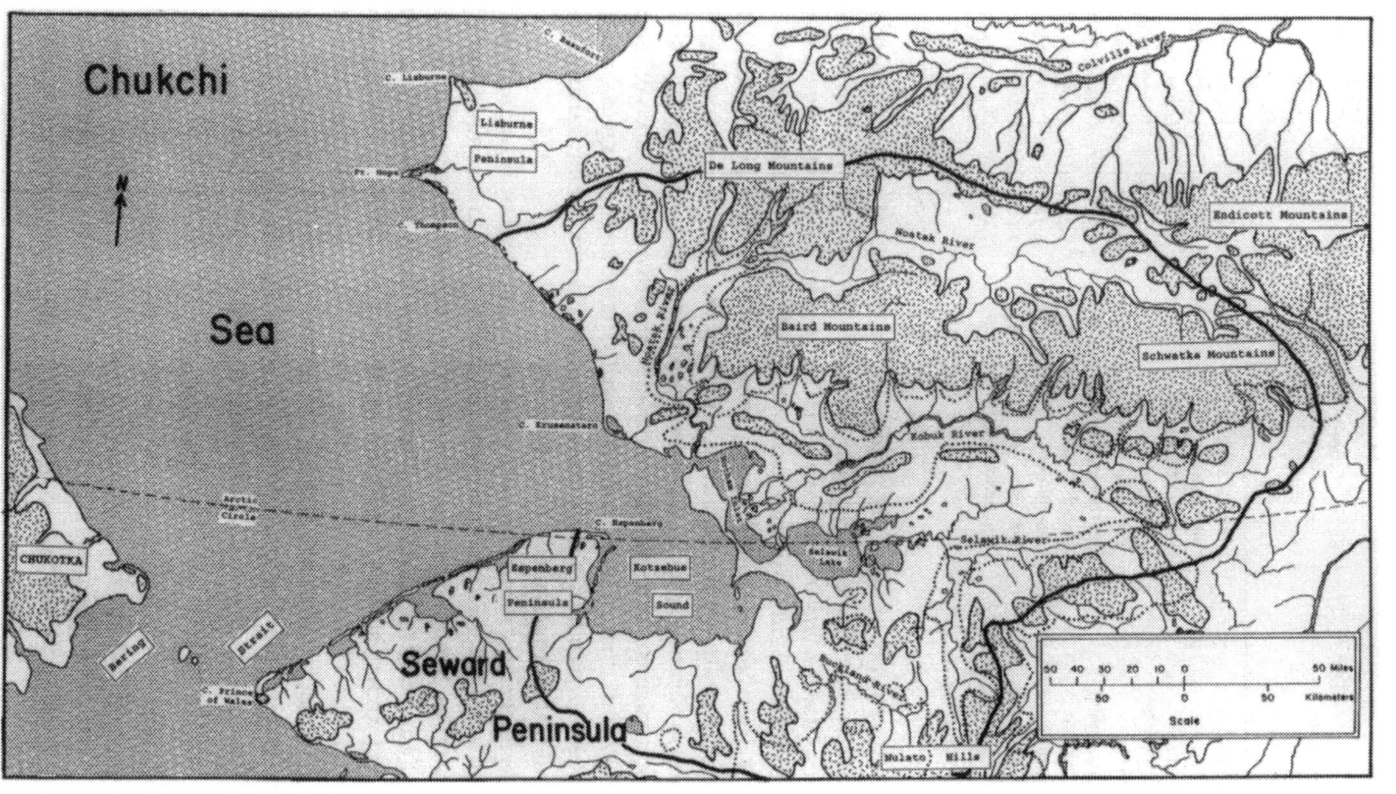

3. Major topographic features of Northwest Alaska.

between those two points (see Map 3). This area nearly coincides with what is now known as the NANA Region, as defined under the Alaska Native Claims Settlement Act (ANCSA). For reasons explained later in this chapter, I usually refer to it henceforth in this book as the NANA Region rather than as Northwest Alaska.

Geographic Setting

The NANA Region encompasses an area of approximately 40,000 square miles (104,000 square kilometers), which makes it slightly larger than South Korea. It is located roughly between 154° and 166° W and 65°30′ and 68°30′ N. The Arctic Circle crosses the region just south of its center. The region's far northern location results in marked seasonal differences in the amount of daylight it receives: there is almost no darkness in June and very little sunlight in December.

The NANA Region has a varied topography that includes broad level plains, rolling hills, and rugged mountains ranging up to nearly 8,800 feet (2,680 meters) in altitude. In the early 19th century the region had an Arctic desert climate, with long, cold winters and short, cool summers.[7] Temperature extremes were nearly +100 to −75°F (+38 to −60°C) in the interior and +85 to −50°F (+30 to −46°C) on the coast. Freshwater was usually frozen from early to mid-October ("freeze-up") until sometime in May ("breakup"). Freeze-up on the ocean usually took place between late November and late December, while breakup there usually came in June. Until very recently, average annual precipitation was about 8–9 inches (20–23 centimeters), most of which fell as rain in late summer. The countryside was usually snow covered from mid-October through May, although snow could fall at any time of year.

The latitudinal tree line meanders across the region from northeast to southwest. Tundra vegetation (lichens, mosses, grasses, sedges) predominates in all districts, although woody shrubs occur in suitable habitat along the waterways and in sheltered areas. The Buckland, Kobuk, lower Noatak, and Selawik Rivers have spruce and other boreal forest trees growing along their banks and along the sides of the adjacent valley floors. Harvestable plants include berries, greens, roots, mosses, shrubs (willow, alder, cottonwood) with edible or otherwise useful leaves, bark, and wood, and trees (especially spruce and birch). Driftwood, originating primarily in regions farther south, was formerly abundant along the coast.

During the early 19th century the Native inhabitants of the NANA Region had hunting-gathering economies based on resources that were relatively rich and varied for a region so far north.[8] Big game included caribou, mountain sheep, and grizzly, black, and polar bears.[9] Furbearers, many of which were harvested for food as well as for pelts, included the arctic and red fox, wolf, lynx, wolverine, river otter, marten, ermine, least weasel, mink, beaver, muskrat, marmot, and arctic ground squirrel. Other terrestrial mammals included hares, porcupines, and possibly a small musk ox population. The nearby waters of the Chukchi Sea were home to a variety of sea mammals, particularly bearded, ringed, and spotted seals and belugas (white whales). Much less common but occasionally present in the outer reaches of Kotzebue Sound and the southeastern Chukchi Sea were bowhead and gray whales and walrus. Anadromous fish included five species of salmon, five species of whitefish, smelt, and Dolly Varden char. Freshwater fish included northern pike, burbot, lake trout, arctic char, grayling, and Alaska blackfish. Sculpin, herring, and arctic and saffron cod were the saltwater fish most important to the Iñupiat. Sea cliff nesting birds, migratory waterfowl (ducks, geese, swans, cranes), gulls, and ptarmigan were the most important birds in the Native economy. In addition, there were a variety of shorebirds, birds of prey, and passerine birds.

Three general characteristics of the resource base are particularly important in understanding traditional Native life in the region. The first is that, while plant resources were harvested and filled important niches in the economies of each of the several nations in the region, they could not even come close to supporting a human population in any of them. Like other Arctic peoples, the Iñupiat of the NANA Region were, and had to be, hunters and fishermen. Second, the relative abundance of the different resource animal and plant species varied from one nation's territory to another. Third, all of the sea mammals and caribou and most of the fish and bird species found in the region are and were seasonally migratory. Caribou and some of the other terrestrial mammals are also subject to major long-term fluctuations in numbers. The animal resource populations on which the Iñupiat depended, in short, were highly variable geographically, seasonally, and over the longer term.

Temporal Setting

The period of interest in this study is the early 19th century or, more precisely, the period 1800–1848. This period was chosen because it is the earliest for which both the documentary evidence produced by Westerners and the oral accounts of Iñupiaq historians can be reasonably applied.

Just when the first humans arrived in northwestern Alaska is unknown, but the earliest evidence of human occupation dates from between 10,000 and 12,000 years ago (Dumond 2001; Kunz and Reanier 1994; Reanier 1995:37–38). People have been living there more or less continuously ever since, although there has been a considerable ebb and flow of peoples of different cultural heritages over time.

Cultures that can be linked directly to early contact Eskimo and Athapaskan societies date from at least 1,250 years ago and probably from another millennium or more before that. (For the Athapaskan interior see D. Clark 1981; for the NANA Region see Anderson 1984, updated by Gal 1997; for Chukotka see Ackerman 1984.) The situation was not static during this long period, but there was a high level of continuity between its beginning and the period of interest here (Anderson 1970; Burch 1979, 1998a, 1998b; Burch et al. 1999; Burch and Mishler 1995; Gerlach and Hall 1988; Gerlach and Mason 1992; Giddings 1952:118, 1965; Hall 1970, 1975a, 1984; Jenness 1928:74, 78; Krauss 1993; Krupnik 1983, 1994; Kunz 1977, 1991:99–100; Mason 2003:225–238). Both the hostile and the peaceful international relations described in this volume had ancient roots (Ackerman 1962:27; Bandi 1995; Collins 1934:2827; Jenness 1928:74, 78; Mason 1998:273, 281, 296, 2003:227, 231).

If the inception date of this study, 1800, was chosen arbitrarily, the same cannot be said of the termination date, 1848. In 1848 American whaling ships and trading vessels began to venture into northern Alaskan waters, their numbers increasing dramatically over the next few years (Bockstoce 1986). Also in 1848 several vessels of the British Royal Navy entered the region to search for the lost exploring expedition of Sir John Franklin, something they repeated for several years in succession (Bockstoce 1985). A Royal Navy ship overwintered near the head of Kotzebue Sound in 1849–50 and just a short distance south of the study region in both 1850–51 and 1851–52. The first epidemic of infectious disease struck in 1850–51.[10] These developments contributed to a dramatic change in the nature of international affairs in northwestern Alaska.

National Boundaries

In his book *Europe and the People without History* Eric Wolf states that "treating named entities such as Iroquois, Greece, Persia, or the United States as fixed entities opposed to one another by stable internal architecture and external boundaries interferes with our ability to understand their mutual encounter and confrontation. In fact, this tendency has made it difficult to understand all such encounters and confrontations" (1982:7). He is right, but whoever said that we have to treat nations as fixed entities? Stability is a variable, not a constant. Complete stability, in the sense of never changing, cannot exist in the real world. The internal architecture and external boundaries of a nation can last for centuries in some cases (e.g., imperial China) but for only a few generations in others (e.g., the Soviet Union).

Since Wolf's book appeared it has become fashionable to deny that national boundaries even exist. Summarizing this trend, Martin Lewis has stated that "humankind is simply not divisible into one-dimensional social entities that fit neatly into geographical space" (1991:605). I beg to differ.

Early in the summer of 1960 I was wandering around West Germany, alternately walking and hitchhiking from Frankfurt to Kiel to attend a German language school for foreigners. One day I took a wrong turn and unexpectedly found myself at the border between West and East Germany. It was marked by two high, parallel, barbed-wire fences; I cannot recall whether they were electrified or not. Between them was a wide space of barren ground that had been ploughed, disked, and harrowed practically to the consistency of powder. At intervals along the opposite side of the border were towers occupied by men with machine guns, so situated that they had interlocking fields of fire. I submit that anyone who claims that what I saw did not signify the existence of a boundary of some kind has a very serious perceptual problem.

Critics might contend that the border between East and West Germany lasted for less than half a century, which is only a moment in the broad sweep of history. They might further note that the people on both sides of the border spoke the same language and shared common historical, cultural, and often even family ties, and that if it were not for World War II and the Soviet occupation of the region, the border would not have been there. A few people actually crossed it without getting shot, blown up, or electrocuted. These points would be correct. But World War II *did* happen, East Germany *was* occupied, and most of the people who tried to cross the border without permission *were* killed. During the 45-year existence of the two Germanys, the boundary between them directly affected the lives of millions of people and indirectly affected the lives of practically everyone on the face of the earth. To claim that this boundary was a figment of someone's imagination is an exercise in self-delusion.

Another boundary serves as a useful contrast, this being the one between the United States and Canada. This boundary is manifested by a border 5,527 miles (8,893 kilometers) long. Commonly referred to as the longest undefended border in the world, it has been beautifully depicted in a volume titled *Between Friends/Entre amis*, which was presented by the Government of Canada to the people of the United States to commemorate the bicentennial of American independence (National Film Board of Canada 1976). In the book's many photographs the border between the two countries can be seen, if at all, as merely a narrow strip of treeless land through the forest.

A U.S. citizen and a member of U.S. society, I have crossed the U.S.–Canada border hundreds of times. I married a Canadian, and I was a legal resident of Canada for eight years. In 1998 Canadians, who numbered just over 30 million people at the time, made 31.9 million day trips to the United States (down from 60 million in 1991), while Americans made 43.9 million visits to Canada (Meredith 1999:11). But when these millions of people crossed the border legally they did so at designated crossing points, places where they were (or were liable to be) subjected to the scrutiny of immigration and customs officials. Persons crossing the border illegally in either direction were subject to incarceration and/or deportation if apprehended. Canadians visiting or living in the United States have rights, privileges, and obligations different from those of U.S. citizens visiting or living in the United States. Similarly, U.S. citizens visiting or living in Canada are subject to many rules different from those to which Canadians who live there are subject. The reason all these things are so is because the United States and Canada are two different nations. This means that there is a boundary between them. It has been there for more than 200 years.

Those who claim that social boundaries do not exist are making at least as serious a mistake as those who treat them as inviolate fixtures. Boundaries do exist, and for many purposes of both social analysis and everyday life they must be taken into account. But as the examples just discussed indicate, there is a considerable range of variation among them with respect to both magnitude and duration. The boundary between West and East Germany was much more profound than the one between the United States and Canada despite the fact that it existed for a much shorter period of time. Why should we expect the boundaries of hunter-gatherer nations to be any less variable than those of modern nation-states?

Historical Interlude

In one way or another this entire book is about national boundaries, primarily but not exclusively as they existed in the NANA Region during the first half of the 19th century. A useful way to introduce the topic is by taking the reader on a brief trip back to that time, specifically, to 1838.

In the summer of 1838 a small party of Russians led by A. F. Kashevarov explored the coast of northwestern Alaska between Chamisso Island and Point Barrow. Traveling by kayak and *umiaq* (pl. *umiat*), a type of large, open, skin boat, instead of the usual European-style ship, the party was apparently considered by the Iñupiat to be a group of Natives and was treated accordingly—usually this meant with considerable hostility. In addition to employing essentially a Native mode of travel, Kashevarov had with him an Eskimo interpreter from Norton Sound named Utuktak who apparently spoke Central Alaskan Yup'ik, Iñupiatun, and Russian. Through him, Kashevarov was able to communicate with the people he met more effectively than had any other Westerner before midcentury.

Kashevarov's party was carried by the Russian ship *Polyphem* to Cape Lisburne, about 50 miles (80 kilometers) north of the primary region of concern in this book but well within the Iñupiaq language area of northwestern Alaska. On July 5 the explorers set out from the ship to explore the coast toward the north. From there I mostly let Kashevarov speak for himself. The text is taken from his journal, as translated into English by David H. Kraus and edited by James W. VanStone (VanStone 1977). More up-to-date renderings of Iñupiaq terms, where known, are placed in brackets.

July 5: [At Cape Lisburne] we were met by savages (20 persons of both sexes with two children and two baydaras [umiat]) who call themselves Tykagmiuts [Tikiġaġmiut]. Their winter settlement is on Point Hope. [VanStone 1977:20]

July 13: At 1:00 we set out again. At 2:30 we put in at a native summer camp consisting of 30 tents. It belongs to the Utukagmiuts [Utuqqaġmiut], whose winter quarters are in the tundra, whence they came down the river that flows into Long Lake to the N of the summer camp, a three day journey. [VanStone 1977:25]

July 14: At 10:00 we set out, moving from the lake into the sea. At 11:00, on passing a sizeable village, we put into shore to calm the frightened inhabitants. The settlement, called Kayakishgvigmiut [Qayaiqsiġviŋmiut], lies on the north side of Icy Cape, from which the coast runs east. The settlement has about 300 inhabitants; they are well built and appear to be healthy; they belong to the Silalinagmiut [Siḷaliñaġmiut] tribe, which begins at this settlement and continues northward along the coast[.] . . . The Kayakishgvigmiuts were friendly; they warned us of the next people, the Kakligmiuts, describing them as evil. [VanStone 1977:26][11]

July 16: At 5:00 we stopped at a settlement situated on a steep bank rising to 20 ft. [6 meters] above the sea. The settlement is called Kalymatagmiut [Qiḷamittaġvigmiut]; it has 25 inhabitants who belong to the Silalinagmiut tribe. In error, they took us for their enemies the Kakligmiuts, but we placated them by giving each person a leaf of tobacco. [VanStone 1977:27]

At 7:00 two native baydaras with 28 men belonging to the Silalinagmiut tribe came to us from the summer camp Tutulivigmiut [Tuttulivigmiut]. The newly arrived savages proved to be bold and strongly inclined to thievery. They live here only in summer; their winter camp is to the north of us and is called Kullyulik; it is the last Silalinagmiut settlement; beyond begins the Kakligmiut tribe. [VanStone 1977:27][12]

July 17: At 6:00 we passed Point Belcher, on which is the first settlement to the N, Atanyk [Ataniq], occupied by a people belonging to the Kakligmiut tribe (which begins at this settlement and continues northward). . . . The inhabitants of Atanik, taking us for their enemies, the Tykagmiuts [of Point Hope], met us with weapons in hand, bows and arrows, but after we had explained our situation through [our interpreter], they made friends with us and each accepted a leaf of tobacco from us. [VanStone 1977:28, 30]

July 21: Savages, about 14 men and eight women, altogether 25 persons with the children, arrived[.] . . . Among them was a man called Pukak, who was revered in Atanik, and two persons from the next settlement to the north of us, Utkiagvik; they all belong to the Kakligmiut tribe. [VanStone 1977:33]

During the period July 21–29 the party was in the Barrow district, which was under the dominion of the Kakligmiut "tribe." During that period the party was troubled by ice and fog and harassed by Natives. As time passed the Natives became progressively more numerous and more menacing toward the explorers, who finally fled south in fear of their lives. They failed to encounter any Siḷaliñaġmiut on the return, possibly because the Natives had gone inland to hunt caribou.[13] The Russians also did not meet any Utuqqaġmiut, evidently because they had already begun their trip up the Utukok River to their own country.

When the explorers arrived back in Tikiġaġmiut country they encountered a small party of Natives at Cape Lisburne whom they passed without incident. A bit farther on they met an old man. "He told us that two of his comrades had set out about a month ago for caribou that had been killed not very far away in the tundra. He assumed that they [his comrades] had been killed by Utukagmiuts whom they sometimes meet in the tundra; they don't know of any other people there[.] . . . He belonged to the Tykagmiut tribe" (VanStone 1977:57).

The explorers then crossed behind the village of Tikiġaq (Point Hope) by traveling across Maryatt Inlet, portaging their boats across the spit back to the ocean. This enabled them, quite fortuitously, to avoid the largest village in northwestern Alaska, although only a few people would have been there at that season. The narrative continues.

August 20: At noon we portaged the baydara to the south shore of Point Hope, which, like the north shore, consists of gravel rising as much as 7 ft. [2 meters] above sea level. The large winter camp Tykaga [Tikiġaq] is on this cape; its inhabitants, according to the savages we met at Cape Lisburne, are quite numerous, comprising a special tribe of Tykagmiuts. They gather at this camp only in winter; they spend the summer and fall hunting caribou in various places. [VanStone 1977:58]

August 20: At 9:00 we put in at Cape Thompson and left the baydara at anchor on the west shore of the cape. Fourteen Tykagmiuts, who lived in a summer camp not far from our landing, approached us; at first they took us for their enemies the Kakligmiuts. [VanStone 1977:58]

August 22: At 11:30 we passed through a third small strait at the mouth of which there was a fairly sizeable summer camp on a spit rising 7 ft. [2 meters] above the sea. Eight baydaras, each with 14 men, approached us from this camp. A crowd of more than 150 persons stood on shore. They, like the inhabitants of the summer camp we passed this morning, comprise a separate tribe and call themselves Kivalinagmiuts [Kivalliñiġmiut], after the name of their settlement, which is in a latitude of approximately 67°40′ N. . . .

The savages who came to meet us, although they did not have arrows with them, each had a knife and they boldly circled us with their baydara, trying to force us to the shore. The wind soon freshened from WSW, forcing them to hasten back toward the shore from which they had come. [VanStone 1977:59–60]

Kashevarov and his men fled southward along the shore, but the rising wind forced them to land about 8 miles (13 kilometers) beyond the Kivalliñiġmiut camp. At 8:00 that evening twenty Kivalliñiġmiut men appeared: "The savages who approached us led us to suspect them of evil intentions toward us and, in addition, not far from us there was another crowd of savages of similar mind (one of the savages, an old man, warned Utuktak of this). Therefore, working the savages into one spot, we surrounded them with our sentries so that they could not signal the other natives. The rest of our crew was on full alert at their guns" (VanStone 1977:61).

Early the next morning the surf moderated enough for the explorers to launch their boats and escape the Kivalliñiġmiut, 60 of whom had surrounded their camp during the night. They traveled southward without encountering anyone else until they rounded Cape Krusenstern at the northern margin of Kotzebue Sound: "**August 26:** At 3:00 we stopped at two winter sod huts 9 miles [14.5 kilometers] to the east of Cape Krusenstern. Here we found about 10 savages belonging to the Kyktagagmiut [Qikiqtaġruŋmiut] tribe[.] . . . From the local savages we purchased several loaches, . . . crowberries, cloudberries, bog whortleberries, and crowberries" (VanStone 1977:62).

Continuing eastward along the northern shore of Kotzebue Sound the Russians "passed some half-dozen sod huts scattered along the coast" but did not encounter any large parties of Natives. At several of these huts they traded tobacco for fish. The explorers then traveled across the sound to Cape Blossom, thereby missing the largest Qikiqtaġruŋmiut village. From there they continued south along the coast and rejoined their ship at Chamisso Island.

Kashevarov's account establishes, at least as a first approximation, four important attributes of the Iñupiaq social systems of northwestern Alaska that are relevant to this volume. First, it contains prima facie evidence of the fact that northwestern Alaska was inhabited by the members of several different nations ("tribes"). As it happens, the specific nations whose members Kashevarov encountered were also identified for the same part of the country by my sources more than 130 years later; their borders, as noted by Kashevarov, were exactly where my sources said they had been. Second, Kashevarov's account shows that the relations between and among those nations were by no means necessarily friendly; some were, and some were not. The aggressive treatment to which Kashevarov's party was subjected in several instances indicates that national borders were taken very seriously by the Natives. Third, the account shows that Iñupiat, if encountered in any numbers in or near their homelands, could be very hostile to strangers. Finally, the account shows that Natives encountered under different conditions, such as in relatively small numbers compared to those of the strangers, were inclined to adopt a more peaceful course of action.

Boundaries

Richard Lee correctly pointed out that "much confusion has arisen from the fact that group boundaries and land boundaries have not been kept separate in analyses of hunter-gatherer organization" (1972b:74). In order to keep the two distinct in the present study, I differentiate between "boundaries," on the one hand, and "borders," on the other. "Boundary" is used solely to refer to the outer limits of a social system. "Border," on the other hand, refers to the outer limits of a unit of land, that is, of a district. The Iñupiaq term for border, thus defined, is *avgun*. As far as I am aware, the Iñupiat do not have a term for boundary as defined here but indicate membership in a particular social system with the infix *-gi-*. Thus, people related on a kinship basis were *iḷagiich*: *iḷa-* (kinship or friendship) + *-gi-* (relationship) + *-ich* (plural). The members of a nation were *nunaqatigiitch*: *nuna* (land) + *-qati-* (possession of) + *-gi-* (relationship) + *-ich* (plural), or people who were related to one another through their (common) possession of land.

Following Francis Sim and David Smallen, I define boundary as "a singular discontinuity between a social system and its environment" (1972:2).[14] Thus defined, a boundary is not an impenetrable barrier. It is not a seal but a locus of transaction between a system and its surroundings (Sim and Smallen 1972:2). In this vein, Lee noted that where boundaries exist there are usually rules for "accommodating" people across them (Lee, Pilling, and Hiatt 1968:157). A boundary, like the skin of an organism, is permeable, but the fact that something can pass through it does not mean that it does not exist.

How does one locate a boundary? One method I have used with considerable success is simply to ask: for example, "Jack, are you Canadian or American?" "To which family do you belong?" "What company do you work for?" All such questions, and usually their answers, concern boundaries. To corroborate the initial findings, one can ask others who know Jack a similar question: "Is Jack a Canadian or an American?" Other, related questions can follow: "What does it mean to be a Canadian as opposed to an American?" "How do you know you are a Canadian?" "How did you become a Canadian?" Usually there is a high level of consistency in the responses.

In general, except in the case of secret organizations or recalcitrant sources, it does not take a great deal of intelligence or very sophisticated research techniques to initiate this type of inquiry. A less obvious consideration is the need to investigate an alleged boundary or border from both sides (Donan and Wilson 1999:22–23). In other words, it is not enough to ask Kivalliñiġmiut sources about the Kivalliñiq–Napaaqtuq border; one must pose the same questions to Napaaqtuġmiut as well.

In the course of the present project I began by asking my most expert sources on a particular district questions like "Who used to live in this valley in your grandparents' time?" Then I asked who lived in neighboring areas. The third step was to pose the same series of questions to experts from neighboring areas. With regard to the NANA Region, my sources always answered decisively, and there was complete consistency in the responses from the several elders with whom I discussed the matter. The results were somewhat less satisfactory for neighboring regions, primarily because I could not afford the time and expense of visiting them before the most expert sources passed away. Fortunately, literary and archival sources provided much of the information I needed to fill in the gaps.

The basic data on the location of national *borders* were supplemented with information concerning the nature of national *boundaries*. It is these that form the subject matter of the present section. I examine several of the "singular discontinuities" reported for early-19th-century northwestern Alaska to see if they circumscribed the same or different social units. If several independent measures circumscribed the same units, and if the units thus identified met the definition of a society as defined by Levy (1966:20 n. 10), then that unit is considered to have been a nation for purposes of this study.

In the following discussion the prefixes "inter-" and "intra-" are separated from "national" by hyphens in an effort to minimize confusion.

FRAMEWORK

The primary social discontinuity separating a nation from its neighbors was a high rate of endogamous residential marriage.[15] From this perspective an

Iñupiaq nation can be conceived of as a deme, or marriage universe. It can also be conceived of as a network in which the nodes were families. Lines between the nodes represented kin ties that were temporarily inactive but that could be activated promptly should the need arise. The outer boundary of a national system was defined by a marked dropoff (although not necessarily a complete break) in the frequency of kin relationships connecting individuals in different local families (Burch 1975a:250).

The endogamy that characterized a traditional Iñupiaq nation was not prescriptive. Inter-national marriage could and did occur.[16] In the majority of cases the woman apparently went to live in her husband's country rather than vice versa, although people visited back and forth to some extent. However, intermarriage was strongly discouraged by parents for two practical reasons. The first and likely more important factor was that an emigrant woman's father, brothers, and male cousins could not effectively come to her aid if she was mistreated by her husband and/or his relatives. The second was that there was always a chance that members of the two nations would find themselves on opposite sides in a battle. In this case men might find themselves trying to exterminate their in-laws or, in the case of a surprise nighttime raid, even their daughter or sister. Mothers would lose the companionship of their daughters not just on a daily basis but perhaps for years at a time; this was usually a situation mothers tried to prevent. Unfortunately, it is impossible to determine just what the rate of endogamy was. Judging from informant statements, it must have averaged 80 percent or higher overall but with occasional fluctuations, which are discussed later.

ECONOMIC DISCONTINUITIES

Economically, there was a discontinuity between nations in the types of transaction that ordinarily took place. Table 2 lists and briefly characterizes the various patterns of property exchange traditionally distinguished in the NANA Region. The six listed in the top section of the table governed intra-national exchanges, whereas the four listed in the lower section governed transactions at the inter-national level. Except for theft, the transactions listed in the intra-national category are almost always lumped together in English under the heading of "sharing." They are notable for the fact that the principle of caveat emptor did not apply. In inter-national modes of exchange, on the other hand, except for transactions between people formally connected as "trading partners" (see Chapter 3), caveat emptor was the dominant principle.

The distinction between inter- and intra-national exchanges was not absolute, but the preponderance on one side or the other was considerable. Theft occurred in both contexts but was considered reprehensible in one while acceptable, sometimes even desirable, in the other. Goods were occasionally

Table 2. Modes of Exchange in Iñupiaq Alaska

Level	Type*	Description
Intra-national	*aitchuq-*	free gift
	atuliq-	loan/gift *with* expectation of a return
	kiuvaanaq-	inherit
	pigriaq-	loan *without* expectation of a return
	simmiq-	direct exchange of similar goods
	tiglik-	theft (unacceptable)
Inter-national	*niuviq-*	exchange between "trading partners"
	tauqsiq-	offering goods for sale
	tunilaq-	unsolicited bid for goods
	tiglik-	theft (acceptable)

Source: Burch 1988a:103–105.
* These terms are verb stems.

offered for sale or independent bid in the intra-national context but not very often; they were usually given or loaned. In the inter-national context, virtually *all* transfers that were not governed by the rules of trading partnerships or kinship were conducted either via theft or in bid or auction situations in which cheating by all parties was a given.

POLITICAL DISCONTINUITIES

Politically (as defined by Levy 1952:468–503), perhaps the most profound discontinuity between nations was in the area of homicide. The general pattern was very straightforward: in general, it was not only acceptable but sometimes even desirable to kill members of other nations. Killing a member of one's own nation was prohibited except under extraordinary circumstances, although it did, of course, occur (Dall 1870:144; Nelson 1899:327; Ray 1967:380). To kill one's own countryman was murder (*iñuaq-*), whereas to kill a foreigner (*tuqut-*) was conceptually not much different from killing a mosquito.

A stranger from another country could be killed simply because he was an alien, although other factors were often involved as well. A murder, that is, an intra-national homicide, ordinarily was committed for a specific reason: conflict over a woman, jealousy, greed, resentment, a power struggle, or to avenge a personal offense of some kind. In this circumstance the evidence was hidden or destroyed to the maximum extent possible, and discussion of the deed was kept to an absolute minimum unless it was a publicly sanctioned execution.[17]

In the inter-national context, a killer felt no shame in telling his countrymen what he had done, although he might keep quiet for a variety of practical reasons. When an inter-national homicide occurred, *any* countryman of the deceased could avenge the death by killing *any* member of the nation to which the killer belonged. At worst, inter-national homicide precipitated a war, which, in principle, involved the entire membership of the two nations involved. Intra-national homicide, on the other hand, could be avenged only by the closest male relative of the deceased. At worst, it precipitated a blood feud involving the members of two local families.[18]

A final aspect of homicide that indicates the discontinuity between one nation and another is in the ritual treatment of the victim by the killer (Dives 1940:27; Hawley 1976b). In the inter-national context no ritual was required. The most that anyone did was to try to get some of the enemy's blood on one's finger and lick it. Even the killing of a seal required more ritual attention.

In the intra-national context, on the other hand, definite rituals had to be practiced, although they apparently varied from one nation to another. Among the Qikiqtaġruŋmiut a killer had to slit the victim's throat. In other districts, according to Knud Rasmussen, "if a man was killed, it was the custom to cut the body to pieces, all joints, sinews, and sever the head. The stomach [cavity?] was then opened and the head put inside after first having removed the jaw. . . . If it happened to be a shaman, a blubber dish was laid over his head and his eyes were smeared with blubber, whereafter the head was laid in a fire" (Ostermann and Holtved 1952:127).

Vilhjalmur Stefansson cites an instance where three men killed a man called Axañak somewhere within the NANA Region: "They then cut off his head, and his arms at the shoulders. They put the head into a bag which Ilav[iñiq] [Stefansson's informant] thinks was the man's own stomach, slit open his thorax along the sternum (one side of it) and put the head in. Then they left the body in a clump of willows. The cutting up, etc., was 'for fear of the dead man's nappata' [spirit]" (1914b:334).

According to Charlie Saġġaaluraq Jensen (1970e), in most parts of Northwest Alaska a murderer cut off his victim's head and then covered it with the victim's stomach, whereas in a battle or raid bodies were simply left where they fell. The basic point is not in the details but in the general fact that, without proper ritual observances, intra-national homicide put the perpetrator at extreme risk from the dead person's spirit, whereas inter-national homicide did not.

DISCUSSION

In principle, the singular discontinuities just described could have varied independently of one another. That is, deme boundaries might not have coincided with those determined on the basis of economic or political criteria, and so on. In fact, they did coincide. System boundaries, as determined on the basis of endogamy, were identical to those delineated on the basis of economic and political criteria. They were also the same ones that circumscribed the nunaqatigiitch identified by my informants. For these reasons I contend that these boundaries were real, not figments of my imagination. I also contend that Kashevarov's experiences, as recounted above, constitute powerful independent evidence in support of this conclusion.

But the units identified on the basis of endogamy, economic transactions, and homicides could also be identified on the basis of other criteria as well. For example, although most of the relevant information has been lost, it is clear that many of the myriad taboos surrounding a person's daily life differed to some extent from one nation to another. Thus, along the Kobuk River a girl was subjected to a full year of isolation upon reaching menarche. Along the Noatak River, however, the period of isolation lasted only a month.

A final matter that needs to be mentioned is the fact that a significant portion of an individual's personal identity was associated with his or her nationality. The members of each nation adhered to an ideology of both distinctiveness from and superiority over the members of other nations. Several years ago I wrote that "the members of each nation thought of their country as being better than that of their neighbors, and of themselves as being more intelligent, stronger, faster, and better looking, and as superior providers, dancers, story tellers, and lovers" (Burch 1980:278). Nothing I have learned since then has caused me to alter this conclusion.

Boundary Expression

There is considerable variation in the extent to which national boundaries are expressed by and hence visible to the members of the social systems involved. Here the possibilities range from physical confrontation and violence through peaceful advertising to no expression at all. Since the next chapter is devoted to hostilities, the discussion here is limited to the more peaceful means of boundary expression.

SPEECH

One oft-discussed (see, e.g., Berndt 1959; Dixon 1976; Peterson 1976:50; Rigsby and Sutton 1980–82:14; Sutton 1991:49) way to advertise one's nationality is through speech, where members can be distinguished from nonmembers on the basis of the language or dialect they speak. Other linguistic devices include distinctive "group" names, place-names, and personal names. Distinctive speech and group names were prominent in this regard in the NANA Region. The former is discussed here, the latter in the following section.

Iñupiatun was and is divided into a number of dialects and subdialects (Fortescue, Jacobson, and Kaplan 1994:viii–ix; Kaplan 1984:13, 2001:250; Woodbury 1984). Nowadays, subdialects are associated with particular villages. During the early 19th century, however, they were associated with particular nations. Subdialects differed from one another primarily (although not exclusively) in their prosodic features, such as intonation contours, rhythm, and speed, which are not phonologically significant in the Inuit language. The differences in speech were so striking, however, that even relatively ignorant Europeans were often aware of them (see, e.g., Collinson 1889:145; Hooper 1881:58, 1884:112). The Natives themselves could very quickly identify the specific nation to which someone belonged solely on the basis of his or her speech. For example, Stefansson, who did research in northern Alaska early in the 20th century, noted that there were "probably seldom five years when an ordinary member of the Noatak group did not see and speak to more than half of the Kuwuk [Kobuk River] group; yet, even so, a Killirk native [from the Killik River on the Arctic Slope] would tell you decisively after hearing a few words, 'this man is from Noatak, that one from Kuwuk' " (1933:314).

Elders I interviewed on the subject seemed to be generally ignorant of dialect differences, but they were highly aware of those at the subdialect level. They had even developed a series of more or less standardized metaphors to characterize different subdialects. For instance, moving from north to south:

> *In the Barrow language they use different words for certain things—especially animals and fish—than the people of the NANA Region, and they talk a lot faster. The Wainwright people speak lower and more slowly. In Point Hope they speak very slowly, slower than anybody else in northern Alaska. At Kivalina they talk at an even rate of speed. In Noatak the language sounds like a rock hitting the water, very low. In Kotzebue they talk fast, and their speech undulates; it is like a washboard, or like waves. On the upper Kobuk they speak slowly. The Selawik language sounds like people walking through shallow water, and the end sound is like a rock dropping in the water.*[19]

All adults recognized these differences, and many people could mimic them effectively. When telling stories, narrators often located the characters socially by mimicking the subdialect associated with the nation concerned.

GROUP NAMES

Students of hunter-gatherers (e.g., Leacock 1969:12; Rogers 1969:46) seem to be particularly interested in identifying "the named group," as though there was only one type of named group in a given population. Whatever the case may be or may have been anywhere else, in northwestern Alaska there was a wide range of named groups. In fact, every group that had any kind of association with a particular place, locality, district, or region considered significant by the Natives had a name associating it with the area concerned. In the larger and more permanent villages people were often identified by group names based on the neighborhood and even the dwelling in which they resided.

Most Iñupiaq group names end with the suffix *-miut*, meaning "people of" the geographic entity to whose name the suffix is appended.[20] Thus, the people living on a point of land, *nuvuk*, might be called Nuvugmiut (people of the point), or the people living on an island, *qikiqtaq*, might be called Qikiqtaġmiut (people of the island). This is simple enough. Unfortunately, it gets more complicated. In many cases, a single term applied on two or more different levels simultaneously. For example, the name for the people who lived in the village at the end of Point Hope spit was Tikiġaġmiut, but the same name also was applied to an entire nation. The village on the end of the spit happened to be the largest one occupied by members of that nation. Natives usually could tell from the context which of the two referents was being discussed; if they could not, they simply asked, being already aware of the fact that there was more than one possibility. A close analogy in the contemporary United States is the state of New York versus the city of New York.

An important point here is that it is outsiders, not Natives, who are confused by Eskimo group names. It is interesting to note in this regard that many of the group and place-names Kashevarov recorded ended in -miut. However, guided by his knowledgeable interpreter, Utuktak, he was able to distinguish between those referring to "tribes" (nations) and those denoting settlements. For example, while amongst members of the Siḷaliñaġmiut "tribe," he visited the settlements of Qayaiqsiġvigmiut and Qiḷamittaġvigmiut, and he was visited by people from Tuttulivigmiut, without getting confused by the terminology (VanStone 1977:27, 33).

PERSONAL APPEARANCE

The members of different nations differed from one another in appearance as well as in speech. These differences were both physical and cultural in nature.

Distinctive patterns of anatomical features probably did not coincide precisely with national boundaries, but apparently they were close enough to serve as a general indicator of an individual's place of origin. Edward Nelson, who visited northwestern Alaska in 1881 after spending four years on Norton Sound, published what amounts to an anatomical tour guide of western Alaska. Diagnostic features he noted were height, build, complexion, chin shape, nose shape, prominence of cheekbones, shape and size of lower jaw, and "development of the superciliary ridge" (Nelson 1899:26–29). The "superciliary ridge" is a "ridge from over the middle of the eye toward the base of [the] nose" (Nelson 1877–81:entry for December 19, 1878). Although one or two features sometimes sufficed, more often it was the whole constellation of features that served to distinguish the members of one group from those of another. Anatomical features were not deliberately modified but were the apparent result of several generations of relatively high levels of inbreeding at the national level combined with more limited outbreeding between or among neighboring populations.

Anatomical differences were not always recognizable at the national level but were distinct enough at the regional level to help an Iñupiaq begin to calculate a stranger's nationality even at a distance. Words and phrases Nelson used to describe the inhabitants of the NANA Region were "tall," "active," "remarkably well built," "finely proportioned," and "athletic." The inhabitants of the upper Noatak and Kobuk valleys specifically were "notable for the fact that a considerable number of them have hook noses and nearly all have a cast of countenance very similar to that of the Yukon Tinné [Athapaskans]" (Nelson 1899:28). John Kelly described the inhabitants of Kotzebue and of the Buckland, Selawik, and Kobuk valleys as being "tall" and "cadaverous," while the people who lived on the upper Noatak were tall and strongly built, "a gigantic race, of a splendid physique that would be remarkable in any part of the world" (Wells and Kelly 1890:15). Those who lived on or near the coast were shorter and less robust. Other writers (e.g., McLenegan 1887:75; Seemann 1853, vol. 2:50; Woolfe 1893:151) made similar observations.

The cultural elements in national differences in personal appearance were more in the domain of adornment rather than in clothing style, although there was that, too. As Kelly reported on the situation existing in the 1880s,

> *each tribe has some peculiarity of dress. Those south of Port Clarence (Cape Douglas) and those north of Point Hope wear shoulder-straps of different-colored furs trimmed with wolverine. Point Hope natives put little white tanned seal-skin tassels around the top of their summer boots, and others do not. The old Eskimos at Point Hope and Point Barrow fashion their boot-soles high, and cut out the upper in one piece, and sew their water-proof boots and mittens without a welt, while the Kavea and Diomedes make the side of their boot-soles low, have the upper in two pieces, and sew with a welt. [Wells and Kelly 1890:17]*

The Iñupiat did not have highly distinctive national or regional costumes, as people do, or did until recently, in many parts of the world. Everyone wore caribou-skin clothing most of the time, and the same basic cut seems to have been used everywhere. However, as Kelly's remarks suggest, the details of workmanship and trim varied to some extent from one nation to another. With clothing, as with speech, national distinctions that might appear subtle to outsiders were obvious to the Natives themselves. Jewelry, including earrings and occasional nose rings, among women and labrets among men were more important in symbolizing national membership. Sometimes tattoos were also significant. In some districts men tattooed the backs of their hands with distinctive patterns, and women in all districts were tattooed on the face, particularly the chin. Again, the differences were not pronounced. Sometimes the only variables were the number and thickness of the lines, but they were quite evident to the Iñupiat.

Unfortunately, knowledge of the exact patterns of anatomical and cultural features that signified membership in particular nations had been lost by the time I did my research. All that my sources could tell me was that their grandparents had said they existed during their childhoods. By the time a person reached adulthood and had learned the patterns, he or she could tell the nationality of a complete stranger simply at a glance.

OTHER INDICATORS

The only other symbolic indicator of nationality that I am aware of is the design pattern painted on paddles and sometimes on the sides of umiat. Examples of the patterns observed on paddles in Kotzebue Sound by Ludovik Choris in 1816 are shown in Plate 1.[21] According to Frederick Beechey (1831, vol. 1:346), paddles used on the starboard side were stained with black, while those on the port ("larboard") side were stained with red.

On the basis of his experience in the Aleutian Islands in 1816, Choris claimed that these patterns symbolized personal ownership rather than nationality. This might have been true in Kotzebue Sound as well. However, in societies small enough for all the members to know one other, personal ownership symbols would have indicated nationality by default if not by intent. Unlike differences in adornment or clothing, these indicators would have been visible at a considerable distance.

Territories

Iñupiaq elders living in northwestern Alaska during the late 20th century claimed that until the ANCSA of 1971 they could go anywhere they wanted and live anywhere they wanted. Furthermore, they would tell you that the same was true in their parents' and grandparents' times. And they were right. That is because the nations whose territories were located in the region ceased to exist during the second half of the 19th century due to depopulation resulting from famine and disease.[22] During the period of interest here, however, inter-district movement was much more constrained.

In discussing the spatial parameters of traditional Iñupiaq nations it is useful to employ the distinction between "estate" and "range" made initially by W. E. H. Stanner (1965:2) for the purposes of understanding Aboriginal territorial organization in Australia.[23] An estate is the geographic area claimed by a set of individuals to be their property, whereas a range is the country over which those individuals ordinarily hunt and forage to sustain life.[24] Together, the two constitute a "domain." For the purposes of the present study, "estate"

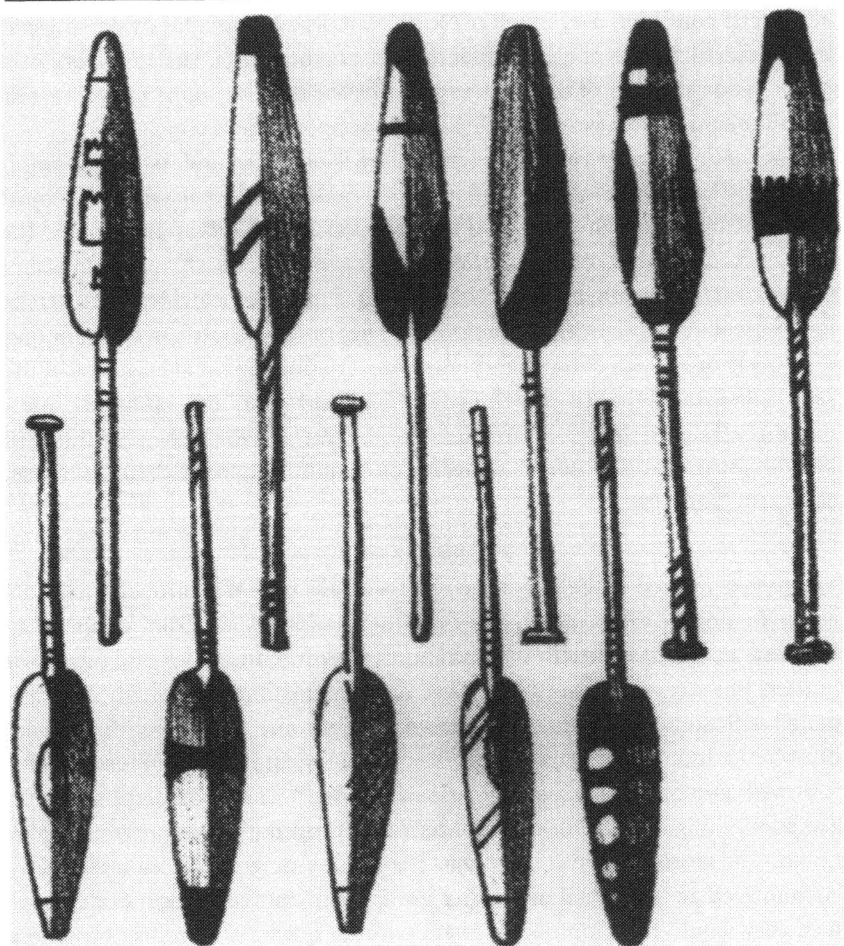

1. Paddles and insignia observed on Kotzebue Sound, 1816 (Choris 1822:pl. 3, fig. 1). Courtesy of the Library of Congress, Washington DC.

and "district" are considered equivalent terms, both referring to the particular real estate over which the members of a particular nation held dominion (Radcliffe-Brown 1952:34).

Writing specifically of the Bering Strait and Norton Sound regions, Ray stated that every nation "was as aware of its [borders] as if fences had been erected" (1967:373).[25] In general, I found the same thing to be true in the NANA Region, although border locations on the eastern margin of the region seem to have been rather less clear.[26] Ray went on to assail the notion of "unused land," which has often been claimed by Westerners to have been the aboriginal condition over much of North America. As Douglas Anderson said in a rather different context (Anderson et al. 1998:265), the members of a given nation used all of their estate some of the time but none of their estate all of the time.[27] My own research strongly supports these conclusions.

The distinction between estate and range is useful in understanding international affairs in early-19th-century northern Alaska because the two almost never coincided. With the possible exception of the Qikiqtaġruŋmiut, the range of the members of every nation in the region was much greater in extent than its estate. In other words, the Iñupiaq nations of northwestern Alaska had mutually exclusive estates but overlapping ranges. Or, to put it yet another way, many or even all of the members of most nations spent at least part of the year in an estate other than their own. It is important in understanding international affairs in the region to know the contexts in which they did this. For present purposes, it is useful to distinguish among three of them: trespass, easement, and license.

TRESPASS

Trespass consisted of the unauthorized use of any part of a particular nation's estate by one or more members of another nation. Apart from deliberately hostile acts, trespass usually involved hunters who ventured beyond their own borders in search of game. There were two circumstances in which this happened with some regularity. One was when men were conducting the crucial hunt for caribou hides for clothing, from mid-August to early September, and followed animals that crossed a national border.[28] This often led hunters in hot pursuit of game to cross the border as well without getting permission to do so. The stories make it clear that if a person or group from one nation encountered an individual or smaller group from another nation in this context, they would try to annihilate them without question or reflection unless they were partners (*niuviġiitch*), cosiblings (*qataŋutigiitch*), or some other kind of relative (*iḷaqatigiitch*) (Dall 1870:144; Ray 1967:381–382; see Chapter 3).

As Charlie Jensen once explained it to me, when Point Hope men were walking up inland, "they didn't want to see a man who belonged to another country. They would kill him even if they didn't know who he was. And other people from Noatak or Kotzebue, Selawik, they always did that before" (1970e). This attitude was reflected above in Kashevarov's account, where the old Tikiġaġmiu (sing.) man who could not find his companions automatically assumed that they had been killed by Utuqqaġmiut despite the absence of any supporting evidence.

A special case of trespass by caribou hunters involved the Akuniġmiut, of the central Kobuk valley. Every summer most of the men and older boys from the central Kobuk district walked north into the upper Noatak River valley, into the estate of the Nuataaġmiut, to hunt caribou. At this particular season, most of the Nuataaġmiut were on the coast (see below). Those who remained behind in their home district tended to hunt caribou on the north side of the valley, while the Akuniġmiut stayed on the south side of the same valley if game conditions permitted. Since this pattern was repeated every summer, everyone involved knew what was going on.

I never heard of summer contacts between Akuniġmiut and Nuataaġmiut caribou hunters. However, I did learn of occasional contacts made when the main body of Nuataaġmiut returned home from the coast, although they usually arrived there after the foreigners had gone. Any Akuniġmiut they encountered were definitely regarded as trespassers and treated accordingly. Knowing this would be the case, Akuniġmiut hunters tried to stay outside the range of Nuataaġmiut activity, although on some occasions parties of Akuniġmiut hunters banded together to ambush Nuataaġmiut working their way upstream.

The other context in which hunters approached or crossed national borders with some frequency was when they hunted seals on the sea ice, the ice broke, and they drifted out to sea. Within the NANA Region, seal hunters often strayed into neighboring estates while on the ice, but this rarely provoked trouble because of easement or license arrangements. Beyond the border of the NANA Region, however, a more stringent standard applied.

Seal hunters could end up far from home when the sea ice was unexpectedly broken up by wind and/or current and moved offshore, which can happen even in the coldest weather. In the waters off northwestern Alaska the prevailing ocean current is from south to north, and many a drifted hunter did not reach shore again until he reached the vicinity of Point Hope, the main village of the Tikiġaġmiut. Such a person was likely to be weak from dehydration and hunger, and his footgear was likely to be in tatters. Once he realized his whereabouts he would try to head south, at least if he had any strength left, for if he was discovered, death at the hands of the Point Hopers was a near certainty.[29] As was true of the errant caribou hunter, his only chance of survival was to establish contact with a partner, cosibling, or other relative who could serve as his guarantor and protector. Sometimes the unfortunate hunter was simply shot or stabbed, and sometimes he was beaten to death. The favorite procedure, however, was for a large crowd to gather, strip the hunter's clothing off, and repeatedly throw him up in the air and let him land on the ground until he succumbed. Sometimes a foreigner who was captured by the inhabitants of a large settlement was pulled apart, his limbs being literally torn from his body.

The assassination of drifted seal hunters was not limited to the Tikiġaġmiut. Nelson recorded that "in ancient time when people were hunting along the north coast from Aziak Island to Cape Prince of Wales it was not uncommon for them to be blown or forced across to the Asiatic shore by wind or ice. The moment they were seen by the natives there they were killed without mercy" (1877–81, journal 11).

Conversely, an unfortunate Chukotkan hunter drifted out on the sea ice sometime early in the 19th century. No one knows how long he was out there, but sometime in mid- to late March he managed to make a landfall on the Alaskan shore, about 15 miles (24 kilometers) north of Cape Krusenstern. As it happened, he got there just after the Napaaqtuġmiut arrived at their spring sealing stations. The Napaaqtuġmiut men were conducting a reconnaissance of ice conditions when they discovered him. They shot him right away with bow and arrow. When I asked why they did that, the response was that they had never seen him before.[30] When I protested that not knowing someone seemed to me to be weak grounds for killing him, the response was, "That's the way people were in those days."[31]

EASEMENT

An easement is the right to use land belonging to someone else for a specific purpose (adapted from Chernow and Vallasi 1993:822). The key elements here are the fact that such use is a right, not a privilege, and that it is for a specific purpose. In Northwest Alaska a specific purpose almost always was associated with a specific season.

Easements were fairly widespread in early-19th-century Northwest Alaska, most relating to the right to cross another estate at certain times of year. Unfortunately, knowledge of how these easements came into being has been lost. By the beginning of the study period they had already been in existence since time immemorial.

One example of an easement involves the use of two other estates by the Nuataaġmiut. Every year, in late May or early June, practically the entire population of that nation descended the Noatak River by boat, traveling right through the estates of the Napaaqtuġmiut and Qikiqtaġruŋmiut in the process. Interestingly, at that particular time of year the relevant portions of the valley had been abandoned by their owners, all of whom were seal hunting on the Chukchi Sea coast. After a few weeks in the Noatak River delta the Nuataaġmiut set up camp at Sisualik, in the heart of Qikiqtaġruŋmiut country, where they hunted beluga whales for several weeks. While the Nuataaġmiut were there the Qikiqtaġruŋmiut were in another part of their estate hunting bearded seals. In late July the Nuataaġmiut were joined at Sisualik by the members of several other nations, including the Qikiqtaġruŋmiut, for a fair,

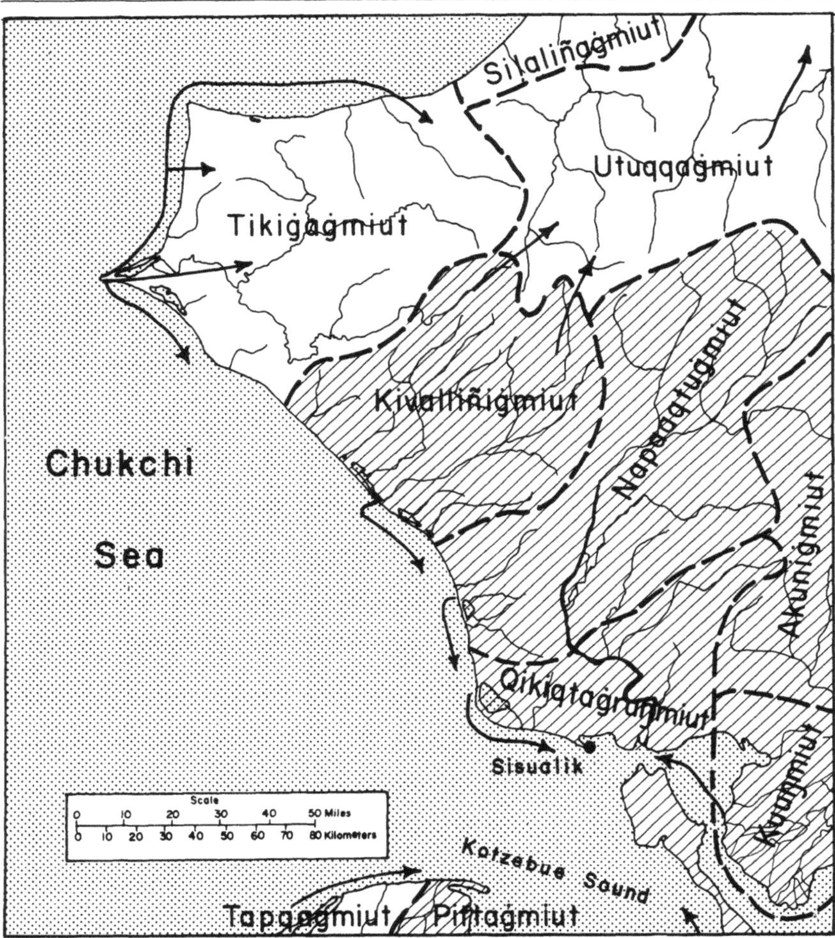

4. Summer movements of the Kivalliñiġmiut and their neighbors. The shading indicates estates within the NANA Region.

an event that is described in Chapter 3. When that was over the Nuataaġmiut returned through the cores of the Napaaqtuġmiut and Qikiqtaġruŋmiut estates to their own country.

The Kivalliñiġmiut also illustrate how easements worked. As Map 4 shows, their estate was along the Chukchi Sea coast just north of Kotzebue Sound, on the northern margin of the NANA Region. Their immediate neighbors were the Tikiġaġmiut and Utuqqaġmiut on the north and the Napaaqtuġmiut on the east and south. In early July a few boatloads of Kivalliñiġmiut went south to Sisualik, passing along the coastal margins of the Napaaqtuġmiut and

Qikiqtaġruŋmiut estates in the process. They had an easement to do this, but the coast was usually uninhabited at that season because the Napaaqtuġmiut and Qikiqtaġruŋmiut preceded the Kivalliñiġmiut in moving south along the coast. Thus, the members of the three nations rarely encountered one another until they reached Sisualik, where a general truce prevailed.

Later in the summer the majority of the Kivalliñiġmiut, who did not go to Sisualik, headed northeast into the Utukok River district (in the Utuqqaġmiut estate) to hunt caribou. They did not have an easement to hunt on Utuqqaġmiut land, however, and were attacked if discovered. As it happened, the overwhelming majority of Utuqqaġmiut were usually on the coast hunting sea mammals and trading at this time of year, so the members of the two nations rarely encountered one another.

Easements applied similarly to other sites where trade fairs were held every summer (see Chapter 3). Each was held in the estate of one specific nation or another but was open to virtually everyone who wanted to attend—as long as people behaved themselves. Free passage along foreign coastlines by traders going to or returning from the fairs was also guaranteed. But after a reasonable length of time for the return trip had passed, this easement lapsed. Tikiġaġmiut traveling by boat along the Kivalliñiġmiut shore in late September, for example, would be suspected of being on a hostile errand. If they were heading south, that is, away from home, such a conclusion was virtually guaranteed, and the travelers would have been treated accordingly.

LICENSE

A license is a privilege that a property owner grants to some other party to make temporary use of his or her land (Chernow and Vallasi 1993:1577). In the early-19th-century NANA Region it consisted of the right that members of one nation granted to the members of another to use their estate for a particular purpose, usually on a one-time basis.

The cases that I have heard of were of two types. The most common was the right for people from one nation to cross another nation's estate on the way to visit the estate of a third. This was usually so that they could attend a feast, but sometimes it was so they could conduct a raid.

The second type was the right of the members of one nation to hunt on another nation's estate, also on a one-time basis. The only instances of this that I have heard about involved people living on the coast in spring requesting and being granted permission to hunt seals on sea ice considered part of another nation's estate.

In the event of famine action was rarely collective on a national level. In this context families separated, each moving to stay with partners or relatives in neighboring countries. This was not license in the sense intended here, since permission was neither requested nor granted. Instead, family heads took advantage of previously existing personal relationships and simply appeared before their partners or relatives to seek their help.

The Wider Social and Geographic Setting

The Iñupiat of the NANA Region were involved in active relations with a variety of other peoples. This section introduces the reader to the peoples involved and provides a general orientation to the wider geographic context in which inter-national affairs took place.

The analysis will proceed at four different geographic levels. The smallest geographic unit is the district, which is the area constituting the estate of a single nation. The second level is the NANA Region, as previously defined, which is also referred to as the "primary study region" or "Northwest Alaska."

The third geographic level includes the regions immediately adjacent to the NANA Region. These include the Arctic Slope on the north, the Koyukuk River valley and a portion of the Yukon River valley on the east, and the southern Seward Peninsula and the eastern shore of Norton Sound on the south. It also includes the upper Kobuk River valley, which is within the NANA Region but which, during the study period, was inhabited by Koyukon Athapaskans. For lack of a better word I call this entire area, *including* the primary study region, "northwestern Alaska." It is the area enclosed by the heavy broken line in Map 5.

Much of the analysis moves back and forth between the broader region of northwestern Alaska and the more restricted one of the NANA Region. I use the label "NANA Region" instead of "Northwest Alaska" in order to reduce confusion as to the geographic level of discussion at any given point.

The fourth and most general level of discussion is north-central Beringia, which consists of the entire area shown in Map 5. "Beringia" is the name that has been given to the entire region lying west of the Mackenzie River, in northwestern Canada, and east of the Kolyma River, in northeastern Siberia (Hopkins 1996:xvii n. 1). It consists of those portions of Alaska, Chukotka, and the platforms of the Bering and Chukchi Seas that were cut off by ice from both Asia and North America during the Pleistocene (Hopkins 1959; Hopkins et al. 1982; Hultén 1937; Morlan 1997).[32] During much of that epoch the entire region was above sea level. For the past 10,000 years or so, however, it has been divided into eastern and western sections by the Chukchi and Bering Seas, which are linked to one another by Bering Strait. Map 5 shows only the north-central sector of Beringia, which is the portion most relevant to the present work.

Knowledgeable Iñupiat had a fairly sophisticated awareness of a geographic and social world that encompassed more than half a million square

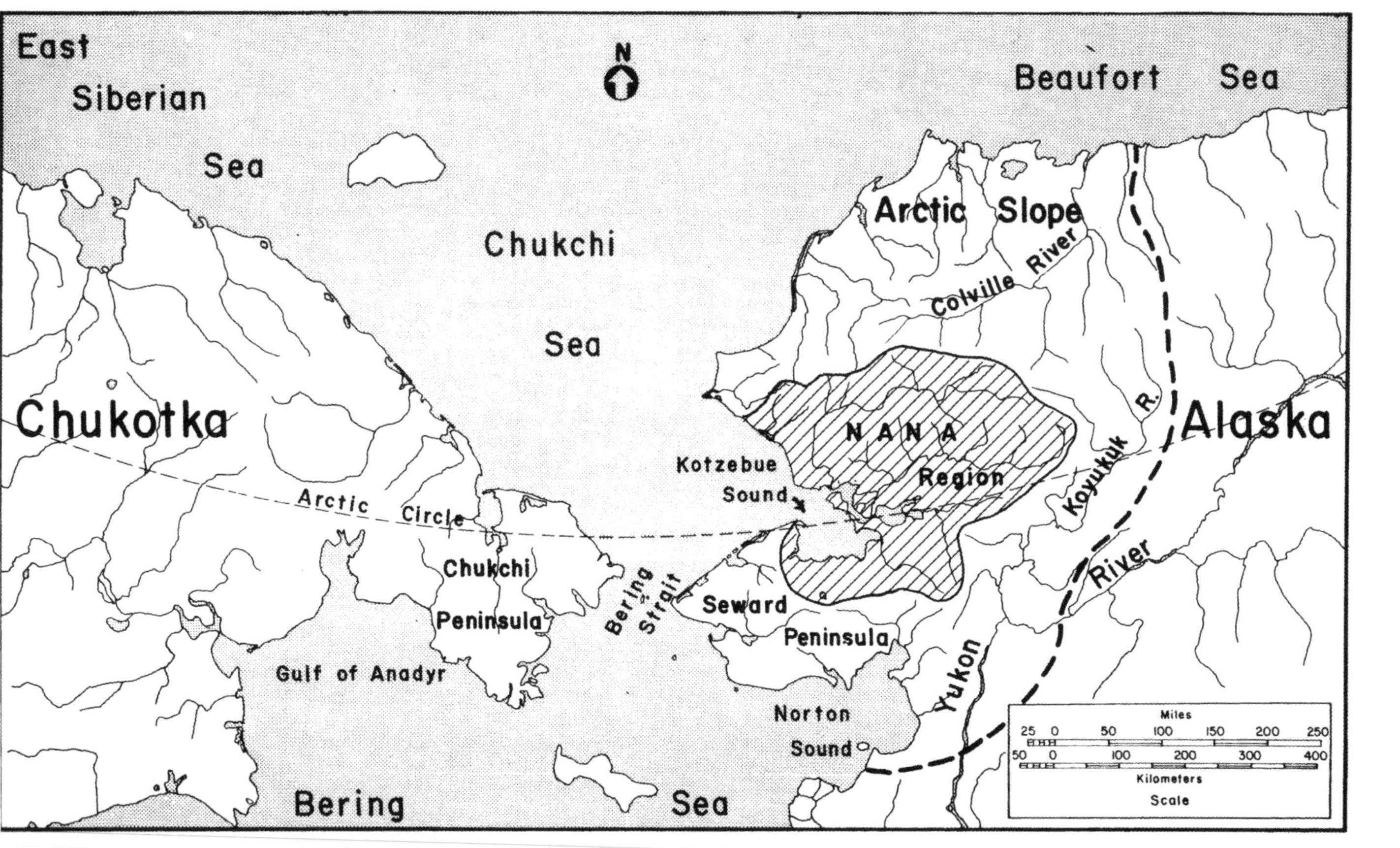

5. North-central Beringia, showing the major geographic areas discussed in the text.

miles (1.3 million square kilometers), an area nearly as large as modern France, Germany, and Spain combined (Beechey 1831, vol. 1:399–400; Simpson 1852–54:entry for November 8, 1853, 1875:233–236, 269–270; VanStone 1977:33). It extended from the Mackenzie River delta, in what is now northwestern Canada, on the east (beyond the edge of Map 5), across Bering Strait to perhaps the middle of Chukotka on the west, and from the Yukon River delta and the northern portion of the Bering Sea on the south to the Arctic Ocean on the north. From the Iñupiaq point of view, this world was inhabited by four basic types of human being: Iñupiat, or Alaskan speakers of the Inuit–Eskimo language; Uqayuiḷat, or speakers of the Central Yup'ik–Eskimo language; Qutlich, or speakers of the Chukchi and/or the two Asiatic Yup'ik–Eskimo languages in easternmost Asia; and Itqiḷḷitch, or Athapaskan Indians, including speakers of both Koyukon and Gwich'in. The borders of the four indigenous language areas are shown in Map 6. During the study period, members of a fifth group, Qatiqtuat, or Westerners, became occasional summer visitors to the region.

Other Iñupiat

Iñupiat lived both north and south of the NANA Region. Those to the north, on the Arctic Slope, were collectively called Siḷaḷiñaġmiut (people of the wide open spaces) by residents of the NANA and Bering Strait regions.[33] They were also known by the names of the specific nations to which they belonged, one of which also happened to be Siḷaḷiñaġmiut. National borders on the Arctic Slope are shown in Map 7.

Siḷaḷiñaġmiut nations were organized along the same basic lines as those in the NANA Region.[34] However, many of those whose estates included sections of coastline had comparatively large populations. These nations were also notable for having large "capital" villages in addition to the smaller ones so typical of the NANA Region. The leader in all respects was the Tikiġaġmiut nation. It is estimated to have had a population of over 1,300 people in the early 1800s, nearly half of whom lived in the settlement of Tikiġaq (Burch 1981:14). Each of the large settlements was occupied by the members of several local families. In some cases, the members of these families were more numerous than the populations of many settlements in the NANA Region.

Structurally, the most distinctive nation in northwestern Alaska was the one whose estate was along the Colville River, the Kuukpigmiut (Burch 1998b:26). In this district resources were clustered in three widely separated patches. None of the patches was rich enough to support the members of an entire nation, but each patch could sustain a substantial percentage of one. Consequently, the members of this nation were divided into three regional bands, one per patch (Burch 1998b:24–25; "regional band" as defined by Helm 1965,

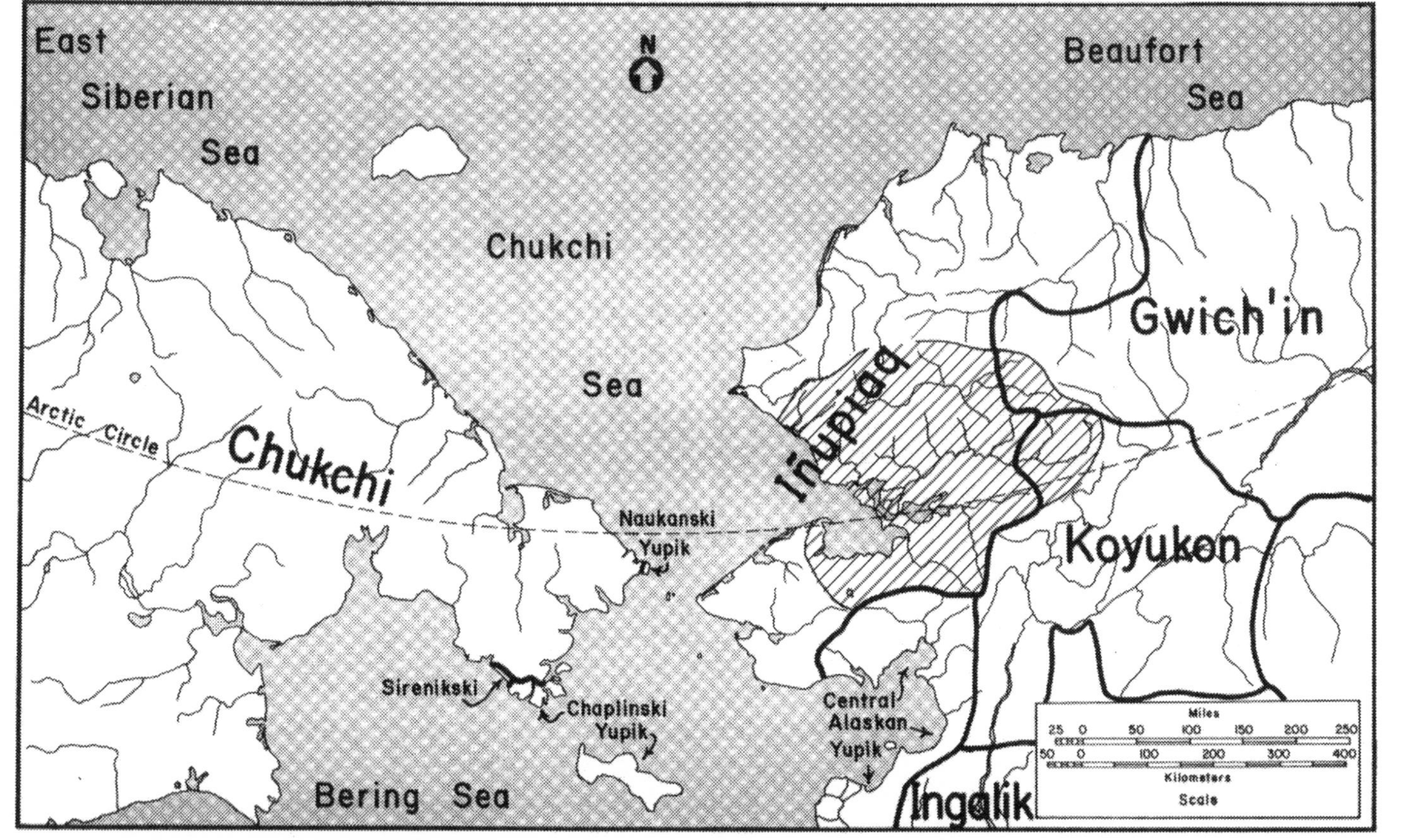

6. North-central Beringia, showing the major indigenous language zones at the beginning of the 19th century. The shaded area is the study region.

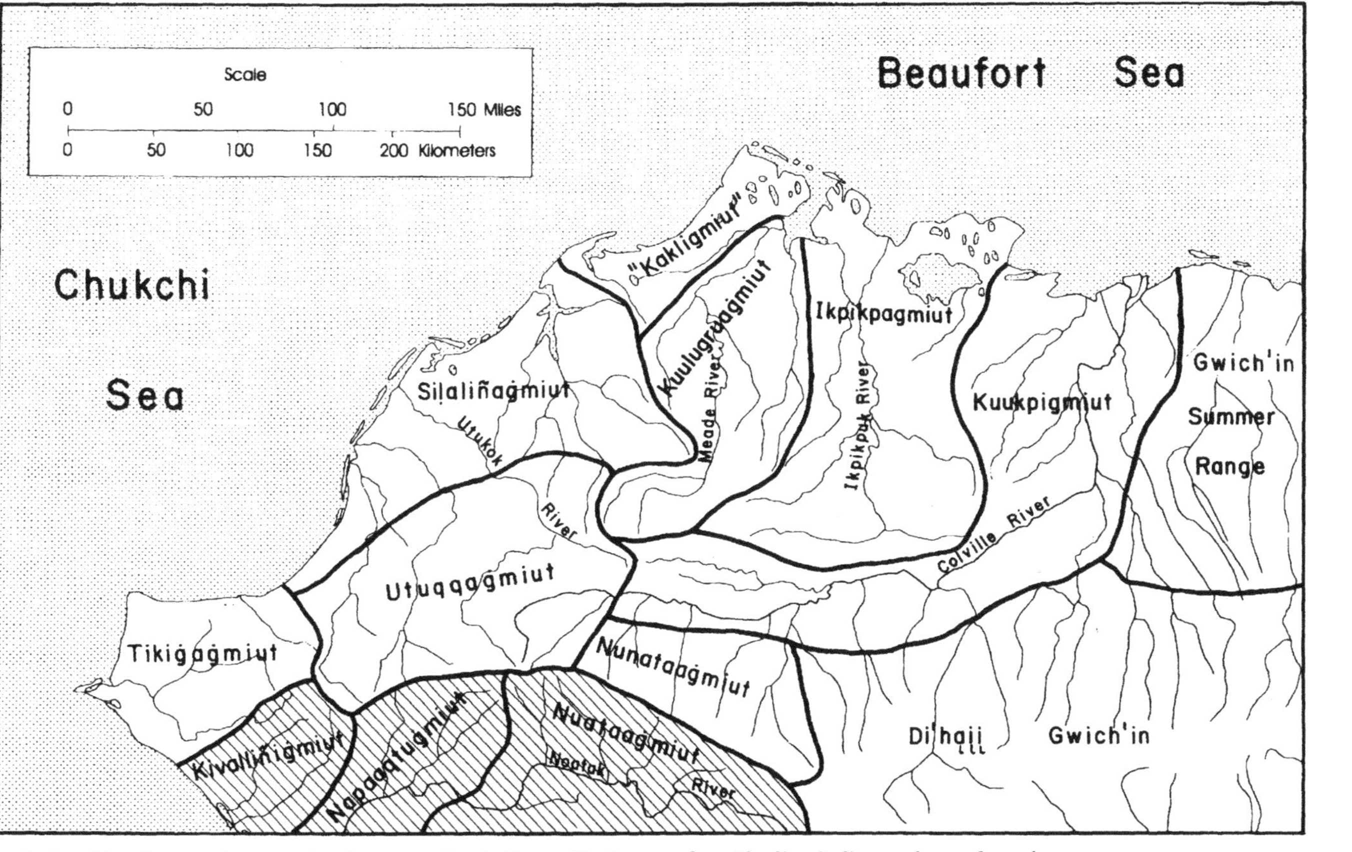

7. National borders on the central and western Arctic Slope, Alaska, ca. 1800. Shading indicates the study region.

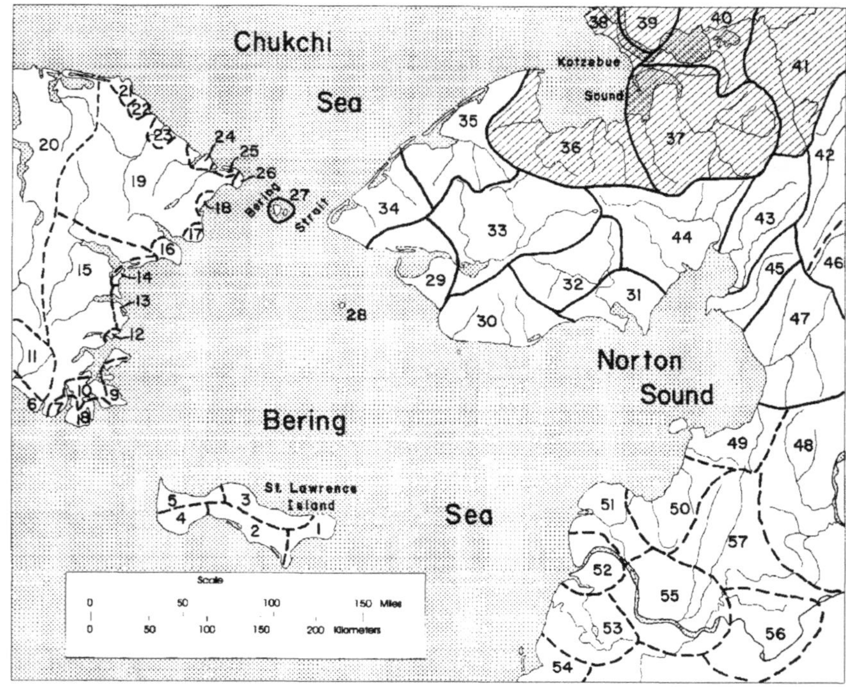

8. National borders in the Bering Strait–northern Bering Sea region, ca. 1800. Solid lines indicate well-defined borders. Broken lines signify either vaguely defined borders or borders concerning which there is limited information. The shaded area is the study region. Keyed to Table 3.

1968). Beginning on the upriver end, these were known as the Kaŋianiġmiut, the Killiġmiut, and the Qaŋmaliġmiut, respectively (Gubser 1965:338–339; Ostermann and Holtved 1952:30, 139, 142; Rasmussen 1933:317; Simpson 1875:234; Stefansson 1914b:9, 199, 208). The members of this society were referred to more frequently by their band names than by their national name, a fact that led to endless confusion on the part of early Western observers and later anthropologists.[35]

The Iñupiaq-speaking inhabitants of the Seward Peninsula living south and west of the primary study region were collectively known as Sakmaliaġruitch by the people of the NANA Region. They were also known by the name of the particular nation to which they belonged. The borders of these nations, as well as those of neighboring districts, are shown in Map 8, and their names are listed in Table 3.[36]

The basic settlement pattern on the Seward Peninsula was a "large village and several smaller ones located on a large river or coastal area within [the]

Table 3. Nations in the Bering Strait–Northern Bering Sea Region (Keyed to Map 8)

1. Kialigagmiit (Y E)	29. Siñġaġmiut (I E)
2. Sikuuvugmiit (Y E)	30. Ayaqsaaġiaaġmiut (I E)
3. Kukuligmiut (Y E)	31. Atnegmiut (Y E)
4. Pauvuilagmiit (Y E)	32. Iġałuiŋmiut (I E)
5. Sivuqarmiit (Y E)	33. Qaviaraġmiut (I E)
6. Sireneghmiit (E)	34. Kiŋikmiut (I E)
7. Avatmiit (Y E)	35. Tapqaġmiut (I E)
8. Qiighwaagmiit (Y E)	36. Pittaġmiut (I E)
9. Uŋazighmiit (Y E)	37. Kaŋiġmiut (I E)
10. Naŋuparaghmiit (C and E)	38. Qikiqtaġruŋmiut (I E)
11. Kurupka River (C)	39. Kuuŋmiut (I E)
12. Yanrakinot (C)	40. Kiitaaŋmiut (I E)
13. Nykhchigen (C)	41. Siiḷviim Kaġianiġmiut (I E)
14. Massigllyt (C)	42. Yunnaka Khotana (A)
15. Southeast Peninsula (C)	43. ðŋlutaləgmiut (Y E)
16. Yanranai (C)	44. Kuuyuŋmiut (Y E)
17. Nuniamo (C)	45. Čaxtuləgmiut (Y E)
18. Puoten (C)	46. "Inkilik Proper" (A)
19. Northeast Peninsula (C)	47. Uŋallaqłiŋmiut (Y E)
20. Yoni (C)	48. Holikachuk (A)
21. Enurmino (C)	49. Tačirmiut (Y E)
22. Seshon (C)	50. Pastulirmiut (Y E)
23. Cheitun (C)	51. Qerauranermiut (Y E)
24. Inchon (C)	52. Kuigularmiut (Y E)
25. Uellyt (C)	53. Qip'ngayarmiut (Y E)
26. Nuvuqaghmiit (Y E)	54. Marayarmiut (Y E)
27. Imaqłit (I E)	55. Kuigpagmiut (Y E)
28. Ukiuvaŋmiut (I E)	56. Iqugmiut (Y E)

Symbols: A = Athapaskan; C = Chukchi; E = Eskimo; I = Iñupiaq; Y = Yup'ik

several hundred square miles" of a nation's estate (Ray 1967:375). The estates of the nations whose members lived on the islands in Bering Strait were much smaller: the Ukiuvaŋmiut of King Island had four villages (Kingston 1999:24–25), while the Imaqłit of the Diomede Islands had five (Heinrich 1963:398). Each of the large villages in the region generally was occupied by several local families and had several permanent community centers, or *qargiich*. Beyond that, the Sakmaliaġruitch and Bering Strait island nations were organized along the same basic lines as those in the NANA Region.[37]

Alaskan Yup'ik Eskimos

Two groups of Yup'ik-speaking Eskimos were known to the people of the NANA Region, those living on the shores of Norton Sound and those on the eastern tip of the Chukchi Peninsula (see Map 8 and Table 3). Whether the Iñupiat recognized both groups as speaking related languages is unclear.

Transcripts of interviews with some of my oldest informants indicated that they once might have, but I failed to investigate this point specifically while they were still alive. In recent years the Iñupiat have lumped both the Eskimo- and Chukchi-speaking peoples of Chukotka together under the general heading of Qutlich. In the present study I either do the same thing or refer to them both as Chukotkans.

The estates of the Yup'ik-speaking people in Alaska extended southward from the Iñupiaq–Yup'ik border on the Seward Peninsula. The inhabitants of this region spoke various subdialects of Central Alaskan Yup'ik and were the northernmost groups of the large Yup'ik-speaking population of southwestern Alaska. It is only those bordering Norton Sound (including Fish River) whose members seem to have had any direct contact with the Iñupiat of the NANA Region. To the people of the NANA Region, the Yup'ik speakers of the Norton Sound area were known collectively as Unalit.

Just how many nations there were in this region at the beginning of the 19th century is uncertain, because in 1838 a smallpox epidemic devastated the population as far north as the eastern shore of Norton Sound and possibly just a bit beyond that (Boyd 1999:128–131; Fortuine 1989:231; VanStone 1979b:58–61). The nations and borders shown in Map 8 and the names listed in Table 3 reflect my somewhat speculative interpretation of the data relating to the period just prior to the epidemic (Ray 1967, 1984; see also Fienup-Riordan 1984; Pratt 1984; Shinkwin and Pete 1984). The pre-epidemic population of the region is unknown, but even the smallest of these nations probably involved more than 400 people. Ray describes the structure of these nations in the same terms she uses for the Iñupiaq speakers of the Seward Peninsula, so one may assume that, in at least their general characteristics, they were very similar to those of the NANA Region.

Chukotkans

The indigenous inhabitants of Chukotka included the Chukchi and three groups (Chaplinski and Naukanski Yupiik, and Sirenikski) of Eskimo speakers.[38] As noted above, modern Iñupiat lump all four of them together under the heading of Qutlich, but whether they did so in the early 19th century is uncertain.[39] What is clear is that Qutlich was used in the 19th century to refer to at least some of the inhabitants of Chukotka (Bockstoce 1988, vol. 1:122, 308). According to a few sources, the Iñupiaq name for Chukotka was Qutlich Nuna, or Qutlich Land (Murdoch 1892:44; Simpson 1875:236).[40]

At one time, perhaps until as recently as the 17th century, Eskimo speakers occupied a very extensive portion of the Chukotkan coast, while the Chukchi lived primarily inland. Subsequently, the Chukchi expanded outward, taking over much former Eskimo territory, apparently as much through assimilation as by conquest (Dolgikh 1972:23; see also de Reuse 1994:296–297; Krupnik 1983). In any event, the members of the two ethnic groups had considerable influence on one another (de Reuse 1994:307). The estates of the early-19th-century Qutlich nations are included in Map 8; the names are listed in Table 3.[41]

Chukchi expansion eastward into former Eskimo territory occurred simultaneously with war against the Russians in Chukotka. Although the Qutlich ultimately prevailed, this warfare was highly disruptive to the Chukchi and probably to several nations of Yup'ik speakers as well. It ceased late in the 18th century, but the ethnic, social, and demographic changes it had initiated were still in the process of being worked out early in the 19th. The estates and names shown in Map 8 and Table 3 are rather speculative as a result and should be regarded with some caution.

The Yup'ik speakers living on Cape Dezhnev (East Cape), the easternmost point in Asia, were the Asiatic Yup'ik speakers who had the greatest contact with the Iñupiat of the NANA Region. This was the estate of a single nation, the Nuvuqaghmiit, whose members spoke the Naukanski Yup'ik language (Fortescue, Jacobson, and Kaplan 1994:vi–ix). Their primary and perhaps only settlement at the time was Nuvuqaq, which may have had a population of some 400 people.

By the late 18th century the Nuvuqaghmiit had become separated from the other Eskimo-speaking peoples of Chukotka by an extensive zone of Chukchi occupation. South of this zone were speakers of Chaplinski (or Central Siberian) Yup'ik (Fortescue, Jacobson, and Kaplan 1994:vi–ix), who were the least affected of all Chukotkan peoples by the Russian invasion. Although the residents of this area and the Iñupiat of northwestern Alaska were probably aware of one another's existence, they were rarely in direct contact (de Reuse 1994:298–299).

Speakers of the Sirenikski (Sighinek) Eskimo language lived just west of the Central Siberian Yup'ik language zone (Fortescue, Jacobson, and Kaplan 1994:vi–ix). Formerly considered a special form of Yup'ik, this language, which is now extinct, was so divergent from the others that it may have constituted a separate linguistic division altogether. In any event, the Sighineghmiit were so far removed from northwestern Alaska that it is doubtful that people from the NANA Region were ever in direct contact with them.

All of the nations of Eskimo speakers in Chukotka were organized differently from the nations of Yup'ik speakers on the Alaskan side. In addition to being divided into a series of local families, they were also organized in terms of preferentially endogamous patrilineal clans.[42] They also had comparatively small estates, the borders of which were precisely defined right along the coast but only vaguely defined more than a few hundred yards inland (Krupnik 1996a, 1996b).

At the beginning of the study period Chukchi occupied the interior and much of the coastal zone of Chukotka. On a general level they divided themselves into two ecological groups, Maritime ("walking") Chukchi and Reindeer ("inland") Chukchi, and it is useful to do that here as well. (I do not know if the Iñupiat made this distinction.) Whether estates coincided with ecological zones is subject to some debate, however. Particularly in the area located between the Naukanski and Chaplinski Yup'ik zones, some nations probably involved both Maritime and Reindeer Chukchi. In any event, there seems to have been considerable freedom of movement between the inland and coastal zones in this area (Bogoras 1904–9:32; Krupnik 1996b; Schweitzer 1993:130–132).

Maritime Chukchi nations exercised dominion over relatively small estates that were intermixed with Asiatic Eskimo estates along the coast of Chukotka (Bogoras 1904–9:28–31). Many of them involved descendants of Yup'ik Eskimos who had been assimilated by the Chukchi or who were still in the process of being assimilated by them during the study period (Dolgikh 1972:23).

Maritime Chukchi nations seem to have been rather similar in size and organization to those Iñupiaq nations in which whaling was an important activity. They were comprised of one large, permanent "capital" village inhabited by the members of several local families and a few smaller satellite villages, most of which were occupied by only a single such unit. They were primarily dependent on sea mammals for subsistence and acquired reindeer skins for clothing through trade with their inland counterparts. Unlike their Eskimo neighbors, the Maritime Chukchi were not organized in terms of clans but in terms of virilocal extended families (Krupnik 1996b; see also Bogoras 1901:101–102). I have never seen estimates of national population size from the study period, but the nations in the vicinity of Bering Strait must have had populations in the range of 250–600 people.

The Reindeer Chukchi lived in the interior of Chukotka and, as the name implies, depended primarily on domesticated reindeer rather than wild fish and game for subsistence (Bogoras 1901, 1904–9; Krupnik 1996a, 1996b). By the early 19th century they had become large-scale reindeer breeders and were the only indigenous people within the scope of this study who were not full-time hunter-gatherers.

Reindeer Chukchi nations held dominion over large estates in the interior of Chukotka. The borders of these estates were apparently only vaguely defined and probably overlapped in many cases (Krupnik 1996a, 1996b). Although the Reindeer Chukchi were herders, they seem to have been organized along the same basic lines as many hunter-gatherers. According to Igor Krupnik (1993:39–40, 93–94, based on earlier work by Bogoras and Dolgikh), they exhibited three levels of organization: the "camp" of 10–25 closely related people; the "neighborhood" of 100–250 closely related people; and the "territorial group" of 200–600 people. These units seem to correspond to my terms "local family," "regional band," and "nation," respectively.

The Iñupiat seem to have been broadly aware of the major divisions of Qutlich but were in direct contact with the members of only a few nations. These include particularly the Nuvuqaghmiit Eskimos of Cape Dezhnev and the Uellyt Chukchi from just around the cape to the north, both of whom were active participants in war and trade across Bering Strait. Some of the Chukchi living just south of the Cape Dezhnev district were also involved in these activities.

Athapaskans

Indians were referred to collectively as Itqiḷḷitch. The Itqiḷḷitch who were in contact with the Iñupiat of the primary study region consisted of two main groups of Athapaskans, Gwich'in and Koyukon. The estates of the Indian nations located within the region defined as northwestern Alaska are shown in Map 9.

Gwich'in were known collectively by Iñupiat as Uyaġaġmiut. At the beginning of the study period the estimated 5,400 Gwich'in were probably organized in terms of a set of independent nations, at least ten in number (Burch 1998b).[43] By the early 1840s, however, population loss due primarily to Western diseases had significantly reduced the membership of the easternmost Gwich'in nations, effectively destroying the demographic base required for them to retain their autonomous status (Burch 1998b; cf. Raboff 1999, 2001). As a result, they changed from independent nations to regional bands within a unified, demographically declining, but geographically expanding Gwich'in nation (Slobodin 1981:514–515). On the west a similar process seems to have occurred about the same time, except that population loss there was due more to warfare with Koyukon and Iñupiat than to disease. By the time the Gwich'in population reached its nadir, in the 1860s, there were only about 850–900 people left (Krech 1978:99), and they all belonged to a single all-encompassing Gwich'in nation.

At the beginning of the 19th century the people of the NANA Region were probably in direct contact with only the westernmost of the Gwich'in nations, the Di'hąįį. Their Arctic Slope counterparts, however, were in direct contact not only with the members of that nation but with the members of two others as well, the Neets'ąįį and the Vantee, who lived farther east.

The Di'hąįį were driven out of the NANA Region by Iñupiat during the

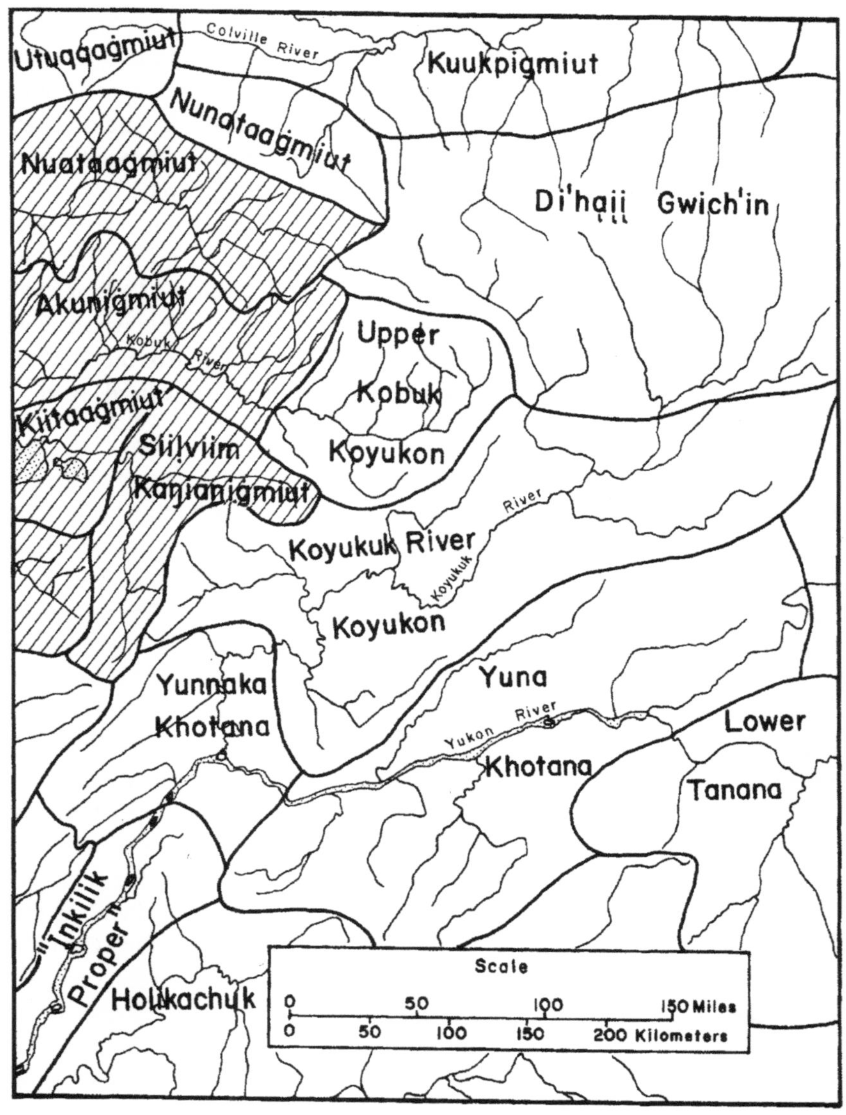

9. National borders in the interior sector of northwestern Alaska, ca. 1800.

1840s and out of most of the rest of their estate by Kuukpigmiut (Iñupiat) and Koyukon (Athapaskans) over the next two decades (Burch 1998b; Burch and Mishler 1995; cf. Raboff 1999, 2001). Most of the few surviving Di'hąįį merged with the Neets'ąįį in the Chandalar River valley in the 1850s, the rest merging with the Neets'ąįį and some groups of Koyukon speakers about 15 or 20 years later.

Very little is known about the Di'hąįį Gwich'in nation. If it was organized along the same general lines as the neighboring Neets'ąįį, it was divided into exogamous matrilineal clans (McKennan 1965:60), and its members spent most of the year living in tiny settlements of only one or two closely related households (Burch and Mishler 1995:164). Beyond that, all we know is that the Di'hąįį were in frequent contact with their Iñupiaq neighbors and that this contact included both hostile and friendly relations.

If the Iñupiat ever had a distinct generic term for speakers of the Koyukon language, it has been lost. Just how many nations of Koyukon speakers there were is uncertain, but there may have been three and possibly four (Arndt 1996:197–199; Burch et al. 1999; A. Clark 1981:582–584; VanStone and Goddard 1981; cf. Raboff 2001:9–19). In three of those four the Koyukon names are unknown, and they are referred to here as the upper Kobuk (River) Koyukon, the Koyukuk River Koyukon, and the Inkilik Proper, respectively. The name of the fourth group, Yunnaka Khotana, is probably an approximation of the indigenous term.

The upper Kobuk Koyukon were assimilated by Iñupiat early in the second half of the 19th century (Burch et al. 1999). Whether they previously constituted a separate nation of Koyukon speakers or were merely a regional band of the Koyukuk River Koyukon is not known. Given the size of the estate they controlled and the nature of the resources normally available there, I am inclined to think that they constituted a separate nation. Based on analogy with the population living in the same district after they had been assimilated, I expect that they could have numbered as many as 500 people. Nothing is known about how they were organized beyond the fact that, even prior to assimilation, their way of life was strongly influenced by that of neighboring Kobuk River Iñupiat (and vice versa).

The Koyukon whose estate apparently encompassed the upper portion of the Koyukuk River valley, shown on Map 9 as Koyukuk River Koyukon, were known to the Iñupiat as Taġraġviŋmiut. Since the place-name Taġraġvik refers specifically to the Koyukuk River, it is unlikely that Koyukon speakers living in either the Kobuk or the Yukon River valleys were included under this term.

Just how many Taġraġviŋmiut there were and how they were organized at the beginning of the study period is unknown. During the 1820s or 1830s this population was struck by a severe famine that left the central part of the valley vacant (Huntington 1993:132–135). In 1842 Lavrentiy A. Zagoskin reported (Michael 1967:153) that the middle portion of the river was essentially uninhabited but that there were people living in the upper part of the valley. In the 1860s the population of the region was very low (only about 300 people); it was organized in terms of four regional bands, each of which was further divided into a set of local families.[44] They were also divided into three exogamous matrilineal clans, and matrilineal ties were paramount in the formation of both local families and regional bands. Settlements tended to be very small (only one or two households, for the most part) and were occupied by the members of only a single local family. Larger aggregations formed from time to time but only for brief periods.

Very little is known about the early-19th-century organization of either the Yunnaka Khotana or the Inkilik Proper. Unlike their Taġraġviŋmiut relatives, they were apparently not divided into clans, and the primary organizational unit was the semisedentary endogamous village.[45] Like their Yup'ik neighbors on the Norton Sound coast, these people were struck by the smallpox epidemic of 1838. After that event they reportedly numbered some 450 people (Loyens 1966:22), a figure that, if correct, suggests a particularly large pre-epidemic population by Alaskan standards.

Westerners

Europeans and others of European cultural and biological ancestry were originally referred to as Qatiqtuat, which means "things without any color" (Cleveland 1970a). Subsequently, they became known as Naluaġmiut. The newer term is bizarre because, according to the Iñupiaq system of identification, the suffix -miut must be appended to a place-name. In this case, however, it is attached to *naluaq*, which means "bleached skin." Nevertheless, the term is attested in the NANA Region as early as 1873 (Smith 1873). African Americans apparently arrived in northwestern Alaska around or shortly after midcentury, when they came as members of whaling crews. They received the label Taaqsipaich (pl.; Taaqsipak, sing.), which refers to their skin color, *taaqsiq* meaning "dark." In this study all nonindigenous visitors to north-central Beringia are grouped together under the term "Westerner." More precise distinctions, such as between Americans and Europeans and among Russians, British, and Americans, are made as appropriate.

The first Westerners to venture into northern Beringia were Russians, a few of whom penetrated western Chukotka during the 17th century. The Russians and their Siberian Native allies tried to subjugate the Chukchi and Asiatic Yup'ik Eskimos by force. They failed, but not before wreaking widespread havoc among the Native population (Bogoras 1901:80, 1904–9:15; Forsyth

1992:143–151; Golder 1971:156–164; Krupnik 1996a, 1966b; Lantzeff and Pierce 1973:214, 218–219; Ray 1975b:11). After pausing to regroup, the Russians turned to trade as a more fruitful way to establish hegemony in the region. Russians also made a few extremely brief exploratory visits to Bering Strait during the 17th and 18th centuries. Only one of them—the Billings expedition in 1791—involved direct contact with Iñupiat on the Alaskan mainland, however (Chernenko 1957; Merck 1980; Sarychev 1806–7, vol. 2:44–52; Sauer 1802:242–248). The English also made one foray into the region during this early period (James Cook's expedition in 1778), but their only contacts with Iñupiat were south of the NANA Region (Cook and King 1784).

It was not until 1816, when Otto von Kotzebue "discovered" the sound that he named after himself, that Westerners began to make direct contact with Iñupiat living in the NANA Region (Chamisso 1986a, 1986b; Choris 1822; Kotzebue 1821, vol. 1:207; VanStone 1960). After a decade of fairly detailed scrutiny and charting of the coastline of northwestern Alaska as well as sporadic summer contact with the Native inhabitants, European exploration of the NANA Region declined until the late 1840s. A Russian trading vessel, however, apparently made annual visits to Kotzebue Sound from about 1840 to the mid-1860s (Black 2004:199).

A major threshold was crossed in 1833, when the Russian-American Company established a trading post at Saint Michael (Mikhailovskii Redoubt) on the southern shore of Norton Sound (Ray 1975b:122–124). The Saint Michael post was roughly 150 miles (240 kilometers) south of the region of primary concern here, but its presence as a relatively close market for furs and as a source of Western goods was nevertheless soon felt in the NANA Region. Of equal if not greater importance was the smallpox epidemic of 1838, which decimated the Yup'ik-speaking Eskimo population of Norton Sound and the Koyukon population of the lower Yukon (Michael 1967:92, 95, 100, 146, 147, 149; Ray 1975b:125–127). For some reason the epidemic stopped south of Iñupiaq territory. However, by depopulating the eastern shore of Norton Sound it greatly facilitated the movement of Iñupiat to the trading post at Saint Michael by eliminating most of the inhabitants of the intervening estates.

A second major threshold occurred between 1848 and 1854, when a series of British expeditions, known collectively as the Franklin search expeditions, visited the region (Bockstoce 1985; Ray 1975b:140–156). Over a five-year period ships overwintered in northwestern Alaska on four occasions. Also beginning in 1848, large numbers of American whaling ships arrived in northwestern Alaska, often accompanied by small trading vessels (Bockstoce 1986:93–102, 182–184; Collinson 1889:132). These developments had a significant impact on the Iñupiat generally and were the beginning of the end of the phenomena I describe in this book.

We are extremely fortunate that most of the Westerners who visited the NANA Region before 1848 came primarily to explore the country and do a bit of trading but not to exploit, missionize, or conquer the Native peoples who lived there. As explorers and observers, most of them kept good records of what they saw, yet they tried to leave the Natives relatively undisturbed even when they were confronted with very hostile behavior. The Westerners also came in relatively small numbers. Somehow they managed to come and go without transmitting any foreign diseases to the members of this "virgin-soil" population, despite the fact that most of Alaska to the south had been devastated by smallpox. It is this situation, combined with the enduring strength of the Iñupiaq oral tradition into the lifetimes of my informants, that made possible the writing of this book.

Some Methodological Notes

Most of this book is based on information provided to me by Iñupiaq elders more than a century after the time the relevant events or phenomena occurred. I understand, because they told me so, that at least some of the leading researchers who have worked in the NANA Region over the past thirty years do not accept historical information provided by oral sources as being true unless they can corroborate it with archaeological or historical evidence. Others reading this book may also wonder whether they should accept the testimony of people who never personally witnessed or experienced the phenomena of which they speak. I have addressed this issue elsewhere (Burch 1981:63–64, 1991, 1998a:12–19), but, since skeptics apparently abound, it is appropriate to deal with it once again.

In the past, Iñupiaq history was transmitted orally from one generation to the next in both formal and informal contexts. The formal context was the storytelling session, during which experts recounted legends and tales before assemblages made up of people of all ages. These took place at all times of year but especially during the long winter nights, when cold and darkness restricted outdoor activities. Informal contexts included conversations and narratives delivered as people traveled about the country, crossing or passing localities of historical interest as they did so. Many historical events were recorded in place-names, of which there was an enormous number and which were known by virtually every adult. Information obtained in this way augmented and reinforced that acquired in a more formal setting.

Sources

Most of the information I obtained on traditional Iñupiaq life was acquired between 1960 and 1990 through formal interviews with 120 people who lived in 14 different villages. Of the total, 45 claimed to be—and were regarded by the Iñupiat as—historians. The rest were not historians, but most of them still provided me with contextual or other useful information.

It is customary in the evaluation of *written* material as a source of historical information to publish detailed critical analyses of both its form and its content. This is not ordinarily done with oral sources because the people in the population from which they are drawn, not to mention the sources themselves, typically find it offensive to be publicly evaluated in this way. After all, they did not publish the material but shared it privately with a researcher in an atmosphere of trust. A critical analysis of orally produced information must be conducted, nevertheless, in order for an investigator properly to assess the information provided by several different individuals. The difference is that the critique of oral sources is not made part of the public record, whereas the analysis of published sources usually is.

In my own research I never accepted anything an informant told me at face value; I always subjected it to critical scrutiny. However, I must also note that by the time I had begun serious historical research, I had learned never to dismiss anything out of hand. Criteria I used to assess the information provided by individual informants included the following: (1) their status as historians within the Native community, where factual accuracy was a major criterion for evaluation; (2) the internal consistency of their information; (3) the breadth of their knowledge with regard to their subject matter; (4) their knowledge of change through time; (5) the consistency of their information with that provided by others; (6) a willingness to admit ignorance; and (7) corroboration by other types of evidence if relevant material was available.

The information provided by all of my sources was evaluated in terms of the above criteria. My most striking finding was how accurate and honest the overwhelming majority of my sources were in assessing their own strengths and weaknesses. Of the 120 people I interviewed formally, only one deliberately tried to mislead me, and only three knew a lot less than they thought they did. Another striking feature was the exceptionally high degree of consistency in the information provided by different people. Even with regard to subjects where a certain amount of falsification might be expected, such as which side won or lost a particular battle, descendants of combatants from both sides agreed on the outcome without any prodding from me. Perhaps most encouraging of all was the fact that, without any exception (other than the four people just noted) that I can recall, where corroboration of informant testimony by other types of evidence was possible, not one of the accounts failed to be confirmed. If oral sources are shown to be telling the truth in every instance where corroboration by independent evidence is possible, it is very difficult *not* to believe them when they speak about subjects where corroboration is not possible.

Stories

A particularly important consideration in my own research was the fact that Iñupiat differentiated between legends (*unipkaat*) and historical chronicles (*uqaluktuat*) (Jenness 1924:1; Ostermann 1942:163; Rainey 1947:269). The former were ancient tales that were *thought* to be true, while the latter were authentic incidents only a few generations old or less. Virtually all of my research focused on historical chronicles. I never asked an informant to tell me stories. I acquired a substantial number of them anyway, but they always emerged when the subject matter of the interview reminded an informant of a story, be it legend or historical chronicle. Some of these stories are recounted in this volume, particularly in Chapter 2, and it is appropriate to make a few general remarks about them here.

My first comment concerns the language in which the accounts are presented, which is English. The quality of the English varies considerably, but the form in which it appears here is almost always more "standard" than the one in which it was originally told to and recorded by me. The reason for this is that "village English" in northwestern Alaska is a special variant of the language, one filled with Iñupiaq terms and with many English expressions meaning something different from what they do in other parts of the English-speaking world (see Jans 1996:33–37). Also, Iñupiaq storytellers make extensive use of hand, arm, and body gestures; they laugh, cry, smile, and frown as appropriate; and they frequently interject songs into their presentations, sometimes with drum accompaniment. Sources from all districts occasionally interjected Iñupiaq passages into what were otherwise village English accounts, and on the upper Kobuk some of the inserted passages were in Koyukon. I did not realize how difficult it is to capture the substance (not to mention the flavor) of such presentations until I hired four expert typists to transcribe tapes of my interviews. They simply could not do it; I had to do it myself. In order that the reader may understand them, I have translated the narratives presented here from village English or combined village English–Iñupiatun to more or less standard English while trying at the same time to keep some of the flavor of the original presentation.

Another thing I do is present "composite" accounts. By this I mean that I present narratives developed from what came to me as two or more separate accounts. In some cases the segments were acquired by me, but in others some or all of the segments were obtained by other investigators. This apparently cavalier approach requires some explanation.

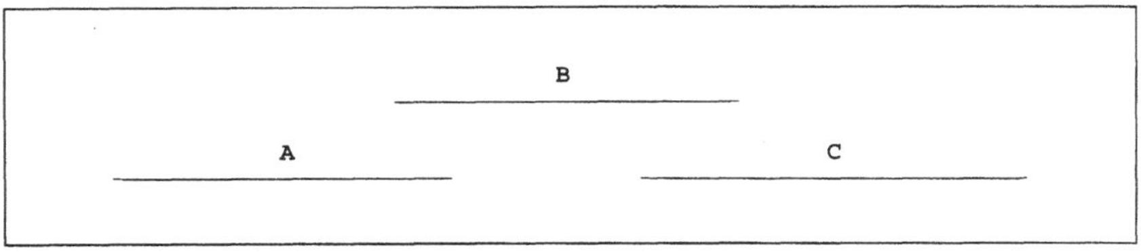

1. Schematic model of relations among story segments.

Many Iñupiaq stories are exceptionally long, taking several hours a night for days or even weeks to complete. Others, while much shorter, still take a long time to tell. One thing that always surprised me about most of the Iñupiaq stories I was told was that, although they seemed to have a more or less distinct beginning, they rarely had an identifiable end. The narrator simply stopped talking. I now realize that when this happened I was getting only a segment of a longer story, even if it had taken the speaker an hour to tell it. The starting point was the place where the story dealt with a person or event relating to what the narrator and I had been talking about in our original conversation. The end was an arbitrarily selected point located somewhere after the part that was relevant to the main subject of our conversation. After hearing many such accounts over the years I became aware of the fact that, in many cases, what I originally thought were two (or more) completely independent stories were linked by a third (or more) into a single account.

This is illustrated schematically in Figure 1, which represents three story segments: A, B, and C. Assume that the first one I heard as a separate story is C. Assume further that four years later I heard story A, possibly dealing with the same people as story C but not otherwise linked to it. Then, at some still later time I heard or read story B. On inspection, story B proves to contain elements of the other two as well as material serving as an obvious link between them. Given this new perspective, it is apparent that these are not three separate one-hour stories but one three-hour story told in three disconnected installments. Segment B serves as a "bridge" to connect A and C.

I am convinced that most anthropologists working in at least the Iñupiaq part of Alaska have failed to get the whole of very many stories. Instead, like me, they acquired one or more segments, each of which was understood by the researcher to be an independent narrative. I am convinced further that most of the collections of "legends," "myths," and "stories" from northwestern Alaska, whether published in Iñupiaq or English, are in fact collections of story segments; the accounts are too short to be anything else.

When I was compiling material for this volume I discovered several instances in which what I thought were separate stories were linked by bridges into single, unitary narratives. Rather than present clearly related segments as independent stories I have combined them here. I have done this even when the segments were given to me by different informants or published by other investigators. I had to take certain liberties when doing this, particularly with regard to style, but in every instance I note the fact that the account is a composite, and I indicate the sources of the segments.

Two additional methodological points concern the names of the people in the accounts presented and the chronology of events. Regarding the first, my sources had not told (or heard) many of these accounts for some years, and the names of individuals in the narratives did not always come readily to mind. That embarrassed them, but at the time I did not think it worth pursuing. I realize now that if I had asked them a week or two later what the names had been, they probably would have remembered some if not all of them. It also did not occur to me until some years after most of this information was acquired to attempt to get a list of the genealogical descendants of the people mentioned in the stories, which would have helped me assign absolute dates to the events in the stories. In addition, I did not realize until later that my informants probably could have told me whether certain incidents occurred before or after certain others, which would have enabled me to compile a relative chronology. When I finally asked about this, well after most of my leading informants had died, two experts on one district told me without hesitation what the sequence of three different battles had been. Such information, when combined with personal names and genealogical data, might have enabled me to sketch a fairly reliable general chronology of major events.

2. Hostile Relations

Hostility is a sentiment that ranges in intensity from mild annoyance through a series of minute gradations to passionate hatred. Its expression in action similarly extends from a frown or a harsh word through a number of intermediate levels to torture and homicide. We cannot know, at this remove in time, how the Iñupiat really felt about foreigners during the early 19th century, but we do have some information on how they acted toward them.

General Demeanor

The stereotyped Western view of Eskimos in general and of traditional Iñupiat in particular is that they were peaceful, happy, smiling, good-natured people who were kind to strangers (Fienup-Riordan 1990:146–153, 1994:321–326). This view has a reasonably solid foundation in many late-19th-century documents. For example, Dr. Irving Rosse, who was aboard the Revenue Marine steamer *Corwin* in the Chukchi Sea in 1880 and 1881, wrote as follows:

> *Perhaps in no other race is the combative instinct less predominant; in none is quarreling, fierceness of disposition, and jealousy more conspicuously absent, and in none does the desire for the factitious renown of war exist in a more rudimentary and undeveloped state. Perhaps the constant fight with cold and hunger is a compensation which must account for the absence of such unmitigated evils as war, taxes, complex social organization, and hierarchy among the curious people of the icy north. The pursuits of peace and of simple patriarchal lives, notwithstanding the fact that much in connection therewith is wretched and forbidding to a civilized man, seem to beget in these people a degree of domestic tranquillity and contentment which, united to their light-hearted and cheery disposition, is an additional reason for believing the sum of human happiness to be constant throughout the world.* [1883:38]

In the same vein, Calvin L. Hooper, commander of the *Corwin* on the 1880 cruise, described the Iñupiat as "remarkably good-natured" and "always smiling when spoken to" (1881:58). In his report on the cruise the following year he noted, "The Innuits are cheerful in appearance, and exceedingly good-natured. They are inclined to laugh at what they do not understand, and when visiting the vessel their faces wore an expression of mingled curiosity and amusement" (Hooper 1884:101). And yet again: "Fortunate it is that these people are good-natured and not inclined to quarrel, for armed as they are and knowing no law, they would be exceedingly troublesome. In the few instances where trouble has occurred between Innuits and white men, it appears to have been the fault of the latter" (Hooper 1884:106).

I do not know just how the arrogant Dr. Rosse came to his conclusion, but it appears as though he was projecting his conception of the Noble Savage on the people of the North. He certainly did not have enough experience to comment on the subject one way or another. But Captain Hooper was clearly being hoodwinked. The Iñupiat smiled at him and were cheerful in his presence because he was in command of an expedition the specific purpose of which was to prevent them from getting the two things they wanted most—whisky and firearms. They wanted to make a good impression on him, and smiling seemed to produce the desired result.

My sources were unanimous in the view that when they were children, which in some cases was just a year or two after Hooper's visits, adults generally wore dour expressions when walking around outside among their own people. It was only when they were inside their houses or community centers (qargiich) that they smiled, laughed, and generally acted in the cordial manner Westerners usually attributed to them. My sources added that everything they had ever heard about still earlier generations indicated that their public demeanor was, if anything, even more serious.

The best-informed sources from the first half of the 19th century corroborate my informants' statements and contradict Hooper's. Frederick Beechey, for example, on the basis of his observations in 1825–26, contrasted the Iñupiat with the eastern Eskimos he had met previously, saying that the Iñupiat were "rather partaking of the warlike, irascible, and uncourteous temper of the Tschutschi [Chukchi]" (1831, vol. 2:303). In 1838 A. F. Kashevarov described the Iñupiat as "warlike," and, as many of the excerpts from his journal cited in Chapter 1 attest, he had ample reason to think so (VanStone 1977:81). Rochefort Maguire, commander of HMS *Plover* during two years at Barrow in midcentury, described the Iñupiat as, "contrary to our preconceived opinion, very troublesome and unfriendly" (1857:416), and he devoted several pages of his report to the presentation of evidence in support of that thesis (1857:416–432).

A general mistrust and fear of strangers underlay Iñupiaq relations with *all* outsiders. On the basis of his extensive experience in northern Alaska and Canada, during which he learned to speak the Inuit language fluently, Vilhjalmur Stefansson wrote that "nothing is more ingrained in the real Eskimo and nothing pervades more thoroughly his traditions and folklore than the idea that strangers are necessarily hostile and treacherous" (1944:426). As Lawrence Hennigh put it, one of the most fundamental principles of Iñupiaq life was that "anyone with whom one is not in a positive social relationship is an enemy" (1972:93). That obviously included most foreigners with whom one was acquainted and virtually all complete strangers. The members of most Iñupiaq nations seem to have believed that they were substantially, if not entirely, surrounded by enemies (*akiḷḷiich*).

Early encounters between Iñupiat and Westerners suggest some factors that may have influenced Native behavior while in the presence of strangers. One important variable was relative numbers. If the Iñupiat outnumbered the explorers, they tended to act in an aggressive, hostile manner. If, on the other hand, they were inferior in numbers, they smiled and were friendly. Several comments from early observers support that conclusion.

The first is by a Chukchi who, in 1816, told Otto von Kotzebue that the "Americans" (i.e., the Iñupiat) "behaved friendly as long as they considered themselves weaker; but robbed and murdered strangers without hesitation, if they were strong enough, and were able to do it without danger; and, for this reason, he thought they wore knives in their sleeves, and use their wives to entice them" (1821, vol. 1:262). The second is by Thomas Simpson, who, with a small party, traversed the Arctic coast from the Mackenzie River delta (in Canada) to Point Barrow and back in the summer of 1837: "I may here remark, that, except at Point Barrow, we invariably found the arrogance of the natives to increase in due proportion to their numbers" (1843:183).[1] The following year Kashevarov observed that "as their numbers increased, so did their audacity" (VanStone 1977:42).

Fifteen years later Maguire came to the same conclusion:

> *When the natives were collected in any numbers the difference of character displayed by them when so, and the reverse, is worthy of remark. In the former case they are bold and overbearing, and when meeting the parties [from the ship] gather around them and apparently in a half playful way commence shoving them about and feeling their clothes, when, if they fail in getting what they want given to them, they help themselves, and with their knives soon remove any buttons that happen to be bright. On the contrary, when they are in small numbers, they are not like the same people, but seem quiet, harmless, inoffensive and obliging, even while displaying these good qualities, should their numbers become increased they lose no time in throwing off their assumed humility to join in any plunder going on.* [Great Britain, Parliament, House of Commons 1854b:171]

John Simpson, who had more experience in northwestern Alaska than any other Westerner prior to the mid-1880s, echoed Maguire: "Whenever we have met them at a distance from the ship in small parties, they have proved tractable and willing to assist when required; but when the numbers were large they were mischievous bullies, threatened to use their knives on the slightest provocation, and, instead of giving assistance, would rather throw impediments in our way" (1875:250).

And finally, I quote Edward Nelson, who traveled widely in western and northwestern Alaska during the period 1877–81: "When among their own tribesmen in large villages they frequently become obtrusive, and the energetic, athletic people about the shores of Bering Strait and northward are inclined to become overbearing and domineering when in sufficient numbers to warrant it. On the other hand, when travelling away from their native places in small numbers, among strangers, they become very quiet and mild-mannered" (1899:300).

The above accounts explain why many of the most peaceful Iñupiaq–Westerner encounters were at small summer camps, while many of the most hostile occurred when the Natives were in a significant majority. John Cantwell, a Revenue Marine officer who explored the Kobuk River valley, found that the people living in the interior were "better morally than their brethern [*sic*] of the coast[.] . . . They are honest in their dealings with strangers and amongst themselves" (1889b:82). But, unbeknownst to him, he was in the country at a time of year when most Kobuk men, particularly the younger ones, were away hunting caribou in the Noatak River valley. He might have come to a different conclusion had he been there in October.

Some of the Iñupiaq–Westerner encounters did not fit the pattern suggested by the above generalizations; hence, other factors must have been involved. One seems to have been the Westerners' willingness (or lack thereof) to trade. Closely associated with this was the Iñupiaq expectation of meeting strangers who might want to trade, which was much higher at some times of year than at others. Strangers encountered around the time of the summer trade fairs or who were obviously going to or returning from such a fair were generally treated well. This was particularly so if they exhibited a willingness to trade with whatever Native group encountered them.

For example, on July 27, 1826, a detachment of eight men and two officers from Beechey's crew set out in a barge to explore the mouth of Hotham Inlet. To get there they had to go to within a few miles of Sisualik, the site of the largest trade fair in all of northwestern Alaska. Some people had already gathered for the fair, and when the barge anchored in the vicinity of their camp the Europeans suddenly found themselves surrounded by 14 umiat containing 150 men. But the Iñupiat were "very orderly and well behaved," and the members of the two groups proceeded to trade without even a hint of trouble (Beechey 1831, vol. 1:351–352). Conversely, on July 14, 1820, a detachment of 20 men from the Vasil'ev–Shishmarev expedition, traveling in a longboat and an Aleut umiaq, happened to find itself among hundreds of people at the main beluga-hunting camp of the entire Kaŋiġmiut nation. International trade virtually never occurred at that time and place. After a peaceful beginning the situation rapidly deteriorated. Ultimately, the Russians had to blow up a Native umiaq with a falconet in order to escape from a situation in which they might all have been killed.

Most variations in demeanor probably can be explained by one or a combination of the above two variables. In mid-July 1838 Kashevarov's expedition stopped at a large encampment of Utuqqaġmiut one day and at the main village of the Silaliñaġiut the next. The former probably had a population between 150 and 200 people, while the latter had one of about 300. Yet Kashevarov and his people were well treated by the members of both encampments. As it happens, that was just about the time a trade fair usually took place near the mouth of the Utukok River, just a short distance away, that would have involved both groups (Rainey 1947:240). Later on, when the party was surrounded by similar numbers of people in the Barrow and Kivalina districts, it was in serious jeopardy. The party was in those districts at the wrong time of year or, in the Kivalina case, probably coming from the wrong direction at that time of year.[2]

Strategy

The evidence from both oral and written sources confirms that the Iñupiat were not the happy, peaceful hunter-gatherers the Western stereotype would have us believe. Instead, they were fiercely independent peoples who conducted external affairs in a very aggressive manner.[3] Armed conflict and the threat of armed conflict were basic facts of life. But why? Why did men from one nation attack people of another? How did they decide which nation and which settlement(s) in that nation's country to attack? How did they decide when to attack? These fundamental questions are appropriately discussed under the heading of strategy. Tactics, which concern how the strategy is actually carried out, are discussed separately below.

Outside Pressure

The notion that Western expansion lay behind indigenous warfare in northwestern Alaska specifically has never been suggested, as far as I know. However, it has been proposed by Service (1968) and by Ferguson and Whitehead (1992:26–28) as a major cause of indigenous warfare everywhere in the world, hence in northwestern Alaska by implication. Their thesis is that warfare among small-scale societies, such as those in northern Beringia, is the direct consequence of pressure being put on them by much larger and more powerful ones, particularly colonialist societies. The frequency and the characteristics of warfare in such societies are caused by the dislocations and culture change resulting from state expansionism. Truly indigenous warfare, therefore, is beyond the reach of ethnographic research.

If the Service–Ferguson and Whitehead hypothesis is correct, then it follows that warfare, as described in the ethnographic record of northern Beringia, did not exist prior to at least indirect contact by nation-states. In addition, if the hypothesis is correct, the more direct the contact with nation-states became, the more frequent indigenous warfare should have become. We are fortunate to be able to test these propositions with evidence from the study region.

The data relevant to this issue are summarized in some detail in Chapter 4, which is where I place the events of the study period into their historical context. Here I summarize the particular conclusions of that discussion relevant to the issue at hand. The first is that archaeological evidence indicates that warfare in northwestern Alaska predates Western contact by at least 300 years and probably by more than 1,000. The second conclusion is that the cessation of warfare in northwestern Alaska occurred very soon after intensified contact, which began in 1848. These findings are exactly the opposite of those predicted by the Service–Ferguson and Whitehead hypothesis.

The situation in Chukotka was radically different from the one in northwestern Alaska. There, the Russians and the Chukchi fought each other for more than a century. The Russians prevailed more often than not, but the resistance mounted by the Reindeer Chukchi in particular was so effective that it led the Russians to decide that their conquest was not worth the cost. Accordingly, they abandoned the country, leaving the Chukchi in command. The Reindeer Chukchi followed up their victory with their own territorial expansion. In Chukotka the Service–Ferguson and Whitehead hypothesis does not account for the origin of warfare, but it is consistent with both the spread and the changing nature of Chukchi warfare during the 18th century. However, since Chukchi expansion eastward was blocked by Bering Strait, it had to take place to the west, far beyond the region of primary interest here.

Territorial Expansion

A second hypothesis concerning the causes of war, this one specifically relating to events in northern Beringia, was proposed by Dorothy Jean Ray: "Each tribe was eager to extend its boundaries, and would have done so if land had not been so carefully guarded" (1967:389). Land *was* carefully guarded, however, with the result that "tribal movements" were "accompanied by strife and bloodshed." Unfortunately, the battles to which Ray refers "are not of record," and it is therefore impossible to know who tried to acquire what territory, how they acquired it, and who succeeded and who failed.

One obvious potential reason for conflict could have been the desire to acquire richer hunting grounds. There are at least two problems with this hypothesis. The first is that the nations with the richest hunting grounds had the largest populations and were quite capable of defending themselves. The second is that, from everything I learned from the elders, the great majority of people thought that their own estates were the best places to live, and they could hold forth at length on what was special about them. Desired goods that could not be obtained locally could be acquired through trade. Besides these two theoretical possibilities, I never heard of a case in which the members of one society tried to exterminate or eject the members of another from their own homeland so that they could occupy it themselves.

Conflicts over land did occur, or are alleged to have occurred, in a few cases, however. One disputed area was the middle and upper Kukpowruk River valley, located along the common border of the estates of the Tikiġaġmiut and Utuqqaġmiut, just to the north of the study region (Burch 1981:12). This district was peripheral to the Tikiġaġmiut and to their interests. They used the area as a caribou hunting ground only in summer, a season when virtually all of the Utuqqaġmiut were on the coast, some distance to the northwest. It was of much greater potential significance to the Utuqqaġmiut as a winter hunting area, and they therefore expended more energy in establishing control over it. They finally succeeded, apparently during the first decade or two of the 19th century, but probably more by default than by actual conquest. The area was not valuable enough to the Tikiġaġmiut and it was too remote from their settlements for them to go to the trouble of defending it.

A second alleged case of land dispute involved the Tikiġaġmiut and the Nuataaġmiut. According to John W. Kelly (Wells and Kelly 1890:10), the former had a rapidly expanding population during the 18th century and incorporated the entire estates of the Kivalliñiġmiut and Napaaqtuġmiut and part of the estate of the Qikiqtaġruŋmiut into their own. He says they were expanding into Nuataaġmiut territory when a combined force from all four nations confronted them in a relatively large scale pitched battle near Cape Seppings. The Tikiġaġmiut were badly defeated, losing something on the order of 200 men. There seems to be no doubt that a major battle took place where Kelly said it did and that the Tikiġaġmiut were badly defeated there, but his claim that the Tikiġaġmiut estate had become as large as he said is not sustained by any other evidence (see Ostermann and Holtved 1952:48). The Tikiġaġmiut may have attempted to establish a sphere of influence (see Chapter 4) over these other societies, but if they succeeded, it had a lifespan of less than a generation.

Other alleged land disputes occurred on the Seward Peninsula during the 18th and early 19th centuries. Some, noted by Ray (1967:391), involved land on the north side of the peninsula, within the NANA Region. However, the accounts are mutually contradictory, and there is not much we can conclude from them. More interesting is the question of what happened to the Yup'ik-speaking peoples who probably occupied the entire southern and western shore of the Seward Peninsula during the 17th and 18th centuries (Krauss 1993). By the beginning of the 19th century these areas were inhabited by Iñupiaq speakers. Were these lands taken through conquest, or did their inhabitants acquire the Iñupiaq language through some other process? At this point there is no way to know, but assimilation should be kept on the list of possibilities along with territorial expansion.

Reindeer Chukchi territories did not have clearly demarcated borders, so the situation in Chukotka was inherently more fluid than it was in Alaska (Krupnik 1996a, 1996b). On the other hand, Chukchi reindeer herds were expanding at a rapid rate both before and during the study period, and this created the potential for a kind of land hunger that was unknown in Alaska at the time (Bogoras 1904–9:706). However, because Bering Strait blocked them on the east, their expansion was to the west and southwest, away from the region of interest here (Bogoras 1904–9:72–73).[4]

Before leaving the subject of territorial expansion it is useful to consider briefly what the possibilities were. One issue is the ecological feasibility of territorial expansion. In most although not all cases the heartland of each national estate was in an area that was resource rich, at least seasonally, while the border was located in an area that was resource poor (Burch 1998a:311). Simple expansion was not a realistic option in such cases because the resource-poor areas had to be incorporated into the enlarged estate along with the resource-rich ones. This would have divided the new geographic unit into two discrete parcels in which the most desirable living areas were a considerable distance apart. It would have been impossible to manage, not to mention defend, such a large area. In contrast, the members of the nations whose estates lay along the Kobuk and Selawik Rivers, which were not separated by unproductive areas, seem to have gotten along quite well. The system the Iñupiat actually developed—a combination of international trade and selective easements for the use of one another's territory—provided a much more effective means of acquiring scarce resources than conquest ever could have.

A second consideration is the demographic feasibility of territorial expansion. A basic principle of territorial conquest is that "no war is over until the infantry of one side occupies the territory [estate] of the other" (Dunnigan and Nofi 1990:17). In northwestern Alaska the question is, Which, if any, of the nations in northwestern Alaska had sufficient manpower to occupy the combined estates of two formerly separate countries, their original one and the one they conquered? There were probably only two, the Kiŋikmiut (Wales, 650 people) and the Tikiġaġmiut (Point Hope, 1,300 people), both of which are outside the study region.[5] But even they had the manpower to occupy only small additional areas, not entire national estates. An alternative to occupying territory, of course, is to subject the leadership of a conquered nation to foreign control. However, the nations of northwestern Alaska were too decentralized for that to work: there were no national leaders for outsiders to control (see Hayden 1995:30–31).

Given the above considerations, one must conclude that territorial expansion, in the sense of one nation actually adding all or part of the estate of another to its own through either conquest or merger, was not a feasible option in northwestern Alaska. This does not mean that the members of a powerful nation could not strongly influence the affairs of a weaker one, and it does not mean that the members of one or more nations could not be culturally and linguistically assimilated by the members of another while still remaining independent. Most apparent cases of territorial expansion in northwestern Alaska were probably instances of alliance or assimilation and not of conquest, merger, or expansion.[6]

Control of Trade

The possibility that economic factors underlay warfare in northern Beringia has been proposed by Malaurie (1974) and Sheehan (1997). Sheehan's model is the more elegant of the two and thus serves as the focus of the present discussion.

Sheehan asserts that warfare in northern Alaska arose out of a need to control international trade. As I understand it, his argument in support of that thesis rests on the following propositions:

1. The estates of the several nations of northwestern Alaska did not contain all of the resources necessary for human survival.
2. Deficiencies were made up through international trade.
3. Over time, population growth outstripped the capacity of the international trade network to distribute commodities to the extent required for the persistence of some or all of the nations concerned.
4. These deficiencies led to restrictions on trade that favored some nations and not others.

5. Nations that were placed at a disadvantage resorted to war in an effort to redirect the international system of trade in ways that eliminated their shortfall.

Economic factors may, indeed, have been occasionally invoked as a cause of war. There is good reason to believe, for example, that some of the battles between Koyukon and Eskimos and between mixed alliances of Koyukon and Eskimos that occurred at the very end of the study period were fought over issues related to the fur trade. The conflicts at Kelroteyit and Noolaaghedoh are examples (see Appendix 1). However, those are the only examples I know of.

There is precious little independent evidence either to support or to challenge Sheehan's model on the general level, and he does not provide any data in support of his thesis. In order to evaluate it, one would need information on population change, the frequency and distribution of warfare, types of commodities that were traded, and the volume of trade in northwestern Alaska for at least 500 years. The data needed to test Sheehan's hypothesis do not exist now, and they are unlikely to exist in the future.

It is worth pausing here to ponder how people from any one nation could effectively control international trade in early-19th-century northwestern Alaska even in theory. As I show in Chapter 3, international trade was structured primarily around partnerships between individuals in different nations, with exchanges taking place primarily at trade fairs in summer and messenger feasts in winter. Any nation whose members tried to control a trade fair would have been confronted instantly by a massive alliance of all the other nations whose members participated in that fair; such an effort would fail almost before it began. Messenger feasts involved relations between people in only one village in each of two nations. Many, possibly dozens, of such feasts were held every winter. It would have taken hundreds and possibly thousands of troops, dispersed over a huge area yet operating under a single command, to take control of such a system. No nation in northwestern Alaska had the manpower or the communications system required to accomplish that.

The system of international trade in northwestern Alaska was simply too decentralized for any of the nations involved to control it. People and assets were, and had to be, widely dispersed in most nations most of the time, and the distribution of people and assets had to fluctuate seasonally if people were to survive. There were no customs or other controls on the international transfer of either people or goods. There were no chiefs, governments, trading cartels, or other centralized institutions that a foreign power could use to dominate, and thus control, another nation's international trade. No *umialik* (chieftain; see Chapter 3) or shaman had such a broad span of influence that, by assassinating, intimidating, or holding hostage a few important individuals, a foreign power could use him to control the members of an entire nation. None of the social mechanisms for dominating international trade available to the members of more complex societies existed among the nations of northwestern Alaska.

A third theoretical possibility was to control trade routes, of which there was a large and complex network (see Appendix 2). The only places where a nation could exercise much control over such routes was at points where a large number of them came together. However, such locations were precisely where the fairs were held, and most of the trade following those routes converged there only just before and after the fairs were in progress. As noted above, any attempt to control a fair was doomed from the start. A possible exception to these generalizations is Bering Strait, which created a bottleneck in the trade between Chukotka and Alaska. Here the Kiŋikmiut (at Wales) may have attempted to control the intercontinental trade flowing south and west from Kotzebue Sound from time to time, and this has been alleged by some late-19th-century writers (Aldrich 1889:29; Hooper 1881:20). However, they could not prevent Chukotkans from sailing past them and traveling directly to the fair at Sisualik, on Kotzebue Sound. South of Wales, intercontinental traders could easily slip past Kiŋikmiut warriors and cross the strait, rendering futile any attempt to control this route as well.

In many parts of the world economic factors contributing to warfare often included the acquisition of booty and slaves. However, very little plunder was involved in Iñupiaq warfare because most raiding and war parties traveled on foot and therefore traveled light. Once a battle or raid was completed, the aggressors usually tried to get home quickly and thus with little baggage, because they could never be sure that fellow countrymen or allies of the defeated force would not suddenly appear and retaliate. Captives were rarely taken, and when they were it was usually only to torture them on the way home. I have no specific data regarding these matters among the Koyukon or Gwich'in, but they probably followed the same procedures as the Iñupiat and for the same reasons.

Because of the substantial carrying capacity of the boats used in northern Beringia amphibious assaults or other encounters involving umiaq-borne troops offered greater possibilities for recovering booty and/or captives than overland expeditions did. It may be for these reasons that Chukotkans frequently took women captive when they made a successful raid in Alaska. There was apparently also a market for slaves in Chukotka, since the reindeer breeders often needed extra people to help with their herds (Schweitzer and Golovko 1997). One would expect boats to have been filled to capacity with warriors, however, leaving little room for booty or prisoners.

Ethnic Enmity

"Ethnic enmity" is a phrase I use to express a special preference for attacking people of a particular linguistic or cultural background different from one's own. The Athapaskan–Eskimo boundary, in particular, is often said to have been the focus of an especially high level of international hostility in northwestern Alaska. Ray, for example, has stated that "Eskimos felt [the] greatest apprehension toward non-Eskimos, who were considered to be chronic and extremely dangerous interlopers" (1967:387). She also asserted that "anxiety toward other Eskimo groups was not as pronounced as toward non-Eskimos" (Ray 1967:388). Although other writers did not state the position so succinctly, at least some of them, including William Healy Dall (1870:144), James Louis Giddings Jr. (1961:124), and Helge Ingstad (1954:108–109), would appear to agree with it. To hear the Natives talk, they sometimes believe it themselves.

My problem in accepting the ethnic enmity hypothesis is based on the fact that none of the evidence I have collected over more than 40 years of research supports it. Even informants who claimed that warfare was greater between Athapaskans and Iñupiat than it was among Iñupiat ended up citing examples that proved them wrong. An analysis of actual cases reveals that the nature and level of violence between Athapaskan and Eskimo nations was not only not greater but not different in *any* respect from what it was within the Eskimo sphere or within the Athapaskan sphere. Specific *nations*, such as the Di'hąįį (Gwich'in) and the Tikiġaġmiut (Iñupiat), were more aggressive than others, but language boundaries had nothing to do with it. At least some other investigators, including Annette McFadyen Clark (1981:596), Edward Curtis (1930:214), John Murdoch (1892:51), and Vilhjalmur Stefansson (1951:114), seem to have come to a similar conclusion. It appears, however, that violent encounters between Iñupiat and Athapaskans continued for a decade or two after they had ceased within each of the two groups, particularly in the Endicott and Philip Smith Mountains (Itaałuk 1980a:1, 1982a:13–14; Morry n.d.).

Vengeance

Iñupiaq historians uniformly regarded revenge as the primary cause of warfare in northwestern Alaska. Included among those espousing this view were Robert Nasruk Cleveland (1970b), who was born in 1884, and Charley Uluġaaġruk Wood (1931), who was born in the 1850s. Charlie Saġġaaluraq Jensen, who was born in 1893, explained it to me this way:

> *This country lost four or five hunting men; they never came home. The people in some other country killed them, and that's why they never came home. Maybe somebody told them who did it, so they know. Maybe someone in this country*

> *[has] a friend over there who told them. And so they know: Kotzebue people killed our friends. And they talked about it. . . . Then a bunch of people got ready to fight. And when these people kill some of those Kotzebue people, they call it* akisaqtut: *they got their revenge.* [1970d]

Della Puyuk Keats explained that even if an offense occurred many generations previously, people never forgot it and ultimately got their revenge: "Akisaqtuuti, they went back and forth" (1970e).

The members of the nations of northwestern Alaska had ample opportunity to acquire grudges against one another. Although the details had to have changed from time to time, the populations that were there in the early 19th century were descended from others that had been in the same general area for many centuries before them. Because they were so familiar with one another, it was usually fairly simple for them to determine who had made a surprise raid and thus to know who should be attacked in retaliation. As if that were not enough, victors usually allowed one or two people to survive a massacre specifically so they could tell their fellow countrymen in other settlements who had perpetrated it. The justification for this was that the surviving members of the defeated nation would be intimidated and never challenge the victors again. The actual effect, however, was to eliminate any guesswork there might have been regarding where retaliatory raids should be directed. The potential for a never-ending cycle of raids and counterraids was thus inherent in the system.

Given the general context of long-term grievances held between many nations, the interesting question concerns the kinds of catalyst that actually triggered military action by the members of one nation against those of another. In reviewing the accounts of raids and battles at my disposal, I could not find any specific evidence on this point. In virtually every case one raid or atrocity precipitated a violent response that led to further retaliation and so on; I never found out what started the chain of events. Sometimes the response was immediate, but in many cases it took place after several years had passed. Perhaps people just waited until they felt ready to retaliate successfully and then sprang into action.

It is hard to believe, however, that immediate factors were irrelevant. Several types of incident might have served as a catalyst, precipitating military action within a general context of hostility. They are listed here without reference to possible relative significance or priority.

1. Being cheated in a trade, insulted, humiliated in an athletic contest, or bested in almost any way by a foreigner could trigger an act of hostility. Such grievances usually developed at trade fairs, although

they were possible at messenger feasts also. Contrary to popular belief, the Iñupiat were highly competitive.

2. The otherwise unexplained disappearance of a hunter was almost always attributed to homicide by the members of another nation. The nation against which the most grudges were held or the one whose estate was closest to the direction in which the missing man had been heading would be considered the most likely culprit, although a shaman might attempt to answer the question through magical means. (The disappearance of a woman might be attributed to wife capture by someone from another country, but this action might not produce a violent response.)
3. Almost any untoward incident, disaster, or failure could be attributed to black magic on the part of people from another nation, particularly if a pattern emerged in series of such incidents.

One of the more notable features of the above list is that most of the possibilities refer to offenses against individuals. However, offenses against an individual by a foreigner tended to produce a sympathetic collective response among the aggrieved party's fellow countrymen. Furthermore, as Charles Lucier has pointed out, "Westerners cannot often imagine the extent traditional Iñupiat went to to even the score. There was a kind of messianic zeal in the pursuit that most Westerners would take as madness" (1997:196). The key, then, was for the offended individual to persuade his countrymen to join him in avenging what began as a personal affront. The only way to do this was to appeal to the fund of grievances that had accumulated over the years in the population at large. If it was great enough, an apparently minor incident could precipitate an attack.

Discussion

In a paper on the evolution of warfare among the Indians of the Northwest Coast, Herbert Maschner (1997) cautions against overly simplistic explanations of warfare. He argues that wars on the Northwest Coast were never fought for a single reason and that "many of the conflicts witnessed in the 19th century were wars that probably had more to do with historical precedence than with any verifiable ultimate cause." In my judgment those same conclusions are applicable to the wars fought in northwestern Alaska. The ultimate causes of warfare may have been outside pressure, economics, land acquisition, and ethnic enmity or some combination thereof, but by the early 19th century most manifestations of international hostility were probably straightforward acts of vengeance. Indeed, some of my informants volunteered the opinion that the Iñupiaq verb *aŋuyak-*, "to make war between nations," meant "to seek vengeance."[7] The brutality that often characterized Native warfare in northwestern Alaska is more readily understood if this likelihood is kept in mind.

It is also worth noting that, in contrast to the situation existing among agrarian nations, laying waste to a territory as a means of striking back at an enemy nation was not a realistic option in northwestern Alaska. The resource base was too mobile and too difficult to control for that to have a useful effect, and the practical problems associated with even attempting to implement such a strategy would have been insurmountable. Given the difficulties involved in territorial expansion, killing or capturing people was the only realistic option as the primary strategic objective.

Capturing people seems never to have been a strategic goal within the study region. If the supply of eligible women was too low at home, one might be captured from another nation and taken home to become someone's wife. But this seems to have been extremely rare, it was carried out by only one or two men, and it was conducted much more in the manner of a kidnapping than in the context of armed conflict. In addition to the risk entailed in the capture itself, there was always the danger that a kidnapping might lead to a more general confrontation. Sometimes women or children were taken prisoner during a raid or battle, but I have not heard of a single case where the acquisition of wives or children was one of the original objectives of the conflict. For whatever reason, women and children were killed in the great majority of cases.

Target Selection

Having determined that an attack should be made on another nation, the next matter to be decided was the type of attack to be made and the person(s) or settlement(s) against which it would be directed. In understanding the various factors involved here, it is helpful to know something about settlement size and distribution in the region. Of particular importance are fall–early winter settlements, the type in existence during the season when most fighting took place. They also constituted the most regular aggregations of people from one year to the next.

The several fall–early winter settlements occupied by the members of a given nation were distributed about that nation's estate in such a way as to take maximum advantage of the resources the country had to offer at that time of year. For example, the distribution of the fall–early winter settlements of the Qikiqtaġruŋmiut is shown in Map 10. The broken line on the main map shows the border of the Qikiqtaġruŋmiut estate. The broken line on the orientation map shows the border of the NANA Region. The smallest circles represent settlements of one to two houses, while the two intermediate-size circles represent settlements of three houses. The largest circle represents a

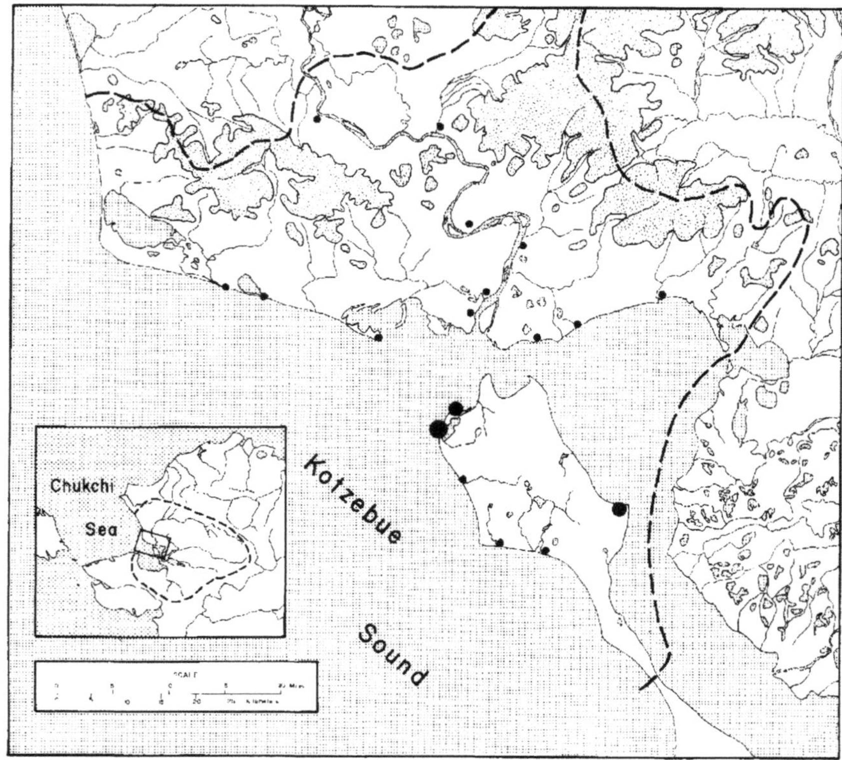

10. Major fall–winter settlements of the Qikiqtaġruŋmiut. The broken line in the main map shows the border of the Qikiqtaġruŋmiut estate. The broken line in the enclosed map shows the border of the NANA Region.

settlement that, until an accident claimed the lives of most of its inhabitants sometime around 1815, contained at least 20 houses and probably more than 160 people; it was the largest settlement in the NANA Region.[8]

The main point here is not the details but the general dispersal of Iñupiaq populations. The Qikiqtaġruŋmiut were chosen to illustrate the general pattern because the locations of their settlements are particularly easy to show on a map. The settlements of most other Iñupiaq nations were distributed in more linear fashion along a river or the seacoast.

The basic problem from the aggressors' point of view was to decide where to strike. If vengeance was directed primarily against particular individuals, then the settlement(s) in which they resided were obviously the prime target(s). In that case, espionage had to be conducted in order to determine the whereabouts of those individuals. The raiders might have to sneak past several enemy settlements in order to reach and withdraw from their intended target. If vengeance was more broadly directed, any enemy settlement might suffice; the raiders might choose to attack the easiest or perhaps the largest. Finally, if vengeance was truly comprehensive in scope and if the aggressors had mustered a large enough force to feel invincible, they might challenge the enemy to an open battle.

The dispersed nature of a nation's population had both disadvantages and advantages with respect to defense. On the negative side, when raiders were discovered to be on the way, residents had to travel several miles to the nearest village to escape or to get help. On the positive side, dispersal made it effectively impossible for an enemy force to attack more than a small percentage of a nation's population in a single engagement. If they tried to exterminate the entire population one settlement at a time, they would be certain to face an ambush before they got very far because news of the first attack would get out. For these reasons, the overwhelming majority of armed confrontations were raids on single settlements, after which the surviving invaders headed for home as fast as they could go.

Tactics

The primary strategic goal of seeking revenge had important tactical implications. Instead of seeking booty, prisoners (*isiqtat*), access to trade, or territorial expansion, military forces sought the physical destruction of the enemy, either of the entire population or of a targeted portion of it. A conclusive victory for one side and defeat for the other consisted in the death of everyone, every man, woman, and child in the target population or everyone in the attacking force. This is expressed in Iñupiatun by the term *tamatkiq-* and in village English by the phrase "clean up [the enemy]." If time permitted, the attack was often followed by the physical destruction of the settlement(s) by means of fire. Sometimes, one or two members of the losing force were left alive (*kisiŋŋuqtaq-*) to tell their countrymen never to challenge that nation again. These harsh objectives were not always realized in fact, of course, but typical settlement size and composition, on the one hand, and the ordinary daily round of village activities, on the other, made them fairly realistic.

It is important to keep in mind that most of the countryside was covered with low-lying tundra vegetation, riparian shrubs, and marshland rather than with large stands of woody trees. This was true even of districts lying within the tree line. This terrain required tactics very different from those that would be appropriate in temperate forests or tropical jungles.

Settlement Size and Composition

The general pattern of fall settlement size in the NANA Region is indicated in Table 4. The left-hand column shows the range of variation in settlement size

Table 4. Estimated Size of Fall Settlements in the NANA Region during the Early 19th Century

Houses in settlement	People in settlement	Number of settlements	Percent of settlements
1	8	73	35.5
2	16	60	29.1
3	24	29	14.0
4	32	15	7.3
5	40	9	4.4
6	48	5	2.4
7	56	4	1.9
8	64	1	.5
9	72	1	.5
10	80	3	1.5
11	88	1	.5
12	96	0	0.0
13	104	1	.5
14	112	1	.5
15–19	120–152	1	.5
20	160	2	.9
		206	100.0

Source: Burch 1998a.

in terms of house numbers, extending from 1 to 20. The next column shows what the settlement population would have been given the indicated number of houses and an average of eight inhabitants per house. The third column shows the number of settlements of each size in the region, and the right-hand column gives the percentage of the total represented by villages of that size. As the table shows, most fall–early winter settlements were very small; nearly 80 percent contained fewer than 32 inhabitants.

The composition of a traditional Iñupiaq settlement is illustrated in Figure 2 with an actual example, the Akuniġmiut settlement of Qalugruaq, ca. 1890. This was a typical NANA Region settlement in both size and composition. Here we see a local family comprised of three brothers and their wives and children as well as a married daughter with her husband and child. The 17 people involved were distributed among three neighboring houses, as indicated. In the early 19th century the most frequent departures from the example would have been fewer children and more adults, with possibly one or two elders and perhaps a married sister in the primary adult group along with her husband and children.

The extremely small size and geographic isolation of the great majority of settlements in the NANA Region made them vulnerable to a well-planned and well-executed surprise attack by only a dozen enemy raiders. On the other

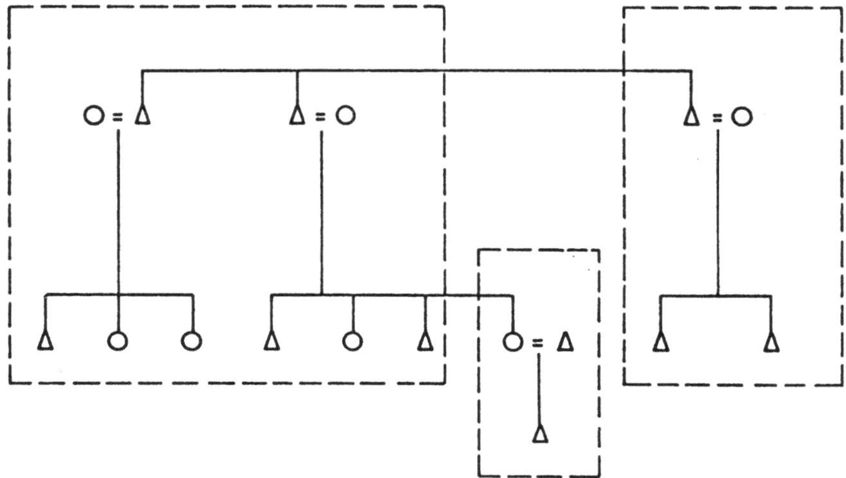

2. An example of an Iñupiaq local family (Burch 1975:258).

hand, being quiet places in which houses were often concealed in thickets of tall shrubs, small settlements were often difficult for foreigners to locate, not to mention approach undetected.

The Daily Round

The characteristic daily round was an important tactical factor because settlements were ordinarily much more vulnerable at certain times of day than at others. Daylight hours usually were the worst time to launch an attack against a village because at least some fully armed men were likely to be out scanning the countryside for game and everything else that might be of interest. The element of surprise was hard to achieve under such conditions. On the other hand, if all the hunters from a settlement were actively engaged in a group effort in one particular locality some distance away, then the village was left completely undefended. Careful scouting, therefore, sometimes revealed unusual opportunities at what were ordinarily poor times for attack.

Normally, raids were made at night, under cover of darkness, when everyone in the target settlement was asleep. A possible flaw in such a plan was that someone might be awake and give the alarm. Another possible flaw was that there might not be enough men in the attacking force to surround each house. If this occurred, the raiders had to exterminate the residents on a house-by-house basis, hoping they could proceed quietly enough to keep from rousing everyone else.

An important consideration was the use of the *qargi*, or community center.

During the day when they were not out hunting men gathered in the qargi to talk and to make and repair equipment. In the larger villages the qargi was usually a separate building erected specifically as a gathering place; the very largest settlements usually had two or more. In medium-size and small villages, such as the overwhelming majority of those in the NANA Region, the qargi was often simply an ordinary house, usually the largest in the village. In all contexts a qargi was usually occupied only by men during the day but was frequently a gathering place for the entire community in the evening. It was the place where the storytelling, dancing, singing, and games that so enriched Iñupiaq life took place.

The aggressors' tactical objective was to trap the residents of an entire village inside the qargi. From the viewpoint of the aggressors, this was the most desirable situation possible. It was not risk free, however. One potential problem inhered in the fact that most of the warriors in the target settlement were usually in the qargi, all of them awake and with weapons at hand. If there was an escape tunnel (as there sometimes was), they might get out and strike the raiders from behind. Another potential risk was that if the raiders had been observed approaching the village, the gathering in the qargi might be staged; the women, children, and some men might be there making a lot of noise while most of the home force hid, ready to strike the raiders from behind the moment the qargi was surrounded.

Preparations

International hostility in northwestern Alaska was expressed through a variety of activities, ranging from spying (*naipiqtuq-*) and harassment to open battle (aŋuyak-). All were very dangerous, and none was undertaken lightly.

General Considerations

One major element in the preparation for armed conflict was education. Stories of armed confrontations, both successful and otherwise, played a central role in Iñupiaq narrative history. By the time a person reached adulthood, he or she had heard countless stories of raids and battles as well as analyses of the strategy and tactics involved in each one. Victorious encounters no doubt held a dominant place in these narratives, but it is hard to believe that disasters would not have been discussed as well. The one or two survivors from a defeated force who were allowed to return home surely reported not only on the general outcome of the conflict but also on which tactics succeeded and which failed. Detailed information on warfare was part of the common fund of Iñupiaq knowledge, shared by men and women, adults and children. It was largely for this reason that I was able to gather the material for this chapter so long after the events described in it took place.

CONDITIONING

Men were in good physical condition as a general rule because, as hunters who traveled hundreds and probably thousands of miles on foot each year, they kept in shape simply by going about their daily tasks. Beginning in early childhood, special exercises designed to prepare them to bear the burdens of hunting in extreme weather were also practiced. Boys were sent out for a time each morning either naked or wearing only light clothing, even in cold or stormy weather, in order to inure themselves to physical discomfort (Brower n.d.:671; Rasmussen 1933:306–307). When fish or game were hard to find, hunters often went for two or three days (or more) without eating, despite having to spend the daylight hours walking about the country. During the long days of late spring and summer they frequently went even longer without sleeping. Through these activities they became accustomed to dealing with hunger, thirst, and fatigue simply as a matter of course.

Many men's games, of which they had a considerable number, were tests of skill, strength, endurance, and/or agility. For example, finger pulling, arm pulling, head pulling, neck pulling, arm wrestling, leg wrestling, several types of high jump, knee jump, and standing long jump contests were frequent, and many could be engaged in even while inside the house or qargi. Outside they held running races and archery contests, lifted heavy weights, and hurled lances and stones (Dall 1870:137). Competitions often lasted for hours or even days.

Another game that helped men keep in good physical condition was Eskimo football (*aqsaurat*), which was like a combination of soccer, rugby, and keep-away played with a soft ball about 8 inches (20 centimeters) in diameter (Brower n.d.:49; Hawley 1973). A player moved the ball by kicking it. He could catch the ball or stop it with his body, but he could not throw it or pick it up and run with it. In addition to kicking the ball away from an opponent, a player could also knock down an opponent or throw him to the ground. A team won when it kept the ball away from the other side for so long that the latter gave up. Women and children played the game solely to have fun, although it was still a vigorous activity. Then it was played on a small "field" and was accompanied by lots of laughter. When it was undertaken only by men, it was a much more serious enterprise. Often the "fields" were several miles long, and games sometimes lasted for many hours, sometimes days. There were no referees. As any adult who has played aggressive physical games without referees knows, such games can get very rough indeed. I never saw an Eskimo football game, but when I first went to Alaska I was impressed by the fact that the respect shown to certain older men was based in part on the prowess they had displayed in fights during football games in their youth.

OFFENSIVE PREPARATIONS

All of the above activities prepared men equally for both ordinary lives as hunters and special careers as warriors. However, there was one activity that was crucial in combat but not in ordinary life: dodging (*igłiq-*) (VanStone 1983:16). Dodging arrows that are intended to kill one requires not only agility but good eyesight and considerable composure.

As far as I am aware, dodging and jumping around were the only activities that were practiced specifically because of their importance in combat. It never occurred to me to ask how the Iñupiat practiced dodging, but Simon Paneak illustrated one technique in a sketch he drew in 1968 (in Campbell 1998:pl. 62). It shows two parallel lines drawn on the ground some distance apart, with a team of men standing behind each line facing their opponents. The objective was for the men on one side to try to hit the men on the other with a mitten that had a stone inside it, apparently taking turns throwing the mitten. A person who was struck had to drop out. The team with the last man standing was the winner. In a handwritten note on the sketch, Paneak says that earlier, in his grandfather's time, the game had been played with bows and blunt-tipped arrows. Presumably, the lines were farther apart when the game was played this way, since even a blunt arrow could cause a serious injury at close range.

Other preparations for a military expedition into enemy territory were relatively few in number, and most of them are obvious. Men made sure their weapons, clothing, amulets, and other equipment were in good order and saw to it that their families had sufficient supplies to last during their absence. The only other thing that seems to have been done with some regularity was to consult a shaman on the prospects for success.

DEFENSIVE PREPARATIONS

In early-19th-century northwestern Alaska people conducted their affairs guided by the assumption that they could be attacked at any time. Accordingly, they took a number of steps to be ready when an enemy put in an appearance.

The most fundamental protection against a surprise attack was careful location of settlements. Houses in most interior settlements were erected in willow thickets, which made them both difficult to find and hard to approach. On the coast settlements were often located on the ends of points or in other exposed positions that were difficult for an enemy to approach unseen. Usually there had to be some kind of trade-off between defensive considerations, on the one hand, and access to fish or game, on the other, but defense was always taken into account.

Defense was also fostered by the quietness of an Iñupiaq village. My senior informants often spoke to me of having been admonished when they were children to be quiet while playing outside so as not to attract the attention of passing strangers. They were also told to listen for strange noises around the village. They claimed that their ancestors had been even stricter during their parents' and grandparents' childhoods. Walter Sigliuna Kowunna (1970) told me that in the old days they used to "listen! Never fool around—that's the way we do long ago. Listen all the time. . . . Never stay out [in the evenings]."

Others echoed that theme. Amos Apuġiña Hawley Sr. put it this way:

> *Just when they stay out, them old-timers, they never laugh much either, nothing. Always watching. Because in those years they have a pretty damn dangers! And right now they forget all about anything. They never even holler much in those years, when I was a kid. They are all the same, them old-timers. Just when they go out, they always be real quiet and watching. And in nighttime, when we stay inside the house, they sure don't want us to be holler around. They want us to be quiet, all the time. To listen. That's the way they are. Right now we forget everything!* [1965c]

Five years later and 200 miles (320 kilometers) away, Robert Cleveland told me, "In the old days, the [Kobuk] people used to be scared all the time. They were scared of attacks by Nunatakers [Nuataaġmiut], Indians, and other peoples. They were scared all the time. They kept a watch out all the time. Not like nowadays. The people right now are just like sleeping people. They aren't afraid of anything at all. But in those days, they kept alert all the time" (1970a; see Anderson et al. 1998:104).

Traditional Iñupiaq villages were so quiet that the enemy could be practically right on top of a settlement without knowing it, occasionally with disastrous results. This is illustrated in a story told to me by Frank Kutvak Glover.

> *One time up at Akuniq, a woman was walking along packing a little baby. It was wintertime. The baby couldn't sleep. It was keeping everybody awake inside the house, and the people didn't like it. So the mother went out, packing the baby in her parka. When she got outside she could see a fire not too far away. There were a lot of men sleeping out in the open beside that fire.*
>
> *The woman decided she'd better go back inside right away and tell the people. She said to herself, "How am I going to wake up my husband without disturbing everyone else? If I try to wake him up gently, he won't get up for a long time. But if I wake him fast by pinching him, he is going to holler and make a loud noise. What am I going to do?"*
>
> *She decided she'd better do it in a hurry, so she pinched him hard on the arm. "Ouch! What the heck are you doing?" he shouted, waking everyone else.*

"I saw a fire out there, with lots of people around it," his wife replied.

Her husband quieted down in a hurry and dressed to go out. He put on his pants and mukluks, and he and the other men in the house went out together. Then they went to the other houses and woke up the people there too.

They could see the strangers all sleeping beside the fire. The Akuniġmiut snuck up on them and started shooting with their bows and arrows. But one of the raiders jumped out of his sleeping bag and managed to escape. The Akuniġmiut pursued him. Pretty soon he started to freeze because he didn't have many clothes on, and the Akuniġmiut caught him. And they shot him right there. [1970c]

Defense was sometimes taken into account in dwelling and qargi construction. Since the single most favored tactic of raiders was to trap people inside their houses or in the qargi, the buildings were sometimes made with secret escape tunnels. Men usually kept their weapons either with them or close at hand all the time, even when listening to stories, feasting, or dancing in the qargi. As Kotzebue (1821, vol. 1:211; see also Ostermann and Holtved 1952:32) observed in 1816, the men's arms were never laid aside, and they were prepared to mount a defense at a moment's notice.

Another protective measure was eternal vigilance. Part of this resulted automatically from the fact that men were out hunting much of the time, and they often covered a fair amount of country when they did so. Even when they were not hunting they spent a lot of time outside, looking around, observing the weather, and making judgments about where game might be. Women too spent a lot of time outdoors, retrieving game their husbands killed, fishing, checking snares set for hares or ptarmigan, or gathering vegetable products. Another frequent outdoor activity for a woman was walking around packing a fussing baby in the back of her parka, as illustrated above in Glover's story. Dogs also served as active sentinels. In the old days most families had only two or three dogs. Those dogs knew who belonged in the village and who did not, and they reacted with hostile noises to strangers who were unaccompanied by a village resident.

Finally, of course, people were specifically on the lookout for strangers or for evidence thereof. Even toward the end of the 19th century, when most of this type of danger had passed, Charles Brower, who traveled widely in northwestern Alaska during the 1880s, said, "I don't think that I ever came in a village day or night that someone was not outside looking to see that no strangers arrived without their knowing" (n.d.:166, see also 143).

The Iñupiat also engaged in espionage. In introducing this subject, I cannot do better than quote a remark of Lucier: "Traditional Iñupiat were intensely focused on knowing everything they could about other people. This was useful, obviously, in warfare and foreign relations generally. Readers may not realize the intensity of their interest in people and all details of their lives, which was manifested in a continuous monitoring of friends, relatives, and foes (past or potential). That which might be considered obsessive awareness and sensitivity in human relations was routine and necessary for Iñupiat" (1997:263). In short, knowing what others were doing was a central tenet of traditional Iñupiaq life, no matter who those "others" were.

Where international relations were involved, the monitoring of other people's activities often took special forms or acquired a more specialized focus. For example, intelligence on enemy settlements and operations must have been gathered by prowlers, whose activities are described in some detail below. But much intelligence gathering was carried out during the course of major international events, such as trade fairs and messenger feasts. In addition to seeing partners and relatives, trading, and generally enjoying themselves on these occasions, most adults were alert for information about possible raids, either against their own nation or against another. Some messenger feasts are said to have been held deliberately for people from a nation suspected of plotting an attack in the hope that the hosts could beguile their guests into unintentionally revealing something of their plans (J. Foster 1970). When any such information was acquired, it was often passed along to other interested parties, particularly at trade fairs. From a political point of view, indeed, a trade fair can be conceived as a giant espionage network.

A special element in international intrigue consisted of women who married foreigners and then moved to their husbands' countries to live.[9] When people from a woman's original homeland were thinking about raiding her husband's country, they often warned her in advance. Conversely, it sometimes happened that a woman living in one country learned that the people there were planning an attack on her native land. She could pass this information on while at a fair. Depending on which way a woman's primary loyalty lay, she could either warn her husband's people, aid in an attempt to destroy them, or maintain a completely neutral stance. Partners and cosiblings were also sometimes involved in sharing such information but apparently with less frequency than expatriate wives.

The final means of defensive preparation were magical. Shamans were the primary focus here, and they sometimes held seances for the specific purpose of determining whether danger from outside attack was to be expected. Another, more permanent procedure was to have magic sentinels (Hadley 1951). Charlie Jensen described how they worked:

> *They used to take a big long stick and put it in the ground. I saw one when I was a boy. And it stood up just like a toy. And a little house was on top, with something inside. Small house up there, just like a little box. Somebody, a person—a woman or man, was inside. Tiny one. Religious. Power!*

> *That fella inside there knew everything that was happening. What was coming. When something good, or something bad, is coming, that fella, he knew. And he told the* aŋatkuq *[shaman]. [1970c]*

Some people also owned magical songs (*mamialaqutiituut*) that would make an approaching enemy turn around and go back, although these were apparently quite rare.

Equipment

Most raiding parties traveled on foot and traveled light. The men wore their ordinary clothing, augmented by protective vests or plate armor. They took along a sealskin bag containing some dried meat or fish, seal oil, extra insoles, and an extra pair of boots. Protective amulets were worn on the clothing. Presumably, the members of war parties also carried some first-aid equipment, such as a lancet, needle and thread, and some medications, although I have no firm information on this. Otherwise, they lived off the land as they went. In summer or early fall they also took along a tarpaulin (*iŋaluk*) made of several seal intestines sewn together; it could not have weighed more than a few ounces. It was used primarily as a shelter in the rain, although it could also serve as a poncho when the men were traveling. Parties traveling by boat could carry much more equipment if they wanted to, but usually the focus was on bringing more men.

The only "uniform" ever worn to indicate a man's role as a warrior was a headband (*niaqun*) and two feathers (*suluuk*-dual). The headband was a simple strap around the head with a bead centered on the forehead, directly above the nose. Worn without feathers, it was simply an item of personal adornment. When warriors were about to launch a raid or ambush or to engage in open battle, however, they often inserted one feather just in front of each ear. I did not think to ask if the feathers were supposed to come from a particular species of bird, but Lucier (1997:175) says they were probably from a golden eagle.

Weapons

The primary weapons used in combat were the bow and arrow and the lance. In general, these were not only the same type but often the very same weapons used in big game hunting, with some exceptions noted below. The warriors carried a quiver (*pisiksisaq* or *qaġruqaġvik*) large enough to hold about 20 arrows (see Plate 2). During combat the quiver was slung across the chest under the arm holding the bow so that another arrow could be quickly withdrawn from it by the free hand after an arrow had been shot (Phebus 1972:98, 99).

BOWS AND ARROWS

The Iñupiat had two kinds of bow (Lucier 1997:127). The more powerful of the two was the *pisiksi* (or *qilluiññaq* in interior districts), which was recurved and

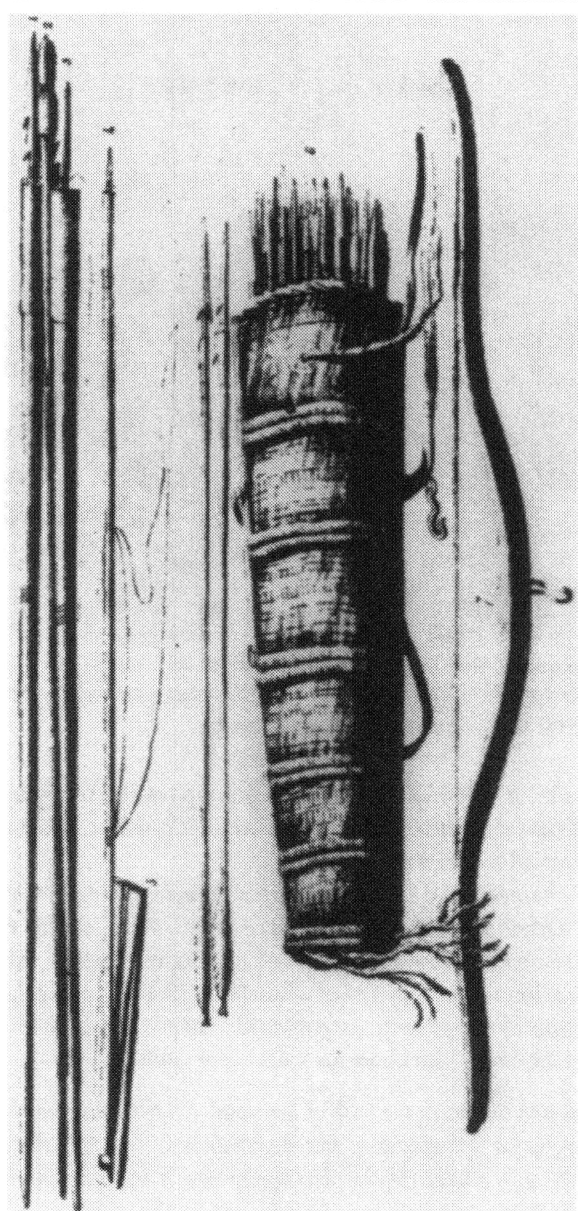

2. Weapons used by people near Bering Strait, sketched by Louis Choris, 1816. Left to right: thrusting spear, throwing spear and throwing boards (not used in combat), arrows, quiver with arrows, and recurved bow. Sketched by Louis Choris (1822:pl. 19). Courtesy of the Library of Congress, Washington DC.

3. Archery demonstration at the Noatak reindeer fair, 1918, using simple bows. Archers, left to right: Suutnaq, Atammak, and Pitniqsaaq. Photographer unknown but possibly Walter Shields. Courtesy of Edith Kennedy.

had sinew backing. A modified version of this type is illustrated in Plate 2. The other type of bow was the simple bow, or *aiyakpak*, which had a simple curve and usually lacked backing (see Plate 3).

Kotzebue characterized Iñupiaq weapons as being "elegantly made" (1821, vol. 1:218).[10] Other authors provided more detail. Beechey, for example, observed in 1826 that bows were made "of drift pine assisted with thongs of hide, and occasionally with pieces of whalebone [baleen] placed at the back of them neatly bound round with a small cord" (1831, vol. 1:340).[11] The following year he elaborated. The bows, he said, were made

> *with sinews and wedges at the back of the wood. On the western coast [of North America] driftwood is so abundant that the inhabitants have their choice of several trees, and are never obliged to piece their implements. It requires some care to bring a bow to the form which they consider best; and for this purpose they wrap it in shavings soaked in water, and hold it over a fire; it is then pegged down upon the earth in the form required. If not attended to when used, the bows are apt to get out of order, and the string to slip out of its place, by which the bow bends the wrong way, and is easily broken.*

In these bows the string is in contact with about a foot of the wood at each end, and when used makes a report which would be fatal to secrecy. The Californians, accustomed to fight in ambush, are very careful to have that part of the string muffled with fur, but I never saw any precaution of the kind used by the Esquimaux. To protect the wrist from the abrasion which would ensue from frequent firing, the Esquimaux buckle on a piece of ivory, called mun-era, about three or four inches [7.6–10 centimeters] long, hollowed out to the wrist, or a guard made of several pieces of ivory or wood fastened together. [1831, vol. 2:309–310]

Berthold Seemann echoed this by reporting that "their bow, made of beech if procurable, is most ingeniously strengthened by thongs of deer-sinew, which are neatly plaited; the string consists of fine deer-sinew threads, laid together like the hairs of a fiddle bow" (1853, vol. 2:53).

Arrows (*qaġrut*) were variously tipped with bone, flint, slate, ivory, and iron (Beechey 1831, vol. 1:340; Seemann 1853, vol. 2:53; Simpson 1843:123).[12] The arrowheads used in combat usually were tanged or barbed, basically the same kind used in hunting big game (Campbell 1998:pl. 37; Giddings 1961:124; Murdoch 1892:195). However, at various points along the coast warriors made arrowheads out of ivory or bone with deliberately weakened bases so that they would break off inside the skin and work their way into the victim's body (Csonka 2000; Paneak 1971b:10; Reinhardt 2000; Reinhardt and Dekin n.d.:52). These were apparently made specifically for warfare. Virtually all of the arrows used in combat had to be surgically removed from victims.

The early explorers saw Iñupiaq bows and arrows in use. In 1827, for example, Beechey was given a demonstration:

The practice of firing at a mark appears to be one of the amusements of the Esquimaux; and judging from what we saw at Chamisso Island, there are some extraordinary performers in this way among the tribe. One day a diver [loon] was swimming at the distance of thirty yards [27 meters] from the beach, and a native was offered a reward if he would shoot it; he fired, but the bird evaded the arrow by diving. The Esquimaux watched its coming to the surface, and the instant his head appeared he transfixed both eyes with his arrow. [1831, vol. 2:308–309][13]

Beechey went on to say, however, that he did not think that Iñupiat in general were expert marksmen.

After a demonstration of Native ability in 1838 Kashevarov declared: "The local inhabitants handle these weapons very skillfully: an arrow released from a bow with ordinary force travels distances of 560 to 630 feet [170–192 meters]. In our presence they hit a target at 67 paces with a stiff cross wind blowing. According to the natives, they can send an arrow straight through a caribou at close range" (VanStone 1977:47, see also 56).

In 1853 the men of the *Plover* expedition watched a Point Barrow Native send "an arrow to a distance of 140 yards [128 meters] into a mound of snow, on which some of the officers had a shooting target: but he gave his arrow so high a flight, that it was doubted that he could have exceeded that distance" (Bockstoce 1988, vol. 1:197). On another occasion a man hit a mark about a foot square at a distance of 40 yards (36.6 meters) about once in ten times, although the same archer demonstrated his bow's power by cracking a piece of sheet iron with a flint-headed arrow (Simpson 1852–54:entry for January 30, 1853). Simpson (1852–54:entry for January 31, 1853) doubted that the best bow could reach 200 yards (183 meters). In 1960 Bob Qipmiuraq Tuckfield (born 1890) and Christopher Tiŋuk Tingook (born 1881?) told Don Charles Foote that the killing distance for caribou with a bow and arrow was about 150 yards (135 meters) (Tuckfield and Tingook 1960); presumably it was about that for humans as well.

A detachment from Beechey's expedition had a more exciting demonstration of Iñupiaq archery during an actual armed encounter that is described later in this chapter. His summation of its effectiveness is as follows:

> *The effect of the arrows was fully as great as might have been expected, and, had they been properly directed, would have inflicted mortal wounds. At the distance of a hundred yards [90 meters] a flesh-wound was produced in the thigh, which disabled the [English] man for a time; and at eight or ten yards [7–9 meters] another fixed the right arm of a marine to his side; a third buried itself two inches and a half [6.35 centimeters] under the scalp. The wounds which they occasioned were obliged to be either enlarged, to extract the arrows, which were barbed, or to have an additional incision made, that the arrow might be pushed through without further laceration. Most of these wounds were inflicted by an arrow with a bone head, tipped with a pointed piece of jaspar [sic]. [Beechey 1831, vol. 2:287–288]*

For perspective, a Prussian experiment with a battalion of line infantry shooting with muskets at a target 100 feet (30.48 meters) long and 6 feet (1.83 meters) high scored 25 percent hits at 225 yards (205.74 meters), 40 percent at 150 yards (137.16 meters), and 60 percent at 75 yards (68.58 meters). In 1846 a British experiment with a percussion musket firing at a target 11.5 feet (3.51 meters) high and 6 feet (1.83 meters) wide scored zero hits at 250 yards (228.6 meters) and 50 percent hits at 150 yards (137.16 meters) (Holmes 2001:198; see also Townsend 1983). Considering these tests as accurate measures of musket range and accuracy and taking into account the time it took to reload muskets and their high rate of misfire, Iñupiaq bows might be considered to have been reasonably effective military weapons for the early 19th century.

Other equipment relating to archery included a wrist guard (*tayagnautmiun*) made of bone or baleen on the arm holding the bow. This protected the forearm from the snap of the bowstring (VanStone 1977:89). Natives also wore a three-fingered glove on the hand that drew the bowstring (Campbell 1998:pl. 37).

LANCES

The thrusting spear, or lance (*pana*), used by the Iñupiat in combat was ordinarily the same type used in hunting.[14] However, by the beginning of the study period imported lances or lance blades had arrived in northwestern Alaska, and some of these may have been used in combat exclusively.

Members of the Billings expedition who reached the western end of the Seward Peninsula in 1791 found the Natives using spears tipped with ivory points 1.5 feet (46 centimeters) long, with two sharp edges. They also had spears tipped with iron, fashioned by themselves, that were sharpened only on one side. In addition, they had some spear points acquired in trade from Chukotka (Merck 1980:189). In 1816 Kotzebue (1821, vol. 1:193, 211, 225) reported the Iñupiat to be using iron spearheads of Siberian manufacture. Ten years later Beechey (1831, vol. 1:340, 359–360, vol. 2:265) was still finding spears tipped with bone and flint, although others were made of iron inlaid with brass.[15] Later still, in 1837, Thomas Simpson (1843:123) found the Iñupiat on the Arctic coast using spears about 6 feet (1.8 meters) long headed with iron or copper. But more than ten years after that members of one of the Franklin search expeditions found people in the same area still using spears tipped with flint, bone, slate, or ivory (Seemann 1853, vol. 2:53).

OTHER WEAPONS

According to my informants, bows and arrows and lances were the only weapons used in combat by the early-19th-century Iñupiat. The fact that they never laid those two types of weapons aside is what convinced Kotzebue that "they are in constant wars with other nations" (1821, vol. 1:211).

The early Western observers also frequently noted that the Iñupiat carried a large knife (*savik*) in addition to their other weapons. Kotzebue (1821, vol. 1:211), for example, reported that the men he encountered on Cape Espenberg carried knives about 2 feet (60 centimeters) long, some in sheaths, others concealed in their sleeves. The members of the Vasil'ev–Shishmarev expedition were threatened by Kaŋiġmiut with large knives apparently carried in sheaths slung over their backs under their parkas (Ray 1983:35). Large iron knives carried in sheaths strapped to the thigh were observed by members of the Beechey expedition (Beechey 1831, vol. 1:308–309, 351–352; Bockstoce 1977:70–71). On the Arctic coast Thomas Simpson noted in 1837 that the

Natives had "formidable iron knives, equally adapted for throwing, cutting, or stabbing" (1843:123). The following year Kashevarov reported that each man carried "a knife—which the savage is never without and which hangs from his side in a sheath" (VanStone 1977:42). On several occasions the Natives refused to trade their very best skins for anything except large knives (Kotzebue 1821, vol. 1:210, 235–236; Ray 1983:33). On the strength of this evidence there is little doubt that knives should be added to the list of basic Iñupiaq military equipment.

Large knives were probably used in combat under any one of three circumstances: (1) as a backup weapon when other arms were not at hand for some reason or had been destroyed or lost, (2) when enemies were in such close proximity to one another that bows and arrows or lances could not be wielded effectively, or (3) in subsidiary confrontations between individuals rather than groups. On one occasion Kotzebue and some men in a small boat were overtaken by hostile Tapqaġmiut in an umiaq. The Natives threatened the Russians with lances while their boat stood off a few feet waiting for a second boatload of men to arrive (Kotzebue 1821, vol. 1:205). Apparently, the Russian and Iñupiaq craft were separated by a distance at which lances could be effectively employed and knives could not. Ten years later Beechey's men, also in a small boat, were approached very closely by three boatloads of Kaŋiġmiut who drew their knives and actually attempted to board the English craft (Beechey 1831, vol. 1:459). In this case the Natives were apparently too close for lances to be effective. In individual encounters some of Beechey's men had knives drawn on them, as had Shishmarev's (Beechey 1831, vol. 2:280, 282–283). One Kaŋiġmiu actually stabbed a Russian with a knife, which moved the Russian to fire a primed but unloaded pistol in the Native's face (Ray 1983:37).

The only other weapon mentioned in the literature was the club (*anaullaun*). None of the early explorers said anything about clubs, but Knud Rasmussen, who passed through northwestern Alaska in 1924, was told that warriors formerly had used "great saw-toothed clubs designed to crush the skull of the enemy" (1933:307). Rasmussen probably got his information from Brower, who described war clubs as "mostly made of bone with teeth like a saw on one edge, about an inch deep, the handle was made so it fitted a mans hand ,and had a thong on it so the owner could not lose it" (n.d.: 672).[16]

Murdoch described a little club (*tiglun*) made of the "butt end of an old pickax head of whale's bone, with the point cut down to a blunt end" (1892:191). He said that it was clenched in the hand and "used for striking blows, probably at the temple" (Murdoch 1892:191). He specifically stated that its purpose was the taking of human life, but it is difficult to see how it could have been used except to deliver a coup de grâce or to strike people on the head as they emerged from a building. My own sources had never heard of clubs being used in combat, although unmodified walrus tusks and penis bones (baculums) would have served well in that capacity. As is noted later, however, both the Koyukon and the Alaskan Yup'ik Eskimos used clubs in warfare, so it is quite possible that Rasmussen's information was correct.

Men shooting bows and arrows would have had a difficult time carrying a spear, not to mention actually wielding one. At a distance bows and arrows were obviously the weapons of choice. At close quarters, however, thrusting spears might have been more useful than bows and arrows, while in hand-to-hand combat knives and clubs might have been more effective than any other weapon. An unanswered question is just how a warrior could transport this entire array of weapons and shift from one to another as appropriate when engaged in actual combat.

Armor

Protection against enemy weapons was provided either by breastplate armor made of plates of ivory or caribou antler (*qatigaġun* or *mannisaq*) or by protective vests or body wrappings made of bird skin, sealskin, or caribou hide (Beechey 1831, vol. 1:340, vol. 2:285; Burch 1988b:230; Nelson 1899:pl. 92; Sheehan 1997:140; Stefansson 1914b:384, 386; Thornton 1931:42; VanStone 1977:89; Varjola 1990:270–272).[17] These garments were either tied around the waist or chest or suspended from a line around the neck or from shoulder straps. As a rule they were worn underneath the parka. Whenever men were in or near enemy territory or when an enemy attack was anticipated they wore this protection all the time, even when sleeping. Proof of the effectiveness of this equipment was offered by a Tikiġaġmiut man named Samaruna, mentioned again in Chapter 3, who murdered a man in Point Hope in 1853. Seeking revenge, relatives of the deceased "shot numerous arrows at him[,] many of which struck him but were turned by a coat of mail he wore under his coat" (Simpson 1852–54:entry for April 5, 1854).

Armor is scarcely mentioned at all by the early explorers. That is understandable, of course, because ordinarily it could not be seen, being worn beneath the parka. One exception is noted in Martin Sauer's report on the Billings expedition. He states that Captain Billings told him that at Cape Rodney in 1791 he "saw their armour, some made of wood, and some of bone" (Sauer 1802:247n.).

Museum collections and archaeological excavations should eliminate any doubt we might have about the existence of plate armor in northwestern Alaska (see, e.g., Burch 1988b:230; Nelson 1899:pl. 92). What is not documented in museum collections is the use of other types of protection against arrows. Therefore, we are fortunate to have Beechey's observation (1831, vol.

2:284–285) of men preparing for actual combat placing eider-duck "frocks" over their regular parkas and even wrapping caribou hides over those. This corroborates my informants' statements about extra layers of skin being used as a kind of flak jacket in districts where ivory was hard to come by.

Defensive Works

The Iñupiat prepared against attack primarily by locating their settlements in places that were difficult for an enemy force to approach without being heard or seen. From time to time they created special defensive mechanisms as well.

The inhabitants of some villages prepared against possible attack by creating and maintaining the rough equivalent of a minefield outside their settlement. It consisted of one or more rows of split and sharpened caribou shinbones and/or baleen spikes (*sukisat*) driven into the ground pointing upward, their tips an inch or so above the surface. They were similar in concept to the pungi sticks used in Vietnam, designed to pierce the boots and feet of attackers and thus disable them. The most elaborate and permanent of these arrays was at Tikiġaq. It consisted of three rows of sukisat extending clear across the landward side of the point from the edge of the beach on the north to the edge of the beach on the south, with narrow winding paths through them here and there. None were placed on the beach itself because the waves would wash them out. Raiders who did not know about the stakes were caught unawares as they approached overland; they could be defeated or driven away before a shot was fired. Raiders who did know of the stakes, however, which was probably the great majority, approached along the water's edge; this was a good tactic anyway because the invaders were harder to see from the settlement at this low elevation. In such cases it was necessary for the defenders to launch a counterattack designed to drive the raiders into the staked area, the precise location of which the attackers did not know. If it succeeded, any wounded enemy warriors were left to suffer overnight and then killed the next morning.

Another defensive work was the stockade (*avaluġun*). This was just what the English name implies, namely, a circular or oval wall of logs and brush strong enough to be proof against arrows and spears. It had to be large enough to hold several people and have an opening through which reinforcements could enter or defenders could escape. I have not heard of many of these, and I have never heard of one large enough to surround even a settlement of two or three houses.

A third type of defensive work, used in the Kobuk valley, was a vestibule loosely constructed of logs located at the front of the entrance tunnel to a house. This structure contained ports through which defenders could shoot at raiders who were investing the house without exposing themselves to enemy fire (Anderson and Gal 1991:15).

A final item that was reportedly used in the Kobuk valley was a *manisuk*. As described by James Louis Giddings, this was "a movable willow framework lined with slabs of slate. Archers remained in its protective lee as it was moved forward towards the enemy" (1961:124–125). This was apparently a device made for defensive use during a daylight encounter, presumably not too far from the defenders' settlement. It must have been very heavy and unwieldy.

Getting There

In order to harass or attack the people of an enemy nation, individuals or war parties first had to travel to that nation's estate. This was often a hazardous enterprise in itself. Warriors traveled by umiaq in summer and on foot at other times of the year.[18] I have never heard of dogs and sleds being used for this purpose. Amphibious campaigns sometimes covered 100–200 miles (160–320 kilometers), especially in and near Bering Strait, but some overland campaigns were considerably longer than that. One example is the Athapaskan raid on Nuvuġaluaq that is described later in this chapter. The raiders had to have traveled at least 250 miles (400 kilometers) one way if they were Gwich'in and quite a bit more than that if they were Koyukon. A Tikiġaġmiut war party once raided a settlement on the Arctic coast a short distance west of the Colville River delta. To get there they had to walk nearly 400 miles (645 kilometers), much of it through foreign territory. In order to participate in an ambush of Tikiġaġmiut traders just south of Cape Thompson, an allied force of Kakligmiut (Barrow), Utuqqaġmiut (Utukok River), and the Kaŋianiġmiut band of Kuukpigmiut (Colville River) had to walk 300, 125, and 225 miles (480, 200, and 360 kilometers), respectively. The Tikiġaġmiut and Nuataaġmiut regularly sent spies and raiding parties into one another's estates, each trip requiring a hike of 125–200 miles (200–320 kilometers) one way. Very few raiders had to travel less than 50 miles (80 kilometers) to reach an intended target, and often the people who had to go the shortest distance had to cross the most rugged terrain in the entire region. These expeditions become even more impressive when one realizes that the above distance estimates are all straight-line calculations; the distances traveled on the ground easily could have been twice as far.

"Getting there" was obviously a problem in itself. Not only did raiders have to hunt and fish for food on the way, they often had to do so in hostile territory. If they passed through friendly territory, on the other hand, they not only were well treated but frequently managed to enlarge their force. Sooner or later, however, they had to enter country controlled by an enemy population.

The hazards of travel for purposes of raiding or harassment can be illustrated by two examples. In the first, a raiding party of Tikiġaġmiut (Point Hopers) walked some 400 miles (645 kilometers) to a place a short distance west of the Colville River delta. Their purpose was evidently to ambush the Kakligmiut on their way to the trade fair at Nigliq. (This was a breach of the general truce that prevailed along the coast during the summer.) As noted in Appendix 1, the several accounts of the confrontation are not in full agreement with one another except for the fact that the entire party of Tikiġaġmiut ended up starving to death.

The second example concerns a party of Nuataaġmiut who were on their way to raid an unidentified nation whose estate was located in the Kobuk River valley, probably, but not necessarily, the upper Kobuk Koyukon.

> *The Nuataaġmiut were coming to fight the Kobuk people. [It is not clear if the Nuataaġmiut were coming to fight the upper Kobuk Koyukon or the Akuniġmiut.] In early autumn a war party crossed the [Schwatka] mountains on foot and came down to the Kogoluktuk River. Hoping to save time, they built a raft in order to float down to the Kobuk River. They passed the first canyon. It was a bad river with many rocks, but they made it. They were glad.*
>
> *However, the Kogoluktuk River has two canyons. The one upriver has rapids, but the downriver canyon has falls. The Nuataaġmiut tried the second canyon. The river is smooth and calm up to the canyon but then suddenly plunges over the falls. On either side of the falls there are only canyon walls; there is no place to go except over the falls. One man had a hooked stick. He jumped from the raft and stuck the hook into a crack in the canyon wall and pulled himself up. The other men went into the huge pool under the falls and drowned. Nothing was seen of them again.*
>
> *The man on the canyon wall finally managed to climb to the top. He looked for his friends but could not find even one of them. That man then had to return to Noatak alone. [Adapted from Foote 1966b:story 11; United States Department of the Interior, Bureau of Indian Affairs 1987c]*

Leadership

The leader of a military force was referred to as the *ataniq* of the expedition. An ataniq was a man who was wiser and more knowledgeable than his or her fellows about certain activities or spheres of life. An ataniq therefore commanded respect and obedience with regard to activities relating to those areas. Informants asked to characterize this role in English used words and phrases like "boss," "judge," "tells other people what to do," and "knows more than anyone else." The term was applied, for example, to local family heads while they were actually acting in the capacity of head, to leaders of caribou or beluga drives, to commanders of military expeditions, and to people in direct command of whaling or seal-hunting crews. Context was crucial here: a person who was ataniq in one setting (e.g., a caribou drive) might not qualify to be one in another (e.g., on a military expedition). A person who was head of a small local family might not be the head of a larger family if two or more units merged. Thus, while there were lots of *atangich* (pl.) in general, there was only one when it came to any given activity. An ataniq's sphere of influence fluctuated accordingly.

People were so well known to one another in an Iñupiaq nation that who would be the ataniq in any given situation was rarely discussed or debated; everyone simply knew from lifelong experience. The question here is, How much authority did an ataniq have in traditional warfare? I was curious and admittedly dubious about this because of the frequency with which stories report "point men" or "champions" (see below) being able to lure members of an enemy force into expending all or most of their arrows in futile shots. It seemed to me that properly led warriors would hold their fire until the right moment and then, on command, shoot a volley that no human being could dodge. My sources agreed with me in principle but claimed that some warriors were so agile that even that procedure would not work.

The elders with whom I discussed the command function of a traditional military force were firm on the point that orders were given and that they were obeyed. But they also contended that the same was true in group activities in contemporary (1960s) village life. In fact, I did observe leaders give orders, even if often in subtle ways, and I saw those orders being obeyed. In general, perhaps more than 95 percent of the time my observations supported the elders' claim, but in the other 5 percent they did not.

For example, the activities of all of the hunters involved in a beluga (white whale) drive must be coordinated if one of these hunts is to be successful. There was one senior hunter in Kivalina who, with his son (but to his son's profound embarrassment), invariably broke prematurely out of the line of boats, tore into the pod of belugas, and killed one or two on his own. This caused the rest of the whales to panic and scatter and completely disrupted the entire hunt. This man was under enormous pressure to stop doing this, but coercive sanctions were not available, and he was tough enough to stand up to the collective disapproval of everyone else in the village. A century and a half earlier he might eventually have been killed by his own relatives for such behavior, but that option was not available in the 1960s. If even a single member of a traditional war party departed so widely from acceptable procedure as this man did during the beluga hunt, the lives of all his companions could have been placed in jeopardy.

Just how the command function of a traditional Iñupiaq fighting force worked in practice remains frustratingly unclear to me. When pondering this matter, however, I often recall a passage in Samuel Hearne's famous account of a Chipewyan raid on a Copper Inuit village in July 1771:

> *It is perhaps worth remarking, that my crew, though an undisciplined rabble, and by no means accustomed to war or command, seemingly acted on this horrid occasion with the utmost uniformity of sentiment. There was not among them the least altercation or separate opinion; all were united in the general cause, and as ready to follow where Matonabbee led, as he appeared ready to lead, according to the advice of an old Copper Indian, who had joined us on our first arrival at the river where this bloody business was first proposed.* [1795:150][19]

Although Iñupiaq individuals and families could be quite independent of one another if they chose to be so, they ordinarily did not make such a choice. They preferred to live in large family units, and such units were inherently hierarchical (Burch 1975a:197–202, 205–209, 223–228). People were also used to obeying the commands of an ataniq during group hunts and other group activities. They were not an undisciplined rabble. If the Chipewyan could form a disciplined fighting force, the Iñupiat certainly could have done so. Raids no doubt were organized and carried out from time to time by a few hotheads annoyed by some grievance or other. But major campaigns would not have been undertaken without the support and guidance of the leading men of the nation and without the leadership of an expert in military affairs.

It is probable that a large military force (by Iñupiaq standards) of dozens or hundreds of men was divided into subunits, each of which had separate leadership. In the case of large whaling villages these units would have been based on qargi membership. In all other cases they would have been based on settlement and/or kinship ties.

The hint of such an arrangement is contained in the record of an encounter between the crew of the *Plover* and the people of Nuvuk (Point Barrow) on October 12, 1852. The Natives had reason to believe that the British were going to attack their village to retrieve some stolen goods. Instead of waiting for an assault, the Iñupiat sallied forth to forestall it, approaching the ship in three columns across the ice. To indicate their hostile intent, the men leading each column were "discharging their arrows ahead of them, as they advanced, & picking them up as they got there" (Bockstoce 1988, vol. 1:101–102). Fortunately, bloodshed was avoided, and the Native force withdrew back to the village "in parties," although the number of retreating parties is not indicated (Bockstoce 1988, vol. 1:103). The following spring John Simpson (1852–54:entry for June 25, 1853) learned that the entire village was divided into three "parties" on the basis of qargi affiliation. This does not prove that each of the three approaching columns had represented a separate qargi, but it does make such an interpretation plausible. If it is correct, then the command structure of the military force would have been identical to the power structure of the village. The only problem would have been for the leaders of the separate units to meet in advance to plan and coordinate their actions.

Prowlers

Prowlers were usually called *iññuqutit* (pl.), but they were also referred to as *iññuqugaurat*.[20] The Iñupiaq terms could be applied to people who got lost or who drifted out on the ice, either alone or in small groups (Ray 1967:380). Ordinarily, however, these terms were reserved for people who set out deliberately to make a secret, unauthorized visit to a country other than their own. Natives speak of them in English variously as "wild people," "runaways," "strange people," and "prowlers." They also refer to them frequently as "Indians," even though they know that most of the prowlers in the NANA Region were Iñupiat. On the Koyukon side of the linguistic border, prowlers were automatically assumed to be Iñupiat unless there was hard evidence to the contrary (Attla and Attla 1991). In terms familiar to most people in the early 21st century, these prowlers are appropriately thought of as having been terrorists.

Iññuqutit are one of the few phenomena discussed in this chapter that still existed during my own time in Alaska, certainly well into the 1960s. Indeed, there were so many incidents involving iññuqutit during the 20th century that few people could recall specific examples from the 19th. However, whenever I asked elders if there used to be any iññuqutit in their great-grandparents' time, I invariably received responses like the following: "Iññuqutit? Lots of iññuqutit in those days. Talk about iññuqutit!"

There is a tendency among Westerners to ascribe mythic status to iññuqutit or to claim that they serve as a convenient explanation for otherwise incomprehensible phenomena (see, e.g., Ingstad 1954:108). That may be true some of the time, but it is not true in general. I have met hundreds of people who have encountered evidence of iññuqutit, dozens who have actually seen them, and a few who have had violent encounters with them. I also know of several people who were killed by iññuqutit but before my time. On the other hand, I have never met a person who admitted to having been an *iññuqun* (sing.) himself, and I know the names of only three individuals who were actually caught acting in that capacity.

Iññuqutit were always male. They usually left their homelands for foreign territory in early or midsummer, hoping to arrive at their destination in mid- to late August, just when the first periods of darkness are returning to the NANA Region after the season of perpetual daylight. According to Martha Nunamiu Swan (1970), they sometimes left home in a group and then spread out when they arrived in enemy territory. In some cases they operated as a group all summer. They usually tried to be back in their own country by early October, before there was much snow on the ground.

Never having interviewed someone who admitted to having been an iññuqun, I am forced to rely on my informants' own speculations as to why people became prowlers. Much of the time, apparently, they were engaged in personal vendettas. Unable to whip up enough enthusiasm for a war party to avenge a wrong they had suffered at the hands of some foreigner, they undertook to do it themselves. Consequently, many iññuqutit were looking for a specific person, the one who had wronged them. In other cases espionage seems to have been involved. The goal was to obtain information on the lay of enemy land and the locations of enemy settlements, all with an eye to planning a future raid. But much of the time iññuqutit seem to have been disgruntled individuals who, unable to express frustration or bitterness in a socially acceptable way at home, decided to do so by terrorizing or even killing members of some other nation, or they may have been in some kind of trouble at home and simply wanted to get away for a while. But iññuqutit with even the most benign of intentions seem to have found it difficult *not* to kill foreigners if presented with an opportunity to do so without being apprehended.

The residents of the NANA Region used to assume that iññuqutit were out and about every summer. Even in the 1960s parties of women out picking berries in August always made sure that an armed man was with them in case an iññuqun put in an appearance. Sometimes iññuqutit were benign, but many were not, and Iñupiat traditionally tried to prepare for the worst. In the 1960s, when a prowler was seen or when fresh evidence of one was found, female berry pickers always, and their male guards sometimes, headed for home. Often, however, a sighting led to the formation of an armed party of men who headed for the place where the iññuqun had been spotted to find out just what his intentions were. In my time none was ever caught.

Perhaps the best way to convey an idea of the range of activities in which iññuqutit engaged is to present a number of specific examples, beginning at the more benign end of the continuum and progressing up the scale of violence.[21] The first example is an experience of my own.

On September 23, 1964, a sudden warm spell made it possible to extend the fall fishing season, so four of us went up the Wulik River and camped at the mouth of Sivuuraq Creek. We managed to catch and put away three tons of fish.[22] On the night of the 27th we were sitting in the tent, exhausted but feeling good after a warm meal and a remarkably successful fishing effort. Suddenly, about ten o'clock I heard a very complex whistling sound, reminiscent of the song of a house wren. It was followed by silence. Then I heard the same kind of sound coming from the opposite direction. My companions didn't move, say anything, or change their facial expressions. More silence. Then I heard the same sounds again. I looked at my companions and said, "What is that?" Their response was, "If you don't ask any questions, you won't get into any trouble." And that was it. There were no more whistling sounds and no further comments from my companions. We put out the light and tried to sleep. The next morning, our mission accomplished, we packed up and returned to the village. I was perturbed by the whistling and by the strange behavior of my companions. Passerine birds do not ordinarily sing several hours after nightfall at any time of year, and all of the ones that had spent the summer in northern Alaska that year had headed south several weeks earlier.

Since my fishing companions refused to talk about the incident, I made discreet inquiries among friends. Their immediate analysis was that we had been surrounded by Indians. Since I had never before heard that Athapaskans signaled each other by whistling, it cannot be said that I had yielded to suggestion.[23] They probably had been watching us the whole time and, knowing that we were getting ready for bed, decided to let us know that they were there. We were completely at their mercy; one reason we were still alive the next morning was because they chose not to kill us the night before.

Altogether there were at least a dozen incidents involving iññuqutit at Kivalina fish camps that fall. They all involved nuisance types of activity, such as throwing stones at a tent in the middle of the night or replacing the white gas in a camp stove with water, but they kept people's nerves very much on edge.

A relatively mild example of an iññuqun encounter was recounted to me by Thomas Aniqsuaq Morris from Deering. Morris was born in 1904, and the event he described apparently occurred 30–40 years before that.

> *One time my grandfather was hunting caribou up around Imuruk Lake, and he was going down to a creek to camp because it was getting dark. As he was going down, he saw someone duck down between the tussocks.*
>
> *My father had a knife. In the early years, before the white people came, they always carried a knife. They used to carry it in a sheath stuck in their belt. They had a rawhide belt, and they carried their knife in a sheath right here in front.*
>
> *And he pulled his knife on that guy. That guy started to run, but my grandfather was an awful fast runner. He ran him down, threatened him with his own knife, and took the prowler's knife away.*
>
> *He told that guy he didn't think he would sleep very well, knowing he would be around during the night. But if he took his knife away, then "it would be better if we sleep together and be friends."* [1970]

Morris's account is the only one I have heard in which an iññuqun was actually caught and let off so easily. Another account, given to me by David Iñuqtaq Adams, is more typical: "One time four Napaaqtuġmiut brothers—Maniksaq,

Tiġigluq and two others whose names I can't remember—were hunting on the Kuugruaq River. They were always alert for iññuqutit and one day happened to discover a man watching them. So they split up and surrounded him. By the time he realized he was surrounded they had him, and he surrendered. He was from Selawik. They let him go but told him that if he ever returned, they would kill him" (1986). Although Adams did not say so, the iññuqun was probably from the lower Selawik district specifically and thus was a Kiitaaġmiu (sing.). If so, he was caught about 140 miles (225 kilometers) from home as the crow flies, and he had had to cross the estate of at least one other nation to get to the Kuugruaq. If he was from the upper Selawik district, he had come even farther.

Sometimes things got violent. Here is a story told to me by Della Keats about an experience of one of her relatives, apparently during the 1930s.

> *One time Thomas was rafting some poles to be used for fish-drying racks down the river to the village. They got stuck in the riverbank, so he went over to break them loose. But they were really stuck, and he had a hard time. After awhile he sat down to take a rest.*
>
> *While Thomas was resting, somebody grabbed ahold of him from behind. All of a sudden! He never even had a chance to see who it was.*
>
> *So, they wrestled. That man tried to push Thomas into the river, into the water. They were on a high bank, and the river was below them. Thomas tried to get away from the edge of the bank, all right. He tried to get away from that man, but the man hung on. So, when he couldn't make it that way, he hit the man with his elbow as hard as he could. And when he did that he heard the ribs snap, like they had been broken. His elbow had gone through. Then he pushed that man into the river.*
>
> *The river wasn't very deep, but it was very fast. That man barely made it to the other side. When he got out of the water he could hardly stand, and he walked with a bad limp.*
>
> *Thomas crossed the river and started to follow him. But he thought maybe there would be others, so he went home instead. Later on we found out that man died. Thomas didn't want to kill him, he was just trying to save himself.* [1970e]

Another story with a similar outcome was also told to me by Keats, although she had originally heard it from Dolly Sheidt. The incident probably occurred during the 1890s.

> *One time Dolly Sheidt's uncle was out hunting in the fall time. He stayed alone in a little tent. One evening, before it got too dark, he went into his tent and tried to go to sleep.*
>
> *But sleep wouldn't come. While he was lying there he heard a stick break and a*

noise in the leaves on the ground. He put his parka in his sleeping bag so that it looked like someone was in it. He made it look just like someone was asleep in that bag. And he went out and hid in the bushes.

Pretty soon this iññuqun came sneaking around and opened the door of the tent. He thought he saw a person sleeping there and started shooting. After the stranger had fired into the sleeping bag a couple of times, Dolly's uncle shot and killed him. He knew that he would not be alive himself if he had been in that bag.

Then he heard a boy crying not too far away. He called to that boy; he called him, all right. And he looked for that boy and found him. It was that boy's father he had just killed.

And he talked to him and gave him some food. And he told him to go back home the way he came. "Don't forget the way you came when you and your dad came over here. I won't hurt you. I just tried to save myself. I was sorry to do that, but I had to or I wouldn't be alive now."

And he sent that boy home. [1970e]

Unfortunately, I forgot to ask whence these people had come.

Still another example recounted by Keats took place on the upper Noatak River. I present it as it was originally recorded in an exchange between Keats (DK) and me (ESB).

DK: One time while they were staying in Anigaaq they were living in an *ivrulik*, a moss hut, in the fall time. They stayed in one place—Kaliksuna, Tagluksaq, and my great-grandma. My great-grandma was from Point Hope. One day she walked some distance from the people with whom she was living and met some men from Point Hope. And she showed them where Tagluksaq and the others were living.

ESB: How did she know the Point Hopers were there?

DK: She knew, all right. Maybe she expected them. And she told them that Tagluksak was there. My mother [born ca. 1875] was a little girl that time. And she heard somebody making a noise outdoors. They could feel the moss shake. They hardly slept. Those strangers knew where Tagluksaq and Kaliksuna were staying. I don't know why they were looking for them. I asked my mother, all right, but she didn't know.

My great-grandmother went out and talked to those Point Hopers, even when she couldn't see them. She was just talking any old way, even toward the bushes. But finally those Point Hopers gave up and went home.

ESB: Those Point Hopers walked all the way up there?

DK: Yes, they walked.

ESB: How did they know where to go? Had they been up there before?

DK: I don't know. They probably had been there before, because they had been iññuqutit before. Those iññuqutit used to go up there all the time. [1970e]

This example looks suspiciously like a case of espionage. Keats's grandmother probably had been contacted by Point Hopers during the trade fair at Sisualik, which is how she knew they were coming. Just for perspective, Point Hope is about 225 miles (360 kilometers), as the crow flies, from Anigaaq.

Another example from the upper Noatak was also told to me by Keats.

My mama told me that one time they were going up the Noatak for the winter. After his wife died, my mother's father, Qaqsi, was going up with my mother's grandma and some others. They were about at Anisaaġiaq. My grandpa was managing the dogs that were pulling the boat.

And the helmsman heard a noise just like somebody running in the willows. He made a knocking noise on the gunwale of the boat to get Qaqsi to turn around and look at him. He didn't call him, he just made a noise to get him to turn around. When Qaqsi turned around, the helmsman motioned to him to indicate that he had heard a strange noise.

Then the helmsman brought the boat to the bank. Qaqsi jumped in, got his bow and arrows, and jumped out again. Qaqsi originally was a Kuuvaum Kaŋiaġmiu, from the upper Kobuk.[24] *He could tell from their tracks that the iññuqutit were from that country. So he ran around in the willows calling the names of his relatives from the Kobuk, even though he couldn't see anyone. He called them, all right, but they never came out of hiding. If my grandpa hadn't been there, maybe those iññuqutit would have killed somebody.* [1970c]

This also might have been a case of espionage, although, as Keats suggested, it might have been considerably more sinister than that. The Nuataaġmiut were fortunate to have a Kobuk River man in the party.

The ability to identify the national origin of iññuqutit by inspecting their tracks is illustrated by another story, this one told to me by Mark Uluatchiaq Cleveland.

Many years ago, in the fall time, way up the Kobuk above Ambler, an iññuqun came every night to one camp and stole a few fish. A lot of dried fish were stored in the cache. The people knew what was happening, but they couldn't catch the thief. Finally, one young man got tired of this and stayed up all night to ambush him. The iññuqun came, and the Kobuk man shot him in the side, right under his arm. But the stranger ran away, and the Kobuk man didn't try to chase him.

The next day, when the men inspected the tracks, they were able to identify the footprints of a specific individual from the upper Noatak. They had noticed some-

thing peculiar about those footprints once during a football game at Sisualik. Since that man was never seen again, it is assumed that he died from his wounds. [1989][25]

The final example is in a story told to me by Frank Glover, an Akuniġmiu from the central Kobuk district who was born in 1886. The fact that a bow and arrows was the primary weapon but that a muzzle-loader was also involved suggests that the events took place during the 1860s.

They killed my aana *[grandmother], those* iññuqutit. *But another time, those Akuniġmiut killed an iññuqun. I will tell you about that one.*

An old man had a daughter. A young man took her for his wife, but her father didn't like him.

One year they had lots of fish in their cache, away back behind the house. And that son-in-law went there. His name was Katŋutauraq. He was getting tired of his father-in-law, his wife's daddy. That old man kept calling him names and saying he was no good. And Katŋutauraq got tired of it. His wife told him not to listen to her father, but he got tired of it and went over to the cache. He took his bow and arrows along with him.

He stayed inside the cache until it was dark. And when it got dark, a stranger started to sneak over to it. He was sneaking over to steal some fish. He didn't know that Katŋutauraq was watching him from inside.

The man stood up and started to climb up into the cache. Just as Katŋutauraq was aiming an arrow, he knocked down some dried fish. That man heard it and stopped. Katŋutauraq wanted to kill him right there, but he bumped those fish, the other man heard him, and ran. He did not dodge but ran straight into the willows. And Katŋutauraq shot him right in the back.

That man started to scream. He made a lot of noise. And he fell down. Suddenly, several people emerged from the willows and got him. They pulled out the arrow and took him away. And they all escaped.

Katŋutauraq went back to the houses and told the people that some kind of Indians were watching them.

There were some Kuuvaum Kaŋiaġmiut [upper Kobuk River people] staying there too, that time. And one of them had a muzzle-loading gun. And when Katŋutauraq told about the strange people, that man heard him, that he had shot someone.

And Katŋutauraq was telling his father-in-law about what had happened. And the old man told him to watch out, and he left the house. And when he got outside he started to holler. He shouted to the iññuqutit *that the person who had shot one of their number was named Katŋutauraq. (That old man was crazy!)*

But the man who had the gun wanted to help Katŋutauraq. After awhile they noticed that lots of people had come down to the riverbank from the willows. Strange people. And the man went down too, with his gun, and hid under an overturned skin boat. And he saw one of those men not too far from the boat, right at the water's edge. So, the old man decided to kill that stranger. He wanted to help Katŋutauraq.

It was an easy shot because it was just a little ways. But his gun wouldn't fire. He pulled the trigger once, but no fire. He readied it again and pulled the trigger, but it misfired once more. So, on the third attempt, he fired into the air. And the gun shot that time. Plenty of fire came out. And those wild men, those iññuqutit, ran back into the willows.

That man with the gun kept watching, and, after awhile, those iññuqutit went down to the river again. They were trying to sneak up on the houses. That man was still hiding under a skin boat, but a different one this time.

And pretty soon one of those strangers got close to him, and that man decided to kill him. Maybe it will shoot this time, he thought. That stranger was right in front of him when he pulled the trigger, but the gun didn't fire. So, he tried it again, with the same result. So, on the third time, he shot up into the air, and the gun went off. I don't know how come he couldn't shoot the iññuqutit. Maybe an aŋatkuq [shaman] was with them. Then the iññuqutit ran away.

Well, the next day they went out to see the tracks of those iññuqutit, and they found the tracks of lots of people. And they recognized them as belonging to Nuataaġmiut. [1970c]

The iññuqutit in this example may have been warriors who happened to be discovered before they could mount a raid. Nonplussed by this fact, the wounding of one of their number, and the presence of even a malfunctioning gun, they may have decided to abandon their original objective and go home. Or it may be that this settlement was not the one they had been looking for in the first place. They could have approached it simply to steal some food but had been caught in the act.

These accounts provide some idea of the range of variation of iññuqutit activities. What is not apparent in the examples is a general trend in my full collection of narratives for the parties of terrorists to get larger as one works backward in time. An iññuqun operating alone is uncommon in the oldest accounts but universal in the most recent ones. This suggests that during the time period of particular interest here, iññuqutit were not isolated trouble-makers but organized groups with national rather than (or in addition to) personal objectives.

There is a very fine line between iññuqutit (prowlers), on the one hand, and *suġruich* (raiders), on the other, in all of the early accounts. The objectives of the iññuqutit seem to have been harassment, terrorism, and espionage, with opportunistic homicide as a possibility. Terrorism certainly was not the least of these goals, for iññuqutit frequently, if not invariably, made a point of letting the local people know they had been there, implying that they could have killed someone if they had felt like it. In contrast, homicide was the primary objective among sugruich, and it was pursued quite systematically. If this analysis is correct, the activities of iññuqutit during the study period are most accurately understood under the heading of "reconnaissance in force." The difference between early-19th-century iññuqutit and sugruich probably was a fine one indeed.

Surprise Attacks

Iññuqutit generally did their work from mid-August to early October, while sugruich usually began operating in September and continued throughout the winter.[26] The main season for surprise attacks, as opposed to open battle, was late September to about mid-November. This was so for five reasons. First, the ground and often the lakes, creeks, and sections of the rivers were frozen by then, making overland travel much easier than it was in summer and also making tracking more difficult than it was when the ground was thawed. Second, the long days of summer have passed by that time of year, and approaches to enemy settlements could be made under cover of darkness. Third, there usually was little snow on the ground in the fall. This made overland travel relatively easy for the aggressors and more difficult for defenders to track escaping raiders. Fourth, during the bitterly cold temperatures of midwinter snow makes a loud crunching noise underfoot, significantly reducing raiders' chances of achieving surprise. Finally, fall was the time of year when food supplies were ordinarily at their greatest and the time when women and youngsters could fish on their own. Consequently, in most years men could leave on a fall raid without worrying about their families being short of necessities.

The usual objective of a raiding party was to exterminate the inhabitants—men, women, and children—of an enemy settlement. Sometimes raiders attacked a specific settlement because certain individuals lived there, but often any settlement in the enemy's estate would do.

The primary tactic was to approach the target settlement under cover of darkness, ideally when everyone was in the qargi, otherwise when they were asleep in their own houses. All the raiders had to do was block the qargi or house doors, and the inhabitants were trapped inside. The raiders then taunted (*pitqusaaq-*) their victims and challenged (*ququula-*) them to come out and fight. If they did, they were shot, speared, or clubbed to death as they emerged. If they did not emerge, the raiders gathered combustible material such as birch bark, lit it, and threw it down through the skylight. Any seal oil that had spilled onto the dirt floor soon caught fire. Eventually, the people inside were either burned to death or smoked out.[27] In some accounts the raiders gave them the choice of dying for certain inside or taking their chances outside (Lucier 1997:204). If everyone was not in the qargi, the raiders waited until people were asleep and then followed essentially the same procedure, except that they trapped family members in their separate houses. After all the doors had been blocked, the inhabitants were exterminated one household at a time.

Of course, raiders never could be absolutely certain that everyone was in the qargi or their houses when the attack was launched, which lent an element of uncertainty to the enterprise. In many accounts someone spotted the raiders as they approached the settlement and shouted "Paaġaasi!" [They are coming at you!] before the raiders could get control of the situation. Immediately upon hearing that cry, the defenders grabbed their weapons, emerged from the dwellings or qargi, and counterattacked. If they did this soon enough, the raid was sometimes aborted right at the outset. Otherwise, they fought it out.

Iñupiat rarely gave up without a fight. After spending several years dealing with people in various parts of northwestern Alaska around the middle of the 19th century, John Simpson formed the opinion that "if once engaged in a fight they would not readily give in, at least if there was anything like equality of weapons; and, under any circumstances, they might be expected to defend their homes to the last extremity" (1875:248). Even a successful raid often resulted in casualties for the aggressors.

If there was sufficient advance warning, people who were about to be attacked could flee to a neighboring settlement or else muster a large defensive force and set out to confront the raiders. If they did not have enough time to flee but they did have the manpower to form a battle line, the men in a settlement that was about to be attacked often confronted the raiders outside the village. They hoped to force the raiders to abandon the enterprise, but, failing that, they would attempt to defeat the raiders without the women and children getting involved.

This tactic is illustrated by some examples reported by John Simpson. In the first, the crew of a schooner, the *Nancy Dawson*, "landed on the ice to shoot birds, [and] the handful of men whose tents were in the neighborhood advanced, bow in hand, to meet them and drive them back. Some of these men have since explained, that fearing the guns, they thought it better to oppose the landing of the strangers than trust them on shore, before knowing them to be friends" (Simpson 1875:248). Simpson's second example is the one described above in which an Iñupiaq force of 80 men issued forth from Nuvuk (Point Barrow) to prevent a British attack on their settlement.

Many of the other early explorers also observed or experienced the courage of the Iñupiat in defense of their homes. For example, in 1816 Kotzebue (1821, vol. 1:225) found an old man and a boy quite prepared to defend their pitiful little camp against a much larger number of well-armed Russians. On August 24, 1826, about 2 miles (3.2 kilometers) west of Point Barrow, a detachment from the Beechey expedition had the following experience: "Nineteen of the natives came down opposite us, armed with bows, arrows and spears, and imagining that it was our intention to land motioned us to keep off, and seemed quite prepared for hostilities. Some of them were stripped almost naked [despite the fact that the temperature was at or below freezing]. They preserved a greater silence than we found customary among them, one only speaking at a time, and apparently interrogating us" (Beechey 1831, vol. 1:426).

As noted in Chapter 1, the members of Kashevarov's party were thought to be Iñupiat because of their mode of travel and were initially confronted as an invading force by the people in several of the settlements where they stopped. On the islands of Bering Strait, where the formation of defensive battle lines was all but impossible because of the steep slopes, foreigners who attempted to land without an invitation, as Mikhail Gvozdev did in 1732, were greeted with "a shower of arrows" (Golder 1971:161).

Flight and advancing to meet the enemy by no means exhausted the alternatives available to the Iñupiat for the defense of their villages. Other tactics, some of them developed on an ad hoc basis to take advantage of certain aspects of the situation, were also employed. An example is provided by an incident that occurred at a place now known as Imauġvik, in Napaaqtuġmiut country.[28] There are several accounts of this raid that differ in their details but that have a common core. What follows is a composite.[29]

> *Early one fall, just after freshwater freeze-up, some residents of the settlement happened to spot Tikiġaġmiut raiders while they were still some distance away from the village. They held a hurried council and devised a plan to defeat the raiders. The village was located near a deep pool in the river that was covered with rather thin ice, thick enough to support one or two people but not strong enough to bear the weight of several. While it was still light one or two women at a time went out on the river to hook for fish through holes in the ice over that pool. Their goals were to convince the hidden Tikiġaġmiut raiders that the ice was solid and to convey the impression that the residents were unaware of the impending attack.*
>
> *As darkness fell the defenders wrapped skins around their bodies to help shield themselves from enemy arrows and put their weapons in order. After it was dark the men crept outside and hid in the thick willows surrounding the houses. The women and children remained inside. The little ones were fed raw salmon eggs, which stuck to their mouths, keeping them distracted and making it difficult for them to talk.*

When it had been dark for quite awhile the raiders crept forward, expecting to trap everyone inside their houses. Just when the raiders reached the dwellings, however, the defenders attacked them from the rear. Caught totally by surprise, the raiders fled across the river, only to have the thin ice over the deep hole collapse beneath them. Those who did not drown were shot to death, except for one man. He managed to cross the water by using the floating bodies of his companions as stepping stones and escaped.

One of the Napaaqtuġmiut chased and eventually caught the escapee, only to find out that he was his *qataŋun* (cosibling). According to most versions of the story, he spared the qataŋun's life but told him never to fight against the Napaaqtuġmiut again because he would be killed for certain if he did. In another version, however, this was the second time the man had been caught fighting against the Napaaqtuġmiut, and so he was killed on the spot (Hunnicutt 1960a; Hall 1975b:97–100).

It is one thing to raid a settlement of 2 or 3 houses (12–18 people) and quite another to attack one of 10, 15, or 20 houses (80–160 people) or more. The same basic tactics could be used, but the size of the raiding party had to be much greater. This made it much more difficult for the raiders to approach without being seen, and it also created the logistic problem of so many men living off the land as they traveled through enemy territory. Raids on large villages were, nevertheless, sometimes attempted.

One famous example is a raid on Taksruq Saaŋa, the major village of the Qikiqtaġruŋmiut, just south of where the modern town of Kotzebue is now located. Once again, there are several accounts of the event that differ in detail but not in basic substance. One important element that is in doubt, however, is the nationality of the raiders, the candidates being Utuqqaġmiut, Nuataaġmiut, and the Kobuk River Koyukon. The person who seemed to have the greatest grasp of the material was Frank Glover, and it is his version that I present here.[30]

One time, long ago, the Kuuvaum Kaŋiaġmiut [upper Kobuk River people] wanted to make war on the Qikiqtaġruŋmiut, so they decided to attack their main village, Taksruq Saaŋa.

When they scouted the situation, they decided that they were outnumbered, so they went to the Kobuk River delta and recruited some Kuuŋmiut to join them. They established a base camp near the Little Noatak [River] and left an old woman and a boy there to fish for supplies.

The warriors headed for Taksruq Saaŋa on a moonlit night. They were wearing feathers on their heads.

The villagers, meanwhile, were enjoying an evening of feasting and dancing.

Everyone was in the qargi except for one bald man named Apausuk, who had a toothache. His wife stayed with him to look after him. This man was a superb warrior.

The Kobukers approached the village from behind a little hill. The Kuuvaum Kaŋiaġmiut went along one side, while the Kuuŋmiut went along the other.

The sick man's wife went outside to do something. In the moonlight she happened to catch a glimpse of the feathers worn by the raiders, who were crawling toward the village on their hands and knees.

The woman ran inside and told Apausuk. He sprang up, got his bow and quiver of arrows, and headed for the qargi. He jumped up on the roof and called the news in through the skylight. All the men emerged with their weapons before the attack could begin.

The Kobukers, meanwhile, had seen Apausuk run to the qargi. They recognized him, and they knew his reputation as a warrior. When they realized they had been discovered, they retreated to hold a council of war. They decided that, since Apausuk was in the village and since they had lost the element of surprise, they would be better off retreating.

So they withdrew. They returned to their base camp on the Little Noatak, got the old woman and the boy, and headed back to the Kobuk. The Qikiqtaġruŋmiut followed the trail of the Kobukers back to their base camp, but it had been abandoned by the time they got there. They decided to give up the chase and went home. [1970b, 1970c]

In this case prudence prevented the attack, and only a very quick withdrawal prevented what might have been a major confrontation.[31]

Another example is a raid on the village of Tikiġaq, which was located at the end of Point Hope spit. Tikiġaq, with nearly 80 inhabited houses and a population of more than 600 people (Burch 1981:14), was the largest settlement in northwestern Alaska. It was situated on the end of a long, barren spit that extends several miles out into the Chukchi Sea and is very difficult to approach without being seen. To raid it was a foolhardy enterprise for anything less than a force formed by the combined manpower of several nations. Since the Tikiġaġmiut were notorious raiders themselves, however, mustering such a force may not have been particularly difficult. On this particular occasion, an alliance had been struck among the Napaaqtuġmiut, Nuataaġmiut, Qikiqtaġruŋmiut, and Kivalliñiġmiut, who together could muster a force of perhaps 350–400 men.[32]

This particular attack came in early fall, after the Point Hopers were back in the village for the winter but before the ground had frozen. The raiders came along the south beach. They wore clothing made from caribou-fawn skins, which is appar-

ently especially difficult to see against a sand and gravel background. They had bare feet, which are quieter than boots when walking on gravel, and they were armed only with lances. A woman who happened to be out with her baby boy performing some kind of ritual saw the raiders approaching, and she ran home and raised the alarm.

The Tikiġaġmiut men issued forth with their weapons and formed a series of battle lines just as the enemy force was launching its attack. Caught by surprise and by the discipline and vigor of the counterattack, the raiders retreated. Ignorant of the precise location of the rows of pungi sticks arrayed around the settlement, they allowed themselves to be maneuvered onto them. The spikes pierced their feet and rendered many of the raiders nearly helpless. Pressed by the Tikiġaġmiut defenders, the other members of the attacking force fled back along the beach, leaving their wounded comrades (ikiḷigaat) behind to be dispatched by the victors.

Open Battle

The ultimate form of combat in northwestern Alaska was a battle in the open (aŋuyak-). Skirmishes typically occurred when men in a village about to be attacked ventured out to confront enemy raiders at a distance from their homes and families, but sometimes these were broken off before the affair got much beyond the posturing stage. Large-scale battles (by northern Alaskan standards), involving armies (*aŋuyaktit*) of dozens or even hundreds of men, also took place. Apparently, these took place either when the animosity on both sides had reached such a high level that the combatants wanted to fight it out in the quickest way possible or when so many troops had been mustered that a sneak attack was not feasible.

Open battles seem to have occurred more frequently in the fall than at other times of year for the same reasons that raids did. However, since surprise was a less important factor, there was no particular need for a military campaign to be undertaken during the short days of fall and early winter. Open battle was very rare in spring, however, because food supplies were usually low then, so attention almost everywhere was on subsistence pursuits. Snow depth was also usually the greatest, at least in early spring, which sometimes made travel difficult and always restricted maneuverability. Open battle also was rare in summer, a season when interdistrict travel and trade were at their height and when a general truce usually prevailed.

Open battles seem to have occurred only in tundra settings and apparently began during daylight hours. I never thought to ask if they continued through the night, and none of the accounts I have obtained mentions nighttime encounters other than raids. Once snow was on the ground, however, there was sufficient light to continue fighting at night, at least in clear weather.

The largest battles in Northwest Alaskan history involved alliances of two or more nations on at least one side. Just how these forces were raised and organized is unknown. It would be consistent with other international events, such as the trade fairs, for the warriors from each nation to constitute a separate subunit of the combined force. Each such unit would have had a separate command structure and possibly distinct subunits of its own based on qargi or family membership. Since the same basic tactics were known and followed everywhere, all the alliance leaders had to do was get together in advance and plan the location and timing of the confrontation.

The wish to engage in open battle was initially signaled at a distance by men walking toward the enemy in a column, with the man in the lead shooting arrows ahead of their line of travel. (For an example of this see Bockstoce 1988, vol. 1:101–102.) As they approached the outer range of enemy fire, the men redeployed in a line, held their weapons above their heads, and shouted challenges and insults at the opposing force.

An open battle was fought by opposing lines of men armed with the full array of weapons and other military paraphernalia available to the Iñupiat. The best archers were usually placed on the ends of each line to protect its flanks. The fact that this was so suggests that the Iñupiat were aware of the general concept of a flanking movement, and they must have had some knowledge of how to execute one.

Presumably, battle was joined when the opposing lines were close to the maximum range of Iñupiaq bows and arrows, perhaps around 200 yards (ca. 180 meters) apart. Under the direction of an ataniq, each unit attempted to maneuver into an advantageous position. This phase of a battle apparently could last for hours or even days, during which the warriors had little or nothing to eat or drink. Elders from one or both sides often attempted to intervene at this point in order to prevent bloodshed, but they were usually ignored.

It would be wonderful to know what went on in the minds of the men viewing one another across the potential battlefield, holding their weapons above their heads, posturing, and shouting imprecations and threats. Each group was there, of course, for the specific and sole purpose of annihilating the members of the opposing force. However, at least some of the men in opposing camps usually knew each other; they might even be friends or relatives. Often one could see among the enemy a partner, a qataŋun, or a brother-in-law or father-in-law. These considerations must have introduced an element of ambivalence into the situation, and members of opposing forces who were related in one of these ways may have been allowed to withdraw, as was the case among the Yup'ik-speaking Eskimos of southwestern Alaska (Nelson 1899:329).

An important part of the preliminary maneuvers was for one or two relatively short and particularly agile young men from each side to advance ahead of the line, taunt the members of the enemy force, and try to lure them into shooting prematurely. The standard procedure was for these men to do the *saliksuq*, a dance performed by bouncing around with a rigid body, legs half-bent with the knees out and arms held stiffly akimbo. Thomas Aniqsuaq Morris once characterized this maneuver for me as "dribbling": "They didn't dodge, they jumped around sideways. Of course, if they saw an arrow they dodged it. But otherwise they jumped around sideways. When he saw an arrow, he jumped sideways. Actually, I would call it 'dribble' in English. You know when they play basketball they dribble the ball? Well, that's what I would call it because they dribbled their whole body. I would call it 'dribble.' That's how you saliksuq" (1970).

The only eyewitness account I have found of this movement comes from the Arctic coast. In the summer of 1849 a small party of English explorers under Lt. William Pullen came under fire by Iñupiat shooting with bows and arrows, so the Englishmen returned fire with their muzzle-loading guns: "[The Natives] cut some ludicrous capers on the occasion, dancing and jumping about, to divert our aim, and dropping, like dead men, the instant they observed the flash" (Hooper 1853:248; see also Phebus 1972:fig. 66).

During the early stages of a battle it was relatively easy for the men "on point" to dodge any arrows that came their way. As the range closed the saliksuq became a progressively more dangerous procedure but also a more productive one: the closer the enemy warriors were, the more they were tempted to shoot; the more arrows they shot, the more they ended up wasting. The objective of this whole preliminary phase of battle was to tempt the enemy to use up as much ammunition as possible (*qaġruiġuttaq-*) with minimum injury to, and minimal expenditure of arrows by, one's own side. In many legends as opposed to actual historical accounts, battles were often resolved during this early stage primarily because of the brilliance of the men on one side who were performing the saliksuq. But there must have been many occasions when this tactic failed, either because one or more of the point men were killed and/or because each side managed to retrieve roughly equal numbers of expended arrows.

If the preliminary maneuvering failed to achieve an advantage for either side, the opposing lines eventually closed to within effective bow-and-arrow range of one another (which seems to have begun at a distance of about 150 yards [135 meters]), and the encounter developed into a firefight (*pisigauti-*). The Iñupiat were fully aware of the importance of maintaining proper intervals in the line, partly so that when an arrow was dodged by one man it would not accidentally hit another, partly so that the dodging men would not bump into one another, and partly so that each man had a clear view of the enemy so that he could see, and therefore dodge, incoming missiles. They also understood the value of directing volleys of arrows against specific individuals. However, they apparently were either too spread out themselves or too lacking in discipline to employ this tactic successfully very often, especially at long range.

Arrows that failed to find their mark could, of course, be shot back again, which only prolonged this phase of the battle. Holding an upwind or uphill position could be crucial because it gave one side greater range and/or greater accuracy than the other. The direction and angle of the sun were also important, since glare affected the men's ability to see incoming missiles. The general condition of the men, their equipment, and their food supplies would also be tested, although I have heard of only one case in which discrepancies in any of those areas determined the outcome.[33] The decisive factors were always the relative sizes of the opposing forces, leadership, dodging ability, and marksmanship.

A classic example of a pitched battle involved, on one side, a force of Koyukon (of unspecified nationality) and, on the other, Iñupiat of the Selawik area. It occurred at a place now called Itqiḷḷiġvik (Athapaskan Place), which I cannot locate precisely but which I believe is on the southern flank of the Purcell Mountains. The Iñupiaq force definitely included Siiḷviim Kaŋianiġmiut warriors, probably some Kiitaaġmiut, and possibly some Akuniġmiut as well. This account is a composite of a version told to me by Johnnie Tuuyuq Foster and a somewhat more fanciful one recorded by Edwin S. Hall Jr.

> *One time up there in the hills, at the place they now call Itqiḷḷiġvik, lots of Selawik men were looking for Athapaskans. It was fall, just after the ground froze, and lots of Indians were coming this way, looking for Selawik people and Kobuk people. They wanted to fight.*
>
> *They met each other way up there on the mountain. They met on the south side; it's kind of a long, steep slope on the south side. I don't know how many Indians there were, but there was a lot of them. And there was a lot of men on the Selawik side too.*
>
> *The Selawik warriors began on the downhill side, and the Indians were on the uphill side, each force strung out in a long line. At the start they were not shooting but jumping around with their bows and arrows ready to fire. And one old man from the Indians was yelling and hollering. He didn't want anybody to fight. He waved his hands in the air and went right between the two lines, while the Indians and the Selawik people were jumping around with their bows and arrows but*

before they started shooting. The Selawik people understood that he didn't want to see people get killed. He talked the Indian language, all right, but the Selawik people could understand him.

The Selawik force had some good shooters placed on each end of their line. The Selawik men also had a good ataniq, who got them turned around so that they got uphill from the Indian warriors. (It is better to shoot downhill.) When they finally got on the uphill side, that's the time the Selawik men started to shoot.

The old man failed to stop the battle. When the warriors started to shoot at each other with bows and arrows he grabbed two boys who were in the Indian line—I don't know how old they were, big enough to follow the men, maybe 14 or 15 years old—and went down to the timber to hide.

So the Selawik men and the Indians fought and fought. But the Selawik people didn't lose even one man, and they cleaned up the whole bunch of Indians. Those that weren't dead already they speared to death, although one shaman wouldn't die until they cut out his heart.

The Selawik people knew that the old man and the boys were hiding down near the creek, but they never bothered them; they let them go. [J. Foster 1970; Hall 1975b:331]

In addition to being almost a textbook case of an open battle, this story shows that the Koyukon and Iñupiat employed virtually identical tactics. When I asked Foster how the Iñupiat managed to outmaneuver the Indians, he responded that they had had a good leader and that the men had obeyed his commands.

Eventually, one of three things happened. The first possibility was for the battle to end in a draw, in which case the leaders of the opposing sides negotiated an organized withdrawal. However, I never heard of an actual instance of this happening. The second possibility was for one side to try to break off the action unilaterally and withdraw. This was extremely dangerous, however, for the Iñupiat had no compunctions about shooting a man in the back. The third possible outcome was for one side to gain a clear advantage over the other. When that happened the side with the advantage switched to shock tactics and pressed the attack. They shot as many members of the weaker force as possible and speared, knifed, or (presumably) clubbed to death the wounded. This is what I call the melee stage of battle, when most of the combat was hand to hand and one on one. Prisoners (isiqtat) were either killed outright or tortured to death. Knowing this, when an advantage for one side had been clearly established, the members of the weaker force usually tried to retreat. Unless the battle had gone on for a very long time, they were usually hotly pursued by the victors, a few of whom, in their haste, sometimes got careless and ended up being killed themselves.

Variations

Previous sections have described the three basic forms of international hostility in 19th-century northwestern Alaska: actions by iññuqutit, raids, and open battles. There were, however, a number of variations on those basic themes. It is useful to convey an idea, without attempting to be exhaustive, of the range of possibilities through a series of specific examples. The reader should be warned that portions of some of the following accounts depict scenes of extreme brutality. They are presented because they are part of the record of international hostility in northwestern Alaska. They were described in the oral accounts passed down from generation to generation during traditional times, as they were included in the stories told to me by Native historians.

Upper Kobuk Koyukon/Nuataaġmiut Exchanges

One raid usually led to another. A well-known series of exchanges involved Koyukon-speaking inhabitants from the upper Kobuk valley, on the one side, and Iñupiat from the upper Noatak valley, the Nuataaġmiut, on the other. The source is Robert Nasruk Cleveland (1965c), who told the story to Don Charles Foote.

One time many years ago, the Kobuk River people had a fight with the Noatak people. After killing several people, they captured two young women. They took them to live with the people on the Kobuk. When the Noatakers came to avenge this raid, they took the two women home. This led to a series of raids back and forth spread over several years in which the same two women were captured repeatedly, first by one side, then by the other. However, they survived, while many others were killed.

One summer the two women were living with many Kobuk women and one old man in a large summer fishing camp along the Kobuk, at Maniḷappaat, near the mouth of the Mauneluk River. All the other men and teenage boys were away hunting caribou. One of the Kobuk women, named Kititiġaaġvaat, had just had a baby. As was the custom, she had borne the child in a parturition hut located some distance from the camp, and she had to stay there for four days and four nights before she could re-enter the camp. One day, when the rest of the women were out fishing, she heard splashing sounds made by Nuataaġmiut warriors crossing the Mauneluk River a short distance upstream. Her time was up, so she returned to the camp, and when the others got back from fishing, she told them about the raiders. The old man said Kititiġaaġvaat was crazy, and told the others to ignore her. A little orphan boy had also seen the enemy warriors, but the old man ridiculed him too.

But Kititiġaaġvaat knew that she was right, so she told her mother to take her other children—the old lady's grandchildren, and flee the settlement. When the others were out picking berries, the old woman put them all in a boat, along with the orphan boy, and paddled away through Łaagurahaat slough and hid.

The next morning the raiders attacked the camp and killed all the women and children remaining there. During the attack, the old man hid inside a cache and managed to wound many of the Nuataaġmiut warriors before he, in turn, was dispatched.

The dead included, through a mistake on the raiders' part, the two unfortunate Nuataaġmiut women who had been taken back and forth so many times. After shoving sheefish into the vaginas of all of the Indian women they had killed, the Noatakers took Kititiġaaġvaat and her baby, and retreated toward the upper Noatak River. They travelled through Tuvaasaq and Quġluqtuq. Finally, when they had almost reached home, the Noatakers gang-raped Kititiġaaġvaat and left her with her baby to die. However, she was very tough, and as soon as the Noatakers were a little way off, she fled with her baby, carefully hiding her trail. After awhile the Noatakers thought better about leaving her alive and returned to kill her. However, she escaped, built a small raft, and drifted down to the Kobuk River with her baby.

Some weeks later, the Kobuk caribou hunters returned home to find the rotting remains of their wives and children and vowed revenge. A year or two after that, they headed north to the upper Noatak to seek it. They soon located a large body of Nuataaġmiut and secretly followed them. One morning the men in the Nuataaġmiut camp spotted a large band of caribou and went off in pursuit. While they were gone, the Kobuk raiders killed every woman in the camp. Then they cut off their vulvas, strung them on a line, and headed quickly toward home. [1965c]

Cleveland's narrative stopped there, but it is hard to believe that revenge raids and counterraids stopped with this incident. The next story, which has certain elements in common with the last one, was evidently part of this series, but there is no way to know whether it occurred before or after the events described above.

One year, after the Nuataaġmiut living at Makpik had put away their big boats for the winter, several Koyukon-speaking Kobuk men came over to the Noatak. One day the Makpik men took their kayaks up to a big lake some distance from the village to spear caribou, leaving behind the women, children, and old men. While they were gone those Kobuk men killed all of them except for two young women, whom they took captive. By accident they also missed an old man and a boy who was with him who were hiding. When the raiding party left the old man sent the boy to tell the other Nuataaġmiut men what had happened while he followed the Kobukers. When the caribou hunters arrived back at camp everyone there was dead, even the little babies. However, two young women were missing, having been taken captive by the raiders.

The Kobuk men quickly headed toward home, taking the two women along. The old man, following the escaping raiders, guided his fellow countrymen by howling at night like a wolf. The Noatakers finally caught up with the fleeing raiders without being discovered. One night, when they got to the forested area on the Kobuk side, the Kobuk men built a fire, thinking they were safe. They sent the two women out to gather wood. One of the Noatakers grabbed one of the women and put his hand over her mouth so that she couldn't scream. He told her to put a lot of wood on the fire so that the Kobuk men couldn't see very far from it, beyond the circle of light. This was done. Then the Nuataaġmiut men slipped small knives to the women when they were fetching wood and told them to cut the Kobukers' bowstrings. When the fire was burning brightly the Kobuk men relaxed, eating and laughing. The Noatak men surrounded them in the dark and killed them all save one, the one who had abused the women the most.

The Nuataaġmiut tied short lines between this man's big toes and the labret holes in his lips, tied his hands behind his back, and made him walk back to Makpik, all hunched over. When he tripped over a tussock or something, the Noatakers poked him with their spears and made him bleed. When they reached the scene of the original massacre the Nuataaġmiut asked their captive how he had treated those two women. Then they killed him.[34]

The Athapaskan Raid on Nuvuġaluaq

Nuvuġaluaq was a Tikiġaġmiut settlement of seven houses located on the coast about 12 miles (19 kilometers) northeast of Point Hope. Its inhabitants probably numbered between 50 and 60 people. One fall night a party of Athapaskans raided it, caught the residents inside their houses, and proceeded to massacre them. Just what kind of Athapaskans they were is unknown. Charlie Jensen, who told me the story, used the generic term for Athapaskan, Itqiḷḷiq (sing.), and I failed to ask him what specific kind of Athapaskans they were. They were probably Di'hą̨į̨ Gwich'in, from the Noatak headwaters region; they had the easiest access to Point Hope of any Athapaskan group.

The Athapaskans killed everyone in Nuvuġaluaq except one old woman. She was mortally wounded, but she managed to stay alive until her son returned from Point Hope, where he had gone for a visit.

When he returned to his home, he saw blood all over the floor. His mother told him, "While you were gone somebody came to our place and killed just about everybody. They pretty nearly killed me too, and I am going to die now. But I wanted to live long enough for you to know that the Indians did this."

She hardly knew what she was saying because she was in such agony. The

Indians had jammed a walrus tusk through her vagina clear into her intestines. And after she spoke, she died.

So the son returned to Point Hope. And many Point Hopers came out to Nuvuġaluaq to bury the dead.

And after the end of the following summer, Navaġiaq—that was the boy's name—took his boat, filled it up with oil, muktuk, and whale meat, and headed up the Kukpuk River, taking a young man with him.

At Auksaakiaq they made a house below the mountain there. And they dug a tunnel underneath the ground from the house to the river.

And after they had finished making the house and the tunnel, the young man returned to Point Hope, leaving Navaġiaq alone at the camp.

One night, after freeze-up, he heard something coming toward him. He listened to it, and the sound kept coming nearer. So he took his bows and arrows, ducked into the tunnel, and closed the door behind him.

When the people got there, he could see that they were Indians, about 15 of them. And they went into the house. And he figured that they were the ones who had killed his mother.

When the first Indian came out of the house, Navaġiaq shot and killed him. The others, who were still inside, didn't know what was happening.

When a second man came out, Navaġiaq killed him too. And so on, until he had killed all of them except one. He wanted one man to stay alive so that he could go home to tell his relatives what had happened to them.

The next day Navaġiaq went to Point Hope and got some men. A lot of them came over, and they buried the Indians and all of their things. [Jensen 1970a]

Auksaakiaq was used as a fall–winter settlement site until very recently, but Nuvuġaluaq has remained uninhabited from that date to this.

Kaŋiġmiut–Kiitaaġmiut Exchanges

Another series of brutal exchanges took place between the Kaŋiġmiut of the Buckland River valley and the Kiitaaġmiut of the lower Selawik River valley (Sunno 1951a). These were Iñupiaq nations whose estates were located next to one another within the primary study region. There are several versions of the following story that, as usual, agree in their general outlines but differ in their details.

Once a very long time ago a group of Kaŋiġmiut women were picking berries near the mouth of the Buckland River. They had stopped to eat lunch when they saw a party of men approaching. They ran to their boats, of which there were two. One of the women, who had been resting in a kneeling position, found her legs had gone to sleep and she couldn't run. The other women left the second boat for her and paddled away across the river.

The raiders, who were from Selawik, caught the lone woman. They gang-raped her, then shoved her onto the stem of the umiaq so that the extension of the gunwale thrust into her vagina. The raiders then headed home, leaving her suspended on the gunwale to die a horrible death.

When the Kaŋiġmiut men found out what had happened, they became enraged and headed toward Selawik to seek vengeance. They discovered two elderly Kiitaaġmiut women fishing near the southeastern corner of Selawik Lake. According to the Buckland version of the story, they killed them, cut the bodies into strips, and hung them on a drying rack, like so many pieces of fish or caribou meat. According to the Selawik version, they inserted a spear into each of their rectums, elevated their bodies over a fire, and roasted them to death.

The story continues:

From then on, the Kaŋiġmiut and Kiitaaġmiut were at war. One day in the early fall a Kaŋiġmiut woman walking along the Buckland River saw a party of men fording it not far above the settlement. Each man was carrying a willow shrub to serve as camouflage. The woman ran back to camp and told everyone what she had seen. But she was an infamous liar, and no one believed her.

But the Kaŋiġmiut did go to an aŋatkuq [shaman] to ask if the woman's story was true. His familiar spirit did not tell the truth, though, and he reported that the woman was lying. Consequently, everyone ignored her.

The woman persuaded her husband that she was telling the truth. So they rowed an umiaq out to a nearby island, turned it over, and hid underneath it with their child.

The raiders snuck up on the village early in the morning, when the Kaŋiġmiut were all asleep. Each one of the raiders had a feather stuck in his hair. The Kiitaaġmiut raiders shot arrows into the houses, down through the skylights. Others waited outside the doors and shot or speared everybody who tried to come out. And they killed everyone, men, women, and children. The three people hiding on the island were the only survivors.

And ever since that time, the place where the massacre occurred has been called Iñuqtat, "place where lots of people were killed."[35]

Siege at Sisualik

Another example of variation in the general pattern of Iñupiaq warfare is an encounter that took place at Sisualik, the site of a very large summer trade fair; it was also the location of a small Qikiqtaġruŋmiut fall–winter village. What follows is a composite of several accounts.

Once, after the big fair at Sisualik, when everyone else went home, a boatload of Tikiġaġmiut men stayed behind and hid up on the lower slopes of the big mountain called Iŋitqalik. From there they sent out people to spy on the Qikiqtaġruŋmiut.

After a period of time, some teenage Qikiqtaġruŋmiut boys went to Aniyaaq to do some fishing. The Tikiġaġmiut men then approached them in their umiaq. Only two men paddled, one in the bow, the other in the stern. The others lay on the bottom of the boat, where they could not be seen by people onshore. But when they got close, they all jumped out and attacked the young men. They killed all but one, and they mortally wounded him.

After a time, the people at Sisualik got worried about the boys. A man called Avaŋuluk went out to look for them.[36] *Just before he got to Aniyaak, he found the survivor, who was his son. His legs had been nearly cut off, most of his insides had fallen out, and he was pulling himself along in the water with his hands and arms.*

"The Tikiġaġmiut killed us, and they cut me up too; they don't know that I am still alive. I wanted to tell you about those people." And the boy died right there.

So Avaŋuluk and his wife went over to the big Qikiqtaġruŋmiut village at Taksruq Saaŋa to get help. And some Qikiqtaġruŋmiut men, and some Kobukers too, who happened to be there, promised to come over.

Avaŋuluk, the man whose son had brought the news, went on alone to the enemy camp and challenged the Tikiġaġmiut ataniq, whose name was Nuguraaluk. Avaŋuluk suggested that they duel with bows and arrows at short range, and his challenge was accepted. According to the custom in those days, the avenger had the right to the first shot, and Avaŋuluk's first arrow smashed Nuguraaluk's pelvis. Immediately, all the other Tikiġaġmiut readied their bows and arrows, but Avaŋuluk was a famous runner, and he escaped safely to Sisualik.

By that time some men from Taksruq Saaŋa had arrived at Sisualik and had built a stockade out of timber and bearded seal skins.[37] *Some Qikiqtaġruŋmiut men were already inside when the Tikiġaġmiut warriors arrived, but there were not enough of them to have an advantage in open battle.*

The Tikiġaġmiut approached the stockade and taunted the Qikiqtaġruŋmiut inside, daring them to come out and fight. "You fellas come out! Hurry up! We want to fix you up!" They called to them like that. "You fellas come out. You're just like ground squirrels in there." They called to the Qikiqtaġruŋmiut like that. The Qikiqtaġruŋmiut responded to the taunts with "We're not ready yet."

Every once in awhile the Tikiġaġmiut shot an arrow up in the air so that it would come down inside the stockade. One came down just right and killed a woman. But the Qikiqtaġruŋmiut still did not go out.

While all this was going on Avaŋuluk made two trips to Taksruq Saaŋa by boat to get reinforcements, right under the noses of the Tikiġaġmiut. After his second trip there were enough men in the stockade to deal with the enemy force.

After awhile one little man named Alaaqatlak came out. He wasn't even a Qikiqtaġruŋmiu (sing.) but a Tapqagmiu (sing.), from the Shishmaref district. He was naked, save only for a fox nose on his forehead and a belt with a white fox tail behind, and he had a little drum. He presented his naked rear to the Tikiġaġmiut and shouted, "Shoot at me!" [38] *The Tikiġaġmiut shot at him but missed because he moved around so fast. They never hit him, and he picked up the arrows that they shot. When an arrow fell down, he picked it up. When he had a whole armful of arrows, Alaaqatlak went back inside the stockade.*

About that time the qataŋun (cosibling) of one of the Kotzebue men, Qargalik, started to holler, "Is my brother in there?"

"Yes, come on inside."

"No, I want to shoot arrows."

And after he said that Qargalik went out, followed by all the other men. The Qikiqtaġruŋmiut were armed with long bows, which were superior to those of the Tikiġaġmiut, all of whom were killed except one. Avaŋuluk ran after him, but he was so fast that even Avaŋuluk couldn't catch him.

But at Ikpikaritch Avaŋuluk discovered another person, a Tikiġaġmiu (sing.) boy. He was hiding, hoping that no one would find him. And Avaŋuluk shot him in the stomach and broke off the arrow. Avaŋuluk picked up the boy's intestines, which were spilling out, and told him to run away. And, as the boy did so, Avaŋuluk held onto his guts and pulled them right out of his body. And he died.

Avaŋuluk said that he made that boy pay because the Tikiġaġmiut had nearly cut his own boy in half. Now they were even.[39]

The use of a stockade (avaluġun) was uncommon in the NANA Region, but the story just cited is not the only instance I have heard of its occurrence.

The English versus the Kaŋiġmiut

In all of the early-19th-century literature from northwestern Alaska there were only two significant cases of bloodshed involving Westerners and Iñupiat. One was an incident in 1820 involving Russians of the Vasil'ev–Shishmarev expedition who unwittingly stumbled into the Kaŋiġmiut beluga-hunting station near the mouth of the Buckland River. The other was a series of encounters between the members of the Beechey expedition and a party of Kaŋiġmiut camped on Chamisso Island.[40] The latter is the closest thing we have to an eyewitness account of Iñupiaq warfare, and, accordingly, it is recounted here in some detail.[41]

The prelude to violence was a series of brazen thefts by the Iñupiat and by British attempts to recover the stolen property. On October 14, 1827, a detachment from the *Blossom*, under the command of William Smyth, went ashore to fill casks with drinking water for the ship. They were met by the Natives on the beach and harassed and physically threatened by them. Since he was authorized to drive the Natives off the island if they proved troublesome, Smyth ordered the British guns to be loaded (Beechey 1831, vol. 2:283). With that, the Natives

> *fled to their baidar [umiaq], and placed every thing in her in readiness to depart on a minute's warning, and then, armed with their bows and arrows and knives, they drew up on a small eminence, and twanged their bow-strings, as before, in defiance. . . . The hostile disposition of the natives on the hill, who were drawn up in a line in a menacing attitude, with their bows ready strung, and their knives in their left hands, obliged Mr. Smyth to arm his people, and, in compliance with his instructions, to proceed to drive them off the island. He accordingly advanced upon them, and each individual probably had singled out his victim, when an aged man of the Esquimaux party made offers of peace, and the arms of both parties were laid aside.*

Here we have several elements of a classic battle as described to me by informants. The warriors seized their weapons, took the high ground, and dared the enemy to fight. An elder then appeared and attempted to establish peace before any blood was shed.

On October 29 the confrontation resumed.

> *The first lieutenant [George Peard] observing a baidar full of men approach the island, despatched Lieutenant [Edward] Belcher to the place with orders to send them away, provided there were any of the party among them who had behaved in so disorderly a manner on the recent occasion. On landing, he immediately recognized one of the men, and ordered the whole of the party into the baidar. They complied very reluctantly; and while our seamen were engaged pushing them off, they were occupied in preparations for hostility, by putting on their eider-duck frocks over their usual dresses, and uncovering their bows and arrows. They paddled a few yards from the beach, then rested in doubt as to what they should do; some menacing our party, and others displaying their weapons. Thus threatened, and the party making no attempt to depart, but rather propelling their baidar sidewise toward the land, Mr. Belcher fired a ball between them and the shore, and waved them to begone. Instead of obeying his summons, they paddled on shore instantly, and quitted their baidar for a small eminence near the beach, from whence they discharged a flight of arrows, which wounded two of our seamen.[42] Their attack was of course returned, and one of the party was wounded in the leg by a musket ball.*
>
> *Until this time they were ignorant of the effect of firearms, and no doubt placed much confidence in the thickness of their clothing, as, in addition to their eider-duck dress over their usual frock, they each bound a deer-skin round them as they quitted their baidar; but seeing the furs availed nothing against a ball, they fled with precipitation to the hills.* [Beechey 1831, vol. 2:284–285]

The British were determined to put an end to the harassment. They started after the Natives, sending one detachment in a boat along the shore and another one on foot overland.

We had not proceeded far, when suddenly four of the marines were wounded with arrows from a small ravine, in which we found a party so screened by long grass that it was not visible until we were close upon it.[43] *The natives were lying upon the ground, peeping between the blades of grass, and discharging their arrows as opportunity offered. In return, one of them suffered by a ball from Mr. Elson; on which I stopped the firing, and endeavoured ineffectually to bring them to terms. After a considerable time, an elderly man came forward with his arms and breast covered with mud, motioned to us to begone, and decidedly rejected all offers of conciliation. Unwilling to chastise them further, I withdrew the party, and towed their baidar on board, which kept them prisoners upon the island. . . . This baidar had a large incision in her bottom, made by the person who last quitted her when the party landed, and must have been done either with a view of preventing her being carried away, or by depriving themselves of the means of escape, showing their resolution to conquer or die.* [Beechey 1831, vol. 2:285–286]

The Natives refused to make peace with the explorers and remained hidden during the rest of the ship's stay near the island.

The next day Beechey examined the "trench":

The ravine was conveniently adapted to the defense of a party, being narrow, with small banks on each side of it, behind which a party might discharge their arrows without much danger to themselves until they became closely beset; to obviate which as much as possible, and to sell their lives as dearly as they could, we found they had constructed pits in the earth by scooping out holes sufficiently large to contain a man, and by banking up the mud above them. There were five of these excavations close under the edges of the banks, which were undermined; one at the head of the ravine, and two on each side, about three yards lower down; the latter had a small communication at the bottom, through which an arrow might be transferred from one person to another, without incurring the risk of being seen by passing it over the top. [1831, vol. 2:287]

Beechey noted that, as a defensive measure, this construction was "as perfect as circumstances would allow." He said it also showed how resourceful the Iñupiat were and that it marked a "determination of obstinate resistance" (Beechey 1831, vol. 2:287).

Aftermath

Total victory meant annihilation of the enemy—men, women, and children—without suffering any losses to one's own side. However, it seems to have been almost as unusual for victors to emerge unscathed as it was for them to massacre the losers to the very last infant. The people in most settlements were too alert to be taken completely by surprise, and those who were caught off guard usually had enough of a response capability to inflict at least some casualties among the members of an attacking force. In open battle it must have been extremely rare for the winning side to walk away without any casualties at all, although it apparently did happen from time to time.

Prudence often forestalled an actual clash of arms. Many an attacking force, realizing that it was undermanned relative to that of the enemy or that the element of surprise had been lost, tried to withdraw without making contact. However, I never heard of an instance of a battle fully joined that did not end in defeat for one side and victory for the other. Defeat often turned to rout. Victors pursued their enemies and simply shot them down. If clubs or spears were used, it was probably to dispatch enemy wounded. The Iñupiat also had a special song (*avataqsiaġaa*) that could deliver the coup de grâce to an escaping but wounded person or animal, and it was sometimes employed at this stage of battle to ease a pursuer's task.[44] Sometimes the apparent victors became spread out and disorganized in the process of trying to massacre the fleeing remnants of an enemy force, and the tables could be turned on them by experienced warriors.

Prisoners were taken rarely and hostages never. Women were sometimes taken as slaves, but in most of the cases I heard about they were raped, tortured, and killed before their captors reached their homes. Occasionally a warrior who had run out of arrows surrendered to the members of a victorious enemy force, but he was killed anyway, usually after being tortured first.

The concept of tactical retreat under fire was understood in northwestern Alaska. One possibility in desperate circumstances was for a battle line slowly to withdraw, with men who were mortally wounded and unlikely to survive the trip home dropping into hiding places and ambushing heedless enemy warriors following in pursuit. Alternatively, the entire force tried to withdraw to a good defensive position. Or, in still another possibility, an apparently defeated force could feign a complete rout. Its members would run away as fast as they could, then hide at some prearranged spot. Any members of the enemy force who came along would be shot from ambush. Unfortunately, my sources could not provide me with any concrete examples of these practices.

If pursued, a retreating unit might be forced to make a stand. Alternatively, a pursuit party sometimes tried to circle ahead of a retreating force and ambush it. In theory, this was a relatively simple matter, since the victors usually knew exactly where the losers were headed, but terrain, weather, and other factors often complicated things. In any event, a retreating force had to maintain maximum security precautions until it reached the very heartland of its own country.

A defeated war party that managed successfully to disengage from the victorious force headed for home as fast as it could. Under such conditions the dead were left behind, but my informants stated emphatically that wounded never were left if it was humanly possible to take them along. If seriously injured, they had to be backpacked, which greatly hampered withdrawal efforts.

Wounded on both sides were tended to as time permitted and urgency dictated. The biggest problem must have been the removal of arrows or arrowheads from the victim's flesh. I do not have specific information on how this was done, but I assume that surgical and first-aid techniques used in tending to casualties of war were similar to those used by the Iñupiat in other contexts (Anderson et al. 1998:17; Geary 1976; Giddings 1961:18; Gray 1976; Kirchner 1983:104; Lucier, VanStone, and Keats 1971:254; Stoney 1900:833). If so, the arrows were removed with a small knife or lancet, and the cut was sewn shut with an ivory or bone needle and thread made from sinew. The cut was cleaned with fresh, warm urine, then covered with blubber or seal oil (near the coast) or with spruce pitch (in the interior). Wormwood leaves, if available, were applied to the wound as a poultice. The various medications were held in place by a strip of softened caribou hide tied over the wound.

Ordinarily it would not take more than a day or two for people living in settlements near a successfully raided village to suspect that something was amiss. If a reconnaissance confirmed their fears, they sent out runners to muster a force larger than the enemy's and prepared to attack it, preferably in ambush, otherwise in open battle. Victors in enemy territory knew this would happen. Accordingly, they usually headed home in a hurry, leaving their dead behind but taking their wounded with them. If they had time, they buried or tried to hide the bodies of their own dead, but they either ignored those of their enemy or threw them all into a big pile.

A possible example of such an assemblage is shown in Plate 4. The scene was captured by Leo Hansen, the photographer on the Fifth Thule Expedition, somewhere near Point Barrow in 1924. It was published by Knud Rasmussen (1933:332) in his general account of the expedition with the caption "battlefields of former days."[45] Since the remains were jumbled together rather than systematically disposed of, they were presumably those of the losing side. According to my count of the skulls, at least 60 individuals are represented here, indicating a major disaster for the unidentified nation whence the warriors came. The bodies of the dead on the winning side, however, were probably in the many fresh graves that Thomas Simpson (1843:153–154) saw in the graveyard at Niksiuraq, a short distance southwest of Point Barrow, in the summer of 1837. If so, the battle was between the Kakligmiut nation and an unidentified nation of inlanders.

4. Human remains on a former battlefield near Point Barrow, Alaska. Photograph by Leo Hansen, 1924. Courtesy of the National Museum of Denmark, Department of Ethnography, Fifth Thule Expedition, negative no. 2886.

If any booty was taken, it was usually limited to items such as labrets, beads, weapons, or clothing—things that could be carried easily by men who could not afford to be encumbered by heavy baggage.

Once home, the victors of a raid or battle commemorated the event with a feast. They played games, danced, and did the blanket toss, all of these activities being characteristic elements of Iñupiaq celebrations. They also composed and sang a revenge song, which recited the details of the encounter and boasted of the number of enemy who had been killed (Eliyak 1931; Wood 1931). According to Lucier (1997:72, 272, 372; see also Ostermann and Holtved 1952:140), men who had distinguished themselves in battle received distinctive facial tattoos in the form of four parallel straight lines on each cheek.[46]

The losers, in contrast, faced a bleak prospect. If they were defeated in their own country, the survivors disposed of their dead according to the local custom, swore revenge, and no doubt participated in a number of rituals, although I do not have any information on this point. If a force was defeated in enemy territory, the relatives and friends of its members had to wait in growing suspense and fear for the one or two men who were usually permitted to survive to return home and report the bad news.

Magic and Ritual

Magic and ritual seem to have played a relatively minor role in early-19th-century Iñupiaq warfare compared to the customs of many other peoples.

This was true of preparations for it, of its conduct, and of its aftermath. My informants volunteered little on the subject, other than describing the consulting of a shaman on the prospects for success, the use of magic sentinels, and the use of magic songs (*avataksiaġaat*) to kill an (individual) enemy or make him turn back. They also did not have much to say when I asked about it. Men wore amulets to protect them from harm, but they did that all the time; I have never heard of special ones to be used solely in battle. People who remained at home used magic to try to learn what the results of a raid were but not to affect its outcome. Mysterious things certainly happened during many armed conflicts, as a few of the examples described in this chapter indicate, but they were rarely reported as being deliberately inserted into the situation by either the participants or the people who remained at home.

Battlefields also were not considered to be haunted places, no matter how many men died there. In fact, one way I first began to learn about Iñupiaq warfare was by elders showing me on a map places where there used to be big piles of human bones; when they were children the people used to play with the bones (Burch 1998a:16–17). Finally, I must mention that I have never heard of the existence of any taboos relating to raids or warfare, which made those activities extraordinarily different from practically every other activity the Iñupiat engaged in.[47]

Shamans did perform black magic, that is, magic intended to harm someone else. In all the accounts I have heard, such magic was directed only against individuals, usually either arrogant chieftains or other shamans. Sometimes these people—particularly other shamans—were members of other societies, but often they were not. In any event, I never heard of black magic being specifically invoked in warfare except in a few myths.

Neighboring Regions

The material presented so far in this chapter relates almost exclusively to Iñupiat, both those living in the primary study region and those living north and south of it. In this section I present brief summaries of what is known about hostilities by and among the peoples of Beringia whose estates were on the periphery of the area of major concern in this study: the Yup'ik-speaking Eskimos of Norton Sound; Koyukon of the upper Kobuk, Koyukuk, and Yukon River valleys; and Gwich'in of the central Brooks Range.

The Alaskan Yup'ik Eskimos

The southern sector of northwestern Alaska was occupied by Central Alaskan Yup'ik–speaking Eskimos during most of the first half of the 19th century. Our interest here is primarily in the period between 1800 and 1838–39, the latter date being that of the smallpox epidemic that exterminated much of the original population of the region and opened the way for Iñupiaq emigration. This depopulation effectively brought major warfare to a halt in the region, although small-scale raids were still taking place as late as 1879 (Nelson 1899:317). Edward Nelson, who spent three years at Saint Michael, from 1877 to 1881, was probably the only Westerner ever to interview Alaskan Eskimos who personally participated in the kind of warfare their stories described. Other important sources on warfare in this region are Ann Fienup-Riordan (1990, 1994), James Kurtz (1984), and Matthew O'Leary (1995a, 1995b).[48]

Fall–winter settlements in the Yup'ik sector of the study area tended to be larger than most of those in the NANA Region. They consisted of substantial semisubterranean sod houses and one or more permanent qargiich. Each village was surrounded by a network of well-established settlements to which the residents resorted at certain times of the year to hunt and fish (Nelson 1899:241).

Nelson noted that prior to the establishment of Russian posts in western Alaska, the Eskimo inhabitants of the region "waged an almost constant intertribal warfare; at the same time, along the line of contact with the Tinné [Athapaskan] tribes of the interior, a bitter feud was always in existence" (1899:327).[49] As in the Iñupiaq sector, the "constant danger from hostile raids caused the people to choose locations for their dwellings which were easy of defense" (Nelson 1899:241, 327), mitigated by the need to be near sources of food and water. A lookout was maintained almost constantly.

Training for war was pretty much the same in the Yup'ik sector of the study region as it was farther north. Boys were prepared through a regimen of activities devoted to developing strength, speed, agility, physical and mental toughness, and spiritual power. Weapons included the bow and arrow, spear, knife, and club. Warriors wore light clothing, sometimes with plate armor underneath the parka, and bent wooden headgear.[50]

Nelson tells us how war parties were organized in the region.

> *When the warriors of one of the . . . villages wished to make up a party to attack an enemy, a song of invitation was made and a messenger sent to sing it in the kashims [qargiich] of other friendly villages; meanwhile the men of the village originating the plot set to work in the kashim and made supplies of new bows and arrows and prepared other weapons while waiting for their friends. The people invited would join the men from the first village and all would set out stealthily to surprise the enemy during the night.* [1899:327]

The preferred tactic here, as farther north, was the nighttime raid. In the Yup'ik zone, however, all the men and teenaged boys slept in the qargi, so that was the only building the raiders really needed to seal off. Once that was accomplished, the raiders shot at the entrapped men through the skylight, dropped burning material down through the skylight, and killed with spears or clubs everyone who tried to escape. However, tunnels between houses and hidden exits from qargiich were often built to provide escape routes for people who had been trapped, so the issue might be in doubt for some time. It was only after the men had been taken care of that attention turned to the women and children. If the raid failed, either the raiders abandoned the attack or an open battle ensued.

Open battles took place primarily in summer. They began with a firefight using bows and arrows and proceeded to a shock encounter employing spears and clubs. The tactics seem to have been almost identical to those employed by the Iñupiat.

Leadership was provided by "some of the older men who had general supervision and control of the expedition" (Nelson 1899:329). At times, volleys of arrows were fired, and occasionally "a man would be shot so full of arrows that his body would bristle with them, and, falling, be held almost free from the ground by their number" (Nelson 1899:329). Dodging skills greatly improved a man's chances of survival, and particularly agile point men seem to have been as valuable among the Uqayuiḷat as among the Iñupiat.

If a battle lasted a long time, so that members of both parties became tired and hungry or sleepy, "a fur coat would be waved on a stick by one side as a sign of truce, during which both parties would rest, eat or sleep, and then renew the conflict. During the truce both sides stationed guards who watched against surprise" (Nelson 1899:329). When a man on either side had relatives on the other side and did not want to participate in the battle for that reason, he "would blacken his face with charcoal and remain a noncombatant, both sides respecting his neutrality" (Nelson 1899:329).

A defeated party was always pursued and, if possible, exterminated. Wounded enemies were issued the coup de grâce with a war club having a sharp spur of bone or ivory on one side. The victors killed all of the males on the losing side, threw their bodies in heaps, and left them to rot. A young man fighting his first battle had to drink some of the blood and eat a small piece of the heart of the first enemy he killed. Women and children were often killed, but sometimes women were taken home by the victors to serve as slaves. In addition, "the conquered village was always pillaged, and if a warrior saw any personal ornament on a slain enemy which pleased him, he seized it and wore it himself, even placing in his lips the labrets taken from the face of a dead foe. If one of the conquerors chanced to see a woman wearing handsome beads or other ornaments, he would brain her and strip them off" (Nelson 1899:329). As in the Iñupiaq area, however, the primary objective of warfare was to exterminate the enemy, not acquire booty or captives.

Koyukon

The Koyukon speakers living in the upper Kobuk drainage apparently shared with neighboring Iñupiaq nations both the propensity for international aggression and the manner in which it was conducted. They are known to have fought with at least the Akunigmiut, the Nuataaġmiut, and the Koyukuk River Koyukon, all of whom, incidentally, were their immediate neighbors. However, that could hardly be the extent of their hostilities, if for no other reason than that the perpetually aggressive Gwich'in were also among their immediate neighbors. Beyond that, there is insufficient evidence to say much about them.

The Koyukuk River Koyukon also were actively involved in international hostilities. Theirs seem to have been primarily with Gwich'in, but just which Gwich'in is almost never stated in the accounts. They fought with other Koyukon speakers living along the Yukon River and in the upper Kobuk River valley and with various Iñupiaq and Yup'ik Eskimo nations. They were involved in so much conflict with Eskimos from Norton Sound that the people living near the mouth of the Kateel River built a fort to protect themselves against Eskimo attacks (de Laguna 1947:31). This fort may be the "bunker" whose ruins were shown to Roger Dayton by his father in 1935: "That bunker wasn't too big. Maybe about twelve feet square with a tunnel going to the next place. The next place was another, the same size and covered over with logs too. There was no windows. Just little holes big enough to shoot arrows through. It was just so high off the ground so they could shoot at their enemy" (1981:16).[51] Although the ruins were substantially filled with debris by that time, Dayton calculated that originally men could have stood up inside the walls. After studying the place for a while he concluded that "those bunkers indicated that they used to fight quite a bit among themselves" (Dayton 1981:16).

The Koyukon living along the Yukon River, like their northern relatives, seem variously to have traded with and fought against almost all of their neighbors, whether Athapaskan or Eskimo. The Russian explorer Lavrentiy Alekseyevich Zagoskin, indeed, characterized them as being even more warlike than the Eskimos (Michael 1967:247).

According to Zagoskin, the weapons of the Koyukon were a simple curved bow of birch or fir (spruce?) and arrows with slate, obsidian, or iron points set in bone; a knife or a pair of knives; a *palma*, or lance, of Yakut workmanship obtained through trade from Chukotka; and clubs made of deer antler or fashioned from a palma. The palma was hafted onto a 4-foot-long shaft. Like the Iñupiat, "under no circumstances are [the Koyukon] separated from their weapons: even for a private excursion into the woods or to check the traps, they carry a lance with them" (Michael 1967:247).

The Koyukon had their own version of iññuqutit, although I did not happen to find out what their term for "prowler" is (Attla and Attla 1991). Members of different Koyukon nations spied on and harassed one another, and they treated neighboring Iñupiaq and Yup'ik Eskimos the same way. They suffered similar harassment in return (Dayton 1981:17). Like the Iñupiat iññuqutit, those of the Koyukon did most of their work from about mid-August to mid-September, winding things up just before raiding season began in the fall.

The nighttime raid, during which the aggressors tried to trap the residents of a village in their houses, was the preferred tactic of the Koyukon (Clark 1974:189–190; Michael 1967:107, 132). Commenting on this fact, Zagoskin said that "their system of fighting is based on surprise attack and for this reason bravery or daring in a savage cannot in any way be compared to the true meaning of courage, based on the scorn of death in the service of home, fatherland, or tsar" (Michael 1967:247). If Zagoskin's views were widely shared by his countrymen, one must conclude that Koyukon tactics were much more rational than those employed by the Russians.

Like the Iñupiat, once the Koyukon had successfully entrapped their enemies in their houses, they threw burning material down through the skylight. The occupants of the building either died from burns, suffocated from smoke inhalation, or were killed as they emerged.

Koyukon also engaged in open battle from time to time. This is shown in the case cited above of the battle at Itqiḷḷiġvik, where a Koyukon war party was outmaneuvered by an Iñupiaq force and massacred.[52] Judging from that single event, it appears as though the Koyukon employed the same basic tactics in open battle as the Iñupiat.

Gwich'in

The Gwich'in having the greatest contact with the Iñupiat of the study region were the Di'hąįį, whose estate lay along the spine of the Endicott Mountains in the Brooks Range. These people engaged in a complex array of peaceful and hostile relations with their Iñupiaq, Koyukon, and other Gwich'in neighbors, although not much else is known about them. Overall, at least with regard to the Iñupiat, hostilities originating largely with the Gwich'in seem to have predominated. Ultimately, this resulted in the near extinction of the Di'hąįį and the withdrawal from the study region of any survivors around or before midcentury (Burch 1998b:28–31; Burch and Mishler 1995).

Unfortunately, nothing specific is known about the way in which the Di'hąįį conducted warfare. However, some information is available about their linguistic cousins and neighbors to the east, who for purposes of the present discussion will have to serve as proxies for them.

Just to the east of the Di'hąįį were the Neets'ąįį, among whom war was "largely a matter of surprise attack" (McKennan 1965:67), a fact that necessitated constant vigilance on everyone's part (McDonald 1862–1913:entries for October 12, 1868, and June 12, 1871). Combat was largely "on a hand-to-hand basis using knives, thrusting spears, and a special pick-like club of caribou horn [*sic*]" (McKennan 1965:67). The accounts of specific examples recorded by McKennan confirm the impression that Gwich'in warfare tended to be smaller in scale than that of the Iñupiat and Koyukon and that more of it tended to be of a hand-to-hand nature (McKennan 1933, 1965:67–70; see also Mishler 1995:4, 90–203). This was also true of the Peel River Gwich'in, still farther east (Slobodin 1960). In other respects, the pattern of international hostilities among the Iñupiat, Koyukon, and Gwich'in seems to have been pretty much the same, even to the point of letting one of the defeated warriors escape unharmed (McKennan 1965:37, 67–70).

The major weapons of the Gwich'in were bows and arrows, lances, clubs, and knives, an array that is now familiar to readers of this work.[53] In the minds of the Gwich'in, however, the greatest of these as an implement of war was reportedly the club, probably because it represented the instrument of hand-to-hand conflict, the one on which the warrior depended as a last resort after the bow and lance had been thrown aside (Osgood 1936:86). Clubs were made from heavy bull caribou antlers from which the secondary tines were removed. The antlers were then boiled and straightened. The result was reportedly a "powerful head-crusher weighing up to ten pounds" (Osgood 1936:86) shaped something like a single-bladed pick.

Lances were long, with sharp points of bone, stone, and occasionally copper (acquired through trade with Athapaskans farther south), and were either thrown like a javelin or thrust. Knives were imported two-edged daggers with handles terminating in flaring, voluted antennae. The bow was a single stave made from birch that was whittled to size, then lashed to a form to give it a curved shape. The Gwich'in were familiar with the recurved sinew-backed bows of the Iñupiat but thought theirs were just as good.

Since they were in such intensive and prolonged contact with the Iñupiat, Koyukon, and Neets'ąįį Gwich'in during at least the first half of the 19th century, it is likely that Di'hąįį warfare consisted of a mixture of Iñupiaq, Koyukon, and Gwich'in tactics. Certainly they are known to have been masters of the surprise attack, which they employed successfully against both Koyukon and Iñupiaq settlements on many occasions. On the other hand, although the Gwich'in are known to have confronted Iñupiat in open battle more than once, they may have been largely ignorant of how to form and maneuver battle lines and of how to conduct open battle at a distance. If true, these were serious deficiencies in their confrontations with Iñupiat. This weakness may have contributed significantly to their ultimate demise.

Chukotkans

"Chukotkans" is used here to refer indiscriminately to speakers of Chukchi and the two Yup'ik languages spoken in the region of concern here. In northwestern Alaska they were known collectively as Qutlich.

The interior of Chukotka was inhabited exclusively by Chukchi, but coastal nations were a mixture of Eskimos, Chukchi, and Eskimos who had been partially or entirely assimilated by the Chukchi. Most adult Asiatic Eskimos seem to have been bilingual in Yup'ik and Chukchi, and virtually all of the coastal settlements had both Yup'ik and Chukchi names (Krupnik and Chlenov n.d.:chap. 5, 8–16).

At the level of generalization of the present analysis, Asiatic Yup'ik Eskimos and Chukchi may be considered to have practiced identical kinds of international hostility, using the same types of equipment and tactics and engaging in the same forms of war preparation. The Chukchi were the more formidable of the two, however, because of what is frequently described as their "irascibility" (e.g., Bogoras 1901:92). They did not suffer defeat easily or gracefully. The Reindeer Chukchi were particularly warlike. Because of their great mobility they could range over much wider areas than either the Maritime Chukchi or the Eskimos, and they could muster large forces on relatively short notice (Krupnik 1996b). They were also powerful enough to get their coastal neighbors to transport them by boat across Bering Strait whenever they wanted to attack Iñupiat.

The Chukchi and the Eskimos were the only indigenous Asiatic peoples who did not succumb to the Russians during the eastward expansion of empire, and the Chukchi and Eskimo residents of eastern Chukotka specifically were the only ones who successfully refused to pay tribute to the czar.[54] The struggle with the Russians began in the mid-1600s and lasted for more than a century. The better-armed Russians usually prevailed, wreaking havoc and destruction upon many a Native village and camp. Less frequently, the Chukotkans retaliated in kind. Total annihilation of both Russian and Chukotkan settlements occurred, and atrocities were common on both sides (Bogoras 1904–9:651–654, 690–696). The Chukchi bore the brunt of Russian attacks but were allied with Eskimos against the Russians on several occasions (Krupnik 1996a; Krupnik and Chlenov 1982). For example, the Eskimo residents of Big Diomede Island joined the Chukchi to fight the Russian commander Pavlutsky and may have participated in the very battle in which he was defeated and killed (Golder 1971:161).

Few details regarding Native tactics against the Russians have been recorded, but it is known that they mounted raids, conducted sieges, and engaged in pitched battles. In the latter context alliances of several Eskimo and Chukchi nations may have put as many as 2,000 or more warriors into the field for a single engagement. These units must have had a relatively well defined command structure, for they were able to form and maneuver battle lines effectively. For example, in March 1730 an unknown number of Chukchi confronted a Russian force of 150 men commanded by the Cossack Afanase Shestakov that included Russians, Yakuts, Tungus, Taui, and Koryaks. "The battle opened by the discharge of firearms by the Russians. It was immediately answered by a cloud of arrows from the Chukchi. Before the Russians could reload the Chukchi swept down on them in a mass, and after driving off the left wing and then crushing the right, concentrated their efforts on the center, which gave way" (Golder 1971:156–157). Thirty-one men on the Russian side were killed, including Shestakov (Golder 1971:156–157).

There is no evidence that Chukotkans ever mustered anywhere near as large forces against one another or against people on the Alaskan side of Bering Strait as they did against the Russians. Among themselves, Chukotkans employed essentially the same array of tactics used among the Iñupiat: harassment, surprise nighttime attacks, and open battle. However, the Chukchi who owned domesticated reindeer had vastly greater mobility than either the Maritime Chukchi or any of the nations in northwestern Alaska (Krupnik 1996b).

According to Bogoras (1904–9:646), where two Chukchi nations were involved, open battle usually amounted to a set of man-to-man combats instead of maneuvering battle lines. If that is true, one has to wonder why the Chukotkans abandoned the more sophisticated tactics of mobility and maneuver they employed so successfully against the Russians when they were fighting one another. In another passage, however, Bogoras (1904–9:151, 646) contradicts himself by stating that the bow was the favorite weapon of the Chukotkans and that agility and dodging were extremely important in Chukotkan warfare. These statements imply that firefights were also an important element in combat, which suggests that maneuvering battle lines and pitched battles may have occurred in Chukotka after all. Among the sedentary coastal people, fortified villages, or fortified redoubts erected near villages, were relatively common, and siege warfare was the frequent result (Bogoras 1904–9:650–651; Krupnik 1996a). In contrast to the Iñupiat, Chukotkans often took captives, usually women, whom they forced into slavery (Bogoras 1904–9:659–661; Fisher 1981:113–114; Golder 1971:152; Sauer 1802:252). They also acquired booty, especially in the form of domesticated reindeer.

Chukotkan men, like their Iñupiaq counterparts, strove to maintain themselves in good physical condition (Bogoras 1904–9:161, 646; Doty 1900:193, 211). They wrestled, ran long distances, pulled heavily loaded sleds, lifted heavy stones and timber, and practiced jumping and dodging. They routinely practiced with bows and arrows and with spears.

Chukotkan weapons consisted of two kinds of bow, arrows, lances, large knives, and slingshots. I have not located any references to clubs, but the Chukotkans probably had a few muzzle-loading guns in the early 19th century. Spears were used primarily for defense, bows and arrows for attack, and slingshots as a backup weapon in both contexts. All of these items are described and illustrated by Bogoras (1904–9:151–161).

Armor was even more important in Chukotka than in northwestern Alaska. There were two basic types: "plate armor, consisting of bone, ivory, antler, or iron plates perforated and lashed together, and band armor, consisting of telescoping bands of hide" (VanStone 1983:3). Within each of the two basic types there was considerable variation. Additional accouterments consisted of helmets, cuirasses, shields, shin guards, and neck protectors. In contrast to the usual Alaskan pattern, Chukotkan armor was worn over ordinary clothing, and it often extended from head to toe (Bogoras 1904–9:161–168; VanStone 1983). It was so strong and covered so much of the body that it made the person wearing it all but invulnerable to arrows except at extremely close range. On the other hand, the armor did not lend itself to rapid maneuver or flight. It was heavy and bulky and had to have been worn only in hand-to-hand combat or when a warrior was in a defensive mode. Armor apparently could be shed fairly quickly in a shift from defense to attack, but it could not be donned with the same rapidity if the tide turned.

Warfare across Bering Strait

Hostilities conducted in and across Bering Strait were subject to conditions different from those occurring within Alaska or within Chukotka because a major water crossing was required. Winter crossings on the sea ice did occur, but the strong wind and ocean current in the strait ordinarily keep the ice there in constant motion. The ice in Bering Strait is very dangerous in winter, and to mount an armed raid across it would have been almost suicidal (Brower n.d.:219; Ostermann and Holtved 1952:143–144).

However, during the early 19th century Bering Strait was probably ice covered for a longer period of time each year, and the ice might have been more stable then than it is now. This is suggested by the fact that, in October 1763, the strait was already frozen so solidly that Nikolai Daurkin could be taken from Chukotka to the Diomede Islands by reindeer sled (Masterson and

Brower 1948:65).[55] Such a procedure is virtually inconceivable nowadays, particularly that early in the season. In 1779 Clerke waited for almost the whole month of July for the southernmost portion of the Chukchi Sea to clear of ice.[56] It never did, so he abandoned the attempt to go north of Bering Strait (Cook and King 1784, vol.3:244 ff.). To have so much ice that far south in late July is also virtually unheard-of today. If ice conditions were different during the study period, winter forays across the strait might have been possible, but they still would have been much riskier than overland or boat expeditions because of the constantly shifting ice.

In general, then, intercontinental raiders had to reach their objective by boat and in relatively good weather.[57] Then the warriors had to make a landing in hostile territory, often during the long summer daylight hours, before proceeding about their business. Even if the raid was successful, they had to return home again before severe weather developed and prevented them from doing so.

The obvious difficulties attending intercontinental raids did not stop people from making them. As early as 1711 Peter Popov was told by Chukchi informants that war had existed between the Chukchi and the residents of Alaska "since time immemorial."[58] Sometimes the Alaskans won, sometimes the Chukotkans won. Popov personally saw 10 Alaska Natives held prisoner by the Chukchi and was told that there were another 20 or so in other locations (Fisher 1981:113–114; see also Golder 1971:152). In 1763 a Chukotkan told Daurkin that the residents of Alaska had "long been at enmity with them, so that they alternately go to war against each other. They fight with lances and bows, and their arrows as well as their lances are tipped with quartz, which is very hard and which they treat with a vegetable poison (lyutsik). If a wound made by such a weapon is not immediately sucked clean, the wounded person is sure to die within twenty-four hours" (Masterson and Brower 1948:66–67).[59] In 1779 Ivan Kobelev, a Cossack explorer, met a Chukchi man who had gone as often as five times to the American mainland for trade and war (Masterson and Brower 1948:94–95). In 1816, when Kotzebue showed a Chukchi man some of Ludovik Choris's portraits of Iñupiat from Kotzebue Sound, he drew his knife and declared that if he met a man wearing labrets, that is, an Alaskan, he would pierce him through (Kotzebue 1821, vol. 1:262).

There is no doubt that warfare took place both within and across Bering Strait (Bogoras 1904–9:656; Garber 1940:169–172; Nelson 1899:330; Oquilluk 1973:215–216; Sauer 1802:252; Weyer 1928:23 [Diomede Islands], 3 [Bering Strait]). Nelson summarized the situation as follows: "In ancient times the Eskimo of Bering Strait were constantly at war with one another, the people of the Diomede Islands being leagued with the Eskimo of the Chukotkan shore against the combined forces of those on King island and the American shore from near the head of Kotzebue sound to Cape Prince of Wales and Port Clarence" (1899:330).

The Nuvuqaghmiit (Eskimos from East Cape) and Uellyt (Chukchi from Uelen) were apparently the nations on the Asiatic side that were most frequently involved in Bering Strait warfare, while the Qaviaraġmiut (Kuzitrin River) and Kiŋikmiut (Wales) seem to have been most frequently involved on the Alaskan side. In addition, as Nelson's comment suggests, the residents of all three inhabited islands in Bering Strait were active participants on one side or the other (see also Koutsky 1976; Morrison 1991b:102–105; Ray 1975b:87–89; Ross 1958:13).

The threat of amphibious attack was sufficiently high in the Bering Strait region for the peoples in the area regularly to post lookouts on high points of land during the season of open water. They also erected man-sized cairns fitted with men's clothing on prominent points to fool raiders into thinking that lookouts were there even when they were not (Koutsky 1981b:26; Weyer 1928:4 [Bering Strait]).

Once the main crossing had been completed, invaders tried to keep their boats close to shore because they were less conspicuous to land-based observers there than they were even a short distance farther out (Koutsky 1981c:45). Complete secrecy was very difficult to achieve, however, since crossings usually had to be made while there was at least some light and because boats had to land in locations where there was virtually no ground cover with which to shield their approach to an enemy village. Once the invaders had been spotted, the alarm was given. The defenders attempted to confront the invaders on the beach, just as they were landing, and to greet them with a shower of arrows (Koutsky 1981c:45; Oquilluk 1973:215). Meanwhile, the women and children fled to designated places—caves stocked with food in some districts—where they could hide during the ensuing encounter (Chernenko 1957:132; Ray 1975b:53; Van Valin 1944:25).

Since surprise was almost impossible to achieve across Bering Strait, raids must have been made by relatively large forces. In modern warfare the planners of amphibious assaults attempt to have substantial superiority in both numbers and firepower over shore-based defenders, and the early contact warriors of Bering Strait may have operated on the same principle. Ten or more umiat holding 140 or more men may not have been an unusually large force for an amphibious invasion. Indeed, in 1791 Kobelev (Chernenko 1957:132; Ray 1975b:53) noted that 150 men in 20 boats had left for a campaign against the Tapqaġmiut.

Since surprise was usually lost, open battle was the typical form of combat. In these encounters each side employed the tactics and equipment they ordinarily used in that context. One special goal of the defenders was the complete or partial destruction of the invaders' boats. This isolated them in enemy territory, where they eventually would be outnumbered and killed (Koutsky 1981c:45–46). If those on the Iñupiaq side won, they presumably killed all of the enemy. If the Chukotkans won, on the other hand, they killed all of the men in the defeated force, took whatever booty they could, and captured some women to keep as slaves.

Discussion

It is now appropriate to address some more general issues concerning international hostilities in northern Beringia. Attention is focused primarily on warfare, which is the most extreme form international hostility can take.

An issue that needs to be addressed before any other is whether or not the peoples of northern Beringia engaged in activities that may be appropriately characterized by the terms *war* and *warfare*. The fact that I have used these terms throughout the book indicates my own opinion that they did. Robert Spencer, however, author of the most influential ethnography ever written on northern Alaska, claimed that "properly speaking, there was no institution of warfare on the Alaskan Arctic Slope" (1959:71). By implication, the institution of warfare did not exist in the rest of the Iñupiaq region as well. Spencer believed that his book described the "traditional way of life" on the Arctic Slope without being particularly careful about when the "traditional period" began and ended. A careful reading of his volume and his field notes reveals that he actually reconstructed the situation existing during the childhood of his informants, that is, during the last two decades of the 19th century (see Bodenhorn 1989:24 n. 19). By that time, the nations whose borders serve as the focus of both his book and the present volume had ceased to exist, and warfare had ceased to exist with them. As a result, Spencer regarded all armed confrontations as "feuds," which "arose between extended families" rather than between nations (1959:71, 72, 98, 281).

Bronislaw Malinowski once defined war as "an armed conflict between two independent political units, by means of organized military force, in pursuit of a tribal or national policy" (1941:523). Iñupiaq nations were independent political units, and their raids and battles were conducted by organized military forces even if some of them involved only a dozen men. If one can accept exacting vengeance as a "tribal or national policy," then war must be considered to have been widespread in northern Beringia during the first half of the 19th century.

The General Character of Beringian Warfare

Many years ago I published a list of 15 attributes of warfare in small-scale societies. It was based partly on my own research and partly on the findings of others (Burch 1974:13).[60] The list provides a useful basis for discussion here.

The first attribute on the list was an emphasis on vengeance as a motive. My associated comment was that territorial aggrandizement was seldom a factor in this type of warfare. As I indicated earlier in this chapter, I still believe these conclusions are supported by the evidence from northwestern Alaska.

The second attribute of warfare in small-scale societies is the militia character of war parties. My comment was that troops are recruited from the village or local group. A more appropriate remark is that in such societies no distinction is made between soldiers and others; every man is a soldier. The distinction the Iñupiat made between suġruich (raiders) and *aŋuyaich* (soldiers) was based on the nature of the confrontation, not different categories of personnel. Some men achieved much greater recognition as warriors than most of their countrymen, but this did not accord them any more special status than, say, someone who made particularly fine sealskin rope.

Considering their general physical strength and the conditioning they acquired from hard physical labor, on the one hand, and the brutal treatment they had reason to believe was inevitable from victorious enemies, on the other, it is a wonder to me that I have hardly ever heard of Iñupiaq women being involved as active combatants even in defensive actions. My questions on this point always received negative responses. The only exception was near Qaviaraq, on the Seward Peninsula, where women sometimes hurled rocks down on invaders from bluffs above the channel through which enemy raiders ordinarily traveled.

Attribute number three concerns the small scale of warring units, which was due to the fact that there simply were not enough men in small-scale societies to muster a large military force. However, the data from northern Beringia demonstrate that the scale of warring units was sometimes augmented through alliances with other nations. This could significantly tip the scales in favor of the alliance. Despite the small absolute size of warring units, however, their size relative to the total size of the populations from which they were drawn was extraordinarily high, sometimes approaching 100 percent of the adult male population.

Extensive use of intelligence is attribute number four, based on the fact that, among small-scale societies, the warring parties usually knew one another well. That was not always the case in northern Beringia, where, for reasons that have not been recorded, people sometimes attacked nations that were hundreds of miles away from their homeland. But most of the time it was true; warriors often knew personally the very individuals they were trying to kill. As indicated in the section on iññuqutit, they sometimes could tell not only the nationality of a prowler but also his personal identity because of the evidence provided by his footprints. As recent analyses of World War II in Europe have shown, however, extensive use of intelligence and subterfuge were hardly distinctive features of warfare in small-scale societies (Brown 1975).

The fifth attribute was the use of unspecialized troops; in other words, each warrior does the same thing as all the others. Initially, I agreed with this proposition. After reviewing the data again for this book, however, it seems to be a slight overstatement for northern Beringia. The information on the Koyukon and Gwich'in is incomplete, but all of the other language groups had some division of labor in a military force. Among the Iñupiat, for example, there was an ataniq, or unit commander; there often were one or two point men who moved out in advance of the others and tried to lure the enemy into wasting all his arrows; and there were two or more flank guards, men on the ends of the line who were particularly proficient marksmen. That is a minimal division of labor, but it is more than nothing, and it made military forces in northern Beringia more formidable than they would have been without it.

Shortness of duration of hostilities is the sixth attribute, based on the assumption that there rarely was an adequate surplus to provision either troops or their dependents for a prolonged campaign. While that still seems to me to be a tenable conclusion in general, it requires some modification in detail. On the one hand, I have not heard of a single raid in the study area during which the actual combat could have lasted more than a few hours or of an open battle of more than two or three days' duration. But the original reference was to campaigns, not battles. One issue is what is meant by "prolonged": if it means seasons or years, then the people of northern Beringia did not have prolonged campaigns in the ordinary sense. In a broader sense, however, some of the series of retaliatory raids we know something about may have their ultimate origin in events that occurred centuries ago, in which case campaigns may be said to have gone on more or less indefinitely.

Viewing things within a somewhat narrower time frame, although battles and raids were relatively brief, it must have taken the warriors two or three weeks to reach their destination and a comparable amount of time to return. In this sense, campaigns may be said to have frequently lasted a month to a month and a half. It took a significant commitment from one of these small nations to provide the manpower for such an operation.

The seventh attribute of warfare among small-scale societies is awareness of the principle of mass; outnumbering the enemy was considered very important. The data from northern Beringia support that conclusion, since even a slight preponderance on one side sometimes caused the other to abandon its attack. Even in Iñupiaq myths, the only time the principle of mass did not apply was when the point men were so extraordinary that they could defeat an enemy practically single-handed. In real life that could not have happened very often, if ever.

Great emphasis on surprise raids is the eighth attribute, based on the apparent fact that there were few alternatives to surprise attacks. Certainly the data from northern Beringia confirm a preference for surprise attacks, but they also demonstrate a willingness to engage in open battle whenever it seemed appropriate or necessary. Given the way people used to live in northern Beringia, the surprise nighttime raid was a highly rational approach much of the time.

The next alleged special attribute of warfare among small-scale societies is effective use of terrain. Settlements were carefully situated, and ambushes were uncommon. Battle lines were maneuvered with considerable attention to terrain. On reflection, however, I fail to see how this attribute distinguishes warfare among small-scale societies from any other kind of terrestrial combat. Effective use of terrain is always an important consideration in terrestrial warfare no matter what the scale.

A weak command function is also supposed to be an attribute of this kind of warfare because leaders lacked sanctions to enforce their directives. Leaders did lack sanctions in northern Beringia, but the conformity aspects of group membership were enormous. Membership in a war party was voluntary, and only a real misfit would have disobeyed orders or acted in such a manner as to undermine his countrymen's efforts. Certainly the Chukotkans, at least when confronting the Russians, appear to have had a very strong command function. Unfortunately, the evidence on the subject is too limited to make many definitive statements on how it was carried out.

Attribute 11 is an emphasis on fire rather than shock tactics. This conclusion was based on the assumption that people had poorly developed techniques for closing with an enemy. As far as northern Beringia is concerned, this hypothesis is untenable. Spears, clubs, and knives were all used as shock weapons, and, as the foregoing analysis showed, all were part of the basic equipment carried by military forces. A surprise nighttime attack, for example, consisted almost entirely of shock encounters. With regard to open battle, I think we are missing some important information here, particularly on the process by which a battle line shifted from fire to shock tactics. Did the men who were gaining the upper hand suddenly charge on command, or did the two sides close gradually? I think they must have charged, but none of my sources ever mentioned it, and I never thought to ask about it.

A stereotyped battle plan is attribute 12, meaning that the same tactics were used in every confrontation. I agree that the principle of the surprise raid was stereotyped, but it was also extremely rational and effective under the circumstances. However, evidence presented earlier in this chapter indicates that warriors in northern Beringia were much more flexible and innovative, in both offensive and defensive modes, than I used to think. I am now prepared to reject stereotyped tactics as a general attribute of warfare in small-scale societies.

The next attribute is minimal development of formations. My comment was that units may have been well formed prior to battle but not during and particularly not after shock encounters. The evidence available to me now suggests that this statement is correct. Battle lines were well formed initially but seem to have fallen apart in closely contested combat. Pitched battles probably devolved into general melees and finally into routs more often than not. Whether this characteristic sharply differentiates war between small-scale societies from that between their large-scale counterparts is open to question, however.

The next to last of the postulated attributes of warfare in small-scale societies is the use of unspecialized weapons; the same ones were used for both fighting and hunting. That was generally true in northern Beringia, except that clubs were rarely used in hunting, and specialized arrowheads were preferred in combat. However, I no longer find this attribute very significant. Obviously, if people made their living using weapons to kill big game, whether with bows and arrows or firearms, they could use those same weapons to kill humans. The people of northern Beringia did, however, have specialized accouterments for warfare in the forms of plate armor and protective vests, and the Chukotkans had a whole array of equipment designed to protect them from enemy missiles.

Finally, we come to the attribute of the frequent violation of the principle of concerted effort. There is allegedly a tendency in this kind of warfare toward a series of individual actions rather than a concentrated attack at the enemy's weakest point. I am not so sure that this rule applies in northern Beringia. The Iñupiat, at least, were well aware of the principle of mass, they were familiar with the notion of firing volleys of arrows at point men that would have been very difficult for those men to avoid, and they understood the concept of attacking the weakest part of the enemy line. Their method of conducting nighttime raids was a highly effective application of the principle of concerted effort. It was only when an open battle reached the melee stage that the focus may have been lost.

The Frequency and Distribution of Warfare

Many years ago I stated that "the combination of circumstances required to start a war occurred *somewhere* in northwestern Alaska at least once a year" (Burch 1974:3). What I meant is there was a war every year—somewhere. In reviewing the evidence again in preparation for writing this book, I was led to modify this conclusion.

The first point to make is that there is no solid basis for making a precise estimate of the frequency of warfare during the study period. All one can say with certainty is that warfare was frequent enough and dangerous enough to be on people's minds almost all the time. Incidents involving iññuqutit probably had a great deal to do with this. At least some iññuqutit probably operated in every national estate every year, but only a few of them were involved in bloodshed. They helped keep the level of international tension at a high pitch, however, and they must have helped persuade people that they were actively surrounded by enemies almost all the time.

The frequency of actual raids or open battles, however, is problematic. Many of the encounters I thought were independent of one another when I wrote my paper on warfare 25 years ago turn out to have been different episodes of a single campaign. This means that many campaigns were more complex than I thought but also that there were fewer of them. That conclusion is supported by other types of evidence as well. One is that many colleagues recorded all or parts of the same events that I did, which suggests that we are dealing with a limited number of cases. Another is that it has been impossible to date almost any of the violent encounters on which information is available, so we do not know for certain if they were spread over 20, 50, or 100 years. The absence of dates does not mean that the events necessarily occurred a long time ago, however. Speaking for myself, I simply failed to seek the kinds of information needed for dating while the individuals who might have supplied it were still alive. I suspect that most other researchers in northwestern Alaska were guilty of the same oversight. Thus, the absence of dates may simply be an artifact of inadequate research methods rather than evidence of antiquity.

Many narratives of warfare contain fanciful passages, which suggested to me that they were in the process of changing from historical chronicles to myths when they were recorded by ethnographers. However, as Lucier pointed out to me, "the presence of fantastic elements in an account can hardly be a definitive basis for attributing great antiquity to the events described in it. Both of us know of many events in northwestern Alaska involving magical or supernatural elements that unquestionably occurred even in the 20th century" (1997:250). He's right. It is probably also true that no type of human activity is more prone to instant mythologizing than battle. Warriors flushed with victory enthusiastically embellish accounts of their triumph, while survivors on the other side are eager to blame their loss on mystical forces beyond their control.

Besides, good stories have marvelous propaganda value. Consider, for example, an episode from the life of Qayiayaqtualuk, the founding father of the Kivalliñiġmiut nation. Qayiayaqtualuk was probably born in the early or mid-18th century (Burch 1998a:367), and the event described in the following passage occurred while he was still relatively young.

> *A party of Kivalliñiġmiut were huddling in a cave, beset by Kakligmiut (Barrow) warriors. Tiring of the harassment, a shaman ordered that a fire be built. When it was burning brightly, she put on new gloves and reached into the fire. When she withdrew her hand, it was holding the heart of one of the Kakligmiut warriors. She repeated this until most of the Kakligmiut were dead. Then her companions told her to stop, because they wanted a few survivors to go home and tell their people not to challenge the Kivalliñiġmiut again.* [Sokonik 1918; A. Hawley 1964a; Swan 1983, 1989:113–114]

Who would dare challenge a nation with a shaman capable of performing such a feat?

Despite the above considerations I adopted a conservative approach in selecting raids and battles for notice in this book. Any narrative containing more than just the slightest hint of fantastic elements was excluded on the assumption that it refers to events that took place before the study period.[61]

At the other end, with only a few exceptions that are specifically noted in Appendix 1, none of the accounts considered here dates from after midcentury. The exceptions apparently all date from the 1850s. It is not at all clear why warfare ceased so abruptly, but there is little doubt that it did. All of the confrontations described to me occurred before my oldest informants' parents were born, although the residue of many battles was still visible when my informants were children. This is consistent with Knud Rasmussen's statement, made in 1924, to the effect that he was "able to collect information about [warfare] from elderly men and women whose parents themselves had taken part in the wars" (Ostermann and Holtved 1952:12–13).[62]

All of the above factors argue against there having been as high a frequency of raids and battles as I formerly thought. On the other hand, almost all of the encounters my colleagues and I heard about were true calamities. When the residents of even a small settlement were annihilated down to the last infant, one was dealing with a disaster of immense proportions for populations of the size of interest here. It was not much of an improvement when it was only the men or only the women and children of a settlement who were massacred, especially when torture or other atrocities were involved. I suspect that my colleagues and I heard about only the most extreme cases and that a whole host of less traumatic ones have disappeared from the record.

In the half-dozen instances in which I interviewed descendants of people on both the losing and winning sides of a raid or battle, they all agreed on the outcome. They might have recalled slightly different details, but they agreed on which nations were involved, how the incident unfolded, and who won. My informants also tried to make clear to me that total victory, which to them meant total annihilation of an enemy force or village, was rarely achieved. This was true primarily because many raids were aborted when the invading force either lost the element of surprise, or found itself numerically inferior, or both. The Kuuvaum Kaŋiaġmiut raid on Taksruq Saaŋa, summarized earlier in this chapter, is an example. On many occasions, war parties encountered some kind of difficulty before launching an attack or before even reaching enemy territory and were forced to abandon the enterprise. The disastrous Nuataaġmiut attempt to raft down the Kogoluktuk River to raid the Kobuk people is an example. My point is that, although we probably know about a substantial proportion of the raids and battles that were carried through to completion, we have little or no information on an even larger number that were not.

It is appropriate to note here that the early explorers' accounts give a false impression of the relative aggressiveness of the several different nations of northwestern Alaska. If one drew a conclusion on that issue based on their observations, one would have to identify the Kaŋiġmiut as being the most warlike people in the region. They would be followed by the Kakligmiut of the Barrow district, with perhaps a tie for third among the Kivalliñiġmiut, the Pittaġmiut, and the Tapqaġmiut. This estimate would completely miss the nations that the Iñupiaq historians to whom I spoke thought were the most aggressive, the Tikiġaġmiut of Point Hope and the Di'hąįį Gwich'in.

This is a simple case of sampling error. Tikiġaq, the capital village of the very aggressive Tikiġaġmiut, was visited by Westerners only during the season in which the settlement was all but devoid of inhabitants. Kashevarov missed it altogether in 1838, crossing the point via the lagoon behind it. Also, of course, the early explorers had no knowledge at all of the many nations whose estates were located in the interior.

Places where raids and battles have been recorded in northwestern Alaska are shown on Map 11 and listed in Table 5; brief summaries of and references

Table 5. Reported Locations of Raids and Battles in Northwestern Alaska (Keyed to Map 11)

1. Pisiktaġvik
2. Agki
3. Tikiġaġmiut
4. Kuupałłuk
5. Niksiurak
6. Avalit kuuk
7. Kaŋitch
8. Ikpitchiaq
9. Kaġmalirak
10. Qanaak
11. Imilik
12. Naparuatchiaq
13. Uivvak
14. Nuvuġaluaq
15. Tikiġaq
16. Auksaakiaq
17. Cape Thompson
18. Aagutauraq
19. Iñuktat
20. Nuvua
21. Imauġvik
22. Sapun
23. Makpik
24. Atłiq
25. Killiq
26. Itigamalukpak
27. Ivisaaqtiġnilik
28. Uqsruuġat
29. Anigaaq
30. Sisualik
31. Taksruq saaŋa
32. Kuupaamiit
33. Iqsiiġvik
34. Igliqtiqsiiġvik
35. Qalugraitchiaq
36. Aglinġauraq
37. Maniiḷappaat
38. Suluppaugaqtuuq
39. Nauyatuuq
40. Aalaatna Tsaalaakkakk'et
41. Aalaatna
42. Alaakkakk'at
43. Too loghe
44. Siłyeeminkk'at
45. Hudakkaakk'at
46. Itqiḷḷiġivik
47. Siktaġvik
48. Aaquaksraatchiak
49. Siŋik
50. Iñuktat
51. Name not recorded
52. Iguaġvik
53. Nunaġiaq
54. Inaaġruk
55. Qigiqtaq
56. Iġiġaġik
57. Yakpatakhaq
58. Piġu
59. Ikpik
60. Miłłitaavik
61. Kiŋigan
62. Masu
63. Tapqaq
64. Qaviaraq
65. Iġałuit
66. Atnaq
67. Nuviakchak
68. Kuintaq
69. Maqłuktuliq
70. Katyauraq
71. Kełroteyit
72. Name not recorded
73. Noolaaghedoh
74. Qikiqtaq
75. Whale Island
76. Cape Stephens
77. Qikertaq

on each conflict are presented in Appendix 1. As the map shows, these incidents were distributed widely over the NANA and adjacent regions, although rather few are indicated for the northern interior. The record of ancient conflicts is poorer for the latter region for at least two reasons. First, the population there at its peak was lower than in the other regions covered, and there were fewer incidents as a consequence. Second, early depopulation of part of

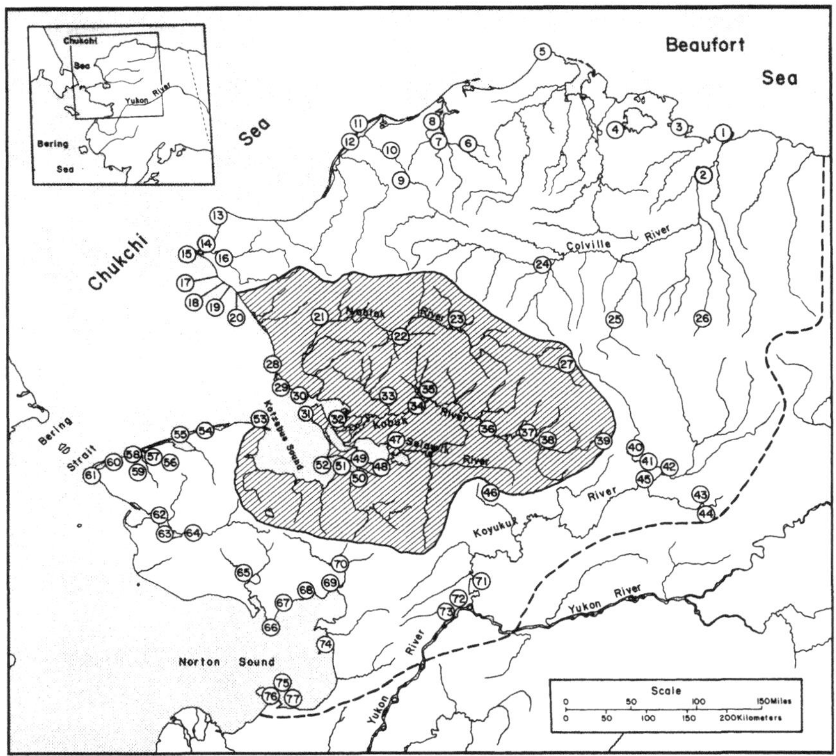

11. Reported locations of battles and raids in early contact northwestern Alaska (see Appendix 1). The shaded area is the NANA Region.

the area and massive population shifts after about 1870 resulted in the loss of knowledge about most of the conflicts that did occur there. I have heard or read about many raids and battles in addition to those noted here, especially in the southern part of the area covered by the map, but either their locations were not specified in the accounts or they were too imprecise for me to place on a map.

The Consequences of Warfare

The primary consequence of warfare in the study region is almost too obvious to have to state: a lower population than there would have been without it. My senior informants all felt that the population of northwestern Alaska would have been much larger than it was in the early 19th century had it not been for warfare, and I can think of no reason to disagree with them. The way war was conducted made this outcome almost inevitable, since the members of a victorious military force tried to kill virtually everyone in the defeated settlement or military unit.

According to Stephen Beckerman and Roberto Lizarralde (1995), a frequent finding in studies of warfare among small-scale societies is a disproportionate number of losses among men, usually young men. I am not sure why they restricted this generalization to small-scale societies, however, since warfare among even the most highly modernized societies leads to a disproportionate number of losses among young men. But I do not think that the generalization applies to warfare in northwestern Alaska anyway.

The ratios of losses among different age and sex cohorts in early contact northwestern Alaska can never be known with certainty. The qualitative evidence suggests that, overall, losses may have been pretty evenly distributed between males and females and among age groups. In open battle all the losses were males but probably spread over a broad range of age groups. In nighttime raids losses in the village would have been spread over all age groups and both sexes, while losses among the raiders would all have been males. In daylight raids on settlements where all the men were away hunting the losses among adults were primarily among women and old men, but among children they were equally distributed among boys and girls.

Paradoxically, warfare seems to have been a major factor underlying international marriages. In fact, it was probably *the* major factor underlying international marriages. When all of the women in a settlement were killed, they left behind a group of men who badly needed wives and who probably could not find enough suitable candidates in their own country. Similarly, when a large number of men were killed in open battle, there suddenly was an urgent need for husbands. Even if the absolute numbers were small, most nations did not have large enough populations to make up the deficits. Spouses had to be sought elsewhere. Since the same factors applied across the entire region, disproportionate losses of men in one district might have been offset by disproportionate losses of women in another, so that the aggregate effect may have been nil. But the consequence for individual nations was to have a disproportionate number of expatriate men or women living in their estate.

Despite the impression the reader might have at this point, the world of the early-19th-century Iñupiat was not a case of the war of all against all, even when the units involved were nations instead of individuals. For example, as far as I can determine, if the Napaaqtuġmiut and Nuataaġmiut were ever involved in the same conflicts, it was always as allies. The Nuataaġmiut were actively involved in hostilities against the Tikiġaġmiut and practically all the nations whose estates were in the Kobuk River valley, but they are never reported to have engaged the Utuqqaġmiut or any of the bands of the Kuukpigmiut in warfare. The Pittaġmiut were in a state of more or less perpetual hostility with the nations to the south, the Qaviaraġmiut and Igałuiŋmiut, but never with their neighbors to the west and east, the Tapqaġmiut and Kaŋigmiut, respectively. The overall pattern is extremely complex, but the basic point is that while some nations were enemies, others were allies. The focus in the present chapter has been exclusively on hostilities, but it is important to keep in mind the fact that they were only half of the story.

Making Peace

While doing the fieldwork on which much of this volume is based, I never thought to inquire as to how members of warring nations made peace. Fortunately, I learned of a few cases anyway. It seems appropriate to summarize them here because they form an appropriate closure to this chapter and provide a bridge to the next. I begin with two examples.

In the first example, seven or eight Tikiġaġmiut (Point Hope) hunters drifted out on the sea ice (A. Hawley 1964b). In contrast to the usual pattern, the wind and current took these men south. A month or so later they reached shore in the estate of the Tapqaġmiut (Shishmaref) in very poor condition. Most of the Tapqaġmiut wanted to kill them in retaliation for all of their own men who had been killed over the years by Tikiġaġmiut under similar circumstances. However, an umialiq (chieftain) argued that this was an unusual opportunity to end the hostility between themselves and the Tikiġaġmiut. Instead of killing these men, he maintained, they should take care of them and nurse them back to health. Eventually, his arguments carried the day. The Tikiġaġmiut hunters recovered and were returned to their countrymen the next summer at the Sisualik fair. From then on relations between the two previously hostile nations improved rapidly.

A second example involved people from two unidentified nations, one Iñupiaq (probably the Akuniġmiut of the central Kobuk district), the other one Athapaskan (probably Koyukon).[63] Several men from the former were rafting down the Mauneluk River on their way home to their families on the Kobuk River after two months of caribou hunting in the upper Noatak River valley.

> *There was thick fog. The mouth of the Maneluk [sic] River was very foggy. They could not see the riverbanks. There was deep water and a good beach just up from the mouth of the Maneluk. They got close to the beach and saw a kayak coming upstream. One man on the raft had a hook made from a willow branch on the end of a pole. (Sometimes in rapids they used a hook to steady the raft.)*
>
> *The kayak near the mouth of the Maneluk got so close that they hooked it and pulled it to the raft. They knew the man. He was an Indian named Katoleelauk. He jumped on the raft. His partner also came near but could not be hooked. He went*

around and around. Finally he was hooked too and pulled to the raft, and he jumped on.

The Iñupiat took Katoleelauk and his partner home. It turned out that they had been prowlers for much of the summer and had terrorized the Iñupiat women so much that they had collected very little food, so they kept them prisoner until freeze-up. Then they met with them and told them that they should stay with them that fall. They would supply everything they needed, and then in the winter they would be sent home. They were to tell their people that they had stayed with the Iñupiat, who wanted to meet peacefully with the Athapaskans. The Iñupiat kept their word, and the Indians did as they were told.

In the long days of March and April many sleds set out. They came to Pah River, and along the river the Indians and Eskimos met. One [Iñupiaq] man was in front of his sled. He took a spear and put it in the trail, point down. That man stood right there. The Indians could not come by. They waited. The Kobuk people watched them. For many hours they waited. They were cold. The man who held them back had lost many brothers and neighbors, killed by Indians. One woman carrying a baby also had lost many brothers and neighbors. She went after the man with the spear. She came to him and asked, "Why do you hold back these people?" She grabbed the spear. She took him home dragging his spear.

Then the Indians came into the village. Each team went to a different Kobuk house. This is the way they met.

Every year after that they repeated this type of gathering, visiting back and forth in alternate years. And after that there was no more fighting between the Koyukuk River Koyukon and the Akuniġmiut.

The above accounts, plus three others I know of, have certain elements in common.[64] This suggests that there was a basic approach to making peace. The first was that people on one side had to have entirely within their power at least one person from an enemy nation. The second was for one or more individuals among the captors to have the idea of initiating peaceful relations by doing something totally unexpected. They not only did not kill the prisoner, they sustained him and eventually returned him in good health to his own people. If this person was successful in persuading the others of the wisdom of this approach, it was done. The freed captive's countrymen would be amazed at this turn of events, and he would give them a favorable report on his treatment. It was apparently considered quite reprehensible for a freed prisoner's countrymen to decline an offer of peace, despite the fact that many among them might have personal vendettas they wished to pursue.

3. Friendly Relations

The terrorism, raids, and battles that characterized international relations in early contact northwestern Alaska and the pervasive animosity and fear they engendered would seem to preclude friendly relations. In fact, friendly relations were at least as widespread as hostile ones, but they had different focal points and connections. Friendly and hostile relations were intertwined in complex and often subtle ways, and one of the most intriguing aspects of early-19th-century life in the region was how the two kinds of relations coexisted.

Preliminaries

Dorothy Jean Ray observed that the members of each nation were "acquainted with an exceptionally large area, and interaction was extensive with numerous other groups" (1975b:87–88; see also Bockstoce 1988, vol. 1:184). Since all of the Native peoples of the region were highly mobile both within and across estate borders, and since they were descended from people who had lived in the same general part of the world for at least a thousand years, no one should find these facts surprising. What is important to keep in mind, however, is that the nature of the interaction varied significantly depending on which nations were involved in each specific case and on the context in which the interaction occurred. Because of the high level of hostility in the region, when people crossed borders for friendly purposes they had to be very careful how they went about it.

The most fundamental rule of international travel was succinctly stated by John Simpson: an Iñupiaq "never undertakes a distant journey unless he well knows the people he is going among, or he goes in company with others on whom he can depend for a welcome" (1875:249). After extensive conversations with elders more than a century later, Ray came to the same conclusion: "No person would enter another group's territory without having relatives there to identify him, or without a guide to take him there" (1964:86).[1] Even when entering the estate of a friendly nation, however, it was necessary for strangers to indicate their intentions to its residents while still some distance away.

5. Men greeting the Beechey expedition near Sisualik, July 1826. Sketch by William Smyth in F. W. Beechey (1831, vol. 1:343).

The most effective way to signal peaceful intentions was to travel openly in a mixed group of men, women, and children. Such a contingent would rarely be regarded as having hostile objectives. However, men, either singly or in groups, also had reason to cross international borders from time to time, and their position was more precarious unless they were well known to and on good terms with the people on the other side. Peaceful intentions were indicated partly by traveling out in the open and partly by making appropriate signals when within view of local residents (Beechey 1831, vol. 1:346; Gough 1973:148; Great Britain, Parliament, House of Commons 1850:15; Hooper 1881:62; Nelson 1899:302; Ray 1983:38; Sours 1987).

One of the appropriate signals involved raising the arms over the head, with the hands empty, then lowering them to the sides. This motion is demonstrated in Plate 5, which shows men in different stages of doing this.[2] Another involved holding the arms out to the side, with elbows bent and forearms raised, then lowering and raising the forearms in a kind of awkward waving motion. A third was to hold one's arms up at an angle of 45 degrees, then to lower them, passing them over the breast and stomach. Additional evidence of peaceful intentions was provided by keeping weapons visible to the members of the resident population but conspicuously *not* ready for immediate use.

When people encountered one another in boats, at least one person in each craft held up furs or perhaps a pole to which an inflated sealskin poke, or bag, was attached, indicating a desire to trade. Others made one or more of the signals listed above. When encountering Westerners the poke was replaced with a fox skin or some other fur, indicating the kind of trade in which Westerners were thought to be interested (Kotzebue 1821, vol. 1:208; Merck 1980:192; Sarychev 1806–7, vol. 2:44; Sauer 1802:248).

Men entering a foreign country with hostile intent also indicated the general nature of their trip in the way they traveled. Instead of traveling openly and in daylight they moved at night, stayed away from major travel routes, and kept on valley floors instead of exposed slopes or ridges. Unambiguous signs of hostile intent when visual contact was made with local residents were for the foreigners to hold their weapons above their heads or to advance toward the residents while shooting arrows ahead of them along their intended line of travel.

Contact

Once the preliminaries were concluded, which was always while the residents and intruders were still some distance apart, the next step was for the members of the two groups gradually to approach one another to a point where direct physical contact was possible. Unfortunately, this subject never occurred to me as one worthy of investigation until I started writing this book, by which time it was too late to investigate in the field. We must assume that there were several possibilities, depending on (1) whether or not the strangers had been invited, (2) whether or not the members of the party were known to the residents, (3) the purpose for which the strangers had come, and (4) whether or not they were passing through on their way to somewhere else. A specific ritual was followed when the strangers were guests arriving for a messenger feast, which is discussed below in a separate section. Beyond that, both the literature and my field notes are singularly uninformative on these matters, so I present what little evidence there is and try to draw a few conclusions from it.

The greeting procedure used with Westerners during the first half of the 19th century was to lick one's hands, draw them over one's face and body, and then draw them over the stranger's face and body. This was followed by an embrace and the rubbing of noses (Beechey 1831, vol. 1:345–346, 391, 429; Bockstoce 1988, vol. 1:169, 215 n. 1; Collinson 1889:67; Hooper 1853:235; Kotzebue 1821, vol. 1:225–226; Murdoch 1892:422; Ray 1983:38; Simpson 1843:155; VanStone 1960:146). This does not strike me as something Iñupiat would do among themselves, however, and I have never seen or heard of them following such a procedure. It may be significant that A. F. Kashevarov, the only Westerner to have been mistaken for a Native during the study period, does not report greetings of this kind (VanStone 1977). On the other hand, identical signals and gestures were employed to greet early Western visitors to the Yup'ik Eskimo region of Saint Lawrence Island, so they must have been in very general use for at least some purposes throughout the entire Bering Strait area (Beechey 1831, vol. 1:331, 332).

A different kind of ritual was observed during the winter of 1854, when W. R. Hobson led a small party from Port Clarence to Chamisso Island: "I observed that before we entered the village the women lit a small fire in the track we were to pass over; they hailed the guide to stop until it was done; I was unable to discover the meaning of this, but conclude it is some superstition regarding the arrival of strangers" (1855:889). This Pittaġmiut village was inhabited only by women and children at the time, the men being away hunting, so they might have been taking special precautions.

Still another type of observance was reported by Charles Brower several decades after the end of the study period. According to him, whenever a stranger from Point Hope came to the Kakligmiut village of Utqiaġvik for the first time he "made for a house as fast as he could run, It did not matter whose house it was as long as he was inside he was safe ,and made welcome ,as long as he stayed there,Allways they knew they were in for a hazeing,sooner or later If they stayed anylength of time,if they only stayed a night they might get away before the villagers were ready for them" (n.d.:485).[3] By "hazeing" he meant run the gauntlet.

Late in the fall of 1884 Brower visited Utqiaġvik in the company of two reluctant guides, a Tikiġaġmiu (sing.) named Kyoocktoo and a Kivalliñiġmiu he had nicknamed Baby. The two Natives managed to get into a house before many people got out to see who they were, and they stayed there. However, just as Brower was getting ready to leave,

> *along in the afternoon Kyoocktoo came to me looking as though he had been through a thrashing machine. About half the village was along with him, the people knowing we would start in a day or two had made him run the gauntlet. Baby was let off as he belonged to another tribe [Baby was a Kivalliñiġmiu], below Point Hope, where it was not customary to treat the Ut-kie-a-vie mutes the same as the Tig-er-rag-a mutes [Tikiġaġmiut] did. The whole village had lined up and Kyoocktoo was made to run between the lines, all the women were the worst, some even sharpening their finger nails to a point, others making small notches in them so they could mark their victim better. The men did not do any damage. All they did was to keep him in line and not let him break away, and get in a house until he had finished his run. Besides scratching him all over the face and body, his skin clothing was torn to pieces. Where ever a woman could get ahold of it she had held on as long as the skin would stand the strain, by this means holding him back as much as possible. Kyoocktoo had managed to get through at last, and get to a house where he was safe. He was now on friendly terms with these people and could come and go as often as he liked and never again would he have to run the gauntlet.*

> *He had to come to me to have some of the women mend his shirts for him, for some reason or other they would not do this for him then. When I saw him, he was almost naked. All that was left of his at-tig-a [parka] was the sleeves.* [N.d.:147–148][4]

Other sources (Nasugluk 1940:18; Quwana 1940:11; Ungarook 1952) indicate that this custom was specific to the Kakligmiut and Tikiġaġmiut.

George Stoney also had some instructive experiences in 1885 and 1886. In December 1885, with one other Westerner and four Kobuk River valley Natives, he approached the village of Isikkuq in the Nigu River valley in the western Endicott Mountains. Before he reached the houses he was stopped by some men who demanded tribute. He refused to pay it and proceeded into the village. There he learned that just a few men had tried to take advantage of him and that most of the residents regarded the affair as a big joke (Stoney 1900:570).

A more serious attempt to exact tribute occurred a few weeks later when Stoney, with two local Natives and an interpreter, was traveling along the upper Kobuk River in February 1886. As he approached the village of Paa,

> *a messenger from Saulogs [Sauġluq], the most influential native of the Putnam [Kobuk], informed me that I could travel no further without paying tribute. My answer was that I would make no payment and that I would keep on. As I drew nearer the village his mother came out and ran ahead of my sled, refusing to notice me or answer my questions. A still worse sign of displeasure and anger was that the inhabitants kept in their houses instead of coming out to greet me. Arriving in the village, Saulogs sent for me; I not only refused to go to him myself, but also forbade my interpreter's going. My entire disregard of Saulogs's presumption, and the position I took, was that I was the greater "oumalik" [umialik] or chief, resulted most beneficially, though probably I was more concerned about the outcome of the matter than he was, being the only white man in my party. I carried my point and he sent his wife to hold a council of peace, which terminated amicably and I proceeded as I desired.* [Stoney 1900:572]

Most of the early explorers offered presents to the Natives they encountered or at least to their leaders in order to elicit a favorable response to their presence. The Natives themselves apparently regarded such gifts as tribute, not as a courtesy, and no doubt this is what Sauġluq had in mind.

A still more aggressive example of greeting comes from King Island, which was visited by Ivan Kobelev and a party of Chukchi in June 1791.

> *In the morning at sunrise we paddled to the island. The Ukipantsy [Ukiuvaŋmiut] saw us already in the ocean and all our baidarkas [boats] stopped. Everybody dressed in kuyak [Chukchi armor], took spears in their hands, and nocked their*

arrows on bow-strings, as warriors should. I asked why are you getting ready for war? We are not going there to fight. At that, [my companions] told me that Ukipantsy always have such greetings, and that they would greet us in the same way. Then the Ukipantsy stopped at the shore, dressed in kuyak, with bows and spears in their hands, and arrows nocked on the bow-strings. We carried our baggage ashore, while the rest were standing at arms. After that the inhabitants took all of us into their yurts [houses]. [Chernenko 1957:133–134]

A final example comes from the Endicott Mountains, where Athapaskans and Kuukpigmiut were frequently in contact. Here the custom was for the men to wrestle one another until exhausted. After that, they visited one another as friends (Itaałuk 1982a:6–7).

These diverse observations, combined with information provided in Chapters 1 and 2, make it possible to derive a few tentative conclusions about the treatment of peaceful foreigners at the point where physical proximity first occurred. First, those who were well known to the residents were initially greeted with a ritualized display of hostility the precise nature of which probably varied from one nation to another. Then they were welcomed and invited into either the qargi or people's houses. Second, poorly known or even unknown foreigners whose country was not actually at war with that of the residents could visit or pass through, either by paying some kind of tribute or else by being subjected to some sort of nastiness, such as running the gauntlet. Third, much depended on the relative numbers of people involved. A large party of visitors was not likely to be challenged by the members of a small settlement, whereas the members of a small party were almost certain to be handled roughly by the members of a large settlement. By the 1880s, being Western probably had much the same impact as being numerous, since by then the Iñupiat were beginning to realize how dangerous even a few armed Westerners could be.[5]

No matter what the specifics were, once they had completed the initial phase of contact, peaceful visitors were enthusiastically accepted. After the initial ceremonies had been concluded, the visitors were invited into the qargi or houses, food and entertainment were provided, and an exchange of gifts ensued. Even the early explorers were frequently offered food and entertained with singing and dancing (see, e.g., Beechey 1831, vol. 1:361–362, 366–367, 390–392, 394–401). When, after the incident described above, Stoney finally entered the village of Isikkuq, the large crowd that had gathered there for a messenger feast surrounded his party, "the men beating tom-toms and the women singing, and for a time we felt anxious; but, their ceremonies over, they gave the hand of friendship and extended the freedom of their village" (1900:570).

Communication

Communication between members of different nations within the Iñupiaq area was not much of a problem (Ballott 1970b; Clark 1975:149; Clark and Clark 1976:198; Commack 1970; Curtis 1930:214; Hall 1975b:249; S. Hunnicutt 1970; Lee 1970; Schneider 1976:257; Smith 1970; Stoney 1900:828; Tickett 1969). Although several dialects and a much larger number of subdialects were spoken in the region (Fortescue, Jacobson, and Kaplan 1994:vii–ix), they were all mutually intelligible, at least after a bit of practice. The interesting areas were language borders. There, bilingualism or multilingualism seems to have been widespread, and trade jargons or pidgins were sometimes used.

Along the Iñupiaq–Gwich'in border, many if not most adults were bilingual. Among the Kuukpigmiut of the Colville River, for example, most adults probably spoke one or more Gwich'in dialects. Many members of the northern Gwich'in nations, but particularly the Di'hą̨į̨, must have been relatively fluent in Iñupiaq, since, in addition to fighting, they exchanged messenger feasts with them, and at least some Di'hą̨į̨ also married Iñupiat. No doubt some Nuataaġmiut also spoke Gwich'in, but I have no specific information on this point.

Bilingualism was widespread along the Koyukon–Iñupiaq border. In the early 19th century the residents of the upper Kobuk River valley spoke Koyukon as their first language and Iñupiaq as their second, reversing the emphasis only after midcentury (Burch et al. 1999). Many of their neighbors immediately downstream, the Akuniġmiut, spoke Koyukon in addition to their native Iñupiaq. At least some Koyukon living in the Koyukuk River valley must have spoken Iñupiaq, because many of them had partners on the Iñupiaq side of the language border. In the Selawik River drainage, particularly the upper portion, many people spoke Koyukon, and the same was true of the Kaŋiġmiut living along the Buckland River (Curtis 1930:220; Sunno 1951d). A trade jargon involving elements of both Koyukon and Iñupiaq was used in some districts by people who were not fully bilingual (Clark 1975:149; Clark and Clark 1976:198; Jones 1991).

A similar pattern of language competence existed along the Iñupiaq–Yup'ik border on the Seward Peninsula. Many residents of Norton Sound were trilingual or multilingual, speaking their own dialect of Central Alaskan Yup'ik plus Iñupiaq and Koyukon and possibly one or two other Athapaskan languages as well. On the Iñupiaq side of the border at least some Kaŋiġmiut spoke Yup'ik, but I have no information about the situation farther west on the Seward Peninsula.

The precise details of the linguistic situation in Bering Strait are unclear because the first language of the inhabitants of the Diomede Islands at the time is unknown. They probably spoke Iñupiaq as their first language, but most of them probably spoke Naukanski Yup'ik as well. The Iñupiaq-speaking inhabitants of the islands in Bering Strait apparently also had some competence in Chukchi. This may be surmised from the fact that the 18th-century explorers Nikolai Daurkin, Mikhail Gvozdev, and Ivan Kobelev were able to communicate with them in Chukchi, and Gvozdev even said that they *were* Chukchi (Golder 1971:161–162; Masterson and Brower 1948:65–67, 93–96). Whether or not any of the Iñupiaq-speaking residents of the Alaska mainland could speak Chukchi or Naukanski Yup'ik or whether any of the residents of Chukotka could speak Iñupiaq is not known with certainty. In later years some members of both groups were multilingual, and they served as interpreters for the others (Northwest Iñupiat Elders Conference 1983:#32A, 7). That situation may have existed in earlier years as well.

Bilingualism seems to have been common in Chukotka among at least the Yup'ik speakers. Most adult Eskimos spoke Chukchi in addition to their native language, but bilingualism was apparently less widespread among the Chukchi, who were the more dominant of the two peoples (Bogoras 1904–9:23; de Reuse 1994:296–297, 306; Schweitzer and Golovko 1995:43–57). Whether or not there was a Chukchi–Yup'ik pidgin is uncertain, although de Reuse claims that there was one based on Eskimo but containing many Chukchi loanwords (de Reuse 1994:319–329; see also Schweitzer and Golovko 1995:84–87).

The evidence indicates that in the early 19th century language differences were not a barrier to international relations anywhere within the study region. Given this fact, one has to question the significance of the so-called silent trade. This was described by Otto von Kotzebue as being the procedure used between people from opposite sides of Bering Strait: "The stranger first comes, and lays some goods on the shore, and then retires; the American comes, looks at the things, puts as many skins near them as he thinks proper to give, and then also goes away. Upon this the stranger approaches and examines what is offered him; if he is satisfied with it, he takes the skins, and leaves his goods instead; but, if not, then he lets all the things lie, retires a second time, and expects an addition from the buyer. In this manner the dealing seems to me to continue without speaking" (1821, vol. 1:228; see also Bogoras 1904–9:53–54; Fisher 1981:32, 44–45).

This procedure was known to everyone, and I do not doubt that it was used from time to time. But it was probably employed only when the specific individuals involved either were not known to one another or were meeting in an unusual context. Although it clearly worked when the individuals involved could not understand each other's language, the silent trade was probably used more frequently as a way to solve a political problem—lack of mutual trust.

There may have been a certain amount of ritual involved in the silent trade. Sidney Huntington (1993:15–17), for example, describes repeated exchanges involving his Koyukon grandfather on one side and an Iñupiaq named Schilikuk on the other. Although the men's transactions apparently were conducted in a manner almost identical to the silent exchanges described by Kotzebue, each man always knew in advance what the other wanted. Furthermore, during Huntington's mother's childhood she accompanied her father on some of his trading expeditions, and she learned to speak some Iñupiaq from Schilikuk. Obviously, the individuals involved here were communicating with one another on several different levels that the phrase "silent trade" does not adequately capture.

Umialġich, *or Chieftains*

An umialik was a rich person. A rich person was one who had lots of equipment, furs, and other goods to trade, sizeable surpluses of food, and a large family. Rich people played a particularly important part in friendly relations among nations in northwestern Alaska. They are mentioned at various points in this chapter, but it is useful to give a basic description of the umialik role here.

An umialik was an effective trader and hunter in addition to being the head of a large local family (Brower n.d.:160–161; Burch 1975a:205–221; Rainey 1947:241; Simpson 1875:272–273; Spencer 1959:151–158). People obeyed an umialik partly out of respect but mostly because he made it worth their while. As Brower said of Kiḷagraq, the umialik at Kotzebue in 1885, he wielded influence "through the ability to supply his neighbors with things they needed during the winter, extending them credit when they were not in a position to pay" (n.d.:160).

The term *umialik* is invariably translated as "chief" by early Western observers in the NANA Region. This was because the men designated by that term were the most influential people they encountered (Bertholf 1899a:24; Dall 1870:556; Maguire 1857:438; Seemann 1853, vol. 2:180; Simpson 1875:272; Smith 1873). *Umialġich* (pl.) were easily recognized because of their elegant clothes, their dignified bearing, and the deference paid to them by their companions. However, having translated umialik as "chief," most of these same observers proceeded to point out that an umialik really had little influence beyond the boundaries of his own (local) family and that "chief" is perhaps too strong a word (Bertholf 1899a:24; Maguire 1857:438; McLenegan 1887:75; Seemann 1853, vol. 2:59–60; Simpson 1875:272). In modern anthropological terms an umialik was not a chief but a "big man" or "chieftain" (Redmond 1998a:3–4; Sahlins 1963:288–294).

The umialik role, unlike the ataniq role, was not context sensitive: a rich man was wealthy whether or not he actually directed a particular activity or crew. For example, although an umialik ordinarily was the leader in most important activities, he was quite willing to pay someone to be the ataniq (boss) of his whaling crew if that person was particularly gifted in that activity. The umialik received the largest share of the proceeds in any case, and it was to his advantage to have the best captain he could recruit.

An umialik's direct influence did not extend beyond the boundaries of the local family he headed, but the families headed by truly wealthy men were always unusually large. This was so almost automatically because the accumulation of wealth depended on the active support of many relatives.[6] Umialġich did not have any institutionalized coercive power, but wealth and an extensive network of personal connections gave them a disproportionate amount of influence over both national and international affairs.

Relationships

International affairs are conducted through relationships between individuals who are members of the nation involved. Even among the most powerful nations in the modern world, "international relations are personal" (Fitzwater 1995:235) in the sense that they are conducted by members of one nation dealing directly with members of another. However, in many societies the most important of the relevant relationships involve individuals representing the governments of or other large-scale organizations in their respective countries. But in the NANA Region as well as in northern Beringia generally there were no governments or other large-scale organizations. International affairs were conducted by individuals acting either on their own or on behalf of their respective families. The relationships in terms of which these affairs were carried out were limited in number and are described below under the headings of "trading partnerships" and "kin relationships."

Before proceeding I wish to clarify my use of two common but important terms that tend to be variably, inconsistently, or all-inclusively used by anthropologists, both in general and with specific regard to the Iñupiat. These terms are *partner* and *alliance*. *Partner* can be used to refer to almost anyone with whom one has any kind of positive relationship, even a husband or wife. For example, writing about Arctic Alaska, Robert Spencer employs it to refer to trading partners (*niuviġiik*) who were not kin and to joking cousins (*iḷḷuġiik*) who were.[7] In the present work, unless otherwise specified, *partner* is used solely to refer to trading partners. *Alliance*, likewise, can be used to designate almost any type of positive relationship. For example, writing about relationships in northern Alaska, Lawrence Hennigh (1983) used the term in exactly that all-inclusive sense, listing as types of ally the following: umialġich, consanguineal relatives, in-laws, trading partners, namesakes, shamans, amulet partners, helpers, and bosses. In the present work *alliance* is used solely to refer to an association between or among separate nations.

Trading Partnerships

The most important relationship in international affairs in early-19th-century northwestern Alaska was the so-called trading partnership (Ahkivgak 1980; Ballott 1970b; Booth 1960:41; Cleveland 1970a, 1970b; D. Foster 1970; J. Foster 1970; Gallahorn 1970a; Green 1969; A. Hawley 1965a, 1967; B. Hawley 1967; Elwood Hunnicutt 1970; Keats 1970d; Kialook 1970; Lee 1970; M. Sage 1965; Smith 1970; Spencer 1952, notebook 2:92; Swan 1970).[8] By "most important" I mean two things. First, it was probably the most common type of relationship operating across national boundaries.[9] Second, it was usually the most active international relationship. Partners ordinarily saw each other at least once a year, often twice, and occasionally more often than that, and they had definite obligations to fulfill each time. These things could not be said about any other type of relationship. The partnership system was the foundation on which peaceful international relations were built.

In much of the NANA Region a trading partner was known as a *niiviq* or *niiviatchiaq*. (Nowadays, a loanword from English, *paatnaq*, is often used instead.) The relationship itself was called *niiviġiik*.[10] Outside the NANA Region but within the Iñupiaq language area the term for the role was *niuviq* and for the relationship *niuviġiik*. Although the primary focus in this volume is on the NANA Region, I use the "standard" form of the term, *niuviq*, following the policy of the Alaska Native Language Center. This word, which is a noun when standing alone, also serves as a verb stem to denote the distinctive type of material exchange that was institutionalized in the relationship.

Partnerships were not necessarily international in character. They could and sometimes did involve people who were members of the same nation, particularly individuals who were skilled craftsmen with different specialties and who were not otherwise related. But before the breakdown of the traditional nations in the late 19th century, the overwhelming majority of partnerships seem to have operated across national boundaries.

The institution of partnership persisted into my time in northwestern Alaska, albeit in modified form. I was a member of such a relationship myself for many years. The account presented here focuses on the traditional pattern, however, not the current one.

CONTENT

A partnership was a voluntary relationship established between two individuals, male or female, who exchanged gifts and agreed to be niuviġiik. The great majority of partnerships involved members of the same sex, but this was not a requirement. If two men were partners, their wives often were partners also, and it was common for the children of partners "to make partners" on their own when they became adults.

An exchange of gifts symbolized the creation of the relationship, but the agreement to be partners obligated the individuals involved to continue to give things to one another from then on. Usually there was an explicit understanding about the basic types of good to be exchanged. To the extent circumstances permitted, these were useful or valuable items that were available or abundant in one partner's country but rare or nonexistent in the other's. A typical pattern was for a person living on the seacoast to provide an inland partner with seal oil and for the inlander to reciprocate with caribou hides. Raw or only slightly modified materials were the most common items exchanged between partners, but manufactured goods such as clothing, pottery, rope, and baskets could be exchanged as well. This was particularly true when the individuals involved were master craftsmen.

The goods that were specified when a partnership was formed were usually few in number, but they constituted a minimal list. When they could afford to partners always gave gifts over and above those mentioned in their initial agreement. Partners also could solicit any kind of good imaginable from one another. If the partner could provide the requested item, he or she was obligated to do so. If the partner could not provide it, as opposed to being unwilling to provide it, that was not considered a defect in the relationship. On the other hand, with the exception noted in the next paragraph, it was considered quite improper for one partner repeatedly to make unreasonable requests of the other partner.

People in a well-established partnership often had fun with the solicitation aspect of the relationship. In addition to the usual items and perhaps an ad hoc list of special goods that were actually needed, partners often requested one obscure or frivolous item that was almost but not quite impossible to provide. The partner from whom such a request was made then spent much of the time between meetings either trying to fulfill the request literally or, perhaps more often, trying to figure out how to do so metaphorically or in some ludicrous way. When the two finally got together again the exchange of these gifts was conducted with elaborate gamesmanship and joking. People sometimes spent almost as much time trying to think of clever requests to make as they did in attempting to fulfill their partners' requests.

The words "giving" and "gift" are not used by accident in the foregoing paragraphs. The English phrase "trading partners" is misleading, since "to niuviq" was to give a free gift to someone who was not kin.[11] "Giving partners" would be a more accurate label. Indeed, when speaking English my informants always used "give" instead of "trade" when referring to exchanges between partners; in their own language they used niuviq- as a verb in this context. Market forces must have had some effect on how partners viewed their relationship, but their exchanges were always made well below the market price.

Support in time of need was another obligation of partnership. If famine struck a particular nation, for example, people had the right to go with their families to live with partners in other countries until the crisis passed. The partners had the obligation to support them to the extent possible. If a man got in trouble at home, he could go stay with a partner in another country until things calmed down—as long as he and the members of his family behaved themselves. Partners thus shared bad times as well as good.

When the people of one nation formed a general alliance with the members of another, the partnerships linking their respective members, particularly those connecting umialġich, provided the framework making that alliance possible. Partnerships involving members of nations who were in a hostile mode toward one another must have been difficult to maintain, but they were feasible for people who attended the same trade fair.

Emotional intensity was an important feature of partnerships, one that is often overlooked by anthropologists. Obviously, there had to have been a range of variation in this regard, but most partnerships of more than a few years' duration were imbued with considerable affection. Good partners were extremely fond of one another and received as much pleasure in giving as in receiving the goods that were exchanged. Partnerships were also a major avenue of international communication. Information on game supplies, weather conditions, foreign intrigue, international affairs generally, and other important matters was transmitted across national borders primarily through the medium of partnerships.

According to Robert Spencer (1959:172, 1984:332–333), partners frequently shared spouses. When I began to think seriously about getting involved in a partnership myself, I investigated this issue with particular care. I found no evidence to corroborate Spencer's statement for either the 19th or the 20th century. This was true even when I interviewed people from the Arctic Slope, which is where Spencer did his research. While my sources agreed that it was theoretically possible for partners to exchange spouses, none of them had ever heard of it happening, and none of them could think of a reason why anyone would do it.[12]

DISTRIBUTION AND NUMBERS

Many, probably most, partnerships involved people who lived in different ecological zones. The advantage of such arrangements is obvious: people could provide their partners with desired goods at relatively little cost to themselves. The inland–coast distinction was particularly important here because that ecotone was the most profound in the entire region. (The specific products that were involved in inland–coast exchanges are discussed below in the section on international trade.) But partnerships were by no means limited to that context.

Some partnerships involved people who lived in different nations within the *same* ecological zone. Coast dwellers had partners in other maritime nations, and inlanders had partners in other interior nations. For example, in February 1853 the officers of HMS *Plover* met a Tikiġaġmiu (Point Hope) umialik who was visiting his Kakligmiut partner in Nuvuk (Point Barrow), yet it is difficult to think of two locations more similar ecologically than Tikiġaq and Nuvuk. The Tikiġaġmiu man supplied his Kakligmiut partner with kettles he had acquired from the Chukchi and received wolverine skins in return (Simpson 1852–54:entries for February 7 and 10, 1853; see also Bockstoce 1988, vol. 1:171).

Partnerships within ecological zones were important because the political aspects of partnerships were just as significant to the early-19th-century Iñupiat as the economic ones. Of primary importance here was the obligation to provide protection for one's partner when asked to do so. It was only toward the end of the 19th century, after both the coastal and inland resource bases had been thoroughly disrupted and after most of the traditional nations had ceased to exist, that economic factors acquired undisputed dominance.

The number of partners an individual could have varied according to how many partnerships he or she could support. A wealthy person obviously could fulfill the obligations of more partnerships than a poor one could, while some people did not have the wherewithal to sustain any. Statements made to me by informants suggest that the ordinary individual in the NANA Region might be involved in one or two partnerships, while an umialik could afford perhaps five or six. Most people tried to have at least one partner from a different ecological zone. However, this was not always possible, especially for people who did not or could not attend the summer fairs.

Whether or not relationships strictly analogous to that of niuviġiik were found among neighboring ethnic groups is not clear from the literature. However, relationships exactly like that of niuviġiik are well known to have linked the Iñupiat to members of all neighboring peoples. Indeed, partnerships seem to have been just about as common across linguistic or ethnic borders as they were within them. According to my informants, Iñupiat from the NANA Region had partnerships with Gwich'in, with Koyukon, with Yup'ik-speaking peoples from Norton Sound, and with residents of Chukotka (see also Anderson 1974–75:68; Clark 1970:20–21, 1974:232, 235, 1977; Clark and

Clark 1976:196; Lucier 1995a; McKennan 1965:25, 63; Osgood 1936:132).[13] Presumably, wealthy Iñupiat living both north and south of the NANA Region were similarly well connected.

Kin Relationships

Kinship ties are those in which membership is based at least in part on the basis of biological relatedness and/or sexual intercourse (Burch 1975a:43–45; Levy 1952:2). The relationships between husband and wife, parents and children, siblings, cousins, in-laws, and the like are common examples of such connections. "Fictive" kinship ties are those in which membership is based on simulated biological relatedness and/or sexual intercourse. Adoption is one of the most common ways in which fictive kinship ties are established.

Kin relationships within the Iñupiaq sector of northwestern Alaska have been described in detail in a separate volume (Burch 1975a). Attention in that study was almost exclusively on the operation of kin relationships within national boundaries; no attention was paid to those involving people living in different countries. Here the emphasis is exactly the opposite, and the treatment is much more general.

The main difference in kin relationships operating between rather than within nations was the much lower activity level of the former. Obviously, in the absence of long-distance means of communication, siblings who lived 300 miles (480 kilometers) apart could hardly maintain as active a relationship as those living in the same village or district. The rights and obligations of kinship ideally were the same in both contexts, but they usually were extremely difficult, if not impossible, to realize in fact at the international level.

Relatives living in different countries, unlike partners, did not have the specific obligation to meet regularly and to exchange particularly desired goods. They might help one another, but they might not. However, in times of crisis, having relatives living in another country could be as advantageous as having partners there, since one could move there with one's family and expect to receive food, shelter, and protection.

The most interesting questions about kinship ties across national borders have less to do with how they operated than with how and why they were created in the first place and just how extensive they were. Unfortunately, hard information on these subjects for the early 19th century is in very short supply. In the following sections I attempt to draw some conclusions from the limited evidence available.

EMIGRATION

One way to establish kinship ties across national boundaries was for a person or family to move from one country to another, leaving a group of relatives behind. The available evidence indicates that international migration did occur, but it was rare and occurred in only a limited number of circumstances. Except in the case of intermarriage, which is discussed below, there had to be a preexisting relationship of some kind between an immigrant and someone in the receiving society in order for migration to occur. Without a guarantor, an immigrant, a family of immigrants, and even a large group of immigrants was almost certain to be either killed or forced into servitude.[14]

Two circumstances seem to have made emigration worth attempting. The first was when a man was in serious trouble in his own country, the usual causes being a blood feud or a dispute over a woman. Under such conditions the risks involved in moving to a foreign land might be less onerous than they would be in staying home. A troublemaker was more likely to be accepted, even with a guarantor, if he brought a wife and children with him than he was if he came alone.

The second circumstance that made emigration worth trying was severe famine in one's own country. There is one well-documented case where famine led to the permanent migration of a relatively large number of people. The disaster struck the Kulugruaġmiut of the Meade River valley on the Arctic Slope during the early years of the 19th century (Burch 1998a:369–372). Several families of refugees moved to the upper Noatak district, where they managed to persist as a relatively discrete community among the Nuataaġmiut. Informants who were descended from these people told me that when they were youngsters, nearly a century after the move, the Nuataaġmiut still regarded them as outsiders.

RESIDENTIAL MARRIAGES

The primary way in which kinship ties were established across national borders was through marriage. International marriages were of two main types, involuntary and voluntary.

An involuntary marriage occurred when a man from one society deliberately kidnapped a woman from another in order to take her for a wife or when a woman was captured during a raid and kept as a wife (Burch 1975a:83). I have heard accounts of both, although neither was very common. Within the NANA Region the former occurred much more frequently than the latter. Most women who were captured in raids were raped, tortured, and eventually killed. One would assume that some years had to pass after an abduction before a visit to the wife's homeland was undertaken, but I have no evidence on the matter.

Voluntary marriages were of two types, residential and nonresidential. A residential marriage was one in which the spouses lived together in the same house. A nonresidential marriage was one in which they did not. The focus here is on the former. Nonresidential marriage, or comarriage, is discussed separately below.

A voluntary residential marriage between individuals from different countries definitely created a positive link between both the individuals and the nations involved. As I noted in Chapter 1, however, there were a number of reasons why parents attempted to prevent their children from becoming involved in outside marriages. This was particularly true when the child went to live in a foreign country. Traditional Iñupiaq nations were family-oriented societies, and to lose a child plus the child's spouse and offspring was a major loss (Burch 1975a:293–295). On the other hand, if the child's spouse was the one who made the move, there was a gain. But immigrants were regarded with suspicion for years and probably even decades after their arrival; one could never know for sure whose side they would choose to support in the event of conflict.

Sometimes there were very good reasons to make an international marriage. The primary one was the difficulty of finding suitable spouses in small populations such as those in northwestern Alaska. Age and gender requirements could not always be met without breaking the incest taboo, which was absolute for siblings and very strong for first cousins. If one could not find a suitable spouse within one's own country, one had to look elsewhere. Going without a spouse was not considered a viable option due to the sharp division of labor between the sexes.

Another circumstance leading to international marriage was the extermination of a disproportionate number of people of one sex during a raid or battle (Swan 1965b). As noted in Chapter 2, this definitely occurred. Spouses for the survivors usually had to be sought outside. It was the opinion of at least one of my informants, Leonard Putuuraq Vestal (1969), that most wives who were acquired by men from the NANA Region under these circumstances came from the Seward Peninsula. No corresponding information about a major source of husbands has come to my attention.

Mutual attraction was the final factor leading to international marriages. Large numbers of young men and women from different countries met at trade fairs and other international gatherings (Keats 1970b; Stefansson 1914b:178). Some of them simply fell in love, and their parents could do little about it. According to my informants, many international marriages were affairs of the heart that rooted and blossomed at a trade fair.

An interesting question is the extent to which people might have become involved in international marriages as part of a deliberate policy of alliance formation or maintenance. Glenn Sheehan (1997:187–188) has raised this as a possibility, although he has not offered any evidence to support it. I agree that it might have made sense for an umialik to do this, particularly with the second or third wife in a polygynous marriage, but I also have no information relating to the point.

The kinship ties created through intermarriage involved general rights and responsibilities regarding support in time of need instead of the specific annual or semiannual duties required in partnerships. They were a kind of insurance, something to draw on in emergencies but not a matter requiring continual attention. For most people partnerships were a more productive form of international connection than kin relationships because the rights and obligations of membership were specifically laid out, whereas kin relationships were functionally diffuse.

Hard information on the frequency of international marriages in the early 19th century does not exist. As noted in Chapter 1, my impression is that the exogamy rate (for residential marriages) was probably less than 20 percent during the relevant period; the qualitative data available to me suggest that it was much lower than that. But let's just say that 10 percent of all residential marriages were across national borders. That strikes me as a very high frequency of international marriages. Theoretically, if international marriage continued at that rate over just a few generations, practically everyone would have had kin living abroad. If the intermarriage rate was higher than that, the number of international kinship ties would have been greater still.

Within nations, kinship ties that were not renewed and strengthened by the members of each generation eventually lapsed. As long as someone recalled the genealogical (including marital) connections involved, however, they could be reactivated at any time. That must have been true in the international sphere as well.

COMARRIAGES

Comarriage is a nonjudgmental term that refers to the Eskimo practice widely known in the West as "spouse exchange" or "wife trading" (Burch 1970b:159–162). Contrary to the popular Western view of the custom, comarriage was an institutionalized form of marriage, one that carried lifelong obligations for the individuals involved. In the early 19th century these were particularly important in the international sphere.

A comarriage was established when the members of one husband–wife relationship exchanged sexual partners with the members of another (for further details and references see Burch 1970b, 1975a:106–111). The various roles and relationships resulting from this arrangement are shown in Figure 3, in which the equal signs indicate regular residential marriages and the double arrows indicate the exchange relationships. (The terms in the relationships column are expressed in the dual number.) The four participants were

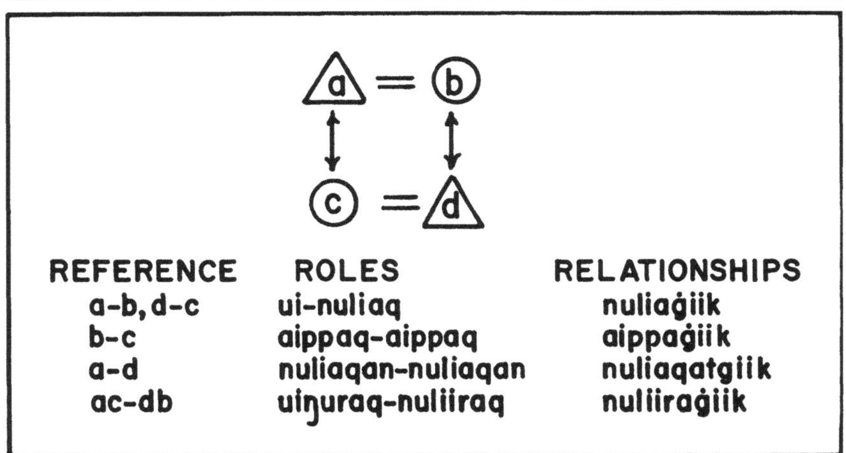

3. The roles and relationships involved in comarriage.

known collectively as *nuliaqatigiich* (pl.). All children ever born to any of them, either before, because of, or after the exchange, were *qataŋutigiich* (pl.), or cosiblings.[15] Even if the sexual exchange occurred only once, and whether or not any of the residential spouses remained together, these relationships lasted throughout the lifetimes of the individuals involved.

Nuliaqatigiich ordinarily did not live in the same settlement, although there was no rule against it.[16] However, as far as I have been able to determine, the two marital pairs involved were not even from the same country in a large number of cases. Most comarriages, like partnerships, were established for the explicit purpose of having links with individuals and families in other countries upon whom one could depend for help in time of need. The responsibilities were much more diffuse than in the case of partnerships, however, being simply the general obligation to help out if asked. In addition to seeing one another at trade fairs and messenger feasts, cospouses and cosiblings visited one another from time to time, occasionally for periods of several months or even whole seasons. Cohusbands or cosiblings who found themselves on opposite sides of a battle were supposed to refrain from harming one another, although they were not required to protect one another.

A variation on the comarriage theme was what I call "comarriage by default." This occurred when a man and a woman had sexual relations outside their residential marriages without the knowledge or consent of the residential spouses. Although the residential spouses might not know they had been jilted, technically they were made cospouses by the affair. More significantly in the present context, any children either of the lovers or their spouses ever had automatically became *qataŋutigiik* (dual). These were the "secret siblings" of Iñupiaq Alaska whose identities were known initially only to the man and woman whose actions created the relationships between or among them. As the children became adults, the knowledgeable parent told them the names of their cosiblings living in other countries. They were to keep this information to themselves, but if they were ever in a difficult situation involving members of another nation where they had a qataŋun, they were to say that person's name aloud and announce that he or she was a cosibling. The qataŋun was then obliged to protect the stranger, to keep him or her properly clothed and fed, and to see to it that he or she was returned home safely, even if the two had never met before. According to the stories, most of the drifted seal hunters who made it back to shore in a foreign land and survived did so only through the intervention and assistance of a qataŋun.

Comarriage seems to have been primarily an Eskimo institution. That is, it was practiced among both Inuit and Yup'ik speakers but not necessarily among their Athapaskan or Chukchi neighbors. However, the Chukchi allegedly practiced "group marriage" (Bogoras 1904–9:602–607). This may have been similar (although not identical) to the Eskimo custom, and it may have filled a similar role in international affairs. I have not seen references to comarriages among the Koyukon or Gwich'in, but oral accounts indicate that there were at least some such connections between various Athapaskan peoples and the Iñupiat.[17]

ADOPTION

Adoption is the creation of relationships between and among individuals who are not connected through sexual intercourse and/or biological relatedness but who act as though they were. Adoption can take a variety of forms, but in most parts of the world and in northwestern Alaska specifically it usually consisted of a married couple acquiring another's child and rearing it as their own.

Adoption within national boundaries was common throughout northern Beringia but particularly among the Iñupiat (Bogoras 1904–9:556–560; Burch 1975a:129–131; Loyens 1966:62–63; McKennan 1965:52; Nelson 1899:290). The question here is, How much adoption occurred between members of different nations? Sheehan (1997:188, quoting Bockstoce 1988, vol. 2:410), citing examples recorded in Rochefort Maguire's Barrow journals, shows that at least some adoption crossed not only national boundaries but also the (apparently) Gwich'in–Iñupiaq ethnic boundary. Other evidence confirms that at least some adoption occurred between Koyukon and Iñupiat as well (Anderson et al. 1998:104; Clark 1970:19; Clark and Clark 1976:210). Sheehan also raises the interesting possibility that most international adoption may have involved umialġich. He is probably correct, but neither one of us has much evidence to support that hypothesis.

The limited available evidence indicates that international and interethnic adoption did occur in early-19th-century northern Beringia but at a very low rate compared to intranational adoption. The international ties created through adoption may have been somewhat stronger than ordinary kinship ties, although in other respects they were the same. It is important to note that, in contrast to the situation in the 21st-century United States and many other countries, Iñupiaq adoption was as much a link between the two sets of adults—the givers and receivers—as it was between the receiving couple and the child.

Discussion

The various kinds of relationships discussed above constituted the social mechanisms through which friendly international relations in early-19th-century northern Beringia were carried out. There were thousands of these relationships linking individuals and families and, therefore, nations throughout the Iñupiaq language zone and between the Iñupiaq language zone and all of the surrounding ones. Of the various possibilities, partnerships carried the greatest functional load because they included specific responsibilities that had to be met according to a fairly precise seasonal or annual schedule. The various kinship ties constituted a kind of social insurance. They were there if needed, but apart from that they did not require much time or effort.

It is no longer possible to chart on a map the international linkages provided by these relationships during the early 19th century. However, enough evidence exists to indicate that the chart would have been an extremely complex network of nodes and lines spread out over a huge geographic area. If we were to focus on this aspect of the system and ignore all other kinds of evidence, we would find it almost impossible to believe that the hostilities described in Chapter 2 could have taken place.

Getting There

Partners and relatives living in different estates usually had to travel considerable distances to meet. In contrast to the interdistrict movements involved in hostile relations, which were carried out by men traveling light, those involved in friendly relations usually were carried out by entire families whose members were encumbered with a considerable quantity of goods. These goods consisted of the food and equipment people needed for material support along the way and a quantity of furs, skins, and other items intended as gifts and/or trade goods at their destination. Full understanding of how the system worked requires at least some knowledge of the means the Iñupiat had at their disposal to transport both themselves and their possessions during these expeditions.

Overland Travel

Overland travel in summer and early fall was carried out on foot, usually with the aid of pack dogs, with almost no technological support. This type of movement was important in the yearly subsistence cycle of many of the Iñupiaq nations of northwestern Alaska but was relevant to international affairs primarily as a limiting factor. In the absence of effective means of overland transportation during the summer and early fall months international trade had to be conducted primarily via waterways during those seasons. Most interdistrict overland travel for peaceful purposes was undertaken during the six to eight months per year when the ground was snow covered and the lakes and rivers were frozen, making the waterways pretty much an extension of the land surface.[18]

The primary conveyance for winter travel was the railed, or basket, sled (*uniapiaq*), in which the bed was raised some distance above relatively thin runners and which had a rail on either side (see Plate 6).[19] Such sleds generally were 8–10 feet (3 meters) long and 16–30 inches (14–75 centimeters) wide, with the details of size and shape varying to some extent from one district to another. Sleds were made of carefully shaped pieces of wood joined or mortised together and held with wooden pins and rawhide lashings.[20] Shoes for the runners varied according to snow conditions and the availability of suitable raw materials (ivory, whale jawbone, birch wood). A large, well-made basket sled could probably bear a load of 600–800 pounds (270–360 kilograms) (Dall 1870:25), but the amount that actually could be drawn depended on the quality of the trail over which the sled had to pass, the number of people and dogs available to pull and push it, the temperature, and the speed with which people wanted to travel.[21]

The typical dog team in the early 19th century was very small, two to four dogs being the norm on the coast but only one or two inland. Dall (1870:25) estimated that dogs in good condition could pull about 100 pounds (180 kilograms) apiece with the help of the driver. Edward Nelson (1899:206), on the other hand, said that a load of 300–400 pounds (135–180 kilograms) required seven dogs, but I suspect that he wished to travel faster than the ordinary Iñupiaq family did.

Working dogs used in the early 19th century were large, weighing perhaps 75–100 pounds (35–45 kilograms). They usually worked alongside people when pulling a sled. An example is a group of Kobuk River Natives George Stoney saw traveling on a tributary of the Alatna River valley in late March or

6. An Iñupiaq family from Kotzebue Sound with a large basket sled. Photographed by E. W. Nelson at Saint Michael, ca. 1880. Nelson Collection, negative no. 3845. Courtesy of the Smithsonian Institution, National Museum of Natural History.

early April 1886: "This party numbered forty souls, and had fifty dogs and twelve sleds. Some of these people presented a rather singular appearance, their sleds being drawn by men, women and dogs all hitched up together. A woman with a child on her back and a single dog with three or four puppies playing beside it would drag a sled, while the man behind pushed and guided, yelling at the single dog as lustily as though his team comprised a dozen or more" (1900:576). Since the Iñupiat usually traveled in family groups when moving from one settlement to another, this may be considered a typical scene. Most groups on their way to a messenger feast would have been similar to this one, except perhaps a bit larger. In reasonably good snow and weather conditions such an aggregation probably progressed at the rate of about 2 miles (3 kilometers) per hour. Berthold Seemann estimated that a typical day's travel was about 25 miles (40 kilometers), but he did not say how many hours it took to go that far or how good the trail had to be to do it (1853, vol. 2:60–61).

Water Travel

The Iñupiat had three basic kinds of boat: a large open freight boat, or umiaq; a decked-over hunting canoe, or kayak (*qayaq*); and, on the Kobuk and Selawik Rivers, a kayaklike but only partially decked canoe (*qayaġiaq*). Of these, only umiat were of any significance in international travel. The time for Umiaq travel extended from late May to early October in most of the interior, from early June to late October or early November in Bering Strait and on the northern Bering Sea, and from July to mid-October on the southern Chukchi Sea.[22]

A traveling umiaq, as opposed to the smaller whaling craft, ranged between about 30–40 feet (7.5–12 meters) in length, 5–8 feet (1.5–2.5 meters) in width, and 2–3 feet (60–90 centimeters) in depth.[23] The draft, even when fully loaded, was less than 2 feet (60 centimeters). Umiat tapered uniformly toward both bow and stern, had flat floors, and usually had four or five seats (see Plate 7). The wooden frame was made of carefully selected and shaped components that were dovetailed and lashed together with sealskin twine or baleen. A cover of bearded sealskins or, in Bering Strait, split walrus hides, sewn together with double waterproof seams, was stretched over the frame. A single mast was set in the floor forward of the center and stabilized with two guylines to both bow and stern. In general, these boats tended to be larger—both longer and wider—in Bering Strait and Norton Sound than they were in the NANA Region, although a few wealthy Nuataaġmiut had boats that must have been at least 40 feet (12 meters) long or even longer. The Iñupiat living on the Arctic Slope probably had the smallest craft used for international travel.

The basic propulsion of an umiaq was provided by paddlers, rarely more than four per side and usually fewer than that in loaded boats. In crosswinds or in river currents a single oar was often employed as well to help keep the craft on course. Because of their shape umiat could not beat into the wind. If travelers were headed into even a moderate breeze, they had to either go ashore and await more favorable conditions or else put their dogs ashore and have them tow the boat along the beach. When traveling downwind they hoisted a large square-rigged sail usually made of several caribou hides. When traveling downriver, which they usually did just after the spring flood, they simply floated, paddling just hard enough to maintain steerageway. The return trip usually required that the boat be towed by dogs and people, although sails were hoisted whenever there was a favorable wind. Guidance in all contexts was provided by a senior man wielding a wide paddle from the stern seat.

The Iñupiat were blessed with waterways that, in general, are conducive to tracking large, heavily laden boats. The coastline, for the most part, consists of smooth gravel beaches, although rocky shores and points occur in some areas. An onshore wind and heavy surf brought coastal travel to a halt, particularly around points of land, but in many areas it was possible for travelers to portage an umiaq and its contents to calmer waters in lagoons behind the outer beach ridge and then proceed on their way.

7. A traditional-style umiaq in the lower Noatak River. Photographed by E. S. Curtis, 1927. Courtesy of the Library of Congress, negative no. z62-89846.

River bottoms in northwestern Alaska characteristically are full of long gravel bars. These are generally covered with water in spring, which is when most Iñupiat descended the rivers. The bars are usually exposed in late summer, however, which is when people returned upstream; if the water was moderately low, the bars were conducive to tracking. If rain caused the water level to rise above the gravel bars during the ascent, the only recourse was to track the boat against the current by walking through the thick brush growing along the riverbank.[24] Very low water also impeded upstream navigation, requiring boats to be dragged over gravel bars, guided around boulders, and/or unloaded, carried, and reloaded far more often than would have been necessary otherwise.

Early Western observers, most of whom were professional sailors, wrote of the umiaq with grudging admiration. While noting that the boats did not handle well in a wind, they marveled at how a craft light enough for just a few men to lift could transport such an enormous payload in the water. Estimates of just what that payload was vary widely. Vilhjalmur Stefansson (1944:37, 1951:106) put it at a ton or a ton and a half (900–1,360 kilograms), although I believe he was referring to the relatively small boats used on the Arctic coast. Stoney (n.d.:162), whose primary experience was with boats used on the

Kobuk and Noatak Rivers, put the figure at 5–7 tons (4,500–6,350 kilograms). In 1959 Doris Saario (1959:7) measured the carrying capacity of an approximately 30-foot (9-meter) umiaq used in the very shallow waters of the Kivalina and Wulik Rivers at 2.5–3 tons (2,270–2,720 kilograms). Harrison Thornton, whose experience was with the large boats at Wales, stated that they were "generally from 35 to 40 feet [10 to 12 meters] long, about 8 feet [2.4 meters] wide at amidships, and approximately 4 feet [1.2 meters] deep." These boats, he said, could carry 15–20 persons or about 5 tons (4,500 kilograms) of freight (Thornton 1931:125).[25] Maguire, in 1854, estimated the size of a Kakligmiut (Point Barrow) boat as being about 30 feet (9 meters) long, 7 feet (2 meters) wide, and 3–3.5 feet (1 meter) high (Bockstoce 1988, vol. 2:358). In 1838 Kashevarov said that the boats of the Kakligmiut (of Point Barrow) could hold up to 12 people (VanStone 1977:89).

Another way to estimate the carrying capacity of an umiaq is to count the number of people in an otherwise empty craft.[26] Several of the early explorers made such counts, which ranged from a low of 7 to a high of 23 people per boat (Beechey 1831, vol. 1:418, 439; Bockstoce 1988, vol. 2:452; Collinson 1889:75; Kotzebue 1821, vol. 1:204, 232; Seemann 1853, vol. 2:55; VanStone 1977:20, 53, 58, 59). Altogether, they saw 404 people in 29 boats, for an average boatload of 14 people. Since all but two of those people were men, one could reasonably multiply that number by an average of 140 pounds (64 kilograms) per person, which yields a total of 1,960 pounds (890 kilograms). Assuming a higher average weight per person would of course increase that total. This calculation concerns a boat's absolute minimum carrying capacity, since people were not piled into boats the same way camping gear, food supplies, and trade goods were.

Since a precise quantitative estimate of the carrying capacity of a 19th-century umiaq is beyond reach, I now abandon the effort to make one and present two qualitative views instead. The first is a general observation made by C. L. Hooper in 1881.

> *The carrying capacity of the oomiac is enormous. When used in traveling it contains a tent of drilling or deer-skin, guns, traps, spears, bows and arrows, a kyack, a seal-skin poke filled with water, a quantity of dried meat or fish, and, in the warm season, a lot of birds and eggs; a sled, several pairs of snow-shoes, a fish-net and some smaller nets for catching birds, a shaman drum, and several bags of skin clothing. Perhaps, in addition, a stock of oil, whalebone [baleen], ivory, or furs is taken along for the purpose of trading.*
>
> *The personnel consists of three or four men, about as many women, and two or three children. Add to these two or three dogs, each with a litter of puppies, and some idea may be formed of what a traveling oomiac contains. The working dogs*

are generally left on shore to follow on foot, which they do, keeping up a continual and most dismal howl. If the wind comes ahead, and the natives desire for any reason to continue their journey, they catch and harness the dogs, and attach them to the oomiac after the manner of a canal-boat and horses, and continue on their way, making four or five miles an hour. When they wish to stop for a night or day they land and pitch the tents; the oomiac is unloaded and turned up on the shore, and the Innuits are as much at home as if in their winter houses. [1884:102]

The second quote is with reference to a specific umiaq owned by some Kiŋikmiut (Wales people) that Frederick Beechey observed being unloaded on Chamisso Island on September 6, 1826.

We watched their landing, and were astonished at the rapidity with which they pitched their tents, settled themselves, and transferred to their new habitation the contents of the baidars (umiat), which they drew out of the sea and turned bottom upwards. On visiting their abode an hour after they landed, every thing was in as complete order as if they had been established there a month, and scarcely any thing was wanting to render their situation comfortable. No better idea could have been conveyed to us of the truly independent manner in which this tribe wander about from place to place, transporting their houses, and every thing necessary to their comfort, than that which was afforded on this occasion. Nor were we less struck with the number of articles which their ingenuity finds the means of disposing in their boats, and which, had we not seen them disembarked, we should have doubted the possibility of their having been crammed into them. From two of these they landed fourteen persons, eight tent poles, forty deer skins, two kyacks, many hundred weight of fish, numerous skins of oil, earthen jars for cooking, two living foxes, ten large dogs, bundles of lances, harpoons, bows and arrows, a quantity of whalebone, skins full of clothing, some immense nets made of hide for taking small whales and porpoises, eight broad planks, masts, sails, paddles, &c., besides sea-horse (walrus) hides and teeth, and a variety of nameless articles always to be found among the Esquimaux. [1831, vol. 1:404–405]

This is as close to a list of the contents of an early 19th-century umiaq as we shall ever have; it indicates even more clearly than raw numbers can the carrying capacity of these vessels.

Venues

Partners and relatives could visit one another more or less any time, but they came together primarily at the so-called trade fairs and messenger feasts. These two venues, particularly the fairs, were also the only contexts in northwestern Alaska where people regularly could meet complete strangers under peaceful circumstances.

Messenger Feasts

"Messenger feast" is the English name for a festival in which the residents of one village invited people from one or more others to come for several days of feasting, trading, and entertainment.[27] The "messenger" part of the name signifies the fact that invitations were conveyed to the guests by messengers sent from the host community. Because of superficial similarities between messenger feasts and a type of festival held on the Northwest Coast, they are often referred to in English as a "potlatch." My Iñupiaq sources referred to this type of feast in their own language as *aqpataq*.[28]

Messenger feasts originated at some time in the legendary past, and they continued to be held into the early 20th century (Curtis 1930:168–177, 197–198). Christian missionaries, who arrived in the NANA Region in the late 1890s, regarded the dancing and other ceremonies associated with the feasts as being the work of the devil and consequently did everything they could to prevent them from taking place (Alġaqsruutit 1983:remarks by Lena Sours; Hawkes 1913:2; Northwest Iñupiat Elders Conference 1983:#83-30, 1). Eventually, the missionaries were successful, and the last messenger feasts conducted along traditional lines apparently were held in the 1920s.

Messenger feasts were held among all of the Eskimo-speaking groups of Alaska except the residents of the Bering Strait islands (Kingston 1996; Lantis 1947:68). They were also held among the Koyukon and between the Koyukon and the Iñupiat (Attla and Attla 1991; Clark 1974:239; Hadley 1960). I have not read about them being held among the Gwich'in, but Di'hąįį Gwich'in were invited to messenger feasts by their Iñupiaq neighbors from time to time. Since they ordinarily reciprocated in kind, at least those particular Gwich'in must have known what messenger feasts were all about (Edington and Edington 1930:292–297; McKennan 1965:25). There were many variations in the details from one ethnic region to another, and the event fit into the annual economic, festival, and ceremonial cycles in different ways.[29] However, messenger feasts played the same basic part in international affairs throughout northwestern Alaska. They have not been reported for the Asiatic Eskimos or Chukchi or between them and residents of Alaska (Krupnik 1996b).

The feasts were structured around partnerships, particularly those involving umialġich. People in the host village did not issue a general invitation to the residents of another village. Rather, the invitations were directed from specific individuals in one village to their partners in another. The invitees brought other members of their (extended) family along, so that the number of people involved could become fairly large, but individual partnerships formed the foundation on which the system was built. No rule stated that messenger feasts had to involve people from two different nations, but in practice it appears that they usually did.

Within a nation the residents of one village could invite people from another for feasts and ceremonies whenever they wanted, and intervillage gatherings were not uncommon. However, such occasions did not include the rituals associated with messenger feasts, and partnerships ordinarily were not involved.

TIMING OF THE FEASTS

In principle, messenger feasts could be held at any time of year. In reality, practical considerations (seasonal variations in weather, hunting and fishing needs, trade fairs) meant that the overwhelming majority took place during the short days of late November to early January. This was the holiday season in northwestern Alaska (Simpson 1875:262; Stefansson 1944:24).

The arrival of the holiday season did not necessarily mean that a messenger feast would be held. Other festivals might be held then instead of or in addition to messenger feasts. In the Yup'ik language sector several other festivals were held during the short days of early winter (Nelson 1899:358). But messenger feasts were more likely to be held then among the Iñupiat than at any other time of year. When Koyukon and Iñupiat hosted one another, however, the feasts tended to be later in the season, even as late as March or early April (Cantwell 1889a:61). The residents of the islands of Bering Strait, the two Diomedes and King Island, could not have messenger feasts in early winter because ice conditions prevented international travel in the region at that time of year (Ray 1967:378–379). Although the residents of these islands had a holiday season, they may never have been involved in messenger feasts because of the travel problem.

CONDUCT OF THE FEASTS

Messenger feasts have been described in some detail in a number of sources.[30] A complete review of this material would require a volume in itself, and it is inappropriate even to attempt one here. Suffice it to say that these sources reveal considerable variation in how messenger feasts were conducted even within the NANA Region, and there is even greater variation if adjacent regions are included.[31] The following account is limited to a brief summary of how the feast was conducted in the region of primary concern in this volume.

The decision to hold a messenger feast had to be made no later than August because of the extensive preparations required. On most occasions the negotiations leading up to a feast were probably begun a year or two in advance of the actual event. The wealthiest man of a small settlement or of a local family in a large one initiated the discussions and made the final decision, but he normally did so in consultation with others who would be involved. It was he who organized the feast and who was considered its "boss," or ataniq.

Each man got to invite one guest (*aqpataq*), virtually always a partner, and in every case I have heard of or read about all of the guests were from the same village. The number of official invitees normally ranged between about six and ten, which, along with accompanying spouses, children, and other dependents, could mean a guest list of anywhere from about 40 to 100 people.

Preparations for the hosts (*kivgiqsuat*) consisted of accumulating a greater than normal surplus of food during the late summer and fall hunting and fishing seasons and constructing a special qargi, one much larger than the ordinary village qargi. It often had two rows of benches around its perimeter, one perhaps 2 feet (60 centimeters) above the floor and another 3–4 feet (90–120 centimeters) above that. Since the building was to be used only for messenger feasts, it was not constructed with the customary craftsmanship or concern for heat retention. Many buildings were used only once and then torn down, but a few were used over periods of several years.

Two messengers (*kivgak*, dual) were selected to carry the invitations. Selection of these messengers was the prerogative of the ataniq, although, as in all things, the choice was usually made only after extensive consultation.

Being a messenger was a major responsibility. It entailed being away from home for an extended period, it sometimes involved arduous travel, and it frequently exposed the incumbents to physical danger from both human and nonhuman sources. Messengers were thus usually men young enough to be strong and vigorous yet old enough to be knowledgeable about both the country through which they had to travel and the subtleties of international diplomacy. Just when they were sent off depended on how far they had to go.

The messengers carried a stick (*ayaupiaq*) about 4 feet (120 centimeters) long that served as both a badge of office and a mnemonic device. In the latter capacity it bore a symbol for each of the individuals who were to be invited to the feast. In some cases these symbols were colored lines, while in others they consisted of small pieces of dried meat impaled on the stick, one piece per guest.

Messengers traveled openly until they approached their destination. Then they resorted to stealth, hiding their dogs and sled and sneaking up on the village. When the opportunity presented itself they ran to the nearest house or the qargi and entered uninvited. Since they could have been mistaken for raiders this was a dangerous thing to do. According to Charles Lucier (1997:318), even when the status of the messengers was correctly interpreted, they were often "harassed and mauled terribly," at least during the first few minutes after their arrival. In any event, their arrival created an uproar, and everyone gathered to find out what was happening.

The invitations were issued formally and publicly. When everyone had gathered, usually in the qargi, the messengers were brought before the crowd. In some districts they were separated from the villagers by a curtain made of skins. One of the messengers then stood at attention, stamped one foot on the floor, and announced that so-and-so in his home village had invited a particular individual in this village to a messenger feast and that he wanted his guest to bring him a particular kind of food. The first invitation was from the ataniq in the host village. When the messenger announced the name of the first guest he declared him to be the ataniq of the entire guest contingent and instructed him to take charge of organizing the others. The named invitee came forward and accepted the invitation. If the invitation was symbolized by a piece of meat, the invitee indicated his acceptance by coming forward and eating it. The messengers then worked their way down the marks on the sticks, identifying each host and guest until all had been named. If an individual did not have the resources to support his participation that year, he would decline.

The prospective guests (*aiyugaakkat*) then began their own preparations. In addition to getting their affairs in order and gathering supplies of meat and fish to consume on their journey, they had to compile a surplus to take to their hosts, any items they wanted to give to their hosts, and anything they wanted to offer for sale.

The most problematic items were the special foods or other goods requested by the prospective hosts (for an example see Dall 1870:154–157). A great deal of humor was involved here. These requests were invariably for obscure foods that were almost impossible to supply because they were either out of season (e.g., fresh salmon), not native to the invitees' estate (e.g., seal liver from an inland district), or in a form in which they were rarely if ever prepared or kept (e.g., rancid ground squirrel fat). Guests frequently tried to fulfill their obligation by acquiring a particularly bizarre or foul-tasting form of the food requested. When Western foods and tools first appeared in northwestern Alaska they made a major contribution to this portion of the messenger feast agenda.

In some districts the messengers stayed with the invitees and then accompanied them to the host village, but if they did, then the hosts would have had difficulty fulfilling any peculiar requests for food. In other districts the messengers went home ahead of the guests to report to the prospective hosts the results of their effort.

The messengers returned with a stick from the ataniq of the guest contingent similar to the one they had carried with the invitations. When they arrived home they went immediately to the qargi, where everyone gathered to hear their report. When all were assembled the messengers told each host the result of his invitation, beginning with the ataniq and working down the list.

In each case they announced the special kind of food that the guest wished to have at the feast.

The trip to a feast required a substantial investment of time and effort. Akunigmiut going to Barrow, for example, faced a one-way trip of nearly 300 miles (380 kilometers) as the crow flies, probably double that on the ground, and they had to cross two major mountain ranges in the process. Trips to neighboring countries on the Kobuk or Selawik Rivers were not as onerous, although a one-way trip of 50–100 miles (80–160 kilometers) could be required even there. Because of the time of year and the high latitude, all or most of the travel had to be done in twilight or darkness.[32] Stormy weather frequently brought movement to a halt, and people who had to travel through mountain passes were subject to the threat of avalanches and rockfalls.

Meanwhile, the prospective hosts were busy hunting and fishing, organizing their food supplies, sending out trading expeditions for what they needed but did not have, and preparing items they wished to give or offer for sale to their guests. They also put the final touches on the qargi and its decorations, composed songs, choreographed new dances, and rehearsed everything they planned to do with and for the guests. The hosts could guess approximately when the guest contingent would arrive, and they kept a constant lookout for it.

The guests halted some distance away from the host village and encamped. Estimates of this distance in the various accounts range from 2 to 15 miles (3 to 25 kilometers). If the messengers had accompanied the guests, they continued on to the village.

When the guests had encamped all the young men of the village organized to go out and greet them (*paaq-*), usually in their finest clothes. They marched out together in a line. When the men reached the guests' camp they asked each person what kind of food he wanted to eat when he arrived at the village. After the responses were noted, young men of both the host and guest contingents raced back to the village. Considerable prestige accrued to the winner of this race, who went straight to the qargi. His party, whether host or guest, was then said to "own" the qargi. When all the racers were in the village they reported to the hosts what their partners wanted to eat when they arrived. After the report was made the host ataniq told the guest runners what the schedule would be, and they returned to their people.

The full body of guests decamped for the village at the appointed time the next day. When they arrived they found the villagers dancing and singing in front of the houses. The visitors halted and sat on their sleds until the performance was over. Guests did not have to lodge with their partners, so as soon as the entertainment was finished villagers dashed into the crowd of visitors and tried to drag people to their own home. Since representatives of several different dwellings could grab a single guest, and since the members of a given family could be dragged in separate directions, this was often a chaotic scene. According to all reports, it was also one enjoyed enormously by the participants. Eventually, the guests were divided among the houses, and calm was restored. Then the visitors' dogs were tied and fed, the sleds were unloaded, and everyone prepared for the evening's festivities.

Everyone went to the qargi at a time chosen by the host ataniq. A prolonged period of dancing and singing followed, with group dances, special performances, special songs, and various forms of entertainment provided by each side for the other. Many dances involved both guests and hosts, especially those who were partners. When people began to tire, the ataniq announced that it was time to eat. The guests sat in a circle on the floor, and each host formally presented his guest and the members of his family some of the specific kind of food they had requested the day before. This probably was the time when the special foods requested at the outset were exchanged, which made it the most humorous part of the entire affair. The hosts then joined the circle and partook of the same meal, which was served by specially designated servers. When dinner was over everyone went home to sleep.

Much of the next day was spent doing chores, visiting, exchanging presents, and playing football. Football in the context of a messenger feast was not the violent affair it sometimes was in other situations. Women and children as well as men played, and games often went on for hours.

Evening brought another round of dancing and feasting but with important differences from the night before. Instead of a wide array of more or less ordinary dances, this was the time for the special messenger feast dance, the wolf dance, which was performed for the guests by the hosts (Curtis 1930:174; Koranda 1964:18–19; for sketches of the wolf dance see Phebus 1972:109–114). Instead of special items of food, the subsequent banquet featured the full array of foods that the hosts had collected for the occasion. These were brought into the qargi in bowls and on platters and placed in the center of the building. Helpers then served individual portions to the participants. After the feast the first round of open-market trading commenced.

The balance of the affair continued at a somewhat reduced but nevertheless vigorous pace. Days were devoted to visiting, trading, and playing football, and evenings were spent feasting, dancing, and engaging in the wide variety of games and contests the Natives had available to them. When food was about to run out, the guests headed for home.

DISCUSSION

A messenger feast was obviously more than a single large meal, which is what the English name for it implies. Rather, it was a series of rituals, dances, songs, feasts, material exchanges, games, and other activities linked together. It was also an enormously time consuming and expensive event to prepare for and conduct on the part of both the hosts and the guests, often leaving both groups short of food for the rest of the winter. On the other hand, messenger feasts reinforced important bonds across international boundaries, provided opportunities for useful exchanges of goods, and usually seem to have been enjoyed by all.

A messenger feast was not a context in which new international connections were established. It was, however, an effective mechanism for renewing and strengthening friendly ties that already existed. Since several of these events were held every year, year after year, the Iñupiat obviously found their benefits to be worth their cost.

It would be impossible to show diagrammatically the full geographic range of international connections maintained through messenger feasts. I do not have enough information to do so, but if I did, the resulting map would be so complex as to be incomprehensible. Instead, I illustrate the general point with a single example, the Akuniġmiut of the central Kobuk River valley. This nation was chosen for three reasons: (1) its central location within northwestern Alaska, (2) the quality of the information available, and (3) the ages of the primary sources. The latter consist of my own informant, Frank Kutvak Glover, who was born in 1886, and Ira Purkeypile's informant, Charley Uluġaaġruk Wood, who was born around 1850 (Glover 1970a; Wood 1931). Information provided by the latter, particularly, provides time depth that I cannot duplicate for any other nation with regard to this particular matter.

The information is summarized in Map 12. The background is a political map of northwestern Alaska ca. 1800. The shading shows the geographic extent of the primary study area. Superimposed on the foregoing is a set of lines connecting Akuniġmiut country with the estates of the ten nations whose members are reported to have exchanged messenger feasts with the Akuniġmiut in the early and mid-19th century. As the map indicates, the total range of these connections spans more than 500 miles (800 kilometers) from north to south and about 300 miles (480 kilometers) from east to west. When it is understood that every nation whose estate is shown on this map was connected to several others in the same way, the complexity of the overall system becomes apparent.

It is important to keep in mind the fact that a messenger feast did not involve all of the members of one nation inviting all of the members of another one to a feast. Rather, it consisted of the wealthiest individuals in one village (or a few neighboring villages) inviting their personal partners in another, with the settlements concerned being in different countries. It

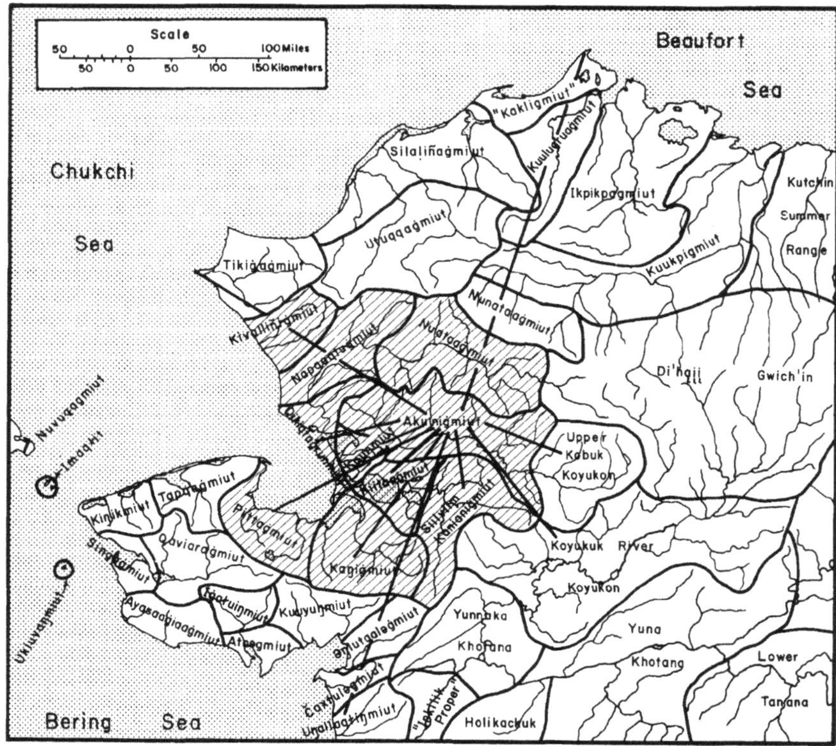

12. International connections maintained by the Akuniġmiut by means of messenger feasts. The shaded area is the NANA Region.

should also be understood that invitations were expected to be reciprocated. Thus, if some Akuniġmiut invited their Tikiġaġmiut partners to a feast on the Kobuk one year, the latter were expected to return the favor in some subsequent year. Theoretically, this reciprocal hosting continued more or less indefinitely.

Another important fact is that any number of settlements in a nation could be involved in a messenger feast, either as hosts or guests, in a given year. For example, the residents of the Akuniġmiut settlement of Qayaina might hold a feast for some Tikiġaġmiut families at the same time that other Akuniġmiut families living at Qalugraitchiaq were attending a messenger feast hosted by Pittaġmiut. On the other hand, during bad years people could not participate in messenger feasts at all as either hosts or guests. Both roles required a substantial surplus of food. If one did not exist, people had to worry about survival, not international diplomacy.

A final issue raised by Map 12 is the fact that sometimes both the messengers and the people they invited had to travel through one or more foreign estates on the way to their destinations. Given the extent and nature of international hostility in northwestern Alaska, one has to wonder how they could do this, particularly if one of the intervening estates belonged to a nation whose members were on the list of active enemies. For example, how did the Nuataaġmiut react to a party of Akuniġmiut crossing their estate on their way to a feast at Barrow? In view of the long history of hostility between these two nations and given the vulnerability of a party that included women, children, and elders, one would think that the temptation to attack would have been almost irresistible. This is one point I actually did think to inquire about in the field. I was never particularly satisfied with the answers I got because they seemed too simple, but they were very consistent with one another. If I understood my sources correctly, getting permission to travel through the estate of an intervening nation, whether enemy or friend, either to issue an invitation or to attend a messenger feast was not a problem. The time of year and the distinctive characteristics of the traveling parties made it obvious that they were on peaceful errands, and the privilege of free passage was automatically granted.

Trade Fairs

Trade fairs were major international gatherings of people that were held annually for the purposes of trade and a variety of recreational activities (Glover 1970c; Keats 1970b; Smith 1970; Swan 1970). Within the Iñupiaq-language sector of northwestern Alaska they were held every summer at Point Spencer on Bering Strait, at Sisualik on Kotzebue Sound, at Sullivik on the Northwest Coast, and at Niġliq at the mouth of the Colville River. They are often referred to in Iñupiaq as *katŋut*, meaning peaceful gatherings of people from different nations.[33] They contrasted with *katirut*, which were gatherings of people from different settlements within the same country. Other terms for a fair were *niuviġiaq*, an occasion during which niuviq-type exchanges occurred, and *taaqsiġiaq*, an occasion during which buying and selling on the open market took place.

THE SISUALIK FAIR

The largest fair in the Iñupiaq-language sector of northwestern Alaska and the only regular fair within the NANA Region was the one held every summer at Sisualik, which is situated near the end of a long sand spit located in the northeastern corner of Kotzebue Sound.[34] This is an excellent location for such a gathering for three reasons. First, it is situated at a place where three major rivers (the Noatak, Kobuk, and Selawik) enter Kotzebue Sound just a few miles apart, providing easy access to people living in the interior. Second, it is located at a spot that is reached easily from coastal districts as far apart as Point Hope to the north and Bering Strait to the south. Finally, large quantities of fish could be caught during the summer at Sisualik; thus, a large number of people could gather there for a week or two without much risk of running out of food.

Sisualik was located in the heart of Qikiqtaġruŋmiut country. However, for about two months each summer both Sisualik and the routes ordinarily taken to and from it were considered neutral ground, much like United Nations properties in New York and Geneva are today. People could go to and return from the fair without being under threat of attack, although the truce was sometimes broken when people who stayed late were on their homeward journey.

The Sisualik fair has been described superficially by a number of observers. However, it was never described at all during the first half of the 19th century or in any detail during the second. Dorothy Jean Ray has explained the deficiency for the earlier period as being due to the fact that the fair was probably "only a very small local gathering at that time" (1975b:98). According to my sources, the fair was at least as large then as it was later on.

The reason that Westerners did not describe the fair is because they were aboard relatively large sailing ships, which could not maneuver among the extensive shoals in the northeastern corner of Kotzebue Sound.[35] They all stayed in the deeper water near Chamisso Island, which is about 50 miles (80 kilometers) southeast of Sisualik. A detachment from Beechey's expedition did get close to Sisualik in the early 19th century, but it apparently traveled along the Baldwin Peninsula rather than the Sisualik side of the entrance to Hotham Inlet.[36] Later on, small American vessels that visited Kotzebue Sound for the specific purpose of trading with Natives got closer, but they conducted most of their transactions aboard ship with Natives who came out by umiaq. In the 1880s detachments from the United States Revenue Marine, who were there to curb the trade in firearms and alcohol, did visit Sisualik, but they had to reach it in small boats.

The Sisualik fair did not start on a specific date; rather, it developed gradually over a period of weeks in midsummer according to a schedule determined by the freshwater ice breakup on the Noatak, Kobuk, and Selawik Rivers, saltwater breakup on Hotham Inlet and Kotzebue Sound, and the spring and early summer hunting programs of the various nations involved.[37] The first people to arrive were Nuataaġmiut, the most distant of whom had traveled some 300 miles (480 kilometers) by boat down the Noatak River to get there. They left home just a few days after the river broke up, which was usually in mid- to late May, descended the river, and camped for a few weeks in the Noatak River delta. In mid- to late June they moved out to Sisualik, where they hunted beluga (white) whales for two or three weeks.

Toward the end of the beluga hunt the Nuataaġmiut were joined by people from the Kobuk River valley, followed by people from the Selawik River valley, then the Qikiqtaġruŋmiut and Napaaqtuġmiut, and eventually by still others whose estates were farther away along the coast. Last to arrive were people from Bering Strait, who usually got there around the end of July or the first week of August and sometimes even later. The sequence of arrivals was pretty much the same from one year to the next.

The fair's conclusion was determined by people's need to return home for late summer–fall hunting and fishing. The first to leave apparently were the Napaaqtuġmiut, who departed around the end of the first week in August so that they could arrive home in time for the major salmon fishery. Others followed, inlanders first, most coastal people second, and Bering Strait residents last. People from Bering Strait often stayed for a week or two after the fair was over in order to fish for salmon and whitefish; sometimes they remained in eastern Kotzebue Sound well into September. As they headed home along the coast they also hunted caribou if they encountered them (Lucier 1997:309).

No Westerner recorded the origin of any of the people who came to Sisualik prior to 1881. Westerners who visited the fair from that year on did record the origins of the participants, but only in vague geographic terms. For details we are thus left with the information provided by my informants plus one of Stefansson's sources.

According to my informants, the fair was attended by people from all of the Iñupiaq nations of the NANA Region, by representatives of all or most of the nations immediately surrounding the region, and by people from Bering Strait. This included, specifically, people from the following nations: Akuniġmiut (central Kobuk River), Imaqłit (Diomede Islands), Kaŋiġmiut (Buckland River), Kiitaaġmiut (lower Selawik River), Kiŋikmiut (Wales), Kivalliñiġmiut (Kivalina), Kuuŋmiut (Kobuk River delta), Napaaqtuġmiut (lower Noatak River), Nuataaġmiut (upper Noatak River), Pittaġmiut (Goodhope Bay), Qikiqtaġruŋmiut (Kotzebue district), Siiḷviim Kaŋianiġmiut (upper Selawik River), Tapqaġmiut (Shishmaref), and Tikiġaġmiut (Point Hope), plus Qutlich (Chukotkans) of unspecified ethnic background and occasional Iñupiat from the Colville (Kuukpigmiut) and/or Utukok (Utuqqaġmiut) Rivers.[38]

In addition, a few Koyukon went to the fair with Iñupiaq partners from time to time (Clark 1996:22). Some of the Athapaskans from the upper Kobuk and middle Koyukuk Rivers traveled with Akuniġmiut partners, while others from the lower Koyukuk or Yukon Rivers attended with their Kaŋiġmiut (Buckland) partners. An occasional Gwich'in probably went to Sisualik with a Nuataaġmiut partner, but if so, the fact went unrecorded. There is a suggestion in the accounts that Yup'ik speakers from Norton Sound also attended from time to time, probably with partners among the Kaŋiġmiut. Imaqłit from the Diomede Islands and, less often, Ukiuvaŋmiut from King Island sometimes came on their own (Kingston 1996).

The only other detailed list of which I am aware was recorded by Stefansson on June 16, 1911 (1914b:314–315; see also Cantwell 1889a:71; Eliyak 1931; Foote 1959–61:box 3, folder 2, 33–34; Hooper 1881:25–26, 39; Northwest Iñupiat Elders Conference 1976:76–08; Nelson 1899:14, 229; Samms 1899–1900:2; Simpson 1875:236). He obtained the information from his Iñupiaq assistant, Ilaviñiq, while they were camped on the Horton River some distance east of the Mackenzie River delta in northwestern Canada. Ilaviñiq was apparently a Nuataaġmiu who had emigrated from the upper Noatak River sometime during the 1885–1900 period, when that district was abandoned due to the crash of the caribou population (Burch 1998a:107–108, 373–374).[39] It is hard to estimate how old he was. In 1911 he was married and had both a 7-year-old daughter and an 18-year-old adopted son living with him, which suggests that he was probably somewhere in his late thirties or early forties. That is important, because it means that he spent at least his childhood years going to the Sisualik fair, and he must have learned a lot about it from his older relatives.

The list Ilaviñiq gave to Stefansson and my interpretations thereof are presented in Table 6. His list is basically the same as the one I presented above. It differs in ways that are easily explained. For example, for the Kobuk and Selawik Rivers he lumped separate nations together as Kuwugmiut (Kuuvaŋmiut, or Kobuk River people) and Silivigmiut (Siiḷviŋmiut, or Selawik River people), whereas I listed them by nation.[40] He did not list the Pittaġmiut nation, but it had become extinct by the time he was born. Some of the survivors lived at the mouth of the Kugruk River, located in the estate of the former Pittaġmiut (hence his Kugrugmiut), and some of the vacated land had been occupied by immigrants from the Kuzitrin River, in the interior of the Seward Peninsula, hence his Kaviaragmiut (Qaviaraġmiut). My informants mentioned King Islanders (Ukiuvaŋmiut) as being occasional participants during the early 19th century, so their being on Ilaviñiq's list is not surprising. He omitted the Kaŋiġmiut, but most of them had migrated to Norton Sound by the time of Ilaviñiq's childhood. The only real anomalies are the omission of the Qikiqtaġruŋmiut, the very people in whose country the fair took place, and the inclusion of the "Kugahigmiut," whom I cannot identify at all. They may have

Table 6. Participants in the Sisualik Trade Fair, as reported by V. Stefansson

Stefansson Name	Burch Interpretation
Imarxlit	Imaqłit (Diomede Islands)
Kaviaragmiut	Qaviaraġmiut (Kuzitrin River emigrants)
Kañianermiut	Kaŋianiġmiut, the regional band of Kuukpigmiut farthest up the Colville River
Kiñigmiut	Kaŋiġmiut (Buckland River)
Kivalinirmiut	Kivalliñiġmiut (Kivalina district)
Kotlit	Qutlich (unspecified Chukotkans)
Kugahigmiut	Unknown, but must be on Koyuk River or Norton Sound, because they sometimes came with Unalit
Kugmiut (not Wainwright Inlet)	Kuuŋmiut (Kobuk River delta)
Kugrugmiut	Residents of the Kugruk River, in former Pittaġmiut country
Kuwugmiut	Kuuvaŋmiut: Anyone from the main Kobuk River valley
Nappaktogmiut	Napaaqtuġmiut (lower Noatak River)
Noatagmiut	Nuataaġmiut (upper Noatak River)
Okouvugmiut	Ukiuvaŋmiut (King Island)
Silivigmiut	Siiḷviŋmiut: Anyone from the Selawik River valley (Kiitaaġmiut, Siiłviim Kaŋianiġmiut)
Sinaragmiut (Port Clarence)	Singaġmiut (Port Clarence)
Tapkarmiut	Tapqaġmiut (Shishmaref)
Tigiragmiut	Tikiġaġmiut (Point Hope)
Unalit	Unalit: unspecified Yup'ik speakers from Norton Sound

Source: Stefansson 1914b:314–315.

been Kaŋiġmiut who had moved to the Koyuk River (near Norton Sound), since he said that the "Kugahigmiut" were occasionally accompanied by a few Unalit (Yup'ik speakers from Norton Sound) when they attended the fair.

Ilaviñiq's list of participants in the Sisualik fair, adjusted for historical circumstances and with the addition of the Qikiqtaġruŋmiut and Kaŋiġmiut, is consistent with the one given to me by my own informants. On the basis of this evidence, we may say that the Sisualik fair was regularly attended by people from 15 nations and occasionally by people from another 7 or 8, for a total of 22 or 23. As the reader may recall from Chapter 2, the members of several of these nations considered themselves to be in a state of war with one another, a point to which I return later.

Determining the number of people who participated in the fair as opposed to the number of nations involved during the early 19th century is difficult because there are no contemporary observations on which to base an estimate. It would have been difficult for an observer on the ground to make an accurate count because the people from each nation were in separate encampments spread out for several miles along the shore. One would have needed an aircraft to get a comprehensive view of the entire assemblage. Also, people came and went, and accurately recording their movements would have been

Table 7. Minimum Number of People at the Sisualik Fair

Nation	Basis of Estimate	Number of People
Akuniġmiut	4 boats	36–53
Imaqłit	3 boats	27–39
Kaŋiġmiut	3 boats	27–39
Kiitaaġmiut	2 boats	18–26
Kiŋikmiut	5 boats	45–65
Kivalliñiġmiut	3 boats	27–39
Kuuŋmiut	50% of population[1]	210
Napaaqtuġmiut	100% of population[2]	300
Nuataaġmiut	80% of population[3]	430
Pittaġmiut	3 boats	27–39
Qikiqtaġruŋmiut	100% of population[4]	390
Qutlich	5 boats	45–65
Siiḷviim Kaŋianiġmiut	5 boats	45–65
Tapqaġmiut	3 boats	27–39
Tikiġaġmiut	5 boats	45–65
Total		1,699–1,864

1. Burch 1998a:179–180.
2. Burch 1998a:67–68, 70–72.
3. Burch 1998a:87–91, 94–95.
4. Burch 1998a:203, 208.

almost impossible. My procedure, therefore, is to develop an estimate based on specific information acquired from elders and then compare the results with observational data from the 1880s.

Table 7 presents my estimate of the minimum number of participants at the Sisualik fair during a normal year during the early 19th century. The nations (or districts) listed in the table are those from which people came virtually every year. The numbers are based on two kinds of evidence. One is a percentage of an estimated total population for the nation concerned, which is used in four cases. The other is the number of boats my sources say regularly came from each district multiplied by an assumed average number of people per boat. There are two figures for average number of people per boat, 9 and 13. The first figure assumes three adult men, three adult women, two children, and one elder of either sex, whereas the latter envisions four men, four women, four children, and one elder.[41] These numbers refer to traveling umiat bringing entire families with all their goods to the fair, in contrast to boats carrying people which came out to visit Western ships.

The totals resulting from the two different assumptions are a minimum of 1,699 and a maximum of 1,864 people, for an average of 1,782. For practical purposes we may speak of roughly 1,800 people as being the standard number of participants in the Sisualik fair.[42] However, that number was frequently augmented by visitors from other districts. As noted earlier, Koyukon from the interior and Yup'ik speakers from Norton Sound attended from time to time, most of them as individuals or families traveling with Iñupiaq partners. Ukiuvaŋmiut (King Island), Utuqqaġmiut (Utukok River), and Kuukpigmiut (Colville River) also appeared on occasion, the first coming directly by boat from their homeland, the second and third after portaging their boats over the De Long Mountains and descending the Noatak River. In any given year the number of participants could have been well over 2,000 people. It is important to note, however, that not all of them were necessarily at Sisualik at the same time. The Napaaqtuġmiut, for example, frequently left before the Bering Strait people (Imaqłit, Kiŋikmiut, Qutlich, and Ukiuvaŋmiut) even arrived. Depending on weather and other conditions, other groups came and went as they pleased or as they deemed necessary.

The only useful estimates to compare with my own are the direct observations made in the early and mid-1880s. In 1880 C. L. Hooper, on the *Corwin*, estimated that 1,000–1,200 people were at "Cape Blossom" on July 17.[43] They had gone there instead of to Sisualik in the hope of meeting American trading vessels.[44] No one was seen at "Cape Blossom" the following year, but Nelson estimated that 600–800 people from the Noatak, Kobuk, and Selawik Rivers were at Sisualik on July 15, 1881, the last two groups no doubt having just arrived (1899:261). After the *Corwin* left Sisualik heading north in both 1880 and 1881, observers on board saw many boats heading south along the coast toward the fair, which supports my contention that their estimates were incomplete (Nelson 1877–81, notebook 12:entry for July 17, 1881).

On August 21, 1884, John Cantwell counted nearly 600 people at Sisualik but was informed that "as many had gone back to their homes" (1889a:71). However, the next day, "after a rapid census," he estimated that there were 1,400 people there, and on the 23rd he reckoned that 1,200 people showed up for a dance to greet new arrivals from Bering Strait (Cantwell 1889a:72). Michael Healy (1887:13) estimated that about 1,000 people were at the fair on August 4, 1885, and Stoney (n.d.:160), having observed the fair on a number of occasions in the early and mid-1880s, made a general estimate of 1,000 to more than 1,200 as being the usual number of participants.

All of the estimates made by outside observers in the 1880s are considerably lower than mine for the early 19th century. However, when additional information is added to the analysis, they make sense. The estimates of 1,200 at "Cape Blossom" in 1880 and 600–800 at Sisualik in 1881 were both made early in the season, when only some of the participants would have arrived. One may state with some confidence that people from only four or five of the nations ordinarily represented at the fair were included in these figures. The Napaaqtuġmiut and Qikiqtaġruŋmiut alone would have added another 500–600 people, and they were just beginning the trip from their spring seal-hunting camps along the coast. Thus, I do not find the figures for these two years significantly at odds with my own general calculation.

The years after 1881 are another matter. The date is crucial because during the winters of 1881–82 and 1882–83 a terrible famine visited the NANA Region, decimating the population (Burch 1998a:47–50). The disappearance of the resources that caused the Great Famine prompted the Iñupiat to increase their commerce with American trading vessels. Among other things, this development led, apparently in 1884, to a shift in the location of the fair from Sisualik to the "Kotzebue peninsula," an appendage of Baldwin Peninsula on which the city of Kotzebue now stands.[45] The fair began to be attended by a greater percentage of the smaller population, and people tended to stay later than they had before. This is why Cantwell found so many people there in late August 1884. Thus, while the post-1883 estimates were much lower than my own for the early 19th century, there are excellent reasons why they should be so.

Most of my sources did not know much about the physical structure of the Sisualik fair prior to its move to the "Kotzebue peninsula." One thing they did know is that representatives of each nation camped together and apart from everyone else and that the Nuataaġmiut camped near the eastern end of the spit.[46] According to Lucier (1987), the Qikiqtaġruŋmiut camped at Sisualigruaq, which is about a mile to the west. Eugene McElwaine (1901:108) confirmed that the members of each nation had their own camp and said that the camps were 1–2 miles (1.5–3 kilometers) apart. The tents were set up in one or sometimes two lines parallel to the beach, with the boats located between them and the shore. The playing fields for football and other large-scale events were behind the tents.

The only general description of the Sisualik encampment by an actual observer was made by Nelson in 1881. He described a portion of the camp as he saw it on July 15, when most of the inlanders—mainly Nuataaġmiut—were there but probably before any coastal people had arrived. At the time it consisted of a row of conical tents more than a mile long.

> *This camp was arranged with almost military precision; along the beach, above high-water mark, with their sterns to the sea, were ranged between sixty and seventy umiaks, turned with bottom upward and toward the prevailing wind, tilted on one rail, the other being supported on two sticks 3½ to 4 feet [1–1.25 meters] long. Seventy-five yards [70 meters] back from the umiaks, in a line parallel to the beach, were ranged over two hundred kaiaks, supported about three*

> *feet [1 meter] from the ground on low trestles made of branching stakes. Below each kaiak, supported on a rest 3 or 4 inches [7.5–10 centimeters] above the ground, was the set of spears, paddles, etc, belonging to the boat. The kaiaks . . . were ranged parallel to each other, pointing toward the sea, in a line with the umiat. Fifty yards [45 meters] back from the kaiaks, and ranged in a line parallel with them, were the conical lodges occupied by the people.* [Nelson 1899:261; *see also* Cantwell 1889a:71]

Nelson went on to say that in his three years in the North he had never before seen an Eskimo camp laid out according to a deliberate plan. But he also noted that "the large number of boats, and the necessity for having clear space to enable each crew to launch without interfering with its neighbors, must have brought about this plan, which could not have been improved, as the entire camp could embark and paddle to a trading vessel in less than five minutes" (Nelson 1899:262). Trading vessels were rare prior to 1848, so that consideration did not apply during the study period. However, since everyone who went to Sisualik for the fair got there by boat, it seems reasonable to assume that the earlier pattern must have been similar to or identical with the one described by Nelson.

A broad range of activities in addition to trading took place at the fair.[47] Indeed, before any trading took place a day of dancing and feasting occurred, and this pattern was evidently repeated each time a new contingent of half a dozen or more boats arrived. Small gatherings were held in a qargi, which in most cases consisted of a windbreak created by tilting an umiaq on its side or from two such umiat with a tarp stretched over poles placed between them. Large events took place in more open settings. As noted above, in 1884 Cantwell (1889a:72) observed a dance held to honor the arrival of several boats from Bering Strait that attracted an audience of 1,200 people.

Feasting, dancing, and trading by no means exhausted the agenda. Athletic competitions were standard fare, including wrestling matches, foot races, jumping contests, feats of strength and agility, spear-throwing and archery competitions, kayak races, and football. Many of the competitions pitted the members of one nation against another, some set two or three nations against two or three others, and others saw inlanders challenging coastal people. Apparently, much of this was ad hoc; someone came up with an idea, and, if others approved, a challenge or the news went out, and in due course people converged to participate or watch. In some events winners were awarded prizes for their achievements (Lucier 1997:315).

Occasionally, it became necessary to replenish food supplies. To do this several families combined their short seines to make a long one and harvested salmon and whitefish, which were usually abundant at that time of year in the waters immediately offshore.

A final activity worth mentioning is sexual intercourse. The fair was the primary context in which sexual liaisons across national boundaries occurred. It was here that many comarriages were created or renewed and trysts were held in secret. As noted earlier, all of the relationships created through these connections had enduring significance.

In the midst of all the hubbub of the fair trade was never forgotten for long. The top priority was exchange between partners. As soon as they could partners got together and, after the preliminary courtesies and festivities, presented each other with their gifts. (Later, before they left, requests were made for the following year.) After partnership obligations had been discharged the individuals involved were free to buy and sell on the open market. A more detailed discussion of both partnership and open-market transactions is presented below in the section on modes of exchange. A discussion of the kinds of goods that changed hands is presented in the section on the international trade network.

The trade fair at Sisualik regularly brought together in a peaceful context substantial numbers of people who previously had tried to kill each other in raids or open battles and who might well be planning to try to do so again. We can only wonder about what thoughts went through a man's mind when he found himself face to face with someone who, less than a year earlier, had confronted him in a battle line or who had participated in a raid on his village during which his wife and children had been killed. At least some encounters like this must have occurred at Sisualik every summer.

Such situations were not the only ones with the potential for trouble. Iñupiaq men tended to be macho types who did not easily tolerate ridicule, teasing, or practical jokes, nor did they appreciate being insulted or shoved around, even when engaged in games such as football.[48] The potential for trouble lay almost everywhere.

Men were not allowed to go about the fair conspicuously armed with bows and arrows or spears, but probably all of them carried concealed daggers.[49] In 1881, by which time warfare had ceased, Nelson (1877–81, notebook 12:entry for July 16, 1881) noticed that most of the men carried revolvers. But even if weapons were not actually in hand they were always close by. Once triggered, violence could escalate quickly.

Sisualik and the waters through which people traveled to get there were considered neutral territory in summertime, and peaceful behavior was very strongly institutionalized. As far as I have been able to learn, the theoretical potential for conflict was never realized in fact. Men who acted in an obstreperous or offensive manner toward foreigners were lectured by their relatives and, if necessary, disarmed and even physically restrained by their fellow countrymen.[50] When a man was observed getting agitated, the news somehow reached his kinsmen very quickly. When he arrived at his tent intending to arm himself and fight, he was subjected to a lecture from a spouse or an older relative and often discovered that his weapons had mysteriously disappeared. If two men insisted on fighting, they had to leave Sisualik to do it. Some paddled by kayak across the bay to the Noatak River delta and settled matters there. Others went to the hills behind the coast west of Sheshalik Spit.

Most of the accounts I have of confrontations at Sisualik are fragmentary, but one told to me by Charlie Saġġaaluraq Jensen is fairly complete. I present it here in full because it illustrates several aspects of the way in which trouble could start and then be contained. Because of the presence of a muzzle-loading gun in the story, the events recounted in it must have taken place rather late, sometime after the purchase of Alaska by the United States in 1867.[51]

Two Point Hopers, Samaruraq and his brother, Kataliña, were at the fair.[52] Kataliña had traded with a Wales man for a sack of Russian leaf tobacco. One whole sack! And for that he paid a sealskin parka.

Kataliña brought the sack back to Samaruraq's tent, which is where he was staying, and leaned it against the wall. Not far from the tent their umiaq was standing on its side, propped up with poles.

Not long afterward Samaruraq was approaching his tent when he heard several men talking very loudly inside. He listened but couldn't quite make out what they were saying. Too many people were talking at the same time. Samaruraq wanted to know what the trouble was so he went inside. There he found his brother and five young men from Wales, two by the door, the rest toward one side, sitting down. Samaruraq saw the sack of tobacco standing against the tent wall right by the door. He sat down on it and listened to the discussion.

He quickly learned that the Wales man who had sold Kataliña the tobacco wanted it back. Kataliña told him he could have it but that he would have to return the sealskin parka first.

Samaruraq took out his pipe and lit it. Just as he was taking his first puff someone pulled the sack out from beneath him, and he fell down on his side. That made him very angry, and he started to shout at the person who did it. One of the Wales men went out. Another tried, but Samaruraq held him back. He had a knife, all right, but Samaruraq held his arm so he couldn't use it. Then he took the knife and let the man go. Two of the other Wales men followed, leaving one still inside.

Samaruraq pretended to chase the men who had gone out. He stopped after about 25 yards [20 meters] because he didn't really want to catch them, he just wanted to scare them.

The Wales man who remained inside was frightened and wanted to leave too, but Kataliña told him, "You stay here. He won't bother you if you stay here." But that man said, "Never mind. I am going out!" He left just as Samaruraq approached the tent. He tried to hide behind the tent, but Samaruraq saw him and chased him. Just when Samaruraq had almost caught him the Wales man tripped and fell, and Samaruraq kicked him hard in the kidney. Samaruraq turned around and headed back toward his tent, while the Wales man limped off, doubled over in pain.

Now, Samaruraq had a qataŋun [cosibling] at Sisualik named Qiyuktaaluk. He was from Kotzebue and was among the many people who had seen the whole affair. And he told Samaruraq, "Qataŋun, we won't sleep now. You have to be careful about making trouble in this place. You have to be careful!" Samaruraq responded that he didn't care, that the Wales man didn't die. "I kicked him, all right, but I didn't kill him." And he showed his qataŋun the knife he had taken.

A couple of days later a group of Wales men came over to Samaruraq's tent. They called, "Samaruraq, come on out! We want to fight. Come on! Take off your armor so we can wrestle." Samaruraq stayed inside and listened. Pretty soon those men started pounding on his umiaq, making holes in it. That enraged Samaruraq, who picked up his muzzle-loading gun and went out. He saw the Wales men over by his boat. They were all standing in a row, and he realized that if he moved fast enough he might hit them all with a single shot. He aimed and fired, but the gun didn't go off.

Frightened, the Wales men fled. Frustrated, Samaruraq returned to his tent. It was only later that he learned that his daughter had removed and hidden the primer to his gun. [Jensen 1970e]

This story shows how easily potentially serious incidents could start. Any open-market transaction could lead to some kind of dispute, and even accidental physical encounters in athletic contests could get out of hand. This was true without even considering the general atmosphere of international hostility that pervaded northwestern Alaska. But the incident also illustrates some of the ways in which trouble was contained. Samaruraq was publicly criticized by his qataŋun for his part in the conflict, an experience that would have chastened most men.[53] Later, when the Wales men raised the conflict to a higher level, Samaruraq was forced to react or lose his boat. If he had actually shot and killed any of the Wales men, however, chaos would have ensued. His determined show of force, which frightened the Wales men, on the one hand, and his daughter's quiet sabotage, on the other, resulted in a peaceful outcome.

The story has a sequel. At the fair the following year Samaruraq and Kataliña heard that the Wales men wanted to fight them with bows and arrows, so they armed themselves, ascended a little hill, and waited. Lots of people milled around to see what would happen, and an old man named Qatsiqayauluk tried to goad the Wales men into going after them. But no one did. Samaruraq and Katalińa stayed on the hill until midnight and finally returned to their tent. That ended the affair, since in the Iñupiaq scheme of things failure to accept a challenge automatically established a truce, even if not a reconciliation.

THE POINT SPENCER FAIR

Another fair was held every summer at Point Spencer, which is a long sand spit on the western end of the Seward Peninsula, just south of Bering Strait. I have no independent information on this fair, but Dorothy Jean Ray's (1964:75, 1975b:98; see also Stefansson 1914a:9) sources claimed that it was established before the one at Sisualik and that in unspecified "aboriginal" times was even larger than its northern counterpart.

Point Spencer certainly was located at a good place for a fair. It was easily accessed from both the Asiatic and Alaskan sides of Bering Strait, from King and the two Diomede Islands, from the interior and coasts of the Seward Peninsula, and from the shores of Norton Sound. No one has published a list of nations represented at this fair, but Ray (1964:75, 1967:387) says that participants came from Chukotka and from all parts of Alaska between Point Hope and Saint Michael. I have never heard of people from Kotzebue Sound or Point Hope attending the Point Spencer fair. They certainly could have, but only in small numbers. At any rate, the fair must have included people from at least the following nations: Nuvuqaghmiit Eskimos and Uellyt Chukchi from Chukotka; Imaqłit and Ukiuvaŋmiut Eskimos from the islands in Bering Strait; Ayasaaġiaġmiut, Kiŋikmiut, Tapqaġmiut, and Siñġaġmiut from the Seward Peninsula coast; Qaviaraġmiut from the Seward Peninsula interior; and Uŋalaqłiŋmiut, Taprarmiut, and probably others from Norton Sound.

Like the Sisualik fair, the one at Point Spencer involved people from nations that were often at war. Also like its northern counterpart, it was institutionalized as a peaceful occasion despite the potential for conflict. According to Oquilluk (1973:102–103), it was the abduction of an Iñupiaq girl by Chukotkans at this fair that initiated the last round of warfare across Bering Strait.

I know of no way to estimate the number of individuals who participated in the Point Spencer fair. According to Ray, "A three mile stretch [of shoreline] would be covered with skin tents, oomiaks, and hundreds of Eskimos from Siberia to Saint Michael" (1964:75). The people from each nation stayed in a separate camp (Oquilluk 1973:103). Like the Sisualik fair, the one at Point Spencer involved a variety of activities in addition to trading, including dancing, feasting, and athletic competitions of all kinds (Oquilluk 1973:101–103). In its basic structure and operation and possibly even its size the Point Spencer fair seems to have been analogous to its counterpart on Kotzebue Sound.

The Point Spencer fair continued to operate for some years after the end of the period of primary interest here. After 1848 many American trading and whaling vessels stopped there, and eventually the site became a coaling and provisioning station for the American whaling fleet (Aldrich 1889:73–77; Whymper 1869a:169, 1869b:162).

THE NIĠLIQ FAIR

The largest fair north of the NANA Region was held at Niġliq, in the Colville River delta.[54] Unlike the fairs at Sisualik and Point Spencer, this one was overwhelmingly dominated by the members of just two nations, the Kakligmiut of Point Barrow and the Kuukpigmiut of the Colville River.[55] According to Maguire (1857:457), as many as 150 of the former might have been present, while Rasmussen (Ostermann and Holtved 1952:30) says that virtually the entire Kuukpigmiut population of 500 people was in attendance. According to my own sources, two or three boatloads of Nuataaġmiut from the upper Noatak River (in the NANA Region) also attended with some regularity, as did a boatload or two of Utuqqaġmiut from the upper Utukok River. A few Gwich'in may also have attended from time to time, probably with Kuukpigmiut partners. Altogether, as many as 700 people may have been present in any given year.

One of Spencer's (1959:21) informants told him that he had counted more than 400 tents at Niġliq and that the camp had included people from Barter and Herschel Islands and the Mackenzie River in addition to the districts mentioned above. According to Spencer, the total number of people involved would have been on the order of 1,500. However, at a reasonable average of five people per tent, that would have totaled 2,000 people. There were not that many people around who *could* attend the fair, never mind *did* attend it. In addition, the Mackenzie River delta people (including the residents of Barter and Herschel Islands) usually traded with the Alaskans at (or near) Barter Island, not at Niġliq. Other problems include the fact that, on the same page, Spencer states that Knud Rasmussen "encountered about 500 Eskimos at the Colville mouth" as late as 1924. In fact, Rasmussen did not see anyone at the Colville River mouth; he was there while the river and ocean were still covered with ice. The inlanders were still up the river, and the coastal people were still at Barrow. His statement was an estimate of the number of inlanders who had attended the fair many years before. In another place Spencer said that it would not have been "unusual" to find 600 people at the Niġliq fair, "although 400–500 would perhaps be a more normal figure" (1959:200). That makes more sense. Unfortunately, these errors and inconsistencies do not inspire confidence in the accuracy of Spencer's estimates, although it should be recalled that his reconstruction was really of the 1880–1900 situation, not the period of interest here.[56]

The Kuukpigmiut left for Nigliq by boat in early to mid-June, shortly after the Colville River ice broke up. Any Utuqqaġmiut and Nuataaġmiut who wished to participate in the fair had to portage their boats over to the Colville River several weeks before that, while snow was still on the ground. The members of the upriver band, the Kaŋianiġmiut, started first (Bockstoce 1988, vol. 2:322). When they reached the mouth of the Killik River they found the members of the Killiġmiut band waiting for them. The two groups continued on together, being joined by members of the Qaŋmaliġmiut band near the mouth of what is now known as the Anaktuvuk River. The flotilla arrived at Nigliq in late June or early July, about ten days after the Kaŋianiġmiut began the voyage. For a week or so after they arrived the Kuukpigmiut spread out over the delta to fish and hunt seals. Then they gathered at the fairground to practice the songs and dances they intended to perform for the Kakligmiut.

The Kakligmiut who headed east to trade were known as Kivaliñaaġmiut. They left Barrow over a period of three or four days in late June or early July. At that season the ocean was still frozen at Barrow, and they had to drag their boats, trade goods, and other paraphernalia on sleds. After five days or so they reached an area where a lead of open water had formed between the land and the sea ice. They left their sleds there and continued on by boat.[57] The total trip took about eight to ten days (VanStone 1977:34). About half a day's journey from their destination the leading boats halted to wait for the laggards. When the last boat arrived the entire party moved en masse to Nigliq, arriving in mid-July.

The Kakligmiut were greeted by an array of Kuukpigmiut singers and drummers.[58] The newcomers remained quietly in their boats until the performance was over and then went ashore. The Kuukpigmiut then helped them unload their vessels and set up camp. According to reports received by John Simpson in the early 1850s, the fairground was "a flat piece of ground on which the tents of the two parties [were] ranged opposite each other between two slight eminences, about a bow-shot apart" (1875:265). A qargi, or community hall, was erected right in the middle of the village to serve as the focus of the various activities (Campbell 1998:pl. 19).

After the camps were in order a feast was held during which the Kuukpigmiut served the Kakligmiut inland foods such as caribou and mountain sheep meat, and the latter reciprocated with seal meat, oil, and *maktak* (bowhead whale skin with blubber attached). The next day was devoted to exchanges between partners and to open-market trades. A week or so of dancing, feasting, athletic contests, and games followed.

The fair concluded, according to Simpson (1875:265), on or about July 26. At that point the Kuukpigmiut began their long trip back up the Colville, taking about twice as long for the upriver trip—about three weeks—as for the trip down (Bockstoce 1988, vol. 2:322). The Kakligmiut, on the other hand, moved out to Oliktok Point, on the eastern edge of the Colville River delta, to prepare for another fair near Barter Island that is discussed in a later section.

OTHER FAIRS WITHIN NORTHWESTERN ALASKA

The three fairs discussed so far do not exhaust the subject as far as northwestern Alaska is concerned. Three others have been noted in the region, and they deserve mention here.

Piġniq is very close to Point Barrow.[59] Not much is known about a fair at this location beyond the fact that there was one, or something like one, toward the end of the 19th century (Spencer 1959:200). If it had been functioning near the beginning of the century, it would have involved several of the Kakligmiut who did not go to Niġliq, most of whom were residents of the village of Utqiaġvik. On the inland side it would have involved representatives of the Ikpikpagmiut and probably the Kulugruaġmiut, both of whose estates were located along rivers crossing the Arctic Coastal Plain.

That this fair does not stand out more in the ethnography of northwestern Alaska may be due to the fact that the Kulugruaġmiut were wiped out by famine during the late 18th or early 19th century, reducing significantly the number of potential participants (Burch 1998a:91, 369–372). It is more likely, however, that the fair was not instituted in the first place until the late 1870s or early 1880s.

The evidence supporting the second of the above hypotheses is of two kinds. First, the reports of HMS *Plover* did not mention any kind of special gathering at Piġniq. This was so despite the fact that the British were within less than 10 miles (16 kilometers) of Piġniq for the better part of two years (1852–54) and in very close contact with the local Iñupiat during most of that period (Bockstoce 1988; Maguire 1857; Simpson 1875). They reported in some detail on the entire trade network of the Iñupiat of northwestern Alaska, but they never once mentioned Piġniq in that context.

One particular event the British did record in 1852, however, was the arrival at Point Barrow of nine boats that came from the east. Their home was on "the mainland near a river where deer abound," and their purpose was to trade caribou meat and fish for sea mammal products (Simpson 1852–54:entry for September 15, 1852; see also Bockstoce 1988, vol. 1:79). For reasons too complex to go into here, I conclude that these boats were manned by Ikpikpagmiut, who, 30 years later, were the primary inlanders who came to Piġniq to trade. But the later traders arrived in early or midsummer and went directly to Piġniq. The ones observed by the British arrived on September 15 and went to Nuvuk. Their visit was not associated with anything going on at Piġniq. If they repeated the visit the following year, it was not recorded, and therefore we do not know if they regularly visited Point Barrow each fall. However, they may have heard that the Kakligmiut were in dire straits that year because of a disastrous whaling season in the spring of 1853 and concluded that the trip would not be worth the effort.

Another type of evidence against an early-19th-century fair at Piġniq comes from Native sources. In 1978, when David Libbey and Cathy Dementieff interviewed elders Arthur Taqtu Neakok and Ida Suksran Numnik, Dementieff asked the following question about the battle of Niksiuraq (see Appendix 1): "Did this war happen before the Nunamiut [inlanders] started going to Piġniq?" The answer was "Yes" (Neakok and Numnik 1978). Both the question and the response to it indicate knowledge of a recent origin for the Piġniq fair. Since the battle probably occurred in the early 1830s, this puts the fair's origin sometime after that. In 1970 Simon Panniaq Paneak volunteered the information to me that Iñupiat from the interior did not start going to the Barrow area in summer to trade until some point in his parents' lifetimes. Since Paneak was born in 1900, that would move the earliest possible date for this fair forward to about 1860.

Murdoch (1892:48) reported that only five or six families of inlanders came to Piġniq in 1882 and 1883, but Herbert Aldrich (1889:149) counted 70 tents there in 1887. These observations suggest that the fair evolved rapidly during the 1880s and was no doubt related to the increasing presence of Westerners near Barrow. The United States Signal Service established a meteorological station there (near Utqiaġvik) in 1881 and ran it for two years (Ray 1883, 1885; see also Murdoch 1988: xiii–xxx). Its base was taken over by the Pacific Steam Whaling Company in 1883 and turned into a shore whaling station. By the winter of 1885–86 it was also a trading post (Bockstoce 1986:232–233). In 1898 D. H. Jarvis recorded that "many of the Colville River people also come to Point Barrow in June and July to exchange furs for seal-oil and ammunition" (1899:99). Putting all of this information together, the conclusion seems inescapable that it was the desire to trade for Western goods that drew people from the upper Colville and Ikpikpuk Rivers to what formerly had been merely a duck-hunting station and that the process began in the late 1870s or early 1880s. By drawing Kuukpigmiut from the upper Colville, this fair must have reduced the number of people participating in the Nigliq fair.

During at least the last two decades of the 19th century a fair was indeed held at Piġniq, although it seems to have been structured more as a messenger feast between the Barrow people, on the one hand, and the inlanders as a group, on the other, than as a trade fair (Brower n.d.:283, 286–289, 460, 588–

565; Murdoch 1892:83–84; Paneak 1970; Spencer 1952, notebook 2:91d, notebook 3:100; Stefansson 1914b:189; Stoney 1900:821–822; Woolfe 1893:144). In 1900 practically all of the inlanders participating in this fair caught influenza and died. The fair was never held again (Brower n.d.:565; cf. Spencer 1959:210–211).

The second fair in the "other" category was one held near Icy Cape, in Siḷaliñaġmiut country (Hopson 1978:96–97; Killigivuk 1960b; Kisautaq and Kean 1981:622–625; North Slope Borough, Commission on History and Culture 1980:160; Rainey 1947:240, 268; Spencer 1959:198, 200). The question, once again, is whether this event was a phenomenon of the early 1800s (or before) or an innovation in the latter part of the century. There is no definitive evidence on which we can base an answer to the question, but I am inclined to believe that it was an early-19th-century (or older) event that persisted. However, I suspect that, although always held in the general Icy Cape area, it was not necessarily held at the same place from one year to the next.

Icy Cape was a good place to have a fair because, like Sisualik and Niġliq, the area was readily accessible to both inlanders and coastal people. The primary inlanders in this case were the Utuqqaġmiut, and the primary coastal dwellers were the Siḷaliñaġmiut, although other nations in both ecological settings also had reasonably good access to the site. To both the Utuqqaġmiut and the Siḷaliñaġmiut the Icy Cape area was much more accessible than either Sisualik or Niġliq. The specific fairground that has been mentioned for the latter part of the century is Sullivik, which was on a barrier island opposite the mouth of the Utukok River just a short distance north of the Utuqqaġmiut summer campground.[60]

A second factor is that on July 13 and 14, 1838, Kashevarov (VanStone 1977:25, 26) encountered 100 Utuqqaġmiut at their summer camp on the coast and 300 Siḷaliñaġmiut at their major settlement at Icy Cape. Those two groups had enough personnel between them for a major inland–coast get-together, and the two sites are only about 20 miles (32 kilometers) apart. Furthermore, there had to have been 200–300 more Utuqqaġmiut around somewhere that Kashevarov missed; they may have been hunting spotted seals on one of the huge lagoons in the district (Larsen and Rainey 1948:31; Spencer 1959:200). He did not, however, report seeing people from other coastal nations traveling along the shore toward Icy Cape.

A third factor underlying my belief that some kind of "fairlike" event was held at least periodically in the Icy Cape district is that on July 23, 1854, the crew of HMS *Plover* saw 95 tents, presumably occupied by 300 or more people, at Ulġuniq (modern Wainwright). At the time Ulġuniq was a relatively small winter settlement about 50 miles (80 kilometers) north of Icy Cape but still within the estate of the Siḷaliñaġmiut. This multitude was composed of people from as far away as Barrow on the north and Point Hope on the south, so it definitely was an international event of some kind (Bockstoce 1988, vol. 2:419). Inlanders, however, were not mentioned.

In sum, there were enough people of different nationalities in or near Siḷaliñaġmiut country every summer to justify the existence of some kind of international event. I assume that one occurred annually. All of the Siḷaliñaġmiut would have attended, since it was in their estate. The great majority of Utuqqaġmiut would have participated in most years, partly because they regularly spent the summer not far from Icy Cape and partly because they ordinarily had the most desirable goods to exchange for coastal products. Other nations, including the Kakligmiut of the Barrow district, Tikiġaġmiut from Point Hope, and Kuukpigmiut from the upper Colville River, probably were also represented. Tikiġaġmiut were probably minor players in this fair during the study period, since they were inveterate enemies of the Utuqqaġmiut.

The first recorded observation of what was definitely a fair at or near Icy Cape was not made until 1886. The festivities that year took place in a large, temporary qargi, which consisted of a large driftwood framework over which a tarp made from 80 caribou hides had been placed. By this time the size of the Siḷaliñaġmiut population had been significantly reduced, although that of the Utuqqaġmiut was apparently more or less at precontact levels. Warfare had ceased, which, combined with the population changes, meant that a gathering of people from many districts was not that problematic. Henry Woolfe (1893:144) affirmed that the 1886 gathering involved both "coast and inland tribes," but he did not say which ones.

The deficit in the number of coastal participants left by the decline of the Siḷaliñaġmiut could have been partially made up by a few boatloads of Tikiġaġmiut, who were known to have been attending this fair by this time, and probably by a few Kakligmiut as well.[61] In an interview Waldo Kusiq Bodfish (1984) indicated that the Utuqqaġmiut had "mixed with" the Siḷaliñaġmiut "long ago, 1700s, 1800s, around then," but started "to mix with" the Tikiġaġmiut "later on," so the evidence seems to support this conclusion.

The third and final fair that took place within northwestern Alaska was an ad hoc event held in winter a long distance inland. It was like a messenger feast in that people from one nation hosted the event. However, it was a katŋut because people from several different nations attended and because it did not include the specific ceremonial procedures that characterized messenger feasts. Unlike the summer fairs on the coast, the winter fairs rarely, if ever, involved the entire membership of any of the nations whose members participated in it.

The winter fair was held at a place in the upper Noatak or upper Colville River valleys that was readily accessible to people from several adjacent districts.[62] It almost always involved Nuataaġmiut from the Noatak River and Kuukpigmiut from the Colville River and often Utuqqaġmiut from the Utukok River as well. Frequent other participants probably included representatives from the Ikpikpagmiut and Kulugruaġmiut nations of the Arctic Coastal Plain. Whether or not Iñupiat from the Kobuk River valley, Di'hą̱į̱ Gwich'in, or upper Kobuk Koyukon were ever included is unknown.

Winter fairs took place on an ad hoc basis because only after an extraordinarily successful fall caribou hunt would enough resources would be on hand to supply so many participants with food. This factor was probably the primary reason that one nation had to host the event, because such success was unlikely to visit more than one district in any given year and even less likely to occur in the same district from one year to the next. It was only after such a harvest had taken place that notices could go out stating that a fair could be held. Unfortunately, beyond these basic outlines, no information on this fair seems to exist.

FAIRS OUTSIDE OF NORTHWESTERN ALASKA

Fairs outside of northwestern Alaska take us a bit far afield in a volume whose focus is the NANA Region, yet they need to be mentioned because it was partly through them that the nations of the primary study region were linked further to the rest of the world. The discussion here is limited to the fairs most closely connected to the residents of northwestern Alaska: Barter Island, Nuklukayet, Saint Michael, and Pastolik.

The first of these fairs took place on an island in extreme northeastern Alaska whose English name derives from the primary activity that formerly took place there (or near there). (Actually, it might have taken place on an island just west of Barter Island.)[63] It is located a short distance west of the border of the Kigiqtaġuġmiut estate, that nation having been the westernmost of those formerly grouped by Westerners under the general heading of "Mackenzie Delta Eskimos" (McGhee 1974:7–18; Smith 1984:347–349; Usher 1971:169–171) but now known by the Native term Inuvialuit (Alunik, Kolausok, and Morrison 2003). The nations regularly represented there included the Kigiqtaġuġmiut from the Mackenzie River delta, the Kakligmiut Iñupiat from Barrow, and a few people from the Vantee (Crow Flats), Dagoo (upper Porcupine River), and/or Neets'ą̱į̱ (Chandalar) Gwich'in. Other Mackenzie Delta Eskimo nations probably were represented there as well.

The Barter Island fair may have been a fairly recent development during the early 19th century. It was started (Franklin 1828:130) or perhaps resumed (Simpson 1875:268) within the lifetimes of two Mackenzie Delta Eskimo men whom John Franklin met on their way home from the event in 1826. Consequently, it must have dated from no earlier than the mid- or late 18th century. Toward the end of the 19th century its location was shifted to Collinson Point, about 30 miles (48 kilometers) to the southwest (Stefansson 1914b:186–187), and, still later, apparently, to Brownlow Point (Agliġuaġruuk) (Kisautaq and Kean 1981:591–596).

The Kakligmiut participants in the Barter Island fair first went to the one at Niġliq. When it was over they traveled slowly down the easternmost delta of the Colville River, their time being spent hunting seals and caribou and fishing for supplies to sustain them on their journey farther east. When they reached Oliktok Point (Jenness 1991:9), just east of the delta, they left the women, children, and most of the boats behind for safety's sake and proceeded swiftly toward their destination. Their Mackenzie Delta Eskimo counterparts from the east and Gwich'in from the south took similar precautions.

When the traders had all arrived at their destination at the very end of July or early August, transactions were handled with dispatch. Fear and distrust were so great that no one slept during the proceedings, and it is probable that all exchanges were made on the open market rather than through partnerships. Then, their business concluded, the various parties immediately headed homeward.

The Nuklukayet fair was held on the bank of the Yukon River near the mouth of the Tanana (A. Clark 1974:209, 1981:583, fig. 1, 1996:31). This site is in the eastern part of Koyukon territory, but it was apparently considered neutral ground (Dall 1870:198). Although various authors have mentioned this fair, they have provided us with precious little information about it.[64] According to Frederick Whymper, the participants in the mid-1860s included representatives of various Koyukon nations as well as Tanana and Gwich'in speakers. As many as 600 people gathered there in some years (Whymper 1869a:176, 1869b:239). Just how far into the past the fair goes is unknown, but it probably predates the period of interest here. Reports of this fair from the 1850s and 1860s describe a system thoroughly enmeshed in the Russian-controlled fur trade (Hudson's Bay Company Archives 1847–48:fol. 35, 1850–51:3d; McDonald 1862–1913, MSS 0196:folder 5, 30–31).

According to Ray, "local markets" were held at Stebbins and Pastolik (Pastuliq) during the 19th century (1975b:98; see also Griffin 1996). Both were the locations of large winter villages (of Yup'ik speakers) before the smallpox epidemic of 1838–39, unlike the fair sites mentioned so far. Ray includes these fairs, together with the those at Point Spencer and Sisualik, under the heading of "local markets" but does not provide information about them.

Stebbins, an old village whose Yup'ik name is Attəġvik (Ray 1984:295), is located on Saint Michael Island at the southwestern corner of Norton Sound. Also located on Saint Michael Island is another old village, Tačik, which is now known as Saint Michael. According to Lavrentii Zagoskin, the fair was at the latter rather than the former location (Michael 1967:100).

Zagoskin states that people from Norton Sound and the Yukon River "used to hold meetings here for exchanging products" (Michael 1967:100; see also Koutsky 1982b:32–34), but this description applies as much to a messenger feast as to a fair. He says that it began in "ancient times," as viewed from his perspective of 1842–44. On the basis of this brief testimony it seems reasonable to conclude that there was some kind of regular trading event on Saint Michael Island during the early part of the period of interest in this volume. It probably was held at Tačik rather than at Stebbins, although it could have moved back and forth between the two.

In 1833 the Russians founded the trading post of Fort Saint Michael a few hundred yards from Tačik. Thus, while the site may have been a center of interregional trade throughout the 19th century, the nature of the trade must have been significantly different after 1833 from what it was before then (Ray 1975b:122–123). Both Native villages on the island were decimated by smallpox in 1838.

Pastuliq, another old Yup'ik settlement, was located about 50 miles (80 kilometers) southwest of Saint Michael. Situated on the Pastolik River near the northernmost outlet of the Yukon, it would appear to have been geographically more suitable as a fair site than Saint Michael, since inlanders and coast dwellers from both north and south could reach it easily. In fact, Pastuliq was a focal point of coastal trade from as far north as the Diomede Islands and as far south as Nunivak Island and from the interior regions of the lower Yukon and Kuskokwim Rivers (Erman 1855:209; Kashevarov 1994:334–342; Michael 1967:100–102; Ray 1975b:128; United States Department of the Interior, Bureau of Indian Affairs 1988; Wrangell 1980:31–32). Pastuliq seems to have been the southernmost point reached on a regular basis by traders who spoke Iñupiatun as their first language, although such visits must have been very rare during the period of interest here.

The Pastuliq fair took place around the end of July and the beginning of August. It mainly involved the Iñupiatun-speaking Ayasaaġiaaġmiut, whose estate was on the southwestern corner of the Seward Peninsula, the Yup'ik-speaking Pastulirmiut in whose village the event took place, and Yup'ik-speaking Kuigpagmiut from just above the Yukon River delta (Kashevarov 1994:336–337).[65] Before the smallpox epidemic struck the region in 1838, some Akulmiut, whose estate was located between the lower Kuskokwim and lower Yukon Rivers, apparently also participated (Kashevarov 1994:336).

The inlanders (Akulmiut and Kuigpagmiut) arrived first, about the time that the Pastulirmiut returned from beluga hunting at the end of July. The Ayasaaġiaaġmiut did not always arrive before the inlanders had to leave, in which case they left their goods on credit with the Pastulirmiut, to be settled later. When the Ayasaaġiaaġmiut traders finally got there they set up camp some distance from the settlement and mounted an armed guard for security. This was followed by two days of nonstop celebrations involving everyone present, with trading beginning on the third day. Kashevarov calculated that no more than 50 boatloads of people attended this event, which could mean upward of 500 people. It is unclear, however, whether that number included the resident Pastulirmiut.

A final trading center worthy of mention here is Aniliukhtakpak, which was located on the lower Yukon River near the point where it most closely approaches the Kuskokwim River. Aniliukhtakpak was not the site of a fair of the type described so far; rather, it was a large, strategically located permanent village where people from both Yup'ik (Eskimo) and Ingalik (Athapaskan) nations gathered in early winter for several days of feasting, entertainment, and trade (Arndt 1996:9, 36, 38–39; Kashevarov 1994:331–332, 340–341; VanStone 1959:14, 1979b:54–55). Although detailed information is lacking, it would appear to have combined the features of an Iñupiaq messenger feast and a trade fair.

Modes of Exchange

Two general modes of exchange have been mentioned in the presentation so far, gift giving and market transactions (see also Burch 1988a:103–105). At the international level the former took place primarily between relatives (including qataŋutigiik) and partners (niuviġiik). Gift giving between kin usually fell under the heading of *aitchuq-*, which meant making a gift with no strings attached. Gift giving between partners was niuviq- and involved fulfilling obligations that were normally spelled out well in advance as well as free gifts.[66]

Actually, if not ideally, long-term reciprocity was expected in every relationship where gift giving was involved. Transactions were always below market level, but everyone was aware of where that level was. In my time there usually was some mental ledger keeping over the years in each relationship where giving was institutionalized, and I expect that the same was true during the study period. Nevertheless, the focus was always on helping a kinsman or partner meet his or her particular needs, not on making a profit; however, no one wanted to suffer much of a loss in the process.

Making a profit was definitely the goal in open-market (taaqsiq-) transactions, although Stefansson (1909:609) claimed that getting a better deal than one's fellows was often more important than making a profit as such. In any event, open-market transactions were mentioned in previous sections, and it is now appropriate to describe just what they entailed.

Open-market exchanges were initiated in one of two ways. One was for a person to offer something for sale (*tuni-*) and invite others to bid (*nallit-*) on it. If the seller was displeased with a bid, he or she could try to get a better one (*akisuniaq-*) or simply reject it. The other was its reciprocal; that is, a person seeking some particular goods would walk around inquiring if anyone had any for sale.[67] Since there was no generalized medium of exchange such as money, the prospective buyer had to offer in exchange something that the seller wished to acquire. Usually, but not necessarily, the item was something that the seller had planned to sell anyway. These conditions set the stage for considerable gamesmanship and prolonged haggling over prices (see Thornton 1931:69, 71–71 for an excellent description of how this worked) as well as for very rapid changes in price (Aldrich 1889:83–84; Beechey 1831, vol. 1:397, 411).

All of the early explorers commented on the Iñupiaq propensity for trading. In 1816 Otto von Kotzebue noted that they were "very expert traders, haggle obstinately, always consult together, and are infinitely happy when they have cheated any body" (1821, vol. 1:211).[68] They were such astute traders, indeed, that both Kotzebue and Beechey thought that they had received some special training in the art from the Chukchi. In 1816 Kotzebue's expedition received a visit from two umiat whose occupants "tried to cheat us every way in the sale of some of their small works, and laughed heartily when they could not succeed. They have probably learnt the common rule in trade, to show the worst goods first, from the Tschukutskoi [Chukchi], as the latter from the Russian merchants" (1821, vol. 1:235).

Similarly, Beechey remarked:

> *From the cautious manner in which the whole tribe dispose of their furs, reserving the most valuable for larger prices than we felt inclined to give, and sometimes producing only the inferior ones, we were induced to suspect that there were several Esquimaux acting as agents upon the coast, properly instructed by their employers in Kamschatka, who, having collected the best furs from the natives, crossed over with them to the Asiatic coast, and returned with the necessary articles for the purchase of others.* [1831, vol. 2:306]

Neither Beechey nor Kotzebue could believe that the Iñupiat had developed these skills on their own.

The Iñupiat were willing to spend hours haggling over prices, to the great frustration of Westerners. They frequently consulted one another before closing a deal and resorted to a variety of other stratagems to come to a decision. Beechey reported:

> *They understood making a good bargain quite as well as ourselves, and were very wary how they received our knives and hatchets, putting their metal to the test by hacking at them with their own. If they stood the blow, they were accepted; but if, on the contrary, they were notched, they were refused. A singular method of deciding a bargain was resorted to by one of their party, almost equivalent to that of tossing up a coin. We had offered an adze for a bundle of skins; but the owner, who at first seemed satisfied with the bargain, upon reflection became doubtful whether he would not be the loser by it; and to decide the doubtful point he caught a small beetle, and set it at liberty upon the palm of his hand, anxiously watching which direction the insect would take. Finding it run towards him, he concluded the bargain to be disadvantageous to him, and took back his goods.* [1831, vol. 1:397]

The haggling that typically accompanied a trade was attested by the earliest explorers, but the fullest accounts come from the second half of the nineteenth century. Nelson described dealing with some Ukiuvaŋmiut who visited Saint Michael sometime during 1879–81:

> *As usual, they were very difficult to trade with on account of their slowness in closing a bargain. A man would bring in a bunch of dried fish, throw it on the floor, and then stand about as if he had no interest in anything going on, until asked what he wished; when the regular price was offered he would almost invariably refuse, and then a long talk would ensue, which ended either by his accepting what was offered or by taking away the fish. This slowness is common with these people.* [1899:230]

On another occasion Nelson was at the head of Norton Bay when an Iñupiaq trader from Kotzebue Sound wanted to exchange some domesticated reindeer skins imported from Chukotka for various articles: "It was in the evening, and after prolonged haggling, and changing one article for another, which lasted until 3 o'clock next morning, half a dozen skins were finally bought from him. We retired and were hardly in bed before the man came back to exchange for other things some of the goods which he had taken. Finally the trader put him off until next day, when he again occupied a couple of hours before he was satisfied" (1899:230–231). He admitted that this might have been an extreme case but claimed that it showed the general Native method of trading.

An amusing account of the negotiation process is contained in the journal of Joseph Grinnell, a participant in the gold rush to the central Kobuk River in 1898–99:

> *I have succeeded at last in trading for two pairs of snowshoes, from some Eskimos who have just come up the river. The dickering engaged the entire afternoon, and I am completely exhausted. It is a stupendous undertaking to attempt to trade for anything. The natives want the earth, and then "some more." The following is an illustration of the proceedings: an Indian [Iñupiaq] brings in a pair of snowshoes and we all rush to see them, commenting on their size and quality. "Mickaninny" (too small); "anganinny" (too big); "naguruk" (good); "caprok pechak" (string loose); "byme by fixem." And then "capsinic" (how much?). The native invariably replies, "You speak." You can never make an Indian state what he wants. You begin by offering him "sox." "Konga" (no). He wants "cow cow" (something to eat). "Flour?" "Capsinic flour?" "Neleuea" (I don't know). Being urged on flour, the native intimates "two sacks." "Oh, apazh, apazh" (too much). One sack flour all right? "No, too small." The [Eskimo] then proceeds to look over the sack of flour brought for his inspection and he finds "potoa" (hole). After this is sewed up he finds that it has been wet at one end and the flour is a little caked in advance at the bottom. He therefore states that the whole thing is "no good," and "dauxic pechak" (no trade). He wants bacon. "So long and so broad," indicating the measurements in the air with his hands. "No, we pechak" (haven't any for him). Then I bring out a shirt to add to the sack of flour. He looks at the shirt and finds a torn place. "Stoney-house" (no good). . . . After two hours of sweating and bargaining the trade is consumated.* [1901:67–68]

Grinnell concluded by saying, "From the foregoing it will be plainly seen that a native is amply able to care for his own interests, and has learned from a probably bitter experience to 'look a leetle out' " (1901:68).

It would be easy to construe these examples as exemplifying the way Iñupiat dealt with outsiders as opposed to with one another. However, Charles Brower, who for all practical purposes became a Native himself, suggests otherwise: "Any one thinking these Eskimos were easy marks soon found out their mistake. They are continually trading among themselves, and any thing they have to sell they would spend hours and days bartering over" (n.d.:140). On a later page he reinforced his earlier statement: "Sometimes they would barter for several days before a trade was finished, no matter who was trading every one seemed to have a say in it, and when there was a dispute either of the O-ma-liks ,as the head men were called would have the settleing of it" (Brower n.d.:244).[69]

There is some evidence, indeed, that this general pattern was not restricted to Iñupiat but was common all over northern Alaska. For example, on April 8, 1874, at a Neets'ąįį Gwich'in camp in the lower Chandalar River valley, Robert McDonald observed that "there is so much talk over each article. And as all take pride in making a good bargain, each of course tries to excel and thus it becomes very tedious" (1862–1913, MSS 0196:folder 3, 19).

Open market trade was conducted on a buyer-beware basis. Traders deliberately withheld goods if they thought the price might rise later (Bockstoce 1988, vol. 1:151; Cantwell 1889a:71; Rosse 1883:42), and they were not averse to raising prices several hundred percent from one day to the next if they felt they had misjudged the market (Beechey 1831, vol. 1:411; Bockstoce 1977:125–126). They were also willing to spend considerable time and effort devising ways to cheat. For example, in 1826 Beechey reported that "on several occasions . . . they tried to impose upon us with fish-skins, ingeniously put together to represent a whole fish, though entirely deprived of their original contents" (1831, vol. 1:391; see also Wolfe n.d.:110).

Shortly after the meteorological station was established at Barrow in 1881, Murdoch reported that some Natives "brought over the carcass of a dog, with the skin, head, feet, and tail removed, and attempted to sell it for a young reindeer; and when we began to purchase seal-oil for the lamps one woman brought over a tin can nearly filled with ice, with merely a layer of oil on top" (1892:41). He also said that clothing and other articles made specially for whites were "very carelessly and hastily made," while the things the Natives made for their own use were very carefully constructed (Murdoch 1892:41). In 1881 the Natives on Kotzebue Sound brought bundles of caribou skins to trade to the crew of the *Corwin* that "upon examination proved to be winter skins and unfit for clothing. They had saved the best skins, supposing that we did not know the difference" (Hooper 1884:39).

One might assume that such blatant efforts to cheat would be greeted with expressions of anger, at least verbal if not physical. However, all of the early sources agree that trading was carried out enthusiastically and in good humor. Beechey said that traders tended to be "noisy and energetic, but good-natured, laughed much, and humorously apprized us when we were making a good bargain" (1831, vol. 1:339). Kotzebue said that "there was so much laughing and joking during the trading that it appeared as if we were surrounded by the lively South Sea islanders, instead of the serious inhabitants of the north" (1821, vol. 1:211). On another occasion Kotzebue's men attempted to trade with eight people in an umiaq, "but the Americans treated us very contemptuously, offering us little rags of rats' and dogs' skins in exchange; but when they observed that we laughed at their goods, they also joined heartily in the laugh, talking much to each other, and at last advised us to put the rags in our noses and ears" (1821, vol. 1:222).

The peaceful nature of the trading may have related to the fact that women and children were usually present while it was going on. Women, indeed, were active players, often as traders and even more frequently as consultants (Beechey 1831, vol. 1:391, 408–409; Bockstoce 1988, vol. 1:97; Kotzebue 1821, vol. 1:211). Whatever the reason, the Iñupiat conducted their negotiations "with surprising tact and ability" (Cantwell 1889a:71).

The International Trade Network

International trade in northwestern Alaska was carried out at the individual and family levels. However, when the full array of interconnections established at those levels is viewed in its entirety, a fairly large and complex system emerges. Having discussed the types of relationship in terms of which international affairs were conducted and the venues where international contacts most frequently occurred, we have reached a point where it is appropriate to look at the system from a broader perspective.

The material as opposed to the social foundation of international trade was based primarily on variations in natural resources from one estate to another. If one country was well supplied with seals (but few caribou), say, and another was endowed with a large caribou population (but few seals), a basis for trade existed as long as people in both nations wanted the other's products. Although raw materials constituted the foundation of international trade and are emphasized in the following discussion, it is important to note that they were by no means the only type of good exchanged. In northwestern Alaska as elsewhere in the world the work of master craftsmen was appreciated and sought after. People capable of producing goods of unusually high quality were usually quite willing to sell them—for the right price. Thus, in addition to raw materials, international trade also included a broad array of manufactured goods: arrows, bows, baskets, bowls, lamps, sleds, rope, kayaks, boots, and parkas, just to name a few of the more obvious possibilities.

Within the study area comparative advantages in resources tended to cluster on a regional more than a national basis because immediate neighbors often shared the same general advantages and disadvantages. This enables me to present the relevant information under a few general headings instead of on a country-by-country basis. The headings are inland–coast, Eskimo–Athapaskan, Alaska–Canada, Alaska–Chukotka, and Native–Westerner.

Inland–Coast Trade

In the NANA Region as in northwestern Alaska generally the major axis of interregional trade was inland–coast (Spencer 1959:14, 124–131). According to Robert Spencer, the primary goods that "were traded between nuunamiut [inlanders] and tareumiut [coastal dwellers] were two—seal and whale oil and caribou hides. These were vital to the economy of each setting and, all things being equal, could not be obtained in sufficient quantity in the native setting" (1959:201).

Spencer's statements are basically correct, but they are also an oversimplification of the exchanges that took place between the two environmental zones during the first half of the 19th century. It is true that inlanders wanted oil, but they were able to satisfy their own needs to a greater extent than is generally recognized. They did so by using tallow from various land mammals, fish oil, and the harvest from their own sea mammal hunts.[70] It is also true that coastal people wanted caribou skins for clothing. However, before the caribou population crashed in the late 1870s and early 1880s they usually were able to satisfy their needs in their homelands to a much greater extent than they could afterward.

The standard view is that the primary coastal product needed by the inlanders was seal and whale oil (Bockstoce 1988, vol. 1:209; Curtis 1930:162; Hopson 1978:93–94; Kisautaq and Kean 1981:596–597; Maguire 1857:413–414; North Slope Borough, Commission on History and Culture 1980:156–157; Northwest Iñupiat Elders Conference 1976:76–07; Ray 1885:39; Simpson 1875:266; Spencer 1959:204; Woolfe 1893:138). There can be no doubt that oil was important, but sealskin rope, sealskin towlines, sealskin boot soles, and sealskins for boat covers were scarcely less so. Other useful sea mammal products included sealskin water bags, snowshoe webbing, beluga sinew, waterproof sealskin boots, maktak, *maktaak* (beluga blubber with skin attached), dried seal meat, and walrus ivory and various items made from it. Arctic fox skins were passed primarily from the coast to the interior, although they probably were not a major item of trade. On the Arctic Slope driftwood was a coastal product highly desired by inlanders living north of the tree line, especially for use in boat construction.

In return for this relatively restricted set of products, the inlanders offered for sale a wide variety of goods desired by coast dwellers. Those of which I have heard or read are listed in Table 8. Caribou hides were the dominant item on the list in terms of both bulk and perceived importance, but it was this entire array of goods, not just caribou hides, that constituted the inlanders' stock in trade. The inlanders brought a lot more to the table than generally has been recognized.

Furs were probably always among the goods offered for sale to coast dwellers, but their value, hence the volume of trade, was probably lower during the 18th century than it was during the 19th. After the Anyui fair was established in western Chukotka in 1789 the Chukchi soon stripped their own country of fur-bearing animals and started buying pelts from Alaska. This steadily raised their value in Alaska, a general trend that persisted right into the 20th century.

While on the subject of the inland–coast trade, it is appropriate to evaluate two figures published by Spencer regarding its volume. The first is the num-

Table 8. Inland Goods Traded to Coastal People

Caribou
bedding
dried meat
hides
sinew
special foods

Dall sheep
dried meat
hides
horns

Furs
arctic ground squirrel
beaver
bear, black
bear, brown
ermine
fox, red (various color phases)
hare
lynx
marmot, hoary
marten
mink
muskrat
otter, land
wolf
wolverine

Minerals
ready-made arrowheads
chert (for arrowheads)
graphite
hematite
kitik (skin-scraping sandstone)
labret stones
marble (whetstones, labrets)
medicinal clay
nephrite (whetstones, labrets)
pyrites
ready-made whetstones

Plant products
birchbark
birchbark baskets
buckets
long, straight poles
spruce pitch
medicinal roots and leaves
tubs
wooden utensils

Miscellaneous
ready-made clothing (parkas, mittens, footgear)
musk ox hair (for thread)
dried fish
feathers for arrows

Sources: Beechey 1831, vol. 1:345, 406; Bockstoce 1988, vol. 2:504; Brower n.d.:242; Hopson 1978:93; Kisautaq and Kean 1981:597; Murdoch 1892:49, 60; Nelson 1877–81, notebook 12; Rainey 1947:268–269; Ray 1885:39; Simpson 1875:266; Spencer 1959:204; Stoney n.d.:159.

ber of caribou hides brought to the coast each summer. Spencer (1959:203) states that it was not unusual for a single umiaq to bring 500–600 hides to the coast for sale in a given year. Now if it is true, as reported above, that 50 Kuukpigmiut boats went to Nigliq each year, and if Spencer's figure is correct, they would have brought 25,000–30,000 hides for sale at Nigliq alone. Even more inlander boats went to Sisualik each year, which would have more than doubled the figures. Without taking into account any hides the Utuqqaġmiut might have taken to the fair in the Icy Cape district, we are talking about a minimum of 60,000 hides being taken every year from the caribou herds of northwestern Alaska simply for the purposes of trade. These figures do not take into account the inlanders' own requirements, which would have been greater than those of the coast dwellers because there were more inlanders.

Altogether, these figures mean that at least 120,000 animals were killed each year for their hides (although much of the meat was consumed as well). Since caribou hides are prime for clothing only in mid- to late summer, most of these animals had to be killed in just two or three months' time. We have to wonder how the Iñupiat could have achieved such an enormous kill in such a brief period. We also have to wonder how they could have done it year after year without exterminating the caribou population.[71] But perhaps Spencer got the number from Nelson, who did, in fact, report that "in the summer of 1880 one man from Point Barrow took about five hundred skins, and many others took nearly as large a number" (Nelson and True 1887:285). But Nelson made this observation in the context of a discussion of how the caribou were being exterminated; it was an extraordinary number, not a typical one.

There are two possible explanations for Spencer's estimate. First, of course, it could be wrong. Alternatively, it could be correct, but for only the latter part of the 19th century. By the late 1870s the Iñupiat had acquired breech-loading rifles and were using them to kill caribou. With these weapons the Iñupiat did, in fact, all but exterminate the caribou populations of northwestern Alaska during the 1870s and 1880s. Thus, they really might have brought as many hides to market as Spencer claims they did (Burch 1994:172–174; Nelson 1899:119; Nelson and True 1887:285; Stefansson 1951:66, 67, 48–49). But his figure is far too high for the time period of primary concern in this study.

A second suspect number is Spencer's figure of 50 pokes of oil as being a possibility for one coastal umiaq to take to the Nigliq fair. My late friend Bob Tuvaaqsraq Hawley Sr. worked for the Kivalina Native Store during his youth, and one of his jobs was to weigh pokes of oil brought in for sale. According to him, small pokes averaged about 100 pounds (45 kilograms) in weight, medium pokes averaged about 200 pounds (90 kilograms), and large pokes averaged 300 pounds (135 kilograms) (Hawley 1970), suggesting an overall average of 200 pounds (90 kilograms) per poke. Fifty pokes of seal oil would have weighed roughly 10,000 pounds (4,500 kilograms), or 5 tons. An umiaq headed toward a fair would have been loaded not only with the pokes but with tents and other camping gear, food, kayaks, several people, and dogs, all of which would add at least another 2,000–3,000 pounds (900–1,360 kilograms) to the load, for a total of 6 tons (5,440 kilograms) or more. The highest estimate I have ever read for the carrying capacity of an umiaq is 5 tons (4,500 kilograms), and that was for one of the very large boats used in Bering Strait (Thornton 1931:125). The boats used in Barrow, which was the primary focus of Spencer's study, had a much lower payload.

Spencer's estimate, therefore, was well above what was physically possible for an umiaq to carry. But there is an additional consideration. When the specific traders regarding whom his figures apply left Barrow they had to go some distance on foot, hauling everything, including their boats, on sleds. The trade goods specifically were carried on small sleds pulled by one or two women and a maximum of two or three dogs (Bockstoce 1988, vol. 2:408; Maguire 1857:457; Simpson 1875:264). It is doubtful that such a sled would have had room for or could have withstood the weight of the number of pokes Spencer indicates. Even if it could, we must further question whether one or two women and a couple of dogs would have had sufficient strength to pull it. In short, while Spencer's estimate of 50 pokes was presented as a maximum figure, it has to be higher than was possible in even the largest boat and very far above the average.

I have gone through this exercise not to pick on Spencer but to introduce some badly needed perspective on the quantities of goods exchanged between coastal and inland nations. Spencer's monograph is a very impressive work, but both he and those who accept his findings uncritically have an inflated impression of the physical magnitude of inland–coast trade. We will never know the exact scale of this trade, but available information indicates that it was substantial enough, and there is no need to exaggerate it.

Another issue that is appropriately addressed here is the degree of dependence by the coastal and inland dwellers on the trade between them. According to Froelich Rainey, the trade was "a fundamental necessity" for the coastal people because without it they would have lacked caribou hides for clothing (1947:240). Spencer went further and maintained that inlanders and coast dwellers were "interdependent," which presumably means that neither one could exist without the other (1959:193, 441–442).[72] Sheehan made the point explicit. According to him, coast dwellers literally could not have survived without caribou skins, and "inlanders might have perished at any time" without seal oil (Sheehan 1997:184). In short, the inlanders and coast dwellers were entirely dependent on one another for survival (Sheehan 1997:11–14).

If these propositions are correct, how did the East Greenland Inuit survive in their harsh environment without caribou skins? How could the Koyukon and Gwich'in have survived for hundreds or even thousands of years in interior northern Alaska without seal oil? The answer is that they survived because there were alternatives. In the absence of caribou the East Greenlanders made clothing from sealskins and polar bear hides (Holm 1914:29–35, 56–57; Petersen 1984:630–631; Thalbitzer 1914:561–580). In the absence of seal oil the Gwich'in and Koyukon acquired the fat they needed from bears, fish, and caribou.[73] Actually, many of the Iñupiat who lived in interior districts preferred land animal fat to sea mammal oil (Brower n.d.:286–287). They placed tallow taken from marmots, ground squirrels, grizzly bears, and Dall sheep into bags made from caribou and sheep stomachs and stored it for the winter (Paneak 1970); among the Kiitaaġmiut and Siiḷviim Kaŋianiġmiut people made extensive use of fish oil (Smith 1970). Even the upper Kobuk Koyukon, who could have traded for seal oil if they had wanted it, preferred bear grease (Wood 1931). Inland–coast trade unquestionably enabled the Iñupiat to live at a higher material standard of living than would have been possible in its absence, but their very survival did not depend on it.

Eskimo–Athapaskan Trade

Trade between the Eskimos (both Iñupiat and Yup'ik) and their Athapaskan neighbors, particularly the Koyukon, probably had a long history in northwestern Alaska, and it was quite active during the first half of the 19th century.[74] Compared to the inland–coast trade among the Iñupiaq nations, however, the trade between the Athapaskans and Eskimos was both small in scale and limited in the variety of products involved.

Most of the Eskimo–Athapaskan trade was carried out in winter, using dogsleds for transportation. In the NANA Region it was conducted almost exclusively in a messenger feast context. On the Arctic Slope most of it seems to have occurred at the Niġliq and Barter Island trade fairs, although the Di'hąįį Gwich'in, on the Athapaskan side, and the Nuataaġmiut and Kuukpigmiut, on the Iñupiaq side, also exchanged messenger feasts from time to time. Moving south, messenger feasts were again the primary venue in the eastern Seward Peninsula and Norton Sound regions, particularly across the Kaltag Portage. A considerable quantity of the Athapaskan trade between the lower Yukon River and the coast was conducted at Tačiq and Pastuliq (Nelson 1899:232). However, most of this involved Yup'ik speakers on the Eskimo side, and, as noted above, I have not been able to determine the specific type of venue involved.

The primary goods Athapaskans had to trade to Eskimos were skins that were rare or absent in Iñupiaq territory and various types of manufactured goods. Beaver and marten were chief among the fur-bearing animals involved here, and both the raw pelts and blankets and mittens made from them were offered for sale. There were no moose in the NANA Region at the time, so moose hide and moccasins made from it were common items of trade from farther east. In return the Iñupiat offered sealskins and sealskin rope, boot soles, waterproof boots, seal oil, walrus ivory, and parkas made from the hides of caribou fawns. Over the course of the 19th century the Western fur trade became progressively more important in exchanges between Athapaskans and Iñupiat, but that subject is dealt with in a separate section.

Alaska–Canada Trade

The Alaska–Canada trade involved Alaskan Iñupiat from Barrow and Inuit-speaking Eskimos from the Mackenzie River delta (Bockstoce 1988, vol. 1:209, vol. 2:505; Franklin 1828:130; Harrison 1908:81; Jenness 1946:62; Kisautaq and Kean 1981:142–143; Morrison 1991a; Murdoch 1892:49, 60; Simpson 1875:267; Simpson 1843:171, 177; Stefansson 1914a:10). In the early 19th century virtually all of it occurred in the context of the Barter Island trade fair.

The material basis for an Alaska–Canada trade was rather meager until Western goods became available from Hudson's Bay Company trading posts during the late 18th century. The people on both sides were coast dwellers who lived in comparatively rich environments, the only differences being that the Alaskans had special access to bowhead whales, while their Mackenzie Delta Eskimo counterparts had special access to beluga. This created one basis of exchange: bowhead whale maktak and oil from Alaska and beluga whale maktaak from Canada. Another item the Canadians had to offer was soapstone, either as a raw material or manufactured into oil lamps, which they had acquired themselves in trade with people living still farther east. The only other distinctive product the Alaskans had to offer was walrus ivory, for which there probably was reasonably good demand in the Mackenzie River delta and for most of which the Barrow traders had to trade themselves with Siḷaliñaġmiut and Tikiġaġmiut to the south. Furs and manufactured goods were exchanged as well, but the primary basis of the Alaska–Canada trade was Western goods entering the system via the Hudson's Bay Company, as discussed below.

Alaska–Chukotka Trade

Trade across Bering Strait no doubt had ancient roots but probably was not all that extensive until Western goods and the fur trade began to penetrate the region.[75] By the time of the study period, furs from the Alaskan side and manufactured Western products and reindeer hides from the Chukotkan side dominated the market.

Native products available in Chukotka that were highly desired by the Iñupiat consisted primarily of domesticated reindeer skins, which have a color pattern different from those of Alaskan caribou, and wolverine and wolf pelts, which for some reason were regarded by the Iñupiat as being of higher quality than those found in Alaska (Lucier 1997:333).[76] In return the Iñupiat offered beaver, fox, muskrat, mink, and land otter pelts, dried fish, ready-made clothing, and manufactured wooden goods of various kinds.

During the early 19th century a special feature of Alaska–Chukotka exchanges was the role played by Western goods. In return for furs and walrus ivory the Chukotkans traded tobacco, beads, and metal goods (e.g., knives, pots, kettles, hatchets, scissors, needles) to the Iñupiat and Yup'ik Eskimos. These exchanges began shortly after the establishment by the Russians of the Anyui trade fair in 1789 near Nizhne Kolymsk, some 800 miles (1,300 kilometers) west of Bering Strait (Forsyth 1992:150; Kotzebue 1821, vol. 1:262–

263; Lantzeff and Pierce 1973:11; VanStone 1977:47). This was where Chukotkans acquired the Western goods that they took to Bering Strait to exchange for Alaskan furs and was the source of the items that so surprised the first Westerners to reach northwestern Alaska.[77]

Stimulated by the expanding supply of Western goods in Chukotka, on the one hand, and a corresponding demand for furs there, on the other, the trade across Bering Strait steadily increased between about 1790 and the mid-19th century. At that point shipborne American traders, whalers, and explorers cruising through Bering Strait began to disrupt the older pattern (Ray 1975b:124; Whymper 1869a:169). Just how this trade fit into the broader historic and prehistoric pattern of aboriginal trade in northern Beringia is discussed in Chapter 4.

Native–Westerner Trade

Native–Westerner trade was of two kinds, indirect and direct.[78] Indirect trade occurred when items of Western manufacture were exchanged for Native products through intermediaries rather than directly between Iñupiat and Westerners. Direct trade, as the phrase implies, involved personal contact between Westerners and Natives.

Most of the Native–Westerner trade in northern Beringia was indirect during the early 19th century, since it depended on the Alaska–Chukotka trade described above. Goods of Western manufacture were acquired by Chukchi at the Anyui fair and then brought or traded through intermediaries to the shores of Bering Strait. From there they were carried to Sisualik, Point Spencer, and other locations for sale to Alaskans. A certain amount of indirect trade also filtered up from Russian outposts in southern Alaska (Michael 1967:100; Miller 1994). There was a marked increase in this trade during the 1830s, when trading centers were established on Norton Sound and the lower Yukon River and when Russian-American Company vessels began almost annual visits to the islands in Bering Strait (Arndt 1990, 1992, 1996; Schweitzer and Golovko 1995:29 n. 16). On the east it was a more recent and more remote phenomenon, the sources of Western goods being the Hudson's Bay Company posts at Fort McPherson, established in 1840 (Hudson's Bay Company Archives 1840–41), and Fort Yukon, established in 1847 (Hudson's Bay Company Archives 1847–48; Murray 1910). This particular trade did not have any noticeable impact on the Iñupiat during the study period.

Direct trade between Westerners and Iñupiat probably began with a few Russian and American traders who visited Kotzebue Sound between about 1810 and 1820 (Howay 1973:84, 96, 97, 150, 192, 194, 196, 203, 205, 206; Ray 1975a, 1983:38). However, during the early years most of it involved infrequent contacts between explorers and Natives. After the Russian post was established at Saint Michael in 1833, direct contact became more frequent. However, it involved only the small portion of the Iñupiaq population willing to go that far to trade, many of whom were not from the NANA Region.[79]

In 1848 explorers involved in the Franklin search expeditions arrived in northwestern Alaska, and their members traded actively with Iñupiat for the next six years (Great Britain, Parliament, House of Commons 1850:paper no. 2, 12, 13; Seemann 1853, vol. 2:130–134). American whalers also arrived off the coast of northwestern Alaska in 1848 (Bockstoce 1986:28–29). They did not have many direct contacts with Iñupiat for the first few years, but they were accompanied by small trading schooners whose crews sought all the trade they could get right from the beginning (Dall 1870:502; Cantwell 1889a:80, 1889b:80; Great Britain, Parliament, House of Commons 1854a:155; Hooper 1881:19–20, 23, 25–26, 42; Nelson 1899:231). In any event, it was only at the very end of the study period that direct trade with Westerners began to have a significant impact on the Iñupiaq way of life.

The primary demand by Western traders was for furs, practically every kind they could obtain, with a secondary interest in walrus ivory. The explorers and later the traders were also interested in acquiring souvenirs in addition to furs, meaning almost any portable item of Iñupiaq material culture they could buy. In return the Natives were willing to part not only with furs but with almost anything they had except their weapons. The Natives either refused to sell their weapons at all or else demanded a very high price for them (Beechey 1831, vol. 1:339, 390, 411, 458; Kotzebue 1821, vol. 1:210). In return they received hatchets, copper and cast-iron kettles, beads, necklaces, knives, scissors, needles, combs, brooches, buttons, and tobacco. The general volume of this trade and its impact on the Iñupiaq way of life are discussed in Chapter 4.

The Overall System

The friendly relations that existed between and among many of the nations of northern Beringia during the early 19th century were the foundation of an active trade network of impressive geographic proportions. As a minimum it extended from the Mackenzie River delta and the Yukon River on the east to Siberia on the west and from the Arctic Ocean on the north to the Bering Sea on the south.[80] At various points along its western, southern, and eastern margins the system was directly connected with Western outposts and thus with that portion of the world system dominated by Westerners. But most of these connections were established toward the end of the period of primary interest here and had not yet had much of an impact on the Iñupiaq way of life.

The trade network of northern Beringia during the early 19th century is summarized in Map 13, which is supported by Tables 9 and 10. The tables list the major points of trade, both Native and Western (Table 9), and the major

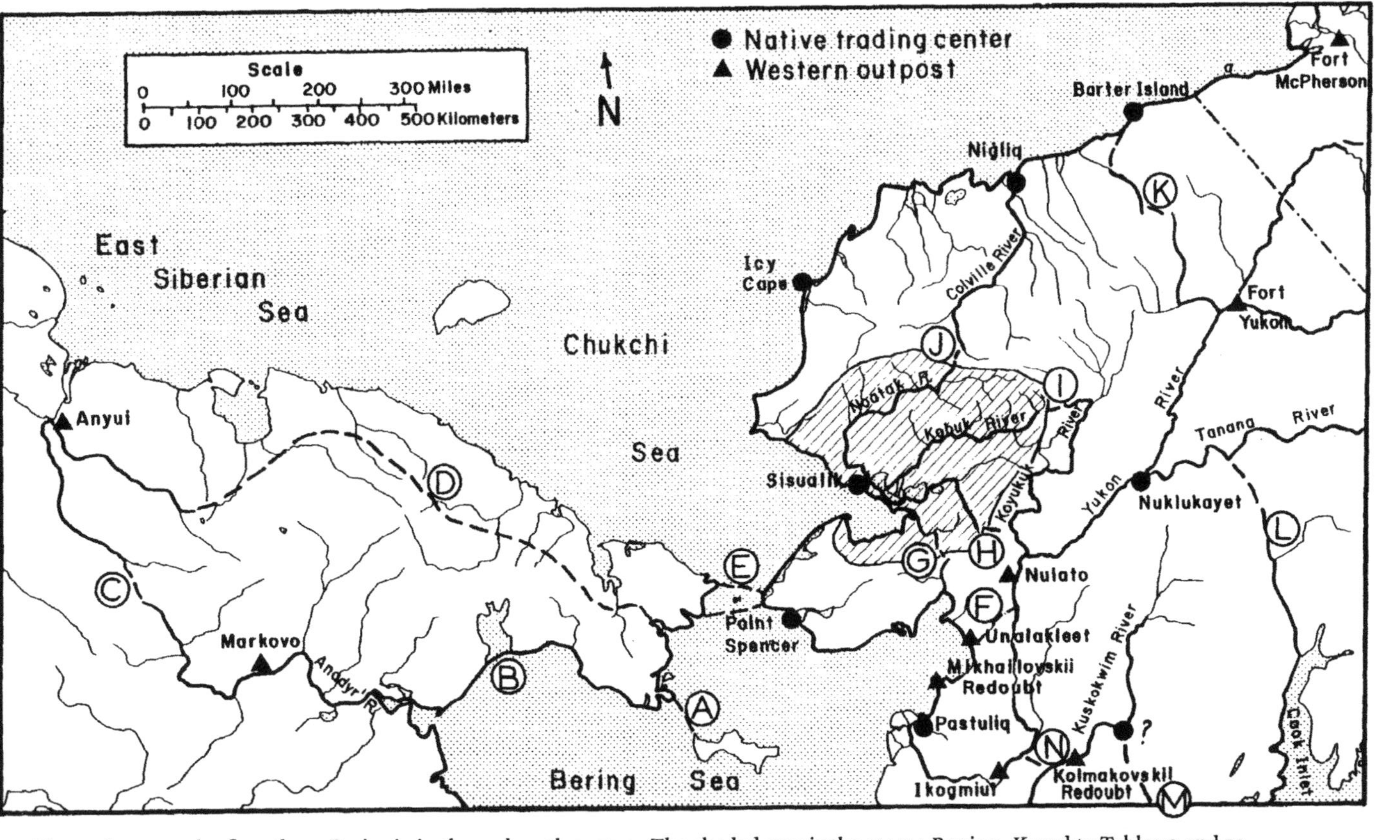

13. The trade network of northern Beringia in the early 19th century. The shaded area is the NANA Region. Keyed to Tables 9 and 10.

Table 9. Western Outposts in Northern Beringia, ca. 1800–1850
(See Map 13)

Outpost	Description and Sources
Anyui	This was a winter trade fair opened in 1789 near the mouth of the Anyui River in western Chukotka. It was run by independent Russian traders under government supervision. This was the main source of European goods acquired in northwestern Alaska during the study period.[1]
Fort McPherson	Opened in 1840 by the Hudson's Bay Company on the lower Peel River, a short distance above the head of the Mackenzie River delta.[2]
Fort Yukon	Opened in 1847 by the Hudson's Bay Company on the Yukon River near the mouth of the Porcupine. Its direct trade was primarily with Gwich'in Athapaskans.[3]
Ikogmiut	This was a Russian-American Company post opened on the Kuskokwim River in 1836.[4]
Kolmakov's Odinochka	A small Russian-American Company post on the upper Kuskokwim established in 1833. It was the precursor of Kolmakovskii Redoubt.[5]
Kolmakovskii Redoubt	This was major Russian-American Company post opened on the Kuskokwim River in 1841.[6]
Markovo	A Russian outpost was established at Anadyrsk in 1649. It was closed in 1764 and was not reestablished until the latter part of the 19th century.[7] However, during the 1820s and 1830s Russian settlers moved into the Anadyr' valley and developed a center at what became Markovo.[8]
Nulato	Established in 1839 by the Russian-American Company.[9]
Mikhailovskii Redoubt	This was an important Russian-American Company post established in 1833.[10]
Unalakleet	An outstation of Mikhailovskii Redoubt was established at this old Yup'ik village in 1837.[11]

1. Erman 1855:203–206; Ray 1975b:98.
2. Isbister 1845.
3. Murray 1910.
4. Michael 1967:81, 275.
5. Arndt 1996:29–30; Kashevarov 1994:331; Oswalt 1963:11, 104; VanStone 1959:46 n. 28.
6. Arndt 1996:29–30; Michael 1967:80, 252–253; Oswalt 1963:11–12, 104–105; VanStone 1984:151.
7. Forsyth 1992:79, 149.
8. Krupnik 1997.
9. Arndt 1996:42–45; Michael 1967:81, 146–147, 183.
10. Arndt 1996:32–33; Ray 1975b:122, 133.
11. Ray 1975b:125.

routes between them (Table 10).[81] The latter include the coastline, the major rivers, and the primary routes taken between watersheds. These were the main, or "trunk," routes, which were supplemented by a large number of smaller, or "feeder," routes (McCarthy 1939a, 1939b, 1939c). The latter are not shown in Map 13 or listed in Table 10, but the most important ones within northwestern Alaska are listed in Appendix 2.

Table 10. Major Trade Routes in Northern Beringia, ca. 1800–1850 (See Map 13)

Map Key	Description
A	Uŋazik (Chaplino)–St. Lawrence Island.
B	Uŋazik–lower Anadyr' River: This was used primarily in summer by Eskimos from Uŋazik to visit Chukchi on the Anadyr' to acquire reindeer hides.
C	Markovo–Anyui: This was an interregional route used exclusively by Chukchi, mostly in winter.
D	Anyui–Bering Strait: This was the main route used by Chukchi traders using reindeer-drawn sleds in winter.
E	Bering Strait: This was used by Chukchi, Asiatic Eskimos, and Iñupiat warriors and traders. Most movement across the strait was made by boat during summer.
F	Kaltag Portage: This was a major winter route between the coast of Norton Sound and the lower Yukon. It was probably used more after the Russian posts were established at Mikhailovskii Redoubt and Unalakleet in the 1830s than it had been previously.
G	Buckland–Koyukuk: This was used by Koyukon and Iñupiat, mostly in mid- to late winter.
H	Selawik–Koyukuk: This route was used by Koyukon and Iñupiat, mostly in mid- to late winter.
I	Kobuk–Koyukuk: This route was used by Koyukon and Iñupiat, mostly in mid- to late winter.
J	Noatak–Colville: Goods and people moved up and down the rivers by boat in summer and crossed the Brooks Range over Howard Pass in winter. This was the main route whereby goods moved between Sisualik on Kotzebue Sound and Niġliq and Barter Island on the Arctic coast.
K	Chandalar–Arctic coast: This was the main route used in summer by Gwich'in traveling to the Barter Island trade fair.
L	Lower Tanana–Susitna and Cook Inlet: This was the route by which coastal products, particularly dentalium, reached the interior from the south coast.
M	Lake Clark–Kuskokwim: This route probably went to the upper Mulchatna River and thence to the Holitna or Stony Rivers and down to the Kuskokwim. There was another route just to the west linking the Nushagak River with the Holitna and Kuskokwim.
N	Kuskokwim–Yukon: The lowlands of the Yukon–Kuskokwim delta made travel between the two rivers fairly easy, but the most frequently used route seems to have been where they were closest together.

Sources: Bogoras 1904–9:57–59:end map; Krupnik 1997; McKennan 1965:25–26; Michael 1967:80; Osgood 1937:75; VanStone 1988:6. Other sources are listed in Appendix 2.

Goods could and did travel the length and breadth of the network shown in Map 13 and beyond. The Iñupiat were aware of the full scope of at least the northeastern portion of the system, and some of them told John Simpson just how it worked during his stay at Point Barrow from 1852 to 1854:

> *At the Colville, the Nu-na-tang'-meun [inlanders] offered the goods procured at Se-su'-a-ling [Sisualik] on Kotzebue Sound from the Asiatics, Kokh-lit' [Qutlich]*

en'yu-in, in the previous summer, consisting of iron and copper kettles, women's knives (o-lu'), double-edged knives (pan'-na), tobacco, beads, and tin for making pipes; and from their own countrymen on the Ko'-wak [Kobuk] River, stones for making labrets, and whetstones, or these ready made, arrow-heads, and plumbago. Besides these are enumerated deer and fawn-skins, and coats made of them, the skin, teeth, and horns of the im'na (argali?) [Dall sheep], black fox, marten, and ermine-skins, and feathers for arrows and head-dresses. In exchange for these, the Point Barrow people (Nu-wung'meun) [Nuvugmiut] give the goods procured to the eastward the year before, and their own sea-produce, namely, whale or seal-oil, whalebone, walrus-tusks, stout thong made from walrus-hide, seal-skins, &c, and proceed with their new stock to Point Barter. Here they offer it to the Kan'g-ma-li en'yu-in, who may be called for distinction Western Mackenzie Eskimo, and receive in return, wolverine, wolf, imna, and narwhal skins (Kil-lel'-lu-a), thong of deer-skin, oil-burners, English knives, small white beads, and latterly guns and ammunition. In the course of the winter occasional trade takes place in these with the people of Point Hope, but most of the knives, beads, oil-burners, and wolverine-skins, are taken to the Colville the following year, and, in the next after, make their appearance at Kotzebue Sound and on the coast of Asia. [1875:266; cf. Woolfe 1893:138][82]

John Simpson's predecessors—Beechey, Franklin, Kashevarov, Kotzebue, and Thomas Simpson—had described separate parts of the system, but he was the first to put it all together.[83]

In a major paper on the historic Beringian trade network, Clifford Hickey (1979:419–420) noted that one of its primary effects was to even out national differences in natural resources and manufactured goods. It did so by moving them from districts where they were abundant to districts where they were not. In early-19th-century northern Beringia, as in the modern world, international trade enabled everyone to achieve a higher material standard of living than would have been possible without it. But it is also important to keep in mind the fact that the system of international easements and licenses permitting people to make selective use of one another's estates was also important to the system's operation. It was the combination of trade *and* international movement that made the system so effective in evening out regional disparities in the resource base.

Alliances

International alliances in early-19th-century northwestern Alaska were formed primarily to establish a united front against common enemies. To a certain extent they also opened up hunting and fishing areas beyond the borders of national estates through easements (Ray 1967:384). With respect to their longevity they ranged from ad hoc to enduring; in regard to their formality they varied between explicit and publicly declared, at one extreme, and casual to almost accidental, at the other.

Relatively formal alliances (*iḷauraaġiiksit-*, "to form an alliance") were created when the several umialġich of the nations involved met, agreed on a particular course of action, and persuaded their followers to accept it. Unfortunately, I do not have any information on exactly how they went about this, but it is reasonable to assume that a formal alliance would have been most easily established when the leading individuals in the nations concerned happened to be partners. Alliances could have been made at fairs, but they were more likely to have been established at messenger feasts, where espionage by or interference from excluded parties could be avoided. Even the most formal alliance, however, was very casual compared to the alliances with which we are familiar today: no governments were involved in their creation, and no formalized international councils or meetings existed to maintain them or guide their conduct (Ray 1967:385).

Informal alliances developed when neighboring peoples just happened to get along well. Consequently, they exchanged feasts, achieved a higher than average level of intermarriage, possibly hunted to some extent in each other's estates, and perhaps even combined forces in war. Over time these alliances became so well entrenched that people forgot how they started; the people probably did not really care. Unless a troublemaker disrupted them, they were simply part of the basic scheme of things.

Judging from Ray's (1967:384–389) research, the most formal and enduring alliances in all of northwestern Alaska may have been in the Bering Strait–Norton Sound area.[84] She lists six alliances there during the study period:

1. The Kiŋikmiut, Siñġaġmiut, and Ukiuvaŋmiut[85]
2. The Kiŋikmiut, Tapqaġmiut, and Pittaġmiut[86]
3. The Kiŋikmiut and Qaviaraġmiut
4. The Qaviaraġmiut, Iġałuiŋmiut, Siñġaġmiut, and sometimes the Ayasaaġiaaġmiut
5. The Ayasaaġiaaġmiut, Iġałuiŋmiut, Ukiuvaŋmiut, and sometimes the Qaviaraġmiut
6. The Atnəgmiut, Čaxtuləgmiut, and Uŋallaqłiŋmiut

A seventh, extending south of Norton Sound, sometimes linked the Uŋallaqłiŋmiut with the Taprarmiut and Pastulirmiut. An eighth alliance linked the Imaqłit of the Diomede Islands with the Nuvuqaghmiit of Cape Dezhnev, the easternmost tip of Chukotka (Nelson 1899:330; Weyer 1962:157). These alliances crosscut one another to such an extent that making them work must

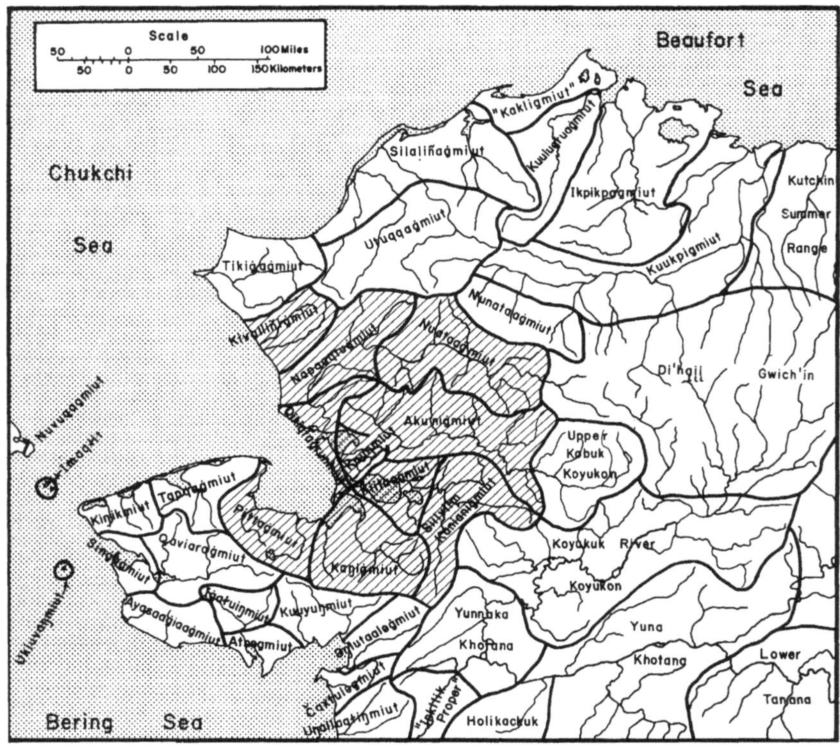

14. A political map of northwestern Alaska, ca. 1800. The shaded area is the NANA Region.

have required remarkable diplomacy. The same characteristics also make it very difficult to depict all of them on a single map, so Map 14 is provided for reference purposes.

Alliances apparently were less formal in the NANA Region than they were in the Bering Strait area and around Norton Sound, although they were not necessarily less enduring. Alliances in this region included the following:

1. The Tapqaġmiut, Pittaġmiut, and Kaŋiġmiut
2. The Akuniġmiut, Kiitaaġmiut, Kuuŋmiut, and Siiḷviim Kaŋianiġmiut
3. The Qikiqtaġruŋmiut and the Pittaġmiut
4. The Napaaqtuġmiut and Nuataaġmiut [J. Foster 1970; Kiana 1969; Stefansson 1914b:10; Wright 1969]

These alliances were apparently so old that knowledge of their origins was lost long ago. An apparently somewhat newer alliance linked the Napaaqtuġmiut, Nuataaġmiut, Qikiqtaġruŋmiut, and Kivalliñiġmiut. The members of these last four nations, it will be recalled, joined forces to attack the capital village of the Tikiġaġmiut, as reported in Chapter 2, and again to fight the Tikiġaġmiut at Nuvua (see Appendix 1). Involving members of four nations, a great deal of travel, and military action that included substantial risk, this alliance must have required either some blatantly aggressive act by the Tikiġaġmiut or else months or even years of negotiation to put together. Whether it endured longer than these two engagements and whether it involved obligations other than mutual aggression against the Tikiġaġmiut is unknown.

An example of an ad hoc alliance involving nations in the NANA Region was established when the Kuuvaum Kaŋiaġmiut recruited some Kuuŋmiut to help them raid the main village of the Qikiqtaġruŋmiut.[87] This one was truly ad hoc, for it did not take place until the initial raid had been aborted, and it ceased to exist only a day or two later. It was evidently based on shared animosity against the Qikiqtaġruŋmiut.

Little information on alliances involving Arctic Slope nations exists. The only alliance I have heard of linked the Nuataaġmiut of the upper Noatak River valley in the NANA Region with the Kuukpigmiut and Utuqqaġmiut of the Colville and Utukok River valleys, respectively. I have never heard of these nations joining forces in war, but their members could hunt in one another's estates to some extent, they frequently exchanged messenger feasts, and families from any one of the three could join the mass of people from one of the others to attend one of the summer fairs. Whether any alliances involving residents of the Arctic Slope existed in addition to this one is unknown. Judging from Kashevarov's account (which was excerpted at length in Chapter 1), at least the coastal nations on the Arctic Slope seem to have had rather strained relations with one another.

In the modern world an alliance promises, as a minimum, peaceful relations between or among the nations involved in it. That was true in northwestern Alaska as well. Given the extent of warfare and raiding in the region, the promise of peaceful relations with even a few other nations was a significant achievement. If the danger from a particular quarter could be reduced or eliminated, a nation's security was greatly enhanced. The members of allied nations did not harass one another, and they could expect to transit one another's estates without fear.[88]

Alliances introduced flexibility into subsistence pursuits when they yielded an easement or license for the members of one nation to use the estate of another to acquire raw materials not available in their own. Permission was key here, because in some areas people used land belonging to another nation without an easement at a specific time of year when its residents usually were somewhere else. Where an alliance was involved, people could hunt and fish in foreign territory even when the residents were there; indeed, members of the different groups often hunted and fished together in the hosts' estate. Such arrangements were particularly valuable to the residents of King Island and the Diomede Islands, who traveled to various parts of the Seward Peninsula each summer to harvest a variety of products that were not available in their own homelands (Ray 1967:385–386).

In the modern world many alliances include a provision for joint defense. In northwestern Alaska, where raids were over almost as soon as they began, distances were great and communication was poor, so cooperative defense was usually impossible. Exceptions could occur, of course, as when people from two or more nations happened to be gathered together for some reason when members of a third nation launched an attack on the settlement where they happened to be. In practice an alliance providing for mutual support in the case of war usually meant that a joint retaliatory effort would be made after a raid on one of the allies. However, allies could conduct espionage on one another's behalf, and if enough advance warning occurred, a joint preemptive strike was a possibility.

4. Conclusions

This book had two main purposes. The first was to describe and analyze the relations of the early contact nations of the NANA Region with one another and with other peoples with whom they were in contact. The second was to extrapolate from the north Alaskan data to a more general model of what an international system in a world inhabited entirely by hunter-gatherers might be like. The first objective has been largely achieved, but two general matters relating to it remain to be discussed. One is to describe how hostile and friendly relations intersected in the real 19th-century world. The other is to explore more fully than heretofore the historical context of the events and processes described in this book; the key issue here is the extent to which they reflected Western influence. Finally, and at somewhat greater length, I relate the subject matter of this book to world systems theory under the heading of "comparative and evolutionary perspectives."

The Intersection of Hostile and Friendly Relations

The two previous chapters produced internally consistent views of hostile and friendly relations prevailing in early-19th-century northwestern Alaska, yet each was the antithesis of the other. How could both have occurred simultaneously? The answer is that, at any given time, each nation was involved in its own unique combination of hostile and friendly relations with its counterparts.

If we focus on individual nations, the way that hostile and friendly relations intersected becomes easy to understand. For example, if we consider the Nuataaġmiut of the upper Noatak valley, we find that they were frequently at war with the Akuniġmiut (central Kobuk), the Di'hąįį Gwich'in (Endicott Mountains), the upper Kobuk Koyukon, and the Tikiġaġmiut (Point Hope). On the other hand, they were allies with the Napaaqtuġmiut (lower Noatak River valley), the Kuukpigmiut (Colville River valley), and the Utuqqaġmiut (Utukok River valley) and frequently with the Kivalliñiġmiut (Kivalina district) and the Qikiqtaġruŋmiut (Kotzebue district) as well. With respect to all other nations, they were on more or less neutral terms. Similarly, if we focus on the Kiitaaġmiut of the lower Selawik drainage, we find them allied with the

Siiḷviim Kaŋianiġmiut (upper Selawik), the Akuniġmiut (central Kobuk River valley), and the Kuuŋmiut (Kobuk River delta) but in a state of war with at least the Kaŋiġmiut (Buckland), the Pittaġmiut (Deering district), and the Koyukuk River Koyukon. If we were to move across the political landscape of northwestern Alaska one nation at a time, we would see that the general pattern exemplified by the Nuataaġmiut and the Kiitaaġmiut would be repeated again and again. Each nation had its own unique set of both enemies and allies, while its relations with all other nations were more or less neutral.

At the level of the region as a whole, the system was a complex array of international relations in which nationalism, which usually contributed to international discord, was offset by other forces that worked to produce harmony. One of the most important of the latter was the universal desire of individuals to have predetermined safe havens to which they could flee with their families in times of turmoil or famine at home. This led individuals and families to establish and maintain partnership and kinship ties with members of other nations, sometimes even nations with which their own was frequently in conflict. The second major force holding the international system together was a seemingly universal obsession with trade, which enhanced the material standard of living of everyone in the region. The desire for trade, in turn, contributed to an extraordinary willingness to suspend hostilities on specific occasions and at certain times of year.

The suspension of international hostilities for messenger feasts and during the trade fair season is, to me, the most remarkable feature of the system. Both types of event were organized around partnerships, but they required the cooperation of practically every individual in northwestern Alaska to make them work. At each of the fairs people who ordinarily were passionate enemies somehow managed to congregate peacefully for a week or two each year. To attend a messenger feast people often had to traverse an enemy estate, but apparently they could do so with little danger if they sought permission to do so in a traditionally approved way. The value people attached to these events was so strongly ingrained that most were willing temporarily to set aside even profound animosity to allow them to take place. When I asked my informants whether people going to or returning from fairs or messenger feasts were ever ambushed by enemy forces, they could think of only a couple of examples.[1]

The picture I have drawn of the intersection of hostile and friendly relations in early historic northwestern Alaska is regrettably static. We have general information on who was allied with whom and on who was at war with whom, but we lack information on the exact pattern existing at any specific period and thus of the nature and frequency of changes over time. Presumably, nations that were allies at one time could be enemies at another and vice versa.

If we choose as a model of international affairs the rapidly changing relations among the Great Powers that has occurred during my own lifetime (1938–present), we must conclude that the situation in early historic northwestern Alaska was probably much more dynamic than I have indicated.

A Temporal Perspective

This study was set within a very specific time frame, 1800–1848. I chose the first date because it is the earliest time I felt I could reliably reach with data from both oral and written historical sources. The second date was selected because it was then that the most significant perturbations in the system for more than 1,000 years began to take place. It is appropriate to reconsider the starting and ending dates of the study within a broader perspective of social change.

Origins of the System

To say that I could not reliably go back farther than 1800 on the basis of oral history does not mean that the system suddenly appeared full blown that year. On the contrary, it was already up and running. The question is, Since when? A related question is, What is the extent to which the system that I have described was the result of Western influence rather than of indigenous factors? If the system can be shown to have been in existence before Western contact, then there is good reason to conclude that it was an indigenous creation.

In 1800 the Russian outpost closest to the NANA Region in Siberia was Nizhne Kolymsk, 800 miles (1,300 kilometers) west of Bering Strait (Forsyth 1992:150; Lantzeff and Pierce 1973:11). The closest Russian posts in Alaska were in extreme southwestern Alaska, some 500 miles (800 kilometers) away; Russian activities at the time were focused on the Sitka region, nearly 1,000 miles (1,600 kilometers) to the southeast (VanStone 1984:149–151). In Canada, although Alexander Mackenzie had already visited the delta of the river now bearing his name, no Western outposts had been established in the delta (Usher 1976:157–159). The nearest Westerners to the east were at least 700 miles (1,125 kilometers) away at the time. Northwestern Alaska in general and the NANA Region in particular were still isolated from Western missionaries, settlers, traders, soldiers, and diseases. The NANA Region Iñupiat were still hunter-gatherers surrounded by other hunter-gatherers.

Despite northwestern Alaska's isolation from the West, "first contact" in the strictest sense of the term had already occurred there by 1800. In most of the New World Western conquerors and missionaries and the diseases they brought with them dramatically transformed the Native way of life within a short period of time. In contrast, Western influence in northwestern Alaska developed in a series of relatively gentle transitions over some 150 years.

Indirect contact with Westerners began late in the 18th century. The Russians began forcefully expanding eastward across Siberia in 1581 (Dmytryshyn, Crownhart-Vaughan, and Vaughan 1985, 1988; Forsyth 1992:30). By 1644 they had reached the western margin of Chukotka, some 800 miles (1,300 kilometers) west of Bering Strait (Forsyth 1992:76). The Russians and their Siberian Native surrogates fought the Chukchi and their Yup'ik (Eskimo) allies off and on for the next 120 years but failed to conquer them. Considerable havoc was wreaked amongst the Chukotkans, but it was at such a high cost to the Russians that they abandoned the effort in 1764 (Forsyth 1992:143–151). At their own initiative the Chukchi established peaceful trade relations with the Russians that same year, and it was via trade, with the Chukchi acting as middlemen, that indirect Russian influence first came to be felt in northwestern Alaska (Forsyth 1992:150).

The Chukchi eventually agreed to become Russian subjects, at least according to the Russian understanding. However, for all practical purposes they remained autonomous until well into the 19th century and possibly even into the 20th (Znamenski 1999). They retained effective control of their territory, pursued their own shamanistic religion, refused to pay tribute to the czar, required both Russians and Eskimos to learn Chukchi if they wished to communicate with them, and continued "to live according to their own customs and laws" (Bogoras 1901:84–85; de Reuse 1994:296–297; Forsyth 1992:150; Lantzeff and Pierce 1973:218–219). John Cochrane, who observed Chukchi traders at the Anyui fair in 1822, stated that, "upon the whole, the Tchuktchi appear to be approaching to Russian subjection," but his own account of their behavior suggests that the opposite conclusion is more warranted (1825, vol. 1:380, 304–325).

In saving themselves from Russian conquest, the Chukchi made an enormous contribution not only to the physical survival of the Iñupiat but to their social and cultural survival as well. By the time the Russians finally reached northwestern Alaska they were seeking trade, not demanding tribute. It is also appropriate to point out that, after the Russians had withdrawn from Chukotka, the Iñupiat were saved from the Chukchi, in turn, by the existence of Bering Strait. Had it not been for the strait, Chukchi reindeer herders, flushed with their victory over the Russians, could easily have expanded eastward into Iñupiaq territory. As it was, they had to expand in the opposite direction.

Depending on the location, the first direct contact between Iñupiat and Westerners occurred in 1732, 1791, 1816, 1826, or 1827. Some dates relevant to this issue are presented in Table 11, which shows that Western explorers got within a few miles of northwestern Alaska as early as 1648 but that no actual contact with Natives in the region occurred until nearly a century later. The

Table 11. Early Western Visits to Northwestern Alaska

Year	Expedition	Comments
1648	Dezhnev	Passed through Bering Strait. No contact.[1]
1728	Bering and Chirikov	Passed through Bering Strait. No contact.[2]
1732	Gvozdev	Brief contacts with residents of King Island and the two Diomedes.[3]
1763	Daurkin	Visited Big Diomede.[4]
1778	Cook	Sailed through Bering Strait to Icy Cape. Only contact with Alaska Natives was on Norton Sound.[5]
1779	Kobelev	Visited the Diomede Islands.[6]
1791	Billings	Explored Chukotka, Bering Strait, and southwest Seward Peninsula.[7]
	Kobelev and Daurkin	Visited the Diomede islands, Wales, and King Island.[8]
1816	Kotzebue	Contacted Iñupiat on north Seward Peninsula and Kotzebue Sound.[9]
1819	Gray	Traded on Kotzebue Sound.[10]
1820	Pigot	Traded on Kotzebue Sound.[11]
1820–21	Shishmarev and Vasil'ev	Explored from Norton Sound to Icy Cape.[12]
1822	Khromchenko and Etolin	Explored shore of Seward Peninsula and Bering Strait islands.[13]
1826–27	Beechey	Explored from Port Clarence to Point Barrow.[14]
1838	Kashevarov	Explored from Point Barrow to Chamisso Island.[15]

1. Fisher 1981.
2. Divin 1993; Golder 1968, 1971:145.
3. Goldenberg 1983, 1990:62; Golder 1971:161–162.
4. Masterson and Brower 1948:64–67.
5. Cook and King 1784, vol. 2:479–484.
6. Masterson and Brower 1948:93–96.
7. Merck 1980; Sarychev 1806–7, vol. 2:44–52; Sauer 1802:242–248.
8. Chernenko 1957; Ray 1975b:52–54.
9. Chamisso 1986a, 1986b; Choris 1822; Kotzebue 1821, vol. 1:200–236.
10. Bockstoce 1986:2; Ray 1983:55–65.
11. Howay 1973:141–142; Ray 1983:55–65.
12. Berkh 1983; Ivashintsov 1980:50–56; Ray 1975:1–66.
13. Arndt 1996:23; VanStone 1973.
14. Beechey 1831, vol. 1:339–459, vol. 2:255–286; Belcher 1825–27; Bockstoce 1977; Gough 1973; Wolfe n.d.
15. VanStone 1977.

first encounter with mainlanders was by James Cook in 1778, but that was in Norton Sound and presumably with Yup'ik speakers rather than Iñupiat. In 1791 Ivan Kobelev and Nikolai Daurkin visited the Diomede Islands, Wales, and King Island but failed to meet anyone on the Alaskan mainland. The Billings expedition visited the southern Seward Peninsula later that same summer, but its contact with Natives was brief.

It was another 25 years before Otto von Kotzebue arrived in the sound that now bears his name, and it was he who made the first documented direct

Western contact with Iñupiat living in the NANA Region.[2] There was a brief flurry of encounters on Kotzebue Sound between 1819 and 1822, but the most extensive ones did not take place until the Beechey expedition, in 1826 and 1827. Frederick William Beechey's expedition also made the first direct contact with people north of Point Hope. All available evidence indicates that not one of these early encounters had any enduring demographic or cultural impact on the Native population of northwestern Alaska.

Assigning a precise date to Western contact with the Iñupiat is partly a matter of interpretation. However, no matter what date one assigns to it, contact falls well after 1600. Evidence indicative of 19th-century-style war and trade from before 1600, therefore, would support the hypothesis that the system described in this volume is indigenous in its origins and basic structure and not a consequence of Western influence.[3]

There is actually no way to determine when the system originated because by the time the evidence becomes very good, the system was already in operation. For present purposes I limit myself to showing that there is good reason to believe that a 19th-century-*type* system of international relations existed in northwestern Alaska at least as long ago as the Birnirk–Punuk period. This means that it was roughly 800 years old by 1600.

Birnirk and Punuk were two different but closely related maritime Eskimo cultures that coexisted in the Bering Strait region during the period 700–1200 (Bronshtein and Dneprovsky 2002; Collins 1937a:66; Dumond 2000:136–140, 2002:350; Gerlach and Mason 1992:65; Mason 1998, 2003:227–234). Punuk sites are primarily (but not exclusively) in Chukotka, and Birnirk sites are primarily (but not exclusively) in northwestern Alaska (Ackerman 1984:109–113; Anderson 1984:90–91; Collins 1964:98; Gerlach and Mason 1992:64; Mason 2000; Rudenko 1961:171–172; Stanford 1976:96–104). There seems to have been considerable interaction between the two (Ackerman 1962; Anderson 1984:90–93; Arutiunov and Fitzhugh 1988:128; Collins 1964:99; Mason 2003:230–235; Morrison 1991b:28–32), and both probably could be considered direct ancestors of 19th-century Iñupiaq culture.

WAR

The first problem to solve is what constitutes evidence of prehistoric warfare. Among hunter-gatherers, who use basically the same weapons for killing game animals as for killing people, this determination is often impossible. In the present instance, however, we are fortunate to have the evidence of armor (see Sheehan 1997:48). Plate armor was made from dozens of ivory plates carved from walrus tusks that have been perforated and linked together with thongs; it is worn like a shirt or vest. The plates are very distinctive items, not likely to be used for any purpose other than armor and not likely to be confused with any other type of artifact (although other objects could be made from the plates). It is inconceivable to me that a man would invest the considerable time and effort required to make them unless he had a major need for physical protection against arrows or spears (see Sheehan 1997:47, 48). Theoretically, that need could relate to feuding, but that was an individual or family affair and unlikely to result in armor production on a very large scale.

The first evidence of plate armor in the area of present interest is in Punuk sites in Chukotka. The same deposits also contained evidence of "refinements in archery equipment (sinew-backed bow, bow braces, sinew twister, wrist guard, new arrow types), and long knives and daggers" (Ackerman 1984:112; see also Arutiunov and Fitzhugh 1988:128; Bandi 1995; Collins 1937b:325–326; Geist and Rainey 1936:142, 159; Rudenko 1961:152–153). To my knowledge, armor plates have not been reported from Birnirk sites in Alaska, however, and warfare may not have been present there at that time. Alternatively, it could be that warfare had arrived but that people had not yet started making plate armor, or the absence of armor plates may be due to sampling error in the excavations.

In any event, large quantities of armor plates have been discovered in a western Thule site at Barrow dating from the 15th century (Sheehan 1995:191, 1997:139, 140; see also Jenness 1928:78), and they have been found in undated Thule sites at Wales and Little Diomede (Morrison 1991b:82). Although these sites are post-Punuk, they date from well in advance of the target date of 1600. Assuming that warfare was present for some time before people started to make the armor, it is highly probable that warfare occurred in northwestern Alaska for as much as 500 years and possibly 1,000 years prior to the period of primary interest in this study.

TRADE

The second problem is to determine what constitutes archaeological evidence of international trade. The most convincing evidence would be the discovery in one district of objects that were demonstrably made in or acquired from another. In the present case we have such evidence in the form of minute quantities of metal—mostly iron, some copper—that were clearly of foreign origin. In fact, iron of Eurasian manufacture was used in engraving tools and as tiny knife blades throughout the Arctic by as early as the beginning of the Christian Era.[4]

An important question in the present context is just how dependent the people of northern Beringia were on this commodity. Allen McCartney addressed this issue as follows:

> *Whether Chukotkan iron and native Alaskan copper should be considered utilitarian or luxury materials depends somewhat upon the definition of its function. Because metal and evidence of metal . . . are primarily seen . . . functioning as manufacturing tools and secondarily as substitute blades for more traditional stone harpoons, lances, arrows, and cutting/skinning knives, early metal use is considered to have a definite utilitarian function. On the other hand, such metal-bladed tools could theoretically have been made with stone blades, as were earlier ones. In that sense metal was not a necessity for Arctic adaptation even though it was widely used.* [1988:77]

Another important matter is the value of iron as an indicator of prehistoric trade—as an index fossil, as it were. What the evidence shows is that both an intercontinental (Eurasian–American) and a pan–North American Arctic trade network was already in existence 2,000 years ago.

By Birnirk times, perhaps 1,000 years ago, the evidence of a widespread trade network was no longer limited to small amounts of metal. Douglas Anderson summarized this additional evidence as follows: "Birnirk-Style weapons (harpoon heads, for instance), have been found over a large area—westward along parts of the northeastern Siberian coast as far as the mouth of the Kolyma River . . . and eastward as far as Atkinson Point, northwestern Canada. This indicates a far-reaching communication network, particularly westward, and calls to mind the extensive trade network of Eskimos around Bering Strait during the nineteenth century" (1984:91; see also Collins 1929:145, 1931:142, 1933:48).

In archaeological sites in the Mackenzie River delta, Robert McGhee sees evidence of the same thing but at a somewhat later time: "[A] Mackenzie–West Alaska relationship was established as early as the 14th and 15th centuries, and was either continuous or sporadically renewed until the historic period" (1976:191).[5] Recently uncovered evidence shows that small amounts of coal were also traded across the North American Arctic as early as 1100 (Kalkreuth and Sutherland 1998).[6]

The transportation technology necessary to support such a trade network existed before Birnirk–Punuk times on both sides of Bering Strait in the form of umiat (Ford 1959:157–158; Geist and Rainey 1936:65, fig. 11; Rudenko 1961:149–150, 175). Sleds and snowshoes were also of ancient vintage, as was at least some use of dogs.[7] Dogs probably were not particularly common, however, since people were observed pulling sleds with their dogs as late as the mid-1880s.

DISCUSSION

The evidence summarized above makes a strong case that the basic structure of the international system existing in northwestern Alaska at the beginning of the study period was almost certainly 500 years old and possibly 1,000 years older than that. It was far too ancient to have been the result of Western influence. It existed long before Westerners got anywhere near the region, and it remained beyond even their indirect influence until shortly before the beginning of the study period. With reference to international trade specifically, I concur with Peter Schweitzer and Evgeny Golovko: what we see in early-19th-century northern Beringia was "not a mere response to the [Western-dominated] expanding world system but the indigenous vehicle through which this expansion took place" (1995:135).[8]

Termination of the System

The final question to be addressed in this section is when the system of international relations described in this volume ceased to exist. Like "contact," termination proceeded gradually. The foundation was laid in the rapidly growing intercontinental trade of the late 18th and early 19th centuries, but it was a series of events that occurred near the close of the study period that signaled the beginning of the end.

The first important development was the establishment of the Russian trading post at Saint Michael (Mikhailovskii Redoubt) in 1833 (Ray 1975b:122–124). Saint Michael is about 150 miles (240 kilometers) south of the NANA Region. It was the first year-round source of Western trade goods to be located anywhere near the region of interest here. During the early years most of the trade between Saint Michael and the NANA Region was probably conducted through Yup'ik-speaking middlemen from nations whose estates bordered Norton Sound. However, the smallpox epidemic of 1838 decimated the Yup'ik-speaking population of southwestern Alaska and much of the Koyukon-speaking population of the lower Yukon (Michael 1967:145–147; Ray 1975b:125–127). Miraculously, it spared the Iñupiat.

After the epidemic Iñupiat from the NANA Region had to visit Saint Michael themselves if they wanted to participate in the trade with that post, although some Russian traders probably visited Bering Strait and perhaps even Kotzebue Sound during the summers (Black 2004:198–199). During the 1840s Kaŋiġmiut especially began to visit the nearly depopulated shores of Norton Sound on their way south to Saint Michael, and some of them decided to stay there (Arndt 1986a, 1986b; Ray 1975b:130–139). Iñupiat did not settle there in any significant numbers until after midcentury, however (Ray 1975b:11).

The year 1848 brought two major developments. One was the arrival in northwestern Alaska of the first vessels of the Franklin search expeditions (Bockstoce 1985). For the next several years they cruised up and down the coast, making frequent contact with Natives. They overwintered in northwestern Alaska on five occasions: twice on the western end of the Seward Peninsula (once with two ships), once in Kotzebue Sound, and twice near Point Barrow (Bockstoce 1985; Ray 1975b:140–156). The crews of the overwintering ships in particular had extensive contact with Iñupiat living in nearby villages.

The second major development of 1848 was the passage through Bering Strait of the American whaling ship *Superior* under Thomas Roys (Bockstoce 1985:21–26). He had an extraordinarily successful season, and other ships soon followed. In the summer of 1850 some 200 whaling ships cruised the waters off northwestern Alaska, and in 1852 their number increased to 220 (Bockstoce 1986:93–102; Seemann 1853, vol. 2:176). The whalers generally stayed well offshore during the early years, but they landed from time to time to collect firewood, and, as noted in Chapter 3, they were usually accompanied by a number of small trading vessels whose captains eagerly sought trade with anyone who would participate, including Iñupiat.

WAR

Warfare apparently came to a halt around midcentury. The cessation of war within the Yup'ik language zone coincided with the smallpox epidemic of 1838, which destroyed the demographic base of the several nations in that region. The reason war ended in the Iñupiaq language area is less apparent.

The Kaŋiġmiut, who had been so aggressive toward both the Russians and the British in the 1820s, had become positively docile by the time HMS *Plover* wintered at Chamisso Island in 1848–49 (Miertsching 1967:36–37). The change was no doubt influenced by their heightened understanding of the power of firearms (and their own lack thereof) and by their increasingly frequent contact with Russian traders at Saint Michael on Norton Sound.

The trend can be seen even more clearly among the Kakligmiut of the Barrow district. They had been extremely hostile to nearly every explorer they encountered in the early part of the century. They continued to be aggressive during the first winter the *Plover* spent there (1852–53) but changed completely the following year. John Simpson described what happened: "We have learned enough from them to believe that they at first looked upon us as a contemptible few whom they could easily overcome, and certainly would have attempted it but for fear of the firearms; but since then, they have gone to the opposite extreme, and invested us with greater powers than we really possess" (Simpson 1875:248).

As a final example of this type, the Western Union Telegraph Expedition set up a base at Port Clarence, in the southwestern part of the Seward Peninsula, in 1865: "The first winter they were there the natives from Cape Prince of Wales [Kiŋikmiut] decided to kill them and take their weapons and other belongings as booty. Thus, a force of fifty men came armed with spears, bows and arrows, and a few flintlock muskets. But when they met the group of twenty-five well armed young men [from the expedition] they changed their mind, made friends, and went home" (Johnshoy 1944:51).

Peace came to Native–Westerner relations in northwestern Alaska because Westerners had firearms and a seemingly infinite supply of prized trade goods, while the Natives had neither. Peace among the Native nations of northwestern Alaska came after that between Iñupiat and whites but probably by less than a generation. Throughout the 1860s and 1870s the residents of Norton Sound were still alert against attack, but raids seem to have been carried out only by individuals or very small groups, and open battle had ceased (Dall 1870:144; Jacobsen 1884:294; Nelson 1899:327). Edward William Nelson, who lived on or near Norton Sound from 1879 to 1881, wrote of warfare in the past tense (1899:327–330), and John Murdoch (1892), Patrick Henry Ray (1885), and George Morse Stoney (1900), each of whom spent at least a year in northwestern Alaska in the early and mid-1880s and who wrote extensive reports on their experiences and observations, did not mention warfare at all. The combined evidence suggests that international warfare in northwestern Alaska declined dramatically during the 1850s, was reduced to a raid or two during the 1860s, and stopped altogether in the 1870s. Prowling, however, continued for another century.

We can speculate indefinitely on why war ceased so abruptly and why it stopped when it did, but before closing this section I will offer my own hypothesis on the subject. It seems to me that the Iñupiaq obsession with trade, which they considered so important that they could meet peacefully with inveterate enemies at least once a year at trade fairs, is one part of the answer. The other part is the vastly increased opportunity for commerce opened up around midcentury by the sudden proximity of Westerners with goods to trade. Western goods acquired previously via the Chukchi had to come a vast distance overland. They were probably so expensive that it was not worth sacrificing other important activities to acquire the means, that is, the furs, to buy them. However, goods brought by ship to Mikhailovskii Redoubt (Saint Michael) and Bering Strait beginning in the late 1820s and to the various trade fairs after 1848 must have been cheap by comparison. From then on, substantial benefits could be achieved through the international trade in furs. Warfare was an obvious impediment to this trade and, after a few unsuccessful confrontations between groups trying to control it, simply was not worth pursuing anymore.

TRADE

At midcentury the Iñupiat were still economically self-sufficient to a high degree despite the long history of international trade and of access through it to goods of Western manufacture. I illustrate this point with regard to firearms and goods made from metal.

The odd firearm had been seen in northwestern Alaska over the years, but at midcentury there probably were fewer than five muzzle-loaders distributed among the entire Iñupiaq population, from Norton Sound around northwestern Alaska to the Canadian border (Bockstoce 1985:101; Bockstoce 1988, vol. 1:156, 174; Burch and Mishler 1995:159; Murdoch 1892:193; Ray 1975a). The Iñupiat were still totally dependent on traditional technology for their harvest of game animals. The situation began to change in the 1850s, when American trading schooners initiated operations in northwestern Alaskan waters. It changed dramatically after 1867, when the Russian prohibition on the sale of firearms to Natives was voided by the sale of Alaska to the United States. By the 1880s large numbers of men were equipped with the latest in firearm technology, although they still made and used bows and arrows (Murdoch 1892:193–195; Nelson 1899:118; Wells and Kelly 1890:26; Woolfe 1893:146).

It was noted earlier that small amounts of metal began to arrive in northwestern Alaska as early as the beginning of the Christian Era. By the beginning of the 19th century there was an active trade in finished metal goods, particularly knives, needles, and containers, across Bering Strait. But the Iñupiat still made their own pots and lamps from local materials as well as those imported from Canada and Chukotka probably until the latter part of the century. They also continued to make and use arrowheads and spearheads, as well as various other items, from stone and bone.

In 1852 Rochefort Maguire reported that only four out of 17 arrows in an abandoned quiver he examined at Point Barrow had metal points (Bockstoce 1988, vol. 1:102). Murdoch (1892:190) also described a quiver from Barrow 30 years later, but in this one 7 out of 13 arrows had metal points. The percentage had increased from 24 to 54, but neither is indicative of an overwhelming dependence on metal. In 1881 Nelson noticed that the people of Point Hope had "an unusually large number of flint arrows, and lance heads, as though they were still [*sic*] or had until lately used them" (1877–81, notebook 12:entry for July 18). A year or two later Murdoch found the people at Barrow still far from dependent on Western goods (1892:52–55). Also on the basis of observations made at Barrow in the early 1880s, Patrick Henry Ray observed:

> *That these people have not yet made the transition from the stone to the iron age is shown by the large number of stone and bone implements still in use among them at the present time. Many of the old conservative men still cling to the habits of their fathers, and believe that stone arrow and lance heads possess virtues that makes them superior to those made of iron. They still teach the young men the art of chipping flint, and over their work tell them of the happy days before white men came to drive away the whales and walrus, and when food was always plenty. An old man, when asked what he would do without the things the white men brought*

> *them, answered that it would be very hard, and then to show us what he could do he showed a pair of boots he had on, and told us with great pride how, when his boots gave out while hunting, he killed a deer, made a needle from a piece of his bone, thread from the sinew, and made himself a new pair of boots from the skin, and asked, Could a white man do that?* [1885:48; *see also* Brower n.d.:170–171; Murdoch 1892:195, 287]

If the Iñupiat were dependent on any Western product by the end of the study period, it was tobacco. The substance was introduced to them by the Chukchi, probably in the mid-18th century.[9] In 1763, on Big Diomede Island, the first request the inhabitants made of Daurkin was for tobacco (Masterson and Brower 1948:65). Cook observed that the residents of Norton Sound were familiar with it in 1778 (Cook and King 1784, vol. 2:479). In 1816 Kotzebue reported that the inhabitants of Kotzebue Sound "prize tobacco highly, and are as fond of chewing as of smoking it" (1821, vol. 1:209). By 1826 tobacco was in widespread use in northwestern Alaska (Beechey 1831, vol. 1:359). The Inuit around Herschel Island in extreme northwestern Canada had been introduced to it but did not like it (Franklin 1828:130–131; cf. Simpson 1843:146–147). By the 1830s some Iñupiat may have been addicted to it (Simpson 1843:147, 157; VanStone 1977:47), but by the 1880s almost all of them were (Woolfe 1893:146).

The precontact trade network continued to operate into the early 20th century (Stefansson 1914a; Woolfe 1893:137–138). However, even though it was as extensive geographically as it had been a century before, the nature of the trade and the Natives' dependence on it had changed in a number of significant ways. For example, by the 1870s the Western goods in greatest demand had become tobacco, whiskey, and breech-loading rifles instead of knives, axes, needles, nails, and drills (Dall 1870:143–144, 382; Murdoch 1892:53, 193; Whymper 1869b:162–163; Woolfe 1893:137, 145–146). By 1885 the caribou population had reached such a low point that the primary source of skins for clothing in much of northwestern Alaska had become domesticated Chukotkan reindeer rather than Alaskan caribou. By 1890 the main sources of Western goods had become whaling vessels, shore-based American whalers and traders, and trading schooners.

DISCUSSION

Between 1880, when the first cutters of the United States Revenue Marine began to patrol north Alaskan waters, and about 1910, when many schools, missions, stores, and other institutions of Western life had been established, the U.S. government asserted its authority over northwestern Alaska and its inhabitants. During this period the traditional Iñupiaq nations ceased to exist as operating systems, bringing to a close the international system described in this book.

Traces of the old system remained, of course, but on the intervillage, not the international level. Subdialects serve to identify a person's place of origin even today, and, in private, people from one village often speak in less than flattering terms about those from another. Battle now takes place on basketball courts and wrestling mats, but the losers survive to join the victors in postevent celebrations. Partnerships are still established but are more signs of friendship than of weighty obligation. As recently as the 1960s some people I knew stayed with a qataŋun (cosibling) when visiting another village. The early winter holiday season is now devoted to the celebration of Thanksgiving and Christmas rather than to messenger feasts; the *qatŋut*, or general gathering of people from several districts, is not the summer trade fair but the annual meeting of the NANA Regional Corporation (established under the Alaska Native Claims Settlement Act), which is held in the same village and at almost the same time as the quarterly meeting of the Friends Church. International affairs are now entirely under the control of the U.S. government.

Comparative and Evolutionary Perspectives

In the introduction I pledged to discuss in the conclusion the implications for world systems theory of the Northwest Alaskan data. The reason I did so is that world systems theorists, while ostensibly dealing with all human societies, have pretty well ignored hunter-gatherers. This is true despite the fact that nations of hunter-gatherers were the only type of society in existence for most of human history. On the other hand, it must be admitted that students of hunter-gatherers have largely ignored world systems theory—except with reference to the relatively recent incorporation of several such societies into the highly centralized world system existing today (see, e.g., Crowell 1997). Before concluding this volume I would like to contribute to at least a preliminary integration of these two perspectives via insights gained through my study of Iñupiaq societies. In the process I also hope to initiate the development of a general model of how international affairs were conducted in hunter-gatherer societies.

A thorough discussion of the disconnect between world system theorists and hunter-gatherer specialists is beyond the scope of the present work. However, a few general observations are in order. On the world systems side the basic question seems to be, Why should we concern ourselves with the study of societies whose members have had no noticeable impact on major world affairs for the past several thousand years? The Roman Empire, the Chinese Empire, and 20th-century Europe, just to name three examples, each affected the lives of more human beings than all the hunter-gatherer societies that ever existed put together. That emphasis is entirely appropriate, in my view, for the reason just stated. However, I also think it is important for people who study civilizations and empires to realize that many of the processes by means of which they emerged and sustained themselves had very ancient roots. These processes are, and always have been, part of the basic human condition.

On the other side, students of hunter-gatherer societies seem to feel that they have nothing to contribute to world systems theory. This is partly because hunter-gatherers have had so little impact on world affairs over the last several millennia. It is also partly because the members of most of the hunter-gatherer societies of historic record were so quickly annihilated by disease, not to mention conquest, that the early contact situation could not be investigated ethnographically. Even in Australia, an entire continent of hunter-gatherers until the first British settlement was made there in 1788, the Aboriginal population was devastated by smallpox not once but at least twice before any ethnographic studies could be carried out there (Butlin 1983; Campbell 2002; Kimber 1988, 1990:165).

Another serious difficulty is what might be called the apples-and-oranges problem. Everyone has heard or read the dismissive assertion that doing such and such is like comparing apples and oranges, meaning that it cannot be done. But of course it can be done. All we need is an encompassing concept to bridge the gap. Both apples and oranges are kinds of fruit, for example, and they can be compared on that basis. Both are also rounded objects, bright-colored objects, objects that grow on trees, and so on; they can be compared to one another, and to many other objects, on these and many other grounds, depending on which of their characteristics are relevant to the issue at hand.

In the present case the apples-and-oranges problem might be rephrased as the empires-and-tribes problem. How can we compare, for example, mid-15th-century Imperial China with early-19th-century Northwest Alaskan Nuataaġmiut? The answer is with concepts that are defined in a sufficiently abstract way as to apply equally to both. If we are trying, as scientists presumably do, to discover the properties that diverse phenomena have in common, we must compare them at a common level of generalization.

The concept of society, as defined by Marion J. Levy Jr., is broad enough to serve this purpose. In this study I have used "nation" as a full equivalent to "society," partly in deference to the wishes of my senior informants and partly to make the point to others that Iñupiaq societies were comparable in their most general features to modern nation-states. This usage also makes it possible to speak just as meaningfully of international affairs in early-19th-century Northwest Alaska or Upper Paleolithic Europe as it does in the modern world of the early 21st century.

Basic Concepts

In proceeding from the particular to the general, it is necessary to introduce and briefly explicate some additional concepts. Wherever possible I have tried to retain terms and definitions used by others, but since there is no universal agreement on either in most cases, I have had to be selective.[10]

SOCIETIES

The basic components of the world system are societies, specifically as defined by Levy:

> A society *is defined as a system of social action: (1) that involves a plurality of interacting individuals whose actions are in terms of the system concerned and who are recruited at least in part by the sexual reproduction of other members, (2) that constitutes a set of social structures such that action in terms of them is at least in theory capable of self-sufficiency for the maintenance of the plurality of individuals involved, and (3) that is capable of existing long enough for the production of stable adult members of the system of action from the infants of the members.* [1966:20–21 n. 10]

This concept has been elucidated at length by Levy (1952:111–148) and will not be elaborated on here.[11] However, it is worth noting that, given his definition, a society is a particular type of social system such that all other types are either subsystems of one society or else the result of interrelationships among the members of two or more societies (Levy 1966:20 n. 10). It is representatives of this last group, that is, intersocietal social systems, that of course are of interest here.

More specifically, the present concern is with relations between and among "microscale" "segmental" societies. I elaborate briefly on these two concepts.

"Microscale" refers to the tiny populations of these societies, which probably ranged between about 300 and 2,000 people. Microscale societies had so few members that virtually every adult knew every other adult. Under ordinary circumstances the members were characterized by a high level of homogeneity, with everyone of the same age and sex speaking the same subdialect, wearing pretty much the same style of clothing, and engaging in the same daily activities. People who married in were under considerable pressure to conform to the general pattern.

The term "segmental" concerns the general way in which these societies were organized; the term "acephalous" is also used by anthropologists to refer to this type of system. As noted in Chapter 1, segmental societies were composed of roughly equal and similar component groups, usually families and/or clans. The most striking organizational feature of this type of society is the absence of a unifying office (e.g., a chief) or organization (e.g., a government) at the top to coordinate or mediate the actions of the members of the several constituent segments.

Most of the microscale societies in world history were probably also segmental and vice versa. It is probably also true that most of the microscale segmental societies in world history were based on a foraging (hunter-gatherer) economy, but I would not be surprised to learn that some of the very first agrarian societies also were of this type. Conversely, it is probably also true that the vast majority of hunter-gatherer societies that ever existed were micro in scale and segmental in structure. However, as noted below, it is known that at least one society of foragers, that of the Calusa, constituted a chiefdom. Thus, while a microscale population and a segmental organization have usually coincided with a hunter-gatherer economy (and vice versa), that is not so by definition, and it has not always been so in fact.

It seems to be difficult for most anthropologists, not to mention people with other backgrounds and training, to conceive of a segmental social system involving fewer than 2,000 people as a society, never mind as a nation. But it was not difficult for my oldest informants, whose parents and grandparents were born into such units, to do so. As Robert Nasruk Cleveland (born in 1884) said to me in the winter of 1970, "They were nations, just like France, Germany, and England are today."

THE WORLD SYSTEM

The "world system" consists of all the relationships existing between and among the members of different human societies at any given time, all over the world. As noted in Chapter 1, this conception is considerably broader than the one used by most world system theorists, who connect "world" and "system" with a hyphen. Most of them analyze under the "world-system" heading what I would regard as subsystems of the world system (without a hyphen). Although some might regard this as terminological gamesmanship, there is a very important issue here: contrary to common belief even among anthropologists, human societies generally have never existed in isolation from one another. The concept of "world system" in the all-inclusive sense captures that important understanding. Until this wider perspective is adopted, hypotheses about the changing nature of international affairs on global and millennial scales are unlikely to be forthcoming.

Subsystems of the world system as I conceive it can be characterized by other, already available terms. A "sector" of the world system can be any arbitrarily selected set of societies at least some of whose members interact with one another. An "interaction sphere" can be a more or less clearly delineated sector in which there is a comparatively high level of interaction between and among the members of the societies included in it but where the level of this interaction falls off markedly at its margin (Caldwell 1964; Chase-Dunn and Hall 2000:88). A "sphere of influence" can be an interaction sphere or a sector of an interaction sphere in which the members of one society or a few closely interconnected societies exercise a disproportionate amount of influence over the members of other societies of the same general type. Finally, an "ecumene" (or "oikumene") can be a sphere of influence in which the dominant society or societies represent a more complex type of social system than most of the others.[12] Most "world-systems" described by other authors would be spheres of influence or ecumenes under these definitions; the latter, particularly, are what have occupied the attention of most world-system theorists, civilizationists, and world historians up to now.

A set of related concepts includes "core," "periphery," "semiperiphery," and "external area." A core, if there is one, is the dominant society in or sector of an interaction sphere. The periphery is the outer margin of an interaction sphere, while the external area is everything beyond that. The semiperiphery is everything between the core and the periphery. Christopher Chase-Dunn and Thomas D. Hall (2000:91) further distinguish between core–periphery differentiation and core–periphery hierarchy. The former exists when the members of "two societies systemically interact and one has a higher population density and/or greater complexity than the other." The latter exists when "one society dominates or exploits the other."

All of the above concepts have measurement problems associated with them (Chase-Dunn and Hall 1997:38–40; Levy 1952:129–134). This is unfortunate but inevitable at the present level of development of the social sciences. In this regard it is appropriate to keep in mind the likelihood that fields like physics, geology, and astronomy would still be at or near their Bronze Age levels of development if their practitioners had allowed measurement problems to hold them back. In those fields, as in science generally, the main issue is the theoretical utility of the concepts involved. If scientific concepts are useful, as determined by the fact that theories formulated with them help people understand the world better than they did without them, someone eventually figures out how to measure their referents (Crosby 1997).

Application to Northwest Alaska

With the conceptual matters behind us we can now turn to a consideration of how the Iñupiaq societies of northwestern Alaska fit into the world system at the beginning of the 19th century. At that time the nations of this region constituted a remnant sector of a geographically extensive and socially complex interaction sphere that apparently had flourished for some centuries beforehand. It began along the coast of northern California, extended up the coasts of Oregon, Washington, British Columbia, and Alaska, then followed the Alaskan coast along the Bering Sea up to and across Bering Strait, then down the west side of the Bering Sea to at least Kamchatka (Fitzhugh and Chaussonnet 1994; Fitzhugh and Crowell 1988; Friesen 1995:270–274; Griffin 1996:99–101; Kowalewski 1996:28; Koyama and Thomas 1981; Maschner 2000; McGhee 1974:7–18, 1976:190–191; Moss 1992; Suttles 1990). The system extended variable distances inland along the major river valleys in North America and westward into interior sections of easternmost Asia. In Alaska an offshoot continued north from Bering Strait into the NANA and Arctic Slope Regions and eastward to (and including) the Mackenzie River delta.

Goods and information flowed from one end of this system to the other through both down-the-line and more general sorts of transactions, interrupted here and there and from time to time by pockets of conflict (Chase-Dunn and Mann 1998:33). This "North Pacific Interaction Sphere" was peopled entirely by hunter-gatherers except on the extreme west, where some of the Asiatic peoples were reindeer-herding pastoralists. With economies based on the efficient exploitation of fish everywhere and sea mammals along the coast, the peoples in this interaction sphere are sometimes referred to as "affluent foragers" (Koyama and Thomas 1981) or "complex hunter-gatherers" (Prentiss and Kuijt 2004:viii–ix) when compared with many other hunter-gatherers in the ethnographic record.

Nested within it, the North Pacific Interaction Sphere contained a number of regional subsystems in which international affairs were particularly intense (see, e.g., Ames and Maschner 1999:165–174; Suttles 1990:9–14). One of these subsystems consisted of the Iñupiaq societies of the NANA Region and their counterparts on the Seward Peninsula and the Arctic Slope. The extent to which the Yup'ik nations of southwestern Alaska were linked to it during the early contact period is unknown because both the establishment of Russian outposts during the 1830s and the smallpox epidemic of 1838 were so disruptive in that region.

During the early 18th century the North Pacific Interaction Sphere was largely intact. By the period of interest here, however, it had been under assault for some time, particularly by Russians in southern Alaska and western Chukotka. Many of the societies comprising the system in 1700 had ceased to exist a century later.

During the period of particular concern in this volume the Russian assault on the southern Alaska sector of the system continued, and the smallpox epidemic of 1838 reached almost to the edge of the study region. However, the sector that included northwestern Alaska, the Mackenzie River delta, and easternmost Chukotka remained intact. The relations between and among the societies whose estates were in this region were still carried out along essentially precontact lines. Accordingly, the system I have described in this book can give us not only theoretical clues but concrete ethnographic evidence as to how an interaction sphere comprised entirely of microscale segmental societies can operate.

Core–Periphery Issues

An astronaut gazing down on northwestern Alaska from a satellite on August 1, 1800, would have immediately identified several apparent cores. They would have been at Niġliq, Sullivik, Sisualik, Point Spencer, Saint Michael, and Pastuliq, that is, the sites of the summer trade fairs. The rest of the countryside would have appeared almost unpopulated by comparison. This would make theoretical sense, because "central places" are usually excellent locations for markets, and markets are usually associated with loci of power. However, the markets in question were themselves international institutions, key integrating elements in the interaction sphere of which they were a part. They were located where they were partly because they were easily reached by traders from several nations and partly because there was enough food available locally to feed the large numbers of people and dogs who gathered there. But these resources were available for only a short time. Once that period had passed people had to disperse to their own homelands or starve.

If our astronaut had gazed again upon northwestern Alaska two months later, on October 1, 1800, the cores observed earlier would have disappeared. Our astronaut would note that people had become concentrated at the few main coastal villages, of which the largest in all of northwestern Alaska were Kiŋigan (Wales) and Tikiġaq (Point Hope), but were otherwise scattered in tiny settlements distributed along the rivers and coast. Although the two large settlements were all but abandoned during the summer, they were home during the winter to the largest populations of any settlements in northwestern Alaska. As a result, the nations of which they were the main settlements, Kiŋikmiut (population ca. 800) and Tikiġaġmiut (population ca. 1,300), respectively, were particularly influential in the NANA Region even though they were located just outside of it.[13] If the "core" concept is to have any useful application to the phenomena described in this book, it is to them that it applies.

When I was working with elders from all over the NANA Region during the winter of 1970, they consistently identified the Tikiġaġmiut as the most warlike Iñupiat any of them had ever heard of in early-19th-century northwestern Alaska.[14] The Tikiġaġmiut included among their enemies at one time or another the Akuniġmiut, Di'hą̨įį̨ Gwich'in, Imaqłit, Kakligmiut, Kivalliñiġmiut, Kuukpigmiut, Napaaqtuġmiut, Nuataaġmiut, Qikiqtaġruŋmiut, Tapqaġmiut, and Utuqqaġmiut, and they were considered a potential threat by practically everyone else. Thus, it is not surprising that, in a case reported by Lawrence Hennigh, "a couple north of Kotzebue returned to camp after visiting relatives to find their children and parents killed and their sex organs strung on a tow line. It was assumed without further evidence that the attackers were from Point Hope" (1972:102). Given their perspective, it was a case of *res ipsa loquitur* (a legal concept meaning "the thing speaks for itself"): who but Tikiġaġmiut would have done such a thing?

On the other hand, not a single one of my sources identified the other major power in northwestern Alaska, the Kiŋikmiut, as being belligerent aggressors. The difference between my informants' views of the Kiŋikmiut, on the one hand, and the Tikiġaġmiut, on the other, was so striking that I finally started posing directed questions on the subject instead of my previous open-ended ones. No matter how I approached the subject, my sources, while admitting that the Kiŋikmiut had been rich, powerful, and perhaps a bit arrogant, claimed that they had never caused an unusual amount of trouble in the NANA Region or on the Seward Peninsula.

The contrast between the Tikiġaġmiut and Kiŋikmiut apparently resided in differences in their respective outlooks on how international affairs should be conducted. The Tikiġaġmiut, who are not known to have formed an alliance with any nation, evidently preferred to pursue their international goals primarily through naked aggression and intimidation; their neighbors responded accordingly.[15] The Kiŋikmiut, on the other hand, preferred diplomacy, and most of their neighbors also responded in kind.

The Kiŋikmiut had alliances with all the nations on the northwestern and central portions of the Seward Peninsula as well as with the King Islanders, and they did not attempt to bother anyone in the countries bordering Norton and Kotzebue Sounds. Accordingly, they could travel just about anywhere they wanted on the Alaska mainland without difficulty. In 1826 and 1827 Beechey encountered parties of Kiŋikmiut at a number of points outside their own estate and concluded that the main Kiŋikmiut settlement of Kiŋigan was "a place which, judging from the respectability of its inhabitants, whom we had seen elsewhere, must be of importance among the Esquimaux establishments upon this coast" (1831, vol. 2:267). (Their primary enemies were on the Diomede Islands and in Chukotka, from which they were separated by the waters of Bering Strait.)

At this remove in time there is no way to know just why the Tikiġaġmiut and Kiŋikmiut differed so much in their basic approach to international affairs. It may have resulted from the difference in scale, since in 1800 the Tikiġaġmiut population was almost twice that of the Kiŋikmiut. Theoretically, this gave them a much greater ability to impose their will on other nations, although, by the time of interest here, they had made so many enemies that they had ceased being effective in doing so. Unfortunately, we also cannot know whether the leaders within either nation consulted one another and developed their international practices out of a deliberate policy or whether things turned out the way they did simply by accident.

At some point shortly before the study period began, the Tikiġaġmiut apparently succeeded in establishing a fairly sizeable sphere of influence in which they were the dominant power. This sphere is said to have incorporated all of the societies whose estates lay along the coast from Kotzebue Sound to Icy Cape as well as others located inland. It thus included much of the northern portion of the NANA Region as well as a portion of the Arctic Slope (Rainey 1947:238; Wells and Kelly 1890:10). Unfortunately, specific information on just how their influence was first extended over such distances and how (and for how long) their dominance was maintained has been lost. What little evidence exists indicates that the Tikiġaġmiut population had been particularly large when the process began. It is also possible that the populations of the other nations had been low then due to famine.[16] Given the Tikiġaġmiut approach to international affairs later on, it is reasonable to assume that their influence was extended somehow through intimidation and probably through brute force as well.

What is known with greater certainty is that their dominance did not last very long. It was destroyed around the beginning of the 19th century in a major battle with an allied force of Kivalliñiġmiut, Nuataaġmiut, Napaaqtuġmiut, and Qikiqtaġruŋmiut. A substantial portion of the Tikiġaġmiut male population was killed during this action, and the Tikiġaġmiut sphere of influence ceased to exist. Thus, even in international systems of only moderately complex hunter-gatherer societies, the "pulsation," or cyclical rise and fall of dominant powers so characteristic of larger-scale international systems, may be said to occur (Chase-Dunn and Hall 1995:116–117). However, pulses in such societies were probably reckoned in generations, not in centuries, as in more recent times.

In general, however, the portion of the interaction sphere described in this volume was so decentralized most of the time as to make core–periphery issues almost meaningless. Populations were too small, mobile, and dispersed, on the one hand, and countervailing alliances were too readily formed, on the other, for any nation or any small group of closely allied nations to achieve and sustain for more than a very brief period the kind of dominance normally associated with a core, not to mention a sphere of influence. Thus, to the question posed by Robert Denemark and his colleagues, "Do all intersocietal systems have center–periphery hierarchies?" (2000:xvi) the answer is "No"; at least those consisting of microscale segmental societies do (did) not.

Evolutionary Implications

The evolution of a world system somewhat more highly centralized than the one described in this book required the establishment of nations that were larger in scale and unitary (i.e., nonsegmental) in structure. These more complex societies are usually referred to as "chiefdoms," which are autonomous political units "comprising a number of villages or communities under the permanent control of a paramount chief" (Carneiro 1981:45).

One of the central claims of this book is that the general processes of confrontation, negotiation, domination, alliance formation, intimidation, rivalry, intrigue, exploitation, trade, and violence have characterized intersocietal relations ever since humans came into existence. Over time, these processes, building on what had gone before, contributed to the incrementally increasing complexity of human societies and of international affairs. However, at certain thresholds they led to changes as profound and abrupt as what physicists call a "phase transition." Everyday examples of phase transitions in the physical world are the transformation of water into ice or steam, both of which, at critical points, require just a one-degree temperature change to produce a dramatic alteration in the physical properties of the basic substance.

The emergence of chiefdoms out of segmental societies was a phase transition. Indeed, Robert Carneiro (1981:38) has claimed that their emergence was probably the most important political development that ever occurred, since it was the first time in human history that the segments making up a human society were unified under a common leadership. He also wrote that "it could not have been an easy step to take because it took some three million years to achieve" (Carneiro 1981:37).

The prerequisites for the evolution of chiefdoms from a world of chieftaincies probably included those that Henri Claessen (2002) listed for the evolution of states but with much lower thresholds. In any event, his list provides a useful framework with which to begin the discussion.

Territory

One of the prerequisites in Claessen's list is that the members of the society making the transition from chiefdom to state had to exercise dominion over a specified territory. This implies that he thinks that that condition was not met in societies less complex than chiefdoms. However, as I have argued in this book, even hunter-gatherers fulfilled this condition; they could not just wander anywhere they wanted. In regions with extremely low population density it may have seemed to Western observers as though people could do so, but those who were native to the region knew better (Williams 1982:146, 148). Except where people moved into uninhabited territory or where a disaster caused major demographic and social dislocations, most of the hunter-gatherer world, like the modern one, was divided into discrete parcels over each of which the members of a particular society exercised dominion. The only partial exception to this rule that I know of is where otherwise uninhabited territory was used by members of two or more different societies during a particular time of year (usually summer) who then withdrew to their own estates when the season had passed.[17]

The borders of hunter-gatherer estates were more or less clearly defined. Within the general area covered in this book, estate borders were perhaps the most clearly defined on the Seward Peninsula, at and just beyond the southern portion of the NANA Region. In Chukotka they were apparently very clearly defined along the coast but progressively less so toward the interior. In contrast, among the five Caribou Inuit Eskimo societies of central subarctic Canada in the late 19th century, borders were not defined at all.[18] Rather, there was a clearly identified heartland in each estate, but who, if anyone, exercised dominion over what land became progressively less certain as one moved outward from there. Then, as one moved into the estate of a neighboring society and toward its heartland, the situation became progressively more clearly defined again.[19] However, despite the vagueness of the (geographic) borders, the (social) boundary of each Caribou Inuit society was absolutely clear-cut: everyone knew who was a member and, by exclusion, who was not (see Cashdan 1984:455).

Population

A second prerequisite for the evolution of chiefdoms was that there had to be a sufficient number of people to form a stratified society. Just how many people are required for this is unclear, but it seems to be at least 5,000, far above the levels found in Northwest Alaska.

Of course, in order for the population to reach the appropriate size in the first place, some sort of nationwide leadership had to be developed so that the necessary coordination and control for stability during the transition could exist. A council of chieftains presumably could meet the requirements. However, in order for a council to work, someone had to lead it, and it would not be a big leap from there to becoming a chief.

In order for the demographic conditions to be met, it was probably necessary for the members of the societies involved to be located in environments with a higher carrying capacity than existed in northwestern Alaska.[20] The nations described in this volume had probably developed as complex a system as they could given the limitations of their far northern setting. This is why the basic structure of the international system in northwestern Alaska had not significantly increased in complexity for more than a thousand years.[21]

Surplus

Claessen's third prerequisite is that the economy had to be productive enough to yield a surplus sufficient to maintain the people filling the privileged roles. In a simple chiefdom there would not have to be very many of these people, but any at all would be more than there were in Northwest Alaska.[22] Even the wealthiest people there were, and basically had to be, producers of at least some of the raw materials and manufactured goods on which their status rested. An umialik and his wife could have the most and the best, but they also had to participate in tasks whereby their wealth accrued.

In addition to having a surplus, a chiefdom had to have a structured way of getting that surplus to the people at the top. There are conceivably many ways to do this, but at least one of them had to be in operation for a chiefdom to evolve, not to mention endure. The Iñupiat had a rudimentary redistribution system that, in principle, could have solved this problem; people gave their produce to the family head or his wife, who then redistributed it unevenly back out again. However, the redistribution network was limited to the local family unit. In a chiefdom it is society-wide in scope and constitutes more a form of taxation by the chief than a sharing of the wealth (Carneiro 1981:58–63).

Ideology

The fourth and last of Claessen's prerequisites is that there had to be an ideology that explained and justified a hierarchical social system. In other words, enough people had to believe that the hierarchical system characterizing the society of which they were members was the right one in order for them to act in appropriate ways.

This condition definitely was not met in Northwest Alaska. Although people were willing disproportionately to share the fruits of their labor with their chieftain and his wife, the dominant ideology was strongly egalitarian. Any chieftain who became too self-important or stingy with his wealth was quickly abandoned by his followers and thereby lost his position.

Circumscription

Another prerequisite to chiefdom formation, one that was not included in Claessen's list but that Carneiro (1970, 1988) has emphasized for decades, is circumscription, both environmental and social. The former may be understood as a shortage of land due to population growth, on the one hand, and to a lack of environmentally suitable space for expansion or emigration, on the other. Social circumscription is similar, but in this case the constraining factor is the presence of other societies exercising dominion over neighboring land that otherwise would be suitable and available for expansion or emigration.

A circumscribed society is one that is boxed in; the growing population problem cannot be solved by either expansion or emigration, those options being closed. The only way to deal with the problem without suffering famine or civil strife is to develop a more effective means of exploiting local resources, to develop a more productive system of international trade and/or movement, or to conquer neighboring societies. The last two options have obvious international implications.

In an extensive region with a temperate climate, abundant resources, and a relatively homogeneous landscape, several nations presumably could become circumscribed more or less simultaneously. Some might cross the evolutionary threshold; others would not. This may be what actually happened in many areas, since the very first chiefdoms were quickly followed by many more (Carneiro 2002:89–90).

Carneiro does not tell us how the degree of circumscription can be objectively measured on a cross-cultural basis, but perhaps a subjective measure is more useful anyway. What one needs to know is the extent to which real people identify a problem of too large a population for the available resources to support. If they perceive themselves as being boxed in, then for all practical purposes they are, since they will seek solutions based on that understanding. Unfortunately, this issue is almost impossible to investigate archaeologically.

Overpopulation was not a problem in the NANA Region during the early contact period. It is conceivable that the sphere of influence the Tikiġaġmiut attempted to (or did) establish shortly prior to the beginning of the study period stemmed from there being too many people in the Point Hope district, but there is no way to know that for certain. During the specific period of interest here, however, warfare, periodic famine, natural disasters such as floods, and accidents kept population levels within tolerable limits.[23]

The Evolutionary Mechanism

Elman Service once noted that "no one has observed the actual origin of a chiefdom" (1962:145). It is more accurate to say that the people who did observe the origin of chiefdoms lived several thousand years ago and had no means of recording what they saw and experienced. But the result is the same: the rest of us are left to conjecture on the subject, using bits and pieces of archaeological data and inference to come to our conclusions.

Carneiro has argued persuasively that chiefdoms had to have evolved through force, because "autonomous political units, whatever their size, never willingly give up their sovereignty" (1998:21). His original theory was that it happened through conquest; the members of one society conquered neighboring societies and incorporated their populations and estates into their own. But this theory does not tell us how the various families or clans of the newly dominant society became subordinate to a single chief in the first place.

More recently, Carneiro has revised his theory. He now believes that the first chiefs were men who were elected to lead an international alliance in war, then somehow retained control over the nations involved after the fighting was over (Carneiro 1998).[24] This seems plausible, because battle seems to offer one of the few occasions when the members of autonomous families or clans, not to mention nations, might voluntarily subordinate themselves to a single leader. And a truly exceptional leader might be able to retain his collective loyalty after the passage of the circumstances surrounding his elevation. An unanswered question at this point is whether the unification of the segments of the dominant society had to precede the incorporation of several societies into the new chiefdom. Perhaps it all happened at once.

One implication of Carneiro's theory is that a chiefdom evolved out of a set of segmental societies in an abrupt leap. What began as a set of autonomous segments distributed among several nations suddenly became subordinate segments of a single nation. At the same time, what began as a set of relatively small estates became incorporated into a single, much larger estate. If this analysis is correct, it should not be surprising to find that a maximal segmental society had a population of no more than 2,500 people, whereas a minimal chiefdom had a population of at least 5,000.

A final point to make here is that the evolution of a chiefdom was not an internal development within just one society but an international event involving many societies. It required not only the unification of the segments of one society under a common leadership but the unification of the segments of several societies under that same leadership. Furthermore, a brand new chiefdom surrounded by segmental societies would presumably quickly come to dominate its neighbors, even if it did not incorporate them; thus, the first more or less sustainable core–periphery hierarchy in the history of the world system came into being.

Comparisons

The Northwest Alaskan situation is usefully compared with other areas occupied by early contact hunter-gatherer societies. Two areas have been chosen for this, the Northwest Coast of North America and north-central California. The people in both areas are sometimes characterized as having been "sedentary foragers," but they are more accurately described as having been "transhumant." That is, they spent most of the year living in fixed settlements but moved seasonally to other locations—mostly within their own estates—to hunt, fish, or harvest vegetable products.[25]

THE NORTHWEST COAST

Most of the prerequisites of a world system of chiefdoms were met in the Northwest Coast sector of the North Pacific Interaction Sphere during the early contact period (late 18th century).[26] There certainly were enough people living there—nearly 200,000 during the mid-18th century—to form several chiefdoms (Boyd 1990:135, 1999:264–265).

Warfare was widespread and frequent (Ames and Maschner 1999:195–218; Donald 2000; Ferguson 1984; MacDonald 1984; Maschner 1997; Maschner and Reedy-Maschner 1998; Mitchell 1984; Moss and Erlandson 1992). It was conducted for a variable mixture of revenge, territorial expansion, access to trade and trade routes, and the capture of slaves. It was often conducted by large formations of men who were transported in 60-foot (18-meter) war canoes, sometimes over long distances. Raids and open battles were contested with bow and arrow, spear, knife, and club by men wearing full body armor and helmets. Defensive measures included careful location of settlements and often the erection of defensive fortifications and palisades.

Warfare as a divisive force was offset by an equally extensive unifying network of friendly international relations (Ames and Maschner 1999:171–174; Drucker 1967; MacDonald 1984:75; Mitchell and Donald 1988:321–328; Oberg 1973:105–111). This was based partly on a pervasive network of kinship connections that were the outgrowth of a system of exogamous clans and partly on international trade. In some areas large trade fairs were held annually. In all areas the substantial competitive giving feasts known in English as potlatches were held from time to time (Barnett 1938; Drucker 1967). Communication was by boat along the coast and on foot via an elaborate network of trails in the interior (MacDonald 1984:75). Evidently, a system of easements and licenses was well established, exemplified most clearly by the peaceful annual international gathering of thousands of people from many different societies to fish for eulachon during their spawning runs (Mitchell and Donald 2001). On the other hand, where easements did not exist people were often charged a fee for using a particular trail in a foreign estate.

Northwest Coast societies were stratified into at least three classes: titleholders, commoners, and slaves (Donald 1997:272–294; Mitchell 1984). There was also an extensive group of craft specialists who did not have to hunt or fish for their subsistence (Ames and Maschner 1999:163–165). The members of these societies definitely believed in an ideology that explained and justified a hierarchical social system. Nevertheless, no Northwest Coast society seems to have evolved into a chiefdom (Mitchell 1983b). Why?

Evidently, the populations of the individual societies simply were not large enough to support the chiefdom level of organization. Even simple chiefdoms have populations in the thousands, while complex chiefdoms have populations in the tens of thousands (Earle 1987:279, 1991:3). Along the Northwest Coast the membership of individual societies ranged between roughly 200 and 2,000 people, about the same as in northwestern Alaska (Donald 1999, 2002). The reason the overall population of the region was so much larger was that the estates of many more nations were crammed into a given amount of space than was the case farther north.

Perhaps the mobility and dispersal of the resource base prevented a large enough permanent concentration of people to permit chiefdoms to form on the Northwest Coast. Perhaps they simply had not invented the type of organization required to establish a chiefdom, or, if they had, they were unable to implement and sustain it. In any event, as far as I am aware the only early contact society of hunter-gatherers to have achieved chiefdom status and to have sustained it for any length of time was that of the Calusa of southwestern Florida, with a population of between 4,000 and 7,000 in the mid-16th century (Widmer 1988:5). Unlike the people of the Northwest Coast, the Calusa were in contact with many chiefdoms having agrarian economies, any one of which could have provided them with the organizational model they needed to evolve into a more complex system.

NORTH-CENTRAL CALIFORNIA

The second comparison focuses on the early contact Wintu-speaking people of north-central California.[27] Like the Northwest Coast Indians, the Wintu were hunter-gatherers surrounded by other hunter-gatherers. However, they lived in the interior instead of along the coast, and they provide a useful contrast. They are also one of the few hunter-gatherer populations to have been analyzed from the world systems perspective (Chase-Dunn and Hall 1997:121–148; Chase-Dunn and Mann 1998).

The early contact (ca. 1800–1830) Wintu numbered about 5,300 people divided among 9 societies.[28] This yields an average national population of just under 590 people. That number is within the range of variation of the Iñupiaq nations of Northwest Alaska although above their average of 470. It is also within the range of variation of the Wakashan societies of the British Columbia coast but below their average population of 786.[29]

The members of each Wintu nation exercised dominion over a discrete estate and spoke a distinct language or dialect. Estate borders apparently were not sharply drawn, however, and consisted of a kind of no-man's-land between estates (DuBois 1935:4). Heartlands, however, were clearly defined (DuBois 1935:6–8).

The Wintu regarded trespass as a cause of grievance but apparently preferred to seek some kind of compensation instead of killing trespassers on sight. They usually tried to do this through negotiation. If that was unsuccessful, an armed confrontation of battle lines frequently resulted (DuBois 1935:36–40). Open battles tended to be firefights during which dodging was an important survival technique; shock tactics were generally avoided. More serious disputes were pursued via surprise attacks, usually made at dawn. These were violent and resulted in killing, the destruction of villages, and the occasional taking of captives. Weapons consisted of bows and arrows, clubs, thrusting spears, and daggers.

International trade was extensive. The Wintu lacked a mechanism analogous to the Northwest Alaskan trade fair, at least in part because the terrain did not lend itself to the movements required for such large gatherings. However, they did have bilateral international gatherings comparable in many respects to Iñupiaq messenger feasts. International trade was thus "down the line," meaning that people exchanged goods with their immediate neighbors, who then traded with theirs, and so on, moving goods over considerable distances through a series of bilateral exchanges (Chase-Dunn and Hall 1997:129). Members of different nations also gathered periodically in one nation's estate to fish for salmon, suggesting the existence of easements, and license was granted from time to time to people seeking to hunt or trade in a foreign estate.

International affairs generally were under the supervision of chieftains. Chieftainship was ideally hereditary but often was not in fact if the incumbent or designated heir was not up to the task. Once in office a chieftain no longer had to hunt and fish but received what he needed from others. If it is true, as Chase-Dunn and Hall (1997:127; see also DuBois 1935:29–34) suggest, that there was usually only one chieftain per society, he must have had much more authority than his Iñupiaq counterparts. Wintu chieftains tended to have two or more wives, some of whom were deliberately recruited from other societies. Marriage was thus an important form of international connection.

Members of some Wintu nations successfully established small spheres of influence from time to time, usually in the context of expanding their estates at the expense of less well-to-do neighbors. However, this expansion occurred at such a slow rate, and the period of domination was so brief, that the core–periphery distinction is not much more useful in describing the Wintu situation than it is the one existing in Northwest Alaska.

Concluding Remarks

When the earth was inhabited solely by hunters and gatherers, the world system was probably not unlike the one described in this volume, at least in its general characteristics. With that as a guiding assumption, I conclude with some hypotheses about what such a world system might have been like.

In a world of hunter-gatherers, the members of neighboring societies were in contact with one another. The notion of the primitive isolate as being the prevailing pattern is a myth. International relations were variously friendly, hostile, or neutral.

Relationships that typically linked the members of different societies together included those created through a low rate of intermarriage, plus one or more others that were not kinship based. At least the leading members of societies whose estates were located along linguistic borders spoke all the languages they needed to in order to communicate with their neighbors. By the end of the Middle Paleolithic and probably before, geographically extensive interaction spheres were probably common, but spheres of influence were probably rare and of only brief duration (Kaufman 2002:490). Ecumenes did not exist. Although chieftains were the dominant force, practically every adult played an active part of some kind in the conduct of foreign affairs.

International trade fairs, or something akin to them, were probably important foci of intersocietal relations wherever the regional landscape facilitated such gatherings and the transportation technology was up to the task of moving sufficient numbers of people and quantities of goods. Alternatively or in addition, bilateral gatherings such as the Iñupiaq messenger feast and the Northwest Coast potlatch were important venues for peaceful international gatherings (Drucker 1967; Vayda 1967). Still another possibility, particularly where both resources and people were highly mobile, was for members of different societies to come together in one society's estate where a substantial concentration of animate resources occurred annually, but for only a brief period. In order for these events to take place, regional systems of easements and licenses were negotiated so that people could cross or otherwise make temporary use of estates in addition to their own. Social boundaries and geographic borders did not keep people locked up in a set of boxes during the Paleolithic any more than they do today; but because of them, cross-border movements had to be undertaken in structured ways, or violence of some kind followed.

The social geometry of regional landscapes changed episodically over time. War, drought, flood, famine, periods of excessive abundance and consequent overpopulation, earthquakes, and climate change, with their associated social and demographic upheavals, kept populations and social systems in flux. Societies rose and fell, and their estates expanded and contracted. Under extraordinary circumstances, such as when the populations of several societies in a region were decimated by the same disaster, survivors may have combined forces to create new societies whose memberships for a time would have been less homogeneous than those of their predecessors. Alternatively, in a prolonged period of great abundance, whether through climatic amelioration or technological advance, the populations of neighboring estates expanded beyond the carrying capacity of their estates and ended up fighting for space.

"BREEDING ISOLATES"

It is appropriate at this point to digress briefly to comment on the implications of this model for the size and structure of "breeding populations" in the hunter-gatherer world system. The literature on this issue, usefully summarized by Robert Kelly (1995:209–210), suggests that the minimum sustainable size of an endogamous population is somewhere around 475–500 people, that is, roughly the average population of the nations of Northwest Alaska. The analyses on which these figures are based apparently assume that the populations in question were truly biologically isolated. But this was probably rarely the case at any particular time and never the case for any extended period of time.

In the discussion of genetic isolation it is important to differentiate between sexual relations involving coresident spouses, on the one hand, and those occurring outside the domestic sphere, on the other.[30] Even 100 percent endogamy among coresident spouses in a society does not guarantee that genes will not flow between members of that society and members of neighboring societies. The rate of coresident endogamy was probably rarely higher than 90 percent in most microscale societies, and a variable number of intersocietal nonresident sexual liaisons occurred in addition to that. It is no accident that the people living in the interior of Northwest Alaska during the 19th century appeared physically to be a mixture of Athapaskan and Iñupiaq despite the fact that mixed coresidential marriages were extremely rare (Nelson 1877–81:entry for July 15, 1881).

The Iñupiat (and Eskimos generally) may have been among the few peoples actually to institutionalize sexual intercourse as a form of international bond (through the system of cospouses and cosiblings), but they could not have been the only people in the world who occasionally looked elsewhere for sexual excitement. Genetic isolates must have been just as rare as social isolates in the hunter-gatherer world system.

PACKING

Over time, the members of many microscale societies invented ever more effective ways to exploit their local resources, and they developed progressively more elaborate systems of international trade and travel (via easements and licenses) to offset the limitations of their own estates. These processes are often referred to collectively as "intensification," although the international element is often overlooked. Over time, continued intensification resulted in an increase in the number of societal estates fitting into a given geographic area. I refer to this as "packing."[31] As the packing level went up, estate size went down.

Packing can be measured by the number of estates to be found in a given amount of space. Since there is no agreed-upon standard for this, I have arbitrarily chosen a standard regional unit (SRU) of 50,000 square miles (ca. 130,000 square kilometers) to illustrate the point. In the Caribou Inuit region of the central Canadian Subarctic, for example, there were only 3.6 societal estates per SRU during the 1880s (Burch 1995:118); average estate size was thus 13,890 square miles (36,114 square kilometers). In Northwest Alaska during the early 19th century, in contrast, there were 12 estates per SRU for an average size of 4,167 square miles (10,784 square kilometers).

In the more benevolent environment of the Wakashan-language sector of the Northwest Coast the number of estates per SRU was nearly 200, or 56 times the level recorded for the Caribou Inuit. The average Wakashan estate would have had an area of about 250 square miles (648 square kilometers). Among the Wintu speakers of north-central California the number of estates per SRU was even higher (242), indicating an average estate size of 207 square miles (538 square kilometers).[32] Presumably, this was about as high a packing level as a sector of a hunter-gatherer world system could achieve. For hypothetical purposes, let's say that the absolute limit was 250 estates per SRU, for an average estate size of only 200 square miles (518 square kilometers). Packing beyond that almost surely required the kind of intensification that can be achieved only through the adoption of agriculture.

International affairs in the Wakashan and Wintu regions were obviously conducted in a much more constricted geographic space than was the case in Northwest Alaska or in the Caribou Inuit region. Indeed, Chase-Dunn and Hall (1997:145) calculated that, in the Wintu region, most international contacts occurred within 50 miles (80 kilometers) of any given starting point. That is less than many *intranational* contacts required in many parts of the Arctic.

In general, it may be assumed that the frequency and intensity of international contacts were dependent at least in part on (1) societal population size; (2) the degree of societal packing; and (3) transportation technology. People living in a region of high density packing could maintain a high level of international contacts even if they had to travel on foot. To the extent that the packing level was lower in a region (hence the distances were greater), more sophisticated transportation technology was a prerequisite for active international affairs. The Iñupiat were blessed with superb watercraft for summer travel and with sleds, dogs, snowshoes, and snow and ice for winter travel. These enabled them to maintain an active international trade network over distances that the inhabitants of temperate climes would have had trouble matching unless they had boats of similar (or greater) capacity and suitable networks of waterways on which to use them. Among the densely packed societies of the Northwest Coast both of those requirements were met; among the Wintu they were not.

VARIATIONS

One type of international link that had no counterpart in northwestern Alaska is one created through a system of exogamous clans such as occurred in Aboriginal Australia and on the Northwest Coast. Over several generations of even a very low rate of intersocietal marriage, many people on both sides of a societal boundary would eventually belong to the same set of clans. The relationships, with their mythical and religious overtones, created through membership in the same clan probably exceeded societal membership as a focus of solidarity (as defined by Levy 1952:341). In such cases it may be difficult for social scientists to locate societal boundaries even if they are looking for them—which they usually are not.

Friendly international relations were counterbalanced by international hostility. Borders were not defended, but estates and (particularly) heartlands were (Cashdan 1984:455). Intrusions that were not in accord with the institutionalized pattern of easements and licenses in the region concerned were considered threats. Some hunter-gatherers may have been especially disposed toward being peaceful, but most of them were no more (or less) so than the rest of humankind (Keeley 1996). International violence, like international trade, was not an invention of large-scale societies (Ember 1978:443; Keeley 1996:vi–ix). However, there is no reason to expect that it was always as lethal as that conducted by the Iñupiat. Hostage and captive taking may have been relatively common, the captives being enslaved in many cases (Donald 1997).

Time was an important variable. International affairs in a region in which many of the societies involved were relative newcomers were likely to be more ad hoc than they were if they (or their progenitors) had been there for centuries. In the former context competition for resources and territorial expansion may very well have been important factors leading to international conflict. However, the longer societies remained more or less in place, the greater the chances that structured means of conducting international affairs would be developed and that they would have included a system of easements and licenses. Where several societies had emerged from a single progenitor these arrangements may have been worked out with particular thoroughness. And, regardless of abstract theories about the causes of war (e.g., Ember and Ember 1992, 1994, 1997), the longer a regional system of societies remained intact, the greater the chances that vengeance would be an important factor contributing to international violence.

If it is true, as has recently been suggested (Stiner, Munro, and Surovell 2000; Stiner et al. 1999), that early Middle Paleolithic human populations were even more widely dispersed than was the case in the study region, then perhaps the Bushmen of southern Africa offer a more appropriate model of international affairs for that period than the societies discussed above (Heinz 1972, 1979).[33]

Bushman societies were comprised of local families who lived in separate settlements most of the year but whose members were linked to one another through intermarriage, age groups, and friendships.[34] The members of each society exercised dominion over an estate having a fairly well defined border, and they spoke a distinctive language, dialect, or subdialect. Borderlands were usually avoided except during times of famine. During such times the members of one society sometimes sought permission to hunt in a neighboring estate, although the frequency of their success in getting it has not been reported. All these features resemble those characteristic of societies in northwestern Alaska. However, among the Bushmen encounters between members of different societies were uncommon, usually accidental, usually peaceful (Silberbauer 1995), and apparently normally conducted on an ad hoc basis (Heinz 1979:478–479). In these respects they depart from the Northwest Alaskan pattern but may approximate that of early Middle Paleolithic Europe. However, for the hunter-gatherer societies that evolved into chiefdoms, the Wintu and Northwest Coast situations are more appropriate models.

No doubt at least some chieftains on the Northwest Coast and in north-central California tried to establish chiefdoms from time to time, but they either failed at the outset or else could not maintain the position once they had achieved it. Leaders among the Wintu had almost achieved chiefly status, but their societal populations were too small, their internal hierarchies were too undifferentiated, and their surplus was too small to permit the development of true chiefdoms.

When the transition to a chiefdom occurred, the tendency toward greater societal packing was reversed. Since then, the long-term trend has been for societies to become progressively fewer in number but with estates and populations that are generally larger (Carneiro 1978). As this happened, core–periphery differentiation and hierarchy became more pronounced and more durable (Chase-Dunn and Hall 1997:36, 130; Chase-Dunn and Mann 1998:89).

The emergence of a chiefdom required some experimentation in the creation of new social forms. The new institutions had to be installed, enough people had to be persuaded of their value to make them work, and some means for their perpetuation had to be devised. No doubt mistakes were made, countervailing forces were set in motion, and many simple chiefdoms rose and fell. Eventually, however, some of them began to endure, and soon they were springing up "in many parts of the world, like mushrooms after a summer storm" (Carneiro 2002:89). It was then that the world system began the long process of evolving from a highly decentralized system of the kind described in this book to the global ecumene we live in today.

Appendix 1
A Gazetteer of Raids and Battles in Northwestern Alaska

The following list is an incomplete record of raids and battles that have been reported for the study region. One reason the list is so short is that a substantial number of incidents were recorded without specific information as to location. Another is that many of the accounts seem to have referred to events that occurred a considerable time before the study period. Finally, many of the references in the unpublished accounts (in land claims and Park Service reports) are simply general statements to the effect that the people who lived at such and such a place used to fight with the inhabitants of certain other nations, but these statements did not refer to specific events. Nevertheless, it is a start and, I hope, will stimulate further investigation of this subject. The numbers in parentheses are keyed to Table 5 and Map 11 in Chapter 2.

Name not recorded (#72): Sometime in the early 1840s a group of Koyukuk River Koyukon living near the mouth of the Koyukuk River were massacred by other Koyukon from the Yukon and Innoko Rivers (Clark 1974:187).

Name not recorded (#51): Unlocated site near the mouth of the Buckland River where Kiitaaġmiut raiders attacked a group of Kaŋiġmiut women who were picking berries. One woman was tortured and killed; the others escaped (Savok 1986).

Aagutauraq (#18): One year a few boatloads of Tikiġaġmiut were returning home from the Sisualik fair. Unbeknownst to them, a party of "Noatak people," presumably either Nuataaġmiut or Napaaqtuġmiut, followed them on land. When the Tikiġaġmiut camped here for the night, the Noatakers attacked them and nearly wiped them out (Attungana 1980).

Aalaatna (#41): Sometime late in the 18th or early in the 19th century there was a series of violent confrontations between the Kobuk River Koyukon and the Koyukuk River Koyukon, the so-called Rabbit Medicine Man wars. At least one of these events occurred near the mouth of the Alatna River. The Kobuk River people are said to have won the battle, although the Koyukuk River people are said to have won the war (Clark 1970:18–19, 1996:62; McFadyen 1995:342, 356, 378).

Aalaatna Tsaalaakkakk'et (#40): Reportedly, there was a big battle here between Kobuk River people (Koyukon?/Iñupiat?) and Koyukuk River Koyukon near the mouth of Siruk Creek. The outcome has not been recorded (Clark 1974:192).

Aaquaksraatchiak (#48): Kaŋiġmiut raiders on their way to the Selawik district encountered two elderly Kiitaaġmiut women at their fishing camp. According to the Buckland (Kaŋiġmiut) version of the story, the raiders killed the women, cut them into strips, and hung their flesh on fish-drying racks. According to the Selawik (Kiitaaġmiut) version, the raiders spitted the women by shoving spears so far into the rectum of each that the points emerged from their mouths and then roasted them over a fire. Aaquaksraatchiak means "two old women." No one remembers the earlier name of the place (NANA Cultural Heritage Project 1975d:9; United States Department of the Interior, Bureau of Indian Affairs 1987a).

Agki(#2): Site on the lower Colville River just above the mouth of the Itkillik River that is "well known for old minor Indian wars" (Ericklook 1977).

Aglinġauraq (#36): Warriors whose origins were not recorded raided a small settlement here and killed all of its inhabitants. Then they found a girl living in an isolated hut, as required by Kobuk River menarche taboos. The warriors wanted to kill her but were afraid to shoot or stab her because of possible taboos relating to blood associated with her condition. They drowned her in a nearby lake instead. The girl's name was Aglinġauraq, which is now the name of the lake. It has been taboo to drink water from this lake since the incident took place (NANA Cultural Heritage Project 1975a:16; United States Department of the Interior, Bureau of Indian Affairs 1987b).

Alaakkakk'at (#42): A force of Gwich'in attacked a Koyukon settlement near the mouth of the South Fork of the Koyukuk River. The Gwich'in were defeated, leaving only four women and a boy in the raiders' community (Burch and Mishler 1995:155–157).

Aniyaaq (#29): A party of Tikiġaġmiut warriors attacked a fishing camp occupied by teenage boys from Sisualik and killed all but one of them. That one survived long enough to tell his father what happened (Lucier n.d.a). This was the prelude to the siege of Sisualik, which is described in more detail in Chapter 2.

Atłiq (#24): A battle between the Kuukpigmiut and a group of Gwich'in, possibly the Di'hąįį, took place here on the middle of the three Smith Mountain lakes. Both sides lost several men, but the Iñupiat prevailed. The loss forced the Gwich'in to abandon the Etivluk–Colville headwaters area (Paneak 1970).

Atnaq (#66): This is the site of a battle between Athapaskans of unreported origin (but presumably Koyukon) and the Atnaġmiut. The Atnaġmiut hid but were discovered, and the Athapaskans killed all but one little boy (Koutsky 1981d:57; Ray 1964:69).

Auksaakiaq (#16): This is the place on the lower Kukpuk River where Naviaġiaq got his revenge on the Athapaskans who had raided Nuvuġaluaq the year before (Jensen 1970a). This incident is described in greater detail in Chapter 2.

Avalit kuuk (#6): Despite the fact that this locality is within Silaliñaġmiut territory, there was a battle here between Utuqqaġmiut and warriors from the Kaŋmaliġmiut band of Kuukpigmiut. The account does not say which side won, but the losers fled far to the east, "to Greenland" (North Slope Borough, Planning Commission and Historical Commission 1976b).

Cape Stephens (#76): In 1836 ten boatloads of warriors, apparently Ayaqsaaġiaaġmiut from the north side of Norton Sound, hid here with an eye to attacking detachments from the Russian trading post of Mikhailovskii Redoubt. Their ultimate goal was to drive out the Russians, who were threatening their position as middlemen in the intercontinental trade between the Yukon and Chukotka. They attacked the members of a wood-collecting expedition, but the Russians managed to keep their casualties to one dead and seven wounded. Discouraged by these results, the raiders abandoned the attack (Arndt 1996:39; Michael 1967:97; Ray 1966:13, 1975b:125).

Cape Thompson (#17): 1. Over the years many Diomeders drifted out on the ice, ended up in the Point Hope district, and were killed by Tikiġaġmiut. The Diomeders tired of this, and one year a boatload of them headed north to seek revenge. However, they were spotted in the vicinity of Cape Thompson by Tikiġaġmiut, who ambushed them and killed all but one woman. Somehow she made it back home and begged the young men to avenge the massacre. Some time later about 30 Diomede men, guided by this woman, returned to the Point Hope district. This time, again in the vicinity of Cape Thompson, they attacked a settlement of Tikiġaġmiut and killed everyone in it (Aġviqsiiña 1940:47).

2. A battle between the Tikiġaġmiut and Kivalliñiġmiut took place here. One party—the source does not say which one—was traveling by boat, the other was on land. The latter ambushed the former. Somehow the combatants managed to work their way to the top of the cape; the account does not say who won (Ostermann and Holtved 1952:49). Another story that may describe the same or a different event claims that the people who carried out the ambush were Kiŋikmiut (Wales) and that the locality was near a cave called Qaiġusuk (Frankson 1980; Kowunna 1980).

Hudakkaakk'at (#45): Just after the ice in the rivers broke up one spring some two dozen warriors identified as Gwich'in (but without further specification) discovered a Koyukon fishing camp and attacked it. Many were killed on both sides, but the Koyukon prevailed, and the few surviving Gwich'in fled (Clark 1974:186; McFadyen 1995:365).

Iġałuit (#66): This is the site of a major battle between the Fish River people (Iġałuiŋmiut) and Yup'ik Eskimos from either Hooper Bay or the Kuskokwim River (Koutsky 1981d:34, 57; O'Leary 1995b; Sheppard 1983:27).

Igliqtiqsiiġvik (#34): This is the site of an encounter between upper Kobuk Koyukon and Akuniġmiut warriors (Mendenhall, Sampson, and Tennant 1989:55–59).

Iguaġvik (Chamisso Island) (#52): Site of a series of armed encounters between Kaŋiġmiut and English explorers under Frederick William Beechey that resulted in six casualties on the English side and at least two, including one death, on the Kaŋiġmiut side (Beechey 1831, vol. 2:280–286; Belcher 1825–27; Bockstoce 1977:126–132; Gough 1973:234–241; Wolfe n.d.:199–203). This encounter is described in some detail in Chapter 2.

Ikpik (#59): Two boatloads of Chukotkans (of unspecified ethnic background) arrived here and were greeted with friendliness. The visiting crews turned their boats on their side, gathered beneath one of them, and chatted with the Tapqaġmiut. Suddenly, the Tapqaġmiut pulled out the support holding up the umiaq shelter, trapping the Siberians beneath it. They then proceeded to kill them (Fair 1998:111; Koutsky 1981a:20, 31–32; United States Department of the Interior, Bureau of Indian Affairs 1996).

Ikpitchiaq (#8): In the early 1800s a party of Silaliñaġmiut ascended the Kuk River by boat to fish. They were discovered by a raiding party from Point Hope, so they moved to an island in the river. They had a net and managed to live on fish. The Point Hopers did not have boats, so they laid siege to the island. But they also lacked nets and, being unable to find any food, starved to death. Many years later over 40 skeletons were counted here (North Slope Borough, Planning Commission and Historical Commission 1976b:10; Schneider 1980). This looks suspiciously like the encounter at Tikiġaġmiut (#3).

Imauġvik (#21): A party of Tikiġaġmiut raiders approaching this Napaaqtuġmiut village was discovered by the inhabitants. However, the villagers deluded the raiders into believing they had not been seen while preparing to mount a counterattack. As soon as the raid was launched that night the defenders drove the attackers onto thin ice. The ice broke beneath their weight, and all but one drowned (Adams 1970, 1986; Hall 1975b:97–100; Hunnicutt 1960b; Stalker 1986; United States Department of the Interior, Bureau of Indian Affairs n.d.). This event is described in more detail in Chapter 2.

Imilik (#11): According to Pamela Ivie and Bill Schneider, a Silaliñaġmiut village here was frequently attacked by Tikiġaġmiut (1988:90–91). Finally, the residents filled the surrounding area with sharp spikes hidden in the grass. The Tikiġaġmiut tried to get past the spikes by digging a trench, but they never finished it. One time a Tikiġaġmiut reconnaissance party discovered that the village was deserted except for a famous warrior named Attaġnaq. The news prompted an assault by a large war party, which trapped Attaġnaq inside his house. They taunted him, challenging him to come out. He responded in kind while preparing for battle by doing stretching exercises. Suddenly, he leaped out and started jumping around, daring the Tikiġaġmiut to shoot him. Many tried, but he always managed to dodge their arrows. When the attackers began to run out of arrows he started shooting back. After several Tikiġaġmiut had been killed the rest fled. However, according to Samuel Agnasagga (1984), the encounter involved the Utuqqaġmiut rather than the Silaliñaġmiut.

Inaaġruk (#54): A battle between the Tapqaġmiut and unidentified Kobuk River people took place along a channel near this site. The outcome has not been reported (Kiyutelluk 1976; Koutsky 1981a:18).

Iñuktat (Buckland estuary) (#50): In response to the outrage perpetrated by Kaŋiġmiut raiders at Aaquaksraatchiak (#48), a Kiitaaġmiut force approached this village very early one fall morning. All the residents were asleep. The raiders trapped them inside their houses and killed all but one woman, who managed to escape (Ballott 1970b; Hall 1975b:388; Lucier 1954:229, 1997:251; NANA Cultural Heritage Project 1975b:1, 1975c:3, 1975d; Savok 1986; Sunno 1951e).

Iñuktat (near Cape Thompson) (#19): There was a battle here between a combined force of Kakligmiut (Barrow), Utuqqaġmiut (Utukok River), and Kuukpigmiut (Colville River) on one side and a Tikiġaġmiut (Point Hope) force on the other. The Point Hopers were on their way to Kotzebue by boat, and the northerners met and defeated them here (Jensen 1970d; North Slope Borough, Commission on History and Culture 1977; Ostermann and Holtved 1952:48, 49). In a previous publication (Burch 1981:14) I confused this encounter with one that took place near Cape Seppings (see Nuvua, #20).

Iŋiġaġik (Ear Mountain) (#56): This is said to have been the site of a battle, possibly several battles, between Tapqaġmiut and Qaviaraġmiut (Kiyutelluk 1976; Koutsky 1981a:30).

Iqsiiġvik (#33): A Nuataaġmiut raid had led people to abandon this settlement. However, over a period of two or three years the Akuniġmiut residents of Qayaina erected at this spot two largely underground houses with tunnels leading to willow thickets. Later, learning that a party of Nuataaġmiut warriors was heading toward the Kobuk, a number of men from Qayaina moved to the houses. The Nuataaġmiut attacked but could not make any headway against the fortified houses. Suddenly, twin brothers, who were excellent warriors, arrived from their home farther up the Squirrel River and drew the raiders' attention. While the Nuataaġmiut concentrated on the twins the men inside the houses escaped through the tunnels, surrounded the enemy, and killed them all (Foote 1966a:story 12; Giddings 1961:110–112; Hunnicutt 1989; Jackson 1989; Tobuk 1981). Elwood Uyaana Hunnicutt tells this story on a videotape made by the Northwest Arctic Television Center for its Iñupiat Heritage Series (n.d.:tape 7, story 4). Knowledgeable viewers in Kiana told me that he got everything right except the name of the place; he said it was Puivlini.

Itigamalukpak (#26): This is the site of a battle between the Kaŋmaliq band of Kuukpigmiut and Di'hąįį Gwich'in just north of Anaktuvuk Pass, one of a recurring series between the two peoples. A few Kaŋmaliġmiut were killed and wounded, but some three dozen Gwich'in were killed. The Gwich'in women built a stockade of poles and hides to protect themselves and finally were permitted to leave. This event caused the Gwich'in permanently to abandon the western and central Endicott Mountains (Gubser 1965:46–47; Hennigh 1972:97–99; Hopson 1978:46–47; Ingstad 1954:113–114; Irving 1950; Kisautaq and Kean 1981:182–183; Paneak 1971a, 1971b). Lawrence Hennigh says that the Iñupiat involved were from the Killiġmiut rather than the Qaŋmaliġmiut band of Kuukpigmiut.

Itqil̥l̥iġivik (#46): This is the location of an open battle between Siil̥viim Kaŋianiġmiut warriors, probably accompanied by Kiitaaġmiut, and possibly some Akuniġmiut on one side and Koyukuk River Koyukon forces on the other. The former prevailed. The locality was named to commemorate the event (J. Foster 1970; Hall 1975b:331). This encounter is described in more detail in Chapter 2.

Ivisaaqtiġnilik (#27): This is a place in the Noatak River headwaters district where the Akuniġmiut took their revenge on a settlement of Di'hąįį Gwich'in and their famous leader, Sayyat. Sayyat and his two wives managed to escape, but many of their companions were killed (Douglas 1986; Foote 1966a:story 10; Giddings 1961:99–103; Hall 1975b:139–141; Mendenhall, Sampson, and Tennant 1989:55–59; Northwest Arctic Television Center n.d.:story 1; Sun 1985:113–117).

Kaġmalirak (#9): This site is listed in the North Slope Borough's Traditional Land Use Inventory as a "minor wars area," but no information is given on either the combatants or the circumstances (North Slope Borough, Planning Commission and Historical Commission 1976b:17).

Kaŋitch (#7): One or two families of Silaliñaġmiut were encamped here one year shortly after freeze-up. Tikiġaġmiut warriors discovered and attacked them, but the inhabitants hid and managed to escape (Ivie and Schneider 1988:46; Schneider 1980).

Katyauraq (#70): A summer and fall village here was abandoned when some unidentified Athapaskans chased the Kuuyuŋmiut who were living here back to the coast (Koutsky 1981e:22).

Kełroteyit (#71): This is the site of an 1846 massacre of Koyukuk River Koyukon by a combined force of lower Yukon Koyukon and Eskimos from Norton Sound. The raiders were apparently attempting to cut off the trade between the Yunnaka Khotana Koyukon and the Kobuk River Iñupiat (Clark 1974:188; Loyens 1966:104–105; VanStone and Goddard 1981:560).

Killiq (location approximate) (#25): This was the site of a battle between Kuukpigmiut and Di'hąįį Gwich'in, one of many in a long series. The Di'hąįį reportedly lost 20 men, while the Kuukpigmiut lost 4 women and 2 men (Paneak 1971a).

Kiŋigan (#61): This, the capital village of the Kiŋikmiut, is the site of many battles with Nuvuqaghhmiit Eskimos of East Cape, Siberia, or Uellyt Chukchi or both. In one specific encounter reported by Garber (1975:169–172), several boatloads of Nuvuqaghhmiit crossed Bering Strait to attack the settlement. However, they were spotted by lookouts posted on Cape Prince of Wales. The women, children, and old men ran to hide in caves on the mountain, while the men prepared for battle. The Nuvuqaghhmiit landed on the beach near the village, equipped with bows, arrows, and large bearded sealskin shields. They were met near the mouth of the creek that flowed between the two segments of the village. The battle raged all day, but the invaders were outnumbered and eventually began to suffer insurmountable losses. Finally, all of them were killed.

Kuintaq (#68): This is listed but unsubstantiated as a battle site (O'Leary 1995a).

Kuupałłuk (#4): Once while an Iñupiat group of unknown nationality was living here a party of Gwich'in raided the camp when the men were away hunting caribou. The raiders killed everyone except two girls, whom they took as captives. When the men returned and saw what had happened they went in pursuit of the raiders. Several nights later the Iñupiat caught up with them. The Athapaskans were seated around a campfire, and the girls were out gathering wood. The Iñupiat signaled the girls to build as big a fire as possible so that the men sitting around it would be blinded by the light. Then they surrounded the Gwich'in and killed all but two, whom they let escape (Arundale and Schneider 1987:47–48, 88, 97). Note that there are striking similarities between this story and the one concerning Makpik (#23).

Kuupaamiit (#32): Athapaskans of unknown origin attacked a small camp in the vicinity of this large village and killed all the women and children while the men were out hunting. The surviving men attempted to reciprocate the following fall, but I did not learn the outcome of their effort (D. Foster 1970).

Makpik (#23): This is the site of an upper Kobuk Koyukon raid on the Nuataaġmiut settlement of Makpik. Attacking while all the men were away hunting caribou, the raiders killed everyone in the camp except two expatriate Koyukon women. Later the Nuataaġmiut men overtook the raiders, killed them all, and recovered the two women (Cleveland 1965c; Curtis 1930:205; Foote 1965b:story 14; Hennigh 1972:100; Lucier 1958:110–111; C. Swan 1965; cf. Bergsland 1987: 344–349). This story is told in greater detail in Chapter 2. Note the striking similarities between this story and the one concerning Kuupałłuk (#4).

Maniiḷappaat (#37): 1. Di'hąįį Gwich'in, under their leader, Sayyat, attacked a summer camp of Kobuk River people (who must have been upper

Kobuk Koyukon). Most of the men and older boys were away hunting caribou in the Noatak River valley. The attackers killed a number of women and children. The nationality (Uyaġaaġmiut, in Iñupiatun) of the raiders was ascertained through an arrow point that had been left behind (Douglas 1986; Foote 1966b:story 10; Giddings 1961:99–103; Sun 1985:113–117).

2. This is also the site of a raid by Noatakers on the Kobuk River people, which is described in greater detail in Chapter 2 (Cleveland 1965c; Curtis 1930:205; Hennigh 1972:100; Lucier 1958:110–111; C. Swan 1965; cf. Bergsland 1987:344–349).

Maqłuktuliq (#69): A confrontation between the Kuuyuŋmiut and an unspecified Athapaskan group is reported to have occurred here. It must have been long ago, because the account has acquired many of the characteristics of a legend (Koutsky 1981e:17, 28–29; O'Leary 1995b).

Masu (#62): Listed but unsubstantiated as a battle site (O'Leary 1995b).

Miłłitaavik (#60): Two boatloads of Chukotkans recruited a Diomede man to watch their boats while they scouted the area, which was in the estate of the Tapqaġmiut. A Tapqaġmiut man spotted the Diomeder and the boats. He shot the Diomeder, and the Chukotkans panicked and fled (Koutsky 1981a:32–33, 1981b:20, 28; O'Leary 1995b; United States Department of the Interior, Bureau of Indian Affairs 1991:5).

Naparuatchiaq (#12): This place is said to have been the scene of some kind of armed encounter, but which nations were involved and what the outcome was were not reported (Agnasagga 1984).

Nauyatuuq (#39): This is the site of a successful Akuniġmiut raid on a small settlement of upper Kobuk Koyukon. It led to a retaliatory raid on the Akuniġmiut settlement of Qalugraitchiaq (#35). This was probably an 18th-century exchange because there are some fantastic elements in the accounts (Cleveland 1970c; Foote 1966a:story 13).

Niksiurak (#5): There was a battle here, one involving large numbers of people, between the Kakligmiut of Barrow and an unidentified inland group. Many people were killed. The place was later characterized as being a graveyard, but it is not clear whether all the bodies interred here derived from this one event (Neakok and Numnik 1978; Schneider, Pedersen, and Libbey 1980:212). Thomas Simpson (1843:153–154) saw so many fresh graves here in the summer of 1837 that his men were afraid that some kind of epidemic had struck the population.

Noolaaghedoh (#73): The residents of both the Koyukon village of Noolaaghedoh and the nearby Russian trading post of Nulato were massacred by members of neighboring Koyukon groups in February 1851 (Adams 1850–51:85, 87; Arndt 1996:103–108; Clark 1974:188–190; Dall 1870:48–52; Joe 1987:16–20; Loyens 1966:104–107; Wright 1995a:60–63, 1995b).

Nunaġiaq (#53): A raid by Qaviaraġmiut (Kuzitrin River) and Iġałuiŋmiut (Fish River) on this important Pittaġmiut spring camp turned into a major battle. The Pittaġmiut won because of the heroics of their champion, who taunted the members of the enemy force into expending all their arrows without killing anyone (Morris 1970).

Nuviakchak (#67): Some Malimiut (meaning Iñupiat from somewhere in the Kotzebue Sound drainage) took control of this Čaxtuləmiut village site by force. A retaliatory raid was successful, and all the Malimiut inhabitants were killed except for a beautiful young girl. She was captured and raped, and then her hands and feet were tied to four kayaks, which pulled in opposite directions, tearing her apart (Jacobsen 1884:291, 1977:132; O'Leary 1995b; Ray 1964:68).

Nuvua (Cape Seppings) (#20): This is the site of a great summer battle between the Tikiġaġmiut on one side and a combined force of Nuataaġmiut, Napaaqtuġmiut, Kivalliñiġmiut, and Qikiqtaġruŋmiut on the other. No details are available, but the Tikiġaġmiut are said to have lost half their male population in this encounter. The battle probably occurred in the late 18th century (Ostermann and Holtved 1952:48; Wells and Kelly 1890:10). In an earlier publication (Burch 1981:14) I confused this encounter with a separate one that took place at Iñuktat, which is closer to Cape Thompson (#17).

Nuvuġaluaq (#14): Unspecified Athapaskans, probably Di'hąįį Gwich'in, massacred a village of Tikiġaġmiut (Jensen 1970a). This encounter is described in more detail in Chapter 2.

Piŋu (#58): A Tapqaġmiu man and his son were attacked here by a boatload of Chukotkans of unknown ethnic background. The son, who was quite agile, drew enemy fire while his father retrieved their arrows. Eventually, the Chukotkans expended all of their arrows. These were then turned against them, with the result that all the attackers were killed (Koutsky 1981a:23, 31; United States Department of the Interior, Bureau of Indian Affairs 1996). This story looks suspiciously like the account of the battle at Nunaġiaq (#53).

Pisiktaġvik (#1): The name means "place where bows and arrows were used," indicating a battleground. Unfortunately, the details have been lost

(North Slope Borough, Planning Commission and Historical Commission 1976a:11). On a sketch map of the Colville River delta prepared for John Campbell Simon Panniaq Paneak locates the spot quite precisely, with the notation that the battle was between the Point Barrow people and the *nunamiut*, which was the general term for people living in the interior (Campbell 1998:pl. 59). On another occasion he said that the inlanders involved were more precisely Kuukpigmiut, or Colville River people (Paneak 1971a:3). Many men were lost on both sides, but the Kuukpigmiut prevailed (Ericklook 1977; Stefansson 1914b:1990). According to Sarah Kunuknana (1977), a man named Atkaaŋ was the leader of the coastal people, and the father of a man named Kullasirak was the leader of the inlanders.

Qalugraitchiaq (#35): 1. Athapaskans of unknown origin arrived in the vicinity of this Akuniġmiut settlement with the intention of massacring its inhabitants. However, they were discovered and defeated by the Akuniġmiut before they could launch their attack (Glover 1970c). 2. This was also the site of a revenge raid by upper Kobuk Koyukon to retaliate for the Akuniġmiut raid on Nauyatuq. The Koyukon killed everyone in the settlement (Cleveland 1970c; Foote 1966a:story 13).

Qanaak (#10): An armed encounter occurred here between Tikiġaġmiut warriors and unnamed opponents (presumably Silaliñaġmiut). There is no information on which side won (North Slope Borough, Planning Commission and Historical Commission 1976b:17).

Qaviaraq (#64): This main village of the Qaviaraġmiut was raided many times by both Uellyt (Chukchi) and Nuvuqaghmiit (Asiatic Yup'ik Eskimos), but the details of most of the battles have been lost. During the final encounter the defenders apparently built a stockade of poles and umiaq covers and managed to kill all of the Chukotkans except two (Hrdlička 1930:117–118; Nelson 1899:330; Oquilluk 1973:215–216; Ray 1975b:31–32; Stefansson 1914b:267; United States Department of the Interior, Bureau of Indian Affairs 1995). Diamond Jenness (1928:78–79) reported on some pictographs, apparently of battle scenes, near a place where the Qaviaraġmiut used to station sentinels.

Qigiqtaq (Shishmaref) (#55): 1. A band of Athapaskans, presumably Koyukon, attacked the village when most of the local Tapqaġmiut men were about 10 miles (16 kilometers) away retrieving supplies of stored fish. When the raiders arrived the women were dancing in the qargi. The Athapaskans blocked the door and threw burning material down through the skylight. The women who emerged were clubbed to death. Most of those who remained inside died of asphyxiation or burns; the few survivors were shot with bow and arrow through the skylight. When the Tapqaġmiut men returned and discovered what had happened, they set out in pursuit of the raiders. They set up an ambush at the place where they expected the Athapaskans to make their last camp before reaching their own village. They guessed correctly, and while the Athapaskans slept the Tapqaġmiut killed them all (Weyer 1928:16 [Wales]).

2. Apparently in a separate event a party of Qaviaraġmiut raided the more easterly of the two settlements on the island. They caught the inhabitants in the qargi and burned them to death. The settlement never recovered from the shock (Nayokpuk 1999; Weyiouanna 1999).

Qikertaq (#77): This is listed but unsubstantiated as a battle site (O'Leary 1995b).

Qikiqtaq (Besboro Island) (#74): Every winter some lower Koyukon came to this island in Čaxtuləmiut country to trade. One year they arrived in unusually large numbers, which made the Čaxtuləmiut suspicious. Before trading the Koyukon were offered a steam bath in the qargi. While the Koyukon were bathing the Čaxtuləmiut checked their sleds and found a large number of weapons hidden in them. They placed guards armed with walrus-tusk clubs at the entrance to the qargi and then poured seal oil through the skylight onto the fire. The resulting conflagration caused the Koyukon to rush out, and they were all clubbed to death as they emerged (Koutsky 1981f:28–29, cf. 1982a:28–29).

Sapun (#22): This is the site of a battle between Nuataaġmiut and unspecified opponents. The outcome of the encounter is unknown (Mills 1960:60).

Siktaġvik (#47): This is the site of an old battleground that is located almost within the modern village of Selawik. The Kiitaaġmiut were on one side of the battle and evidently prevailed. Their opponents might have been from the upper Kobuk River valley. If they were, in fact, from that district, they were likely Athapaskans. The attackers' dead were thrown into a small lake nearby (NANA Cultural Heritage Project 1975c:2; Smith 1970).

Siłyeeminkk'at (#44): This was a Koyukon settlement whose inhabitants were killed in a raid by a party of Gwich'in of unknown nationality (allegedly from the east). This raid might date as late as the mid-1850s (Andrews 1977, vol. 2:358; Clark 1996:62–63; McFadyen 1995:369).

Siŋik (#49): A small party of Russians under M. N. Vasil'ev encountered several hundred Kaŋiġmiut here at their major beluga-hunting site. After friendly initial contacts the Natives became overbearing. As the Russians tried to escape the Natives fired on them with bows and arrows and allegedly with firearms (of unknown origin). The Russians retaliated by firing a falconet (a small cannon) at one of the boats that was chasing them. The ball ripped out the entire side of the boat and wounded one man. The Kaŋiġmiut then abandoned their attack (Ray 1983:34–37). The Native use of firearms in this incident is a complete anomaly as far as the study period is concerned. A few years later Beechey encountered people from the same nation who he claimed were ignorant of the use of firearms.

Sisualik (#30): A Tikiġaġmiut attack on Qikiqtaġruŋmiut, who were protected by a stockade, ended with a battle, which the attackers lost (Curtis 1970; Gallahorn 1970a, 1970b; Harris 1952; Jensen and Jensen 1980; Lucier n.d.a, n.d.c, 1958:109; Mendenhall, Sampson, and Tennant 1989:65–71; Ostermann and Holtved 1952:67–68). This encounter is described in greater detail in Chapter 2.

Suluppaugaqtuuq (#38): There was an encounter here between upper Kobuk Koyukon from Pah River and unidentified Iñupiat. The Iñupiat killed all but one of the Koyukon (Foote 1966a:story 8).

Taksruq saaŋa (#31): This raid by a force of Iñupiat of uncertain origin was aborted when they were discovered advancing on the settlement. This event probably dates from after 1850 (Gallahorn 1970b; Glover 1970c; Elwood Hunnicutt 1970; Jensen 1970c). It is described in greater detail in Chapter 2.

Tapqaq (#63): This site is located near Qaviaraq, the main village of the Qaviaraġmiut, which was often attacked by either Uellyt (Chukchi) or Nuvuqaghmiit (Asiatic Yup'ik) or both. Lookouts were often stationed along Tuksuk Channel, and many battles and skirmishes occurred here and in the vicinity over the years. Women and children hid in caves along the channel during battles, but the women also occasionally got involved by throwing rocks on the Chukotkans from the steep sides of the channel as they paddled by. Sometimes the women swam underwater and slashed the Chukotkan boats with knives, causing them to sink. Whenever the Qaviaraġmiut won, they placed the severed heads of the dead Chukotkans on a level area near the channel (O'Leary 1995b; Oquilluk 1973:215–216; Ray 1964:76; United States Department of the Interior, Bureau of Indian Affairs 1995).

Tikiġaq (#15): There was a raid on Point Hope (Tikiġaq) by a combined force of Napaaqtuġmiut, Nuataaġmiut, Qikiqtaġruŋmiut, and Kivalliñiġmiut, who were defeated (Frankson 1980; Jensen 1970d; Jensen and Jensen 1980; Rainey 1947:240; Rock 1940:4). This encounter is described in greater detail in Chapter 2.

Tikiġaġmiut (#3): There are at least four versions of this confrontation. In the first a party of Tikiġaġmiut (Point Hopers) arrived at this site bent on attacking a group of Kakligmiut from Barrow. However, the Kakligmiut found out they were coming and fled by boat to an island about a mile offshore. Since they had both boats and nets, the Kakligmiut were able to fish for food. The Tikiġaġmiut had neither, so they could not fish. There was no game in the area, and they starved to death (Evok 1970). A variant of this version is that the Kakligmiut found a lot of dried meat on the island that enabled them to survive (Ekowana 1978). In the second version it was the Point Hopers who were on the island. The Kakligmiut stole their boats, which left them isolated there, where they eventually died (Jenness 1991:15; North Slope Borough, Planning Commission and Historical Commission 1976a:8). Still a third version agrees that the Tikiġaġmiut were the ones on the island but claims they were trapped there by breakup and did not have the appropriate gear to survive (Gal 1997). The fourth, reported by Robert Spencer on the basis of information provided by Andy Ungarook, indicates that there was an open battle during which the Tikiġaġmiut were maneuvered onto a sand spit, isolated there, and allowed to starve (Spencer 1952, notebook 2:80, 1959:281). (Spencer's published account confounds stories of two different encounters as recorded in his field notes.) All four versions concur that the Tikiġaġmiut starved to death and that the place has been called Tikiġaġmiut ever since to commemorate the event.

Too loghe (#43): This Koyukon settlement near Olson's Lake was attacked at least once by Iñupiat and twice by Gwich'in (of unspecified nationality). During the last attack only elders happened to be there, and the Gwich'in killed them all. Tiring of the persistent raids, the survivors moved to the mouth of the South Fork of the Koyukuk. At least some of the Gwich'in had firearms during this raid, which suggests a mid-19th-century date (Jones 1991; McFadyen 1995:367).

Uivvak (#13): Tikiġaġmiut living here had advance warning of a Qikiqtaġruŋmiut raid and advanced to meet the raiders in the hills behind the settlement. However, the Tikiġaġmiut were decisively defeated by the Qikiqtaġruŋmiut, and all but one man was killed. He escaped and carried the news to the people at Tikiġaq. This is evidently the battle whose remains were discovered by Aleksandr Kashevarov in 1838 (Jensen and Jensen 1980; VanStone 1977:54).

Uqsruuġat (#28): There was an open battle between Tikiġaġmiut on the one side and either the Qikiqtaġruŋmiut or the Napaaqtuġmiut on the other. The Tikiġaġmiut, who may have been on their way to avenge their loss at Sisualik (#30), were all killed (Edna Hunnicutt 1960b, 1970; Elwood Hunnicutt 1970; Hall 1975b:97–99; Stalker 1986; United States Department of the Interior, Bureau of Indian Affairs 1987c).

Whale Island (#75): Sometime before the Russians arrived on Norton Sound a large village here was attacked and destroyed by raiders from south of the Yukon. This probably occurred during the 18th century (Nelson 1877–81, notebook 4:entry for January 20, 1880, 1899:263–264).

Yakpatakhaq (#57): A former village here suffered a devastating attack by unidentified Chukotkans. The place is named after the only survivor of the attack (Koutsky 1981a:23, 32).

Appendix 2
Overland Travel Routes in Northwestern Alaska

International relations in northwestern Alaska were conducted via travel along the coast, up and down the major rivers, and between watersheds. The coastal and major river routes are obvious to anyone looking at a map, but the overland routes are not. Information on the latter is summarized here as a detailed counterpart to Map 13, which shows the major trade routes in northern Beringia. The routes are characterized as "travel routes" here because they were used for all kinds of travel, not just trade. This appendix recapitulates, augments, and updates previously published material (see Burch 1976, 1990:200, 208, 214, 217).

Norton Sound–Yukon Drainage

The dominant topographic feature of this area is the Nulato Hills. They are not particularly high (3,900 feet [1,200 meters]) or rugged, and the elevations of the major passes are 1,500 feet (460 meters) or less. Distances, too, are not great. For example, route 3 between Unalakleet and Kaltag is less than 80 miles (130 kilometers) long (see Map 15). The major obstacles to winter travel in this zone are deep snow and overflow (water on top of the ice), not topography as such (Osgood 1958:62). (Basic information on routes in this district was obtained from Correll 1971, 1972:148–153; Koutsky 1982a:26.)

1. Saint Michael–Anvik: From the Saint Michael area one traveled east to the mouth of the Klikitarik (Qiqiqtaġuk) River and ascended to its eastern headwater section. The trail then led over the divide to the Golsovia River, crossed it, and then crossed another divide to the middle of Otter Creek. From there the route lay down Otter Creek and the Anvik River (see also Dall 1898:216; Osgood 1958:62).
2. Unalakleet–Anvik: The route lay up the Unalakleet River to the mouth of the Chirosky River, ascended the Chirosky to its head, crossed an easily traversed divide to the upper Anvik, and then led downstream the rest of the way. This route seems to have been less important than routes 1 and 3 but was nonetheless regularly used by people traveling to the Anvik area from central or northern Norton Sound (see also Dall 1898:216).

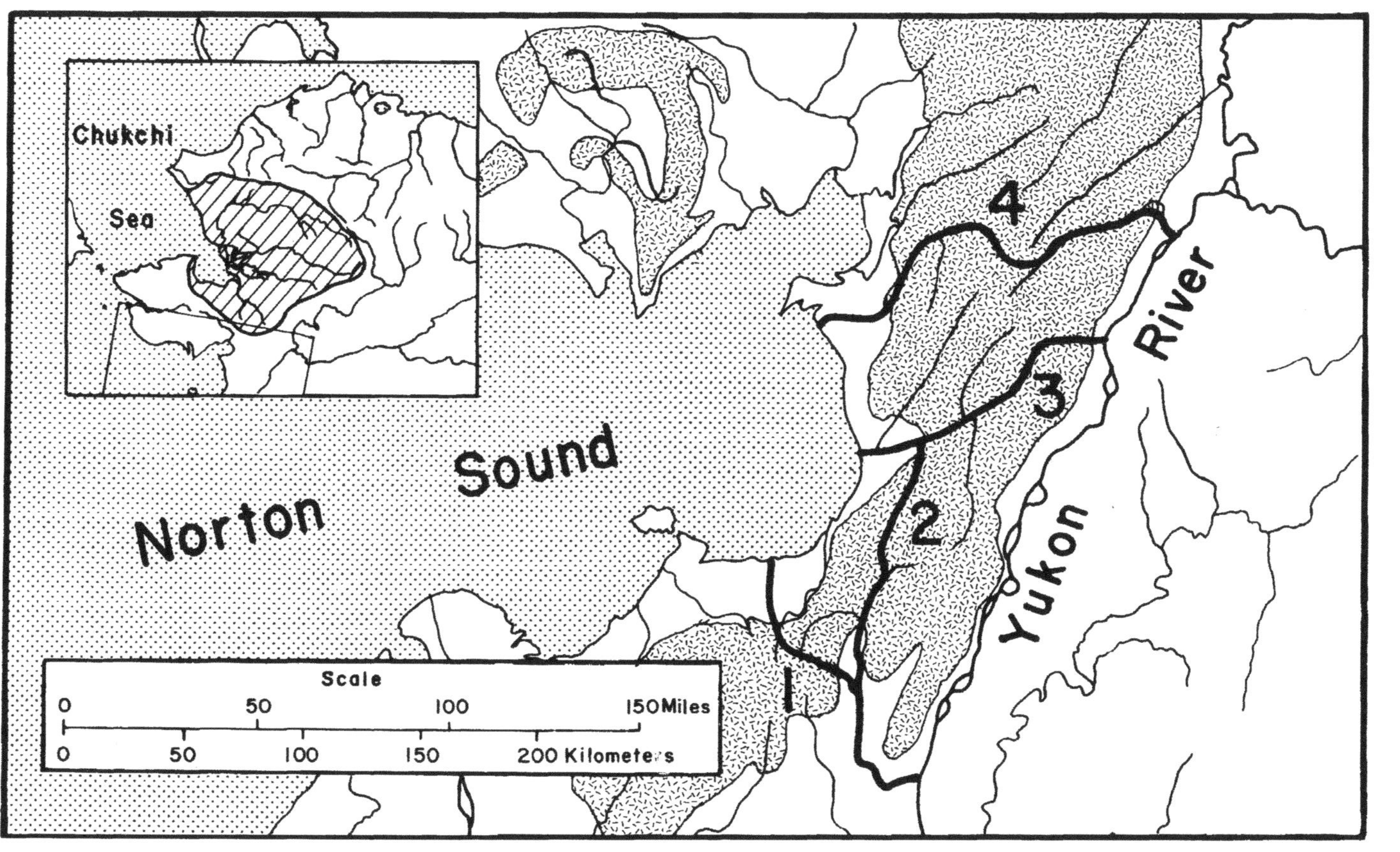

15. Major travel routes between Norton Sound and the lower Yukon River.

3. Unalakleet–Kaltag: A major travel route extended up the main branch of the Unalakleet River to its head and then crossed, via a branch of the Rodo River, to the head of the Kaltag River, which it descended to the Yukon. This "Kaltag Portage" was a major avenue for movement between the interior and Norton Sound. Early in the second half of the 19th century, if not before, at least three villages were scattered along the trail, two of which were occupied by Athapaskans as well as by Eskimos (see also Dall 1898:39, 144; Foote 1965a:map 20; Loyens 1966:24; Stoney 1900:806–807; Stuck 1914:125).
4. Shaktoolik–Nulato: A route of secondary importance ascended the Shaktoolik River almost to its head, crossed a short divide to the head of the Nulato River, and descended it to the Yukon.

Seward Peninsula

The Seward Peninsula is the westernmost projection of Alaska and separates the Chukchi Sea on the north from the Bering Sea on the south. The northern portion of the peninsula consists of an extensive coastal plain, and the western interior is occupied by a lowland basin. The latter is bordered on the south, east, and north by upland areas. The highest elevations occur in the southern half of the peninsula, where, ranging from west to east, the Kigluaik, Bendeleben, and Darby Mountains form the major obstacles to overland travel. Of these, the Kigluaik Range is the highest (4,721 feet [1,439 meters] at Mount Osborn) and most rugged and is the only really significant barrier to travel in the entire zone (Hopkins and Hopkins 1958). Overland travel was not particularly difficult anywhere else, and the region was crisscrossed by a network of trails (Map 16). (Basic information on routes in this area is in Koutsky 1981d:55–56, 1981e:66, 68; Ray 1967:66, 68.)

5. Koyuk–Buckland: This route ascended the Koyuk (Kuyuk) River, continued up the east fork for a short distance, then cut north to the headwaters of the west fork of the Buckland River and thence down to the coast. The divide here is only about 600 feet (180 meters) above sea level, and the route was a major avenue of contact between the Iñupiaq-speaking Eskimos on the north and the Yuplik-speaking Eskimos on the south (see also Bertholf 1899b:110–111; Jacobsen 1884:292, 295–318; Foote 1965a:map 20; Mendenhall 1901:217; Ray 1964:66, 85).
6. Koyuk–Kiwalik: This route followed the main branch of the Koyuk River to the Peace River, ascended it, and crossed to the head of the Kiwalik (Kuugaaluk) via Sweepstake Creek. The route then continued down the Kiwalik to the coast.

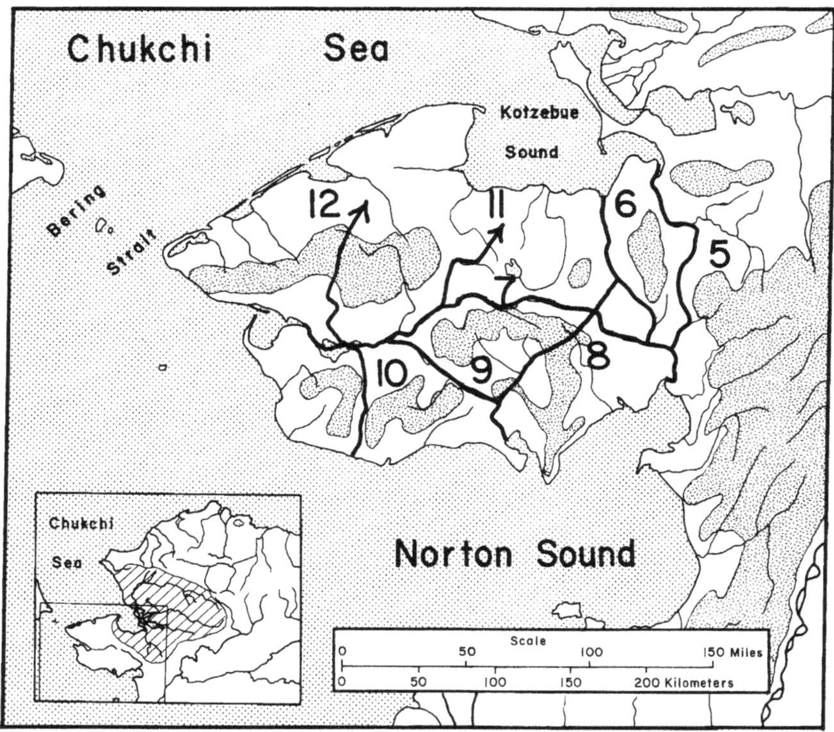

16. Major travel routes across the Seward Peninsula.

7. Koyuk–Kuzitrin: This route ascended the Koyuk to its head and crossed the divide to the westward-flowing Kuzitrin (Kuuzitqiun) drainage. From there one could head directly toward any one of a number of settlements in the area. An offshoot of this route extended from where this one struck the Kuzitrin watershed north to the Kugruk, as in route 11.
8. Golovnin–Kiwalik: This route ascended the Fish River to the northeast side of the basin along its upper course, crossed the divide north of the Omilak mines to the head of the Tubutulik, and then extended to the upper Koyuk via a low pass. From this point a number of routes to the Kiwalik (e.g., route 6) were available (see also Brooks 1901:216; Mendenhall 1901:216–217).
9. Golovnin–Port Clarence: This route began at Golovnin Bay, ascended the Fish River, headed northwest across the south side of the flats along the lower Niukluk River, and then ascended the Niukluk to a point just below the mouth of the north fork. From there it headed west to Sherette Creek, which it descended to the Pilgrim River. From the lower Pilgrim one could

cross the flats to Mary's Igloo (Qaviaraq) or head farther west to Port Clarence. This route was perhaps the most important artery of interregional travel on the Seward Peninsula during the 19th century (see also Brooks 1953:244, 371; *Esquimaux*, no. 8 [1866–67]:35, no. 9 [1866–67]:37–38; Foote 1965a:map 20; Jacobsen 1884:253–294; Mendenhall 1901:216; Michael 1967:124; Seemann 1853, vol. 2:137; VanStone 1973:78).

10. Nome–Mary's Igloo: This route ascended the Nome River to its head, crossed Salmon Lake to the Pilgrim River, and descended it as in route 9. This route offered a shortcut around the eastern end of the Kigluaik Mountains.
11. Mary's Igloo–Kotzebue Sound: This route went up the Kuzitrin to the Noxapaga (Naksampaaga) and from there across the divide to either the Goodhope, the Inmachuk (Ipnatchiaq), or the Kugruk (Kuugruk) Rivers (see also Hobson 1855).
12. Imuruk Basin–Shishmaref Area: From the Imuruk Basin the route ascended the lower Agiapak River, thence up the American River, and across the divide to Bonanza Creek. From there a number of local routes to the coast were available.

Selawik River–Kobuk River

Travelers between the Selawik River drainage on the south and the adjoining Kobuk River drainage on the north had to cross the Hockley Hills on the west or the Waring Mountains on the east. Neither group of uplands is particularly high. The Waring Mountains have gentle slopes and can be crossed almost anywhere. The Hockley Hills, on the other hand, have a rugged spine and are most easily crossed via the routes noted here (Map 17).

13. Oblaron Creek–Portage Creek: To go from the Selawik area to the Kiana region on the Kobuk River one traveled up Oblaron Creek through an abrupt break in the Hockley Hills and down Portage Creek, striking the Kobuk River near the modern village of Kiana. If one wanted to go to the head of the Kobuk River delta farther west, the route lay around the western slopes of Hotham Peak (Aasrigragaaŋiq).
14. Naluk Creek: Naluk Creek originates in the eastern Hockley Hills and flows east, then north, to the Kobuk River. About 4–5 miles (6–8 kilometers) below the head there is a wide gap in the upland between the Hockley Hills on the west and the Waring Mountains on the east. From the Selawik side this gap can be comfortably reached via both Singauruk River to the west and the western branch of the Fish River on the east.

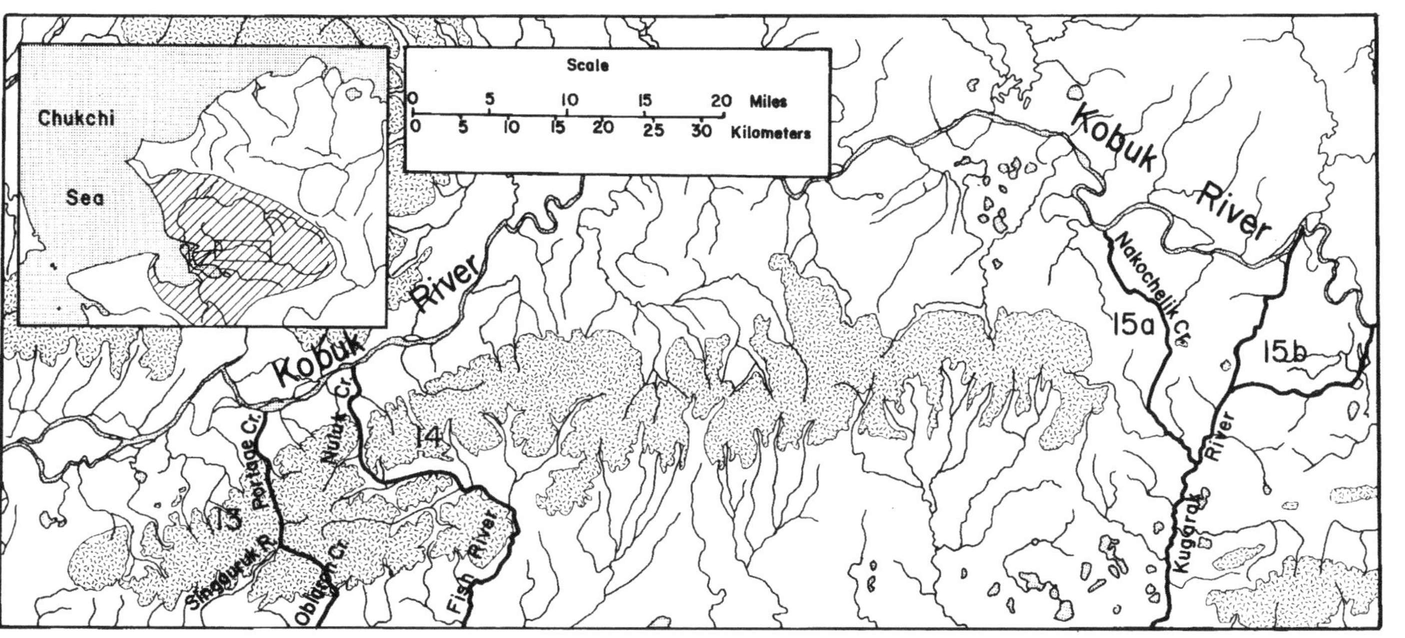

17. Major travel routes between the Selawik River drainage on the south and the Kobuk River drainage on the north.

15. Kugarak River–Kobuk River: This route extended from the Selawik River up the Kugarak (Kuugruaq) and then to the latter's head. From there one heading toward the central Kobuk would cross the eastern end of the Waring Mountains (Iñġitchiaq) and take Nakochelik Creek (15a) or any one of several alternatives to the Kobuk. Travelers heading east to the upper Kobuk River valley (15b) traveled east along the north slope of the Rabbit Hills (Uqallium iñġii) and then descended any one of several tributaries to the Kobuk.

Kotzebue Sound–Yukon Drainage

The rivers flowing into Kotzebue Sound are separated from the Yukon drainage by the northern Nulato Hills, the Purcell Mountains, the Zane Hills, and an extensive area of relatively low upland having very moderate relief. Of these, only the Purcell Mountains were a significant obstacle to travel, and they were readily bypassed. Elsewhere travelers could take almost any route they wanted, but the ones listed below were used most frequently. More important than topography as a hindrance to travel were deep snow in winter and extensive areas of muskeg in summer (Map 18). (Basic information on routes in this area was obtained from Ballott 1970a; Smith 1913:24; Williams 1991.)

16. Buckland–Nulato: This route went up the south fork of the Buckland River to its upper reaches, then east past Wrench Lake and across the divide to the upper Tagagawik (Taġraġviim kuuŋa) River. On the upper river it merged with route 17.
17. Selawik–Nulato: This route lay south from the Selawik area up the Tagagawik River (Taġraġviim kuuŋa) to Derby Creek (Sulukpaugaqtuq), then east across the divide and the south fork of the Huslia River to the Kateel River. From there travelers either went southeast to Nulato (cutting across the drainage pattern) or else followed one of the several rivers flowing roughly northeast to communities on the lower portions of the Koyukuk River (Ballot 1970a).
18. Selawik–Koyukuk: A secondary route between the Selawik district and the Koyukon ascended the Selawik River to its head and then divided. One could go either east across Zane Pass (1,181 feet [360 meters]), the Pah River Flats, and the Hogatza River to the Koyukuk or else southeast along the western slopes of the Zane Hills (Asiksit) to a point farther downriver (see also Foote 1965a:map 20).
19. Kobuk River–Koyukuk River (via the Pah River portage): The divide between the upper Kobuk and the Koyukuk Rivers is low and relatively level. The only major obstruction to travel is thick forest,

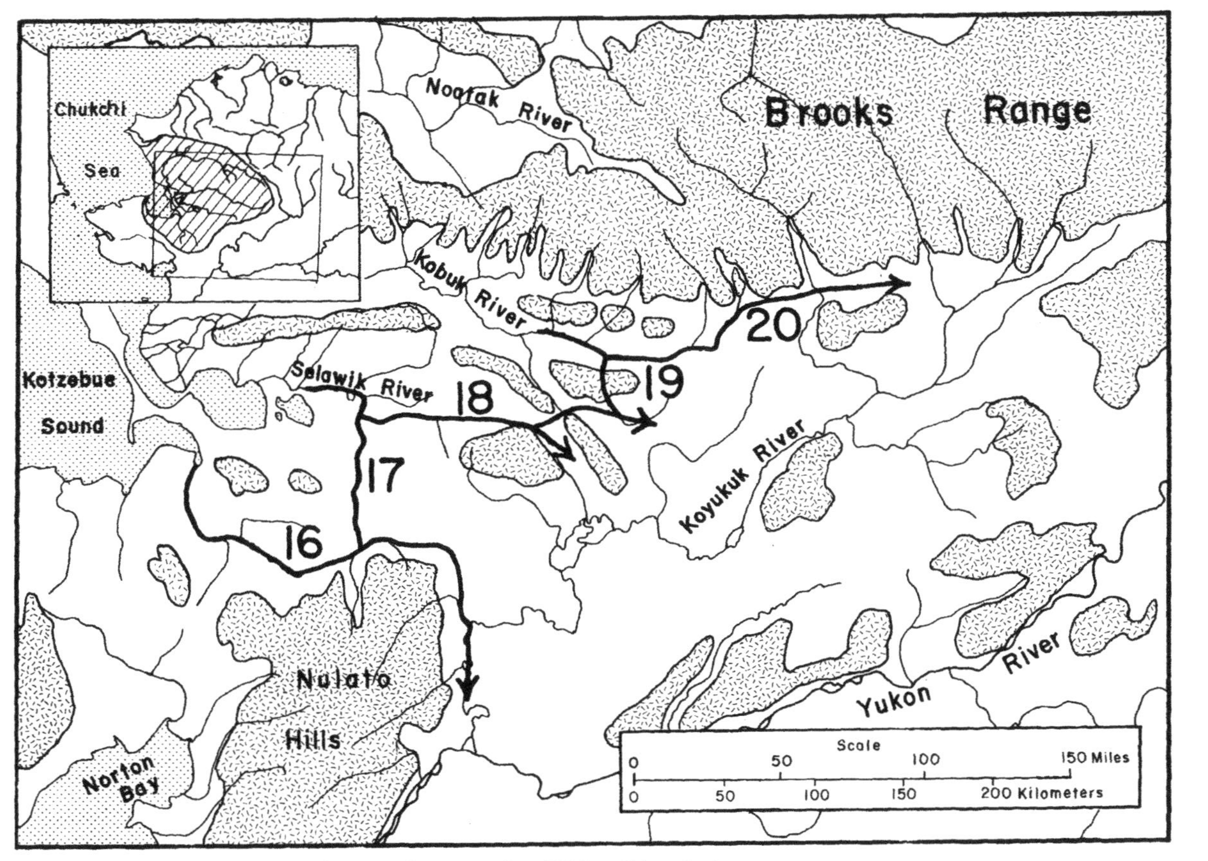

18. Major travel routes between the Kotzebue Sound and Yukon River drainages.

particularly on the Koyukuk side. One could go almost any way one pleased between the two rivers. The main route from the Kobuk lay up either the Pick or the Pah River to the Pah River Flats, where it merged with route 18 (Cantwell 1887:310; Foote 1965a:map 20; Lee 1970; Mendenhall 1902:26; Stoney 1900:802–805, 809–810).

20. Kobuk River–Koyukuk River (via the Alatna portage): To get to the Alatna (Aalaasuq) from the upper Kobuk, one usually traveled upriver to the vicinity of Walker Lake (Orth 1967:map 2), then east across the divide to the Alatna River. The slope here is very gentle, and the only significant obstacles to travel are trees and deep snow in winter. This route (which connected with routes 42 and 43) was also the first part of the route between the upper Kobuk and the Endicott Mountains (see also Cantwell 1887:39; Johnson n.d.:12; Mendenhall 1902:9–10; Smith 1913:33; Smith and Mertie 1930:35; Stoney 1900:573; Stuck 1914:70–72, 1920:49–51).

Baird Mountains

The Baird Mountains are the southwesternmost sector of the Brooks Range, which angles toward the northeast across northern Alaska from near the northeastern corner of Kotzebue Sound. They constitute a moderately rugged upland that rises abruptly from the Kobuk River valley on the south and the lower Noatak River valley on the west to a subsummit upland along the crest of the range. Most of the summits are between 2,500 and 3,000 feet (760 and 910 meters) in altitude, although groups of higher peaks, with altitudes of 3,500–4,500 feet (1,070–1,370 meters), are located in various parts of the range. Toward the north the Bairds slope rather gently downward to the central portions of the Noatak valley, while on the east there is an abrupt increase in relief where they approach the western end of the Schwatka Mountains. Passes through the range that link the Noatak and Kobuk drainages are relatively low and level toward the west. Toward the east they become gradually higher and acquire a much steeper gradient. In all sectors the rise is abrupt on the Kobuk side and relatively gentle on the Noatak side (Map 19). (Basic information on routes through the Baird Mountains was obtained from P. Atoruk 1989; Coffin 1970; Glover 1970a; Sampson 1970; Walker 1969a.)

21. Kiana–lower Noatak: From the Kobuk this route ascended the main branch of the Squirrel River (Siksriktuuq) to its head and then crossed the divide to the closest tributary of the Agashashok (Iġġiitch Isuat) River, which it descended to the plain of the lower Noatak. Once on the plain one could go in almost any direction one pleased.

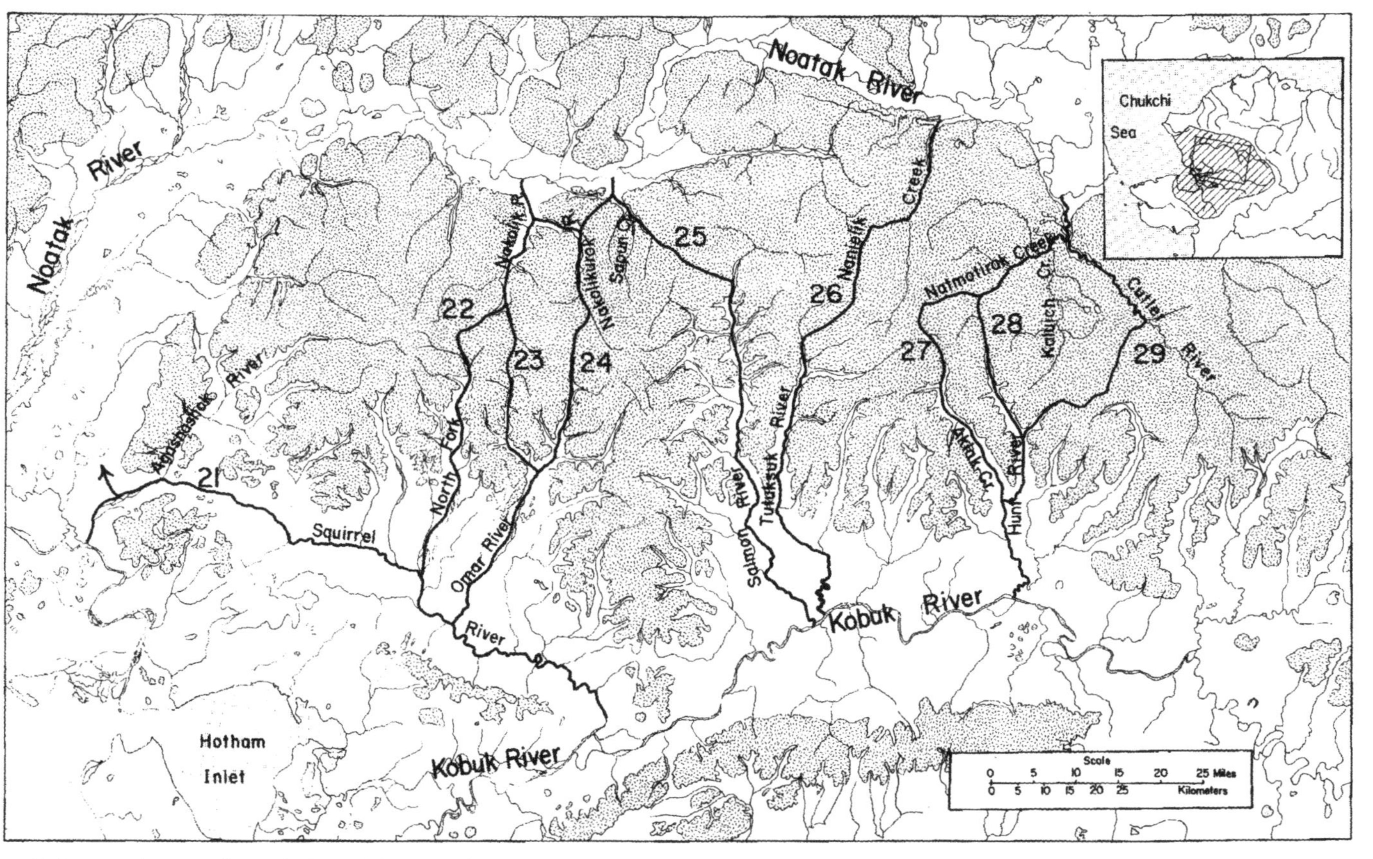

19. Major travel routes through the Baird Mountains.

22. Niaquligruaq Pass: This route went from the North Fork of the Squirrel River on the Kobuk side to Nakolikurok Creek on the Noatak side. The intervening pass is approximately 1,200 feet (365 meters) in altitude. It was good in both summer and winter.
23. Aŋayukalik Pass: This route went from the head of the Omar River (Uumman Kuuŋa) on the south and crossed Aŋayukalik Pass (1,400 feet [425 meters]) to the head of Nakolik Creek (Niaquliim Kuugauraŋa) on the north. It is an easy trail in both summer and winter.
24. Niaquligauraq Pass: This route went from the head of the Omar River across a pass about 1,200 feet (425 meters) in altitude to Nakolikurok (Niaquligauraq) Creek on the north. This route offers a very easy trail in both summer and winter. From where the latter makes an abrupt bend to the west, the route lay across the shoulder of the Angayukalik Hills to Sapun Creek and thence to the Noatak (see also Smith 1913:23).
25. Qalugruaq Pass: The route went up the Salmon (Qalugruaq) River to its upper reaches, then up a tributary extending northwest, across the divide (2,500 feet [769 meters]) to the head of Sapun Creek, and down it to the Noatak (or else cut across the shoulder of the Angayukalik Hills, as in route 21). This route was characterized by very gentle grades on both the Kobuk and Noatak sides and was very easy to traverse. It was the best and most heavily used winter trail from the middle Kobuk to the upper Noatak Basin (see also Mendenhall 1902:26).
26. Tuutaksrak Pass: This route went from the Kobuk up the Tutuksak (Tuutaksrak) to its head, crossed the divide to the head of the west branch of Nanielik Creek, and descended it to the Noatak. This trail has gentle grades but considerable overflow and icing in winter and so was used primarily in summer.
27. Akirum Pass: This route went up Akiak Creek (Akirum Kuugauraŋa), a western tributary of the Hunt River, and crossed Akirum Pass (Akirum Naksraŋa) to the head of Natmotirak Creek (Natmutigruam Kuugauraŋa). It descended the latter to Cutler River and eventually the Noatak. This was one of the less frequently used passes across the Baird Mountains.
28. Kuugruaq Pass #1: This route ascended the Hunt River to its head and crossed the divide (1,300 feet [395 meters]) to the middle of Natmotirak Creek. From there it descended to Kaluich Creek and thence to the Cutler River (Qaluq) and on to the Noatak. This route is almost impassable in winter because of icing.
29. Kuugruaq Pass #2: This route ascended the main tributary of the Hunt coming from the east, crossed the divide (1,900 feet [580 meters]) to the closest tributary of the Cutler, and then continued downriver. As in route

28, the main problem here was not the gradient but the overflow; people had to travel through water much of the time even in the coldest weather. This route is also steeper than route 28, which has the same name.

Schwatka Mountains

The Schwatka Mountains extend for some 75 miles (120 kilometers) from the eastern end of the Baird Mountains on the west to the vicinity of Walker Lake on the east. They form the highest and most rugged sector of northwestern Alaska, with summits ranging from altitudes of 4,000 feet (1,220 meters) in the western portion of the range to above 8,000 feet (2,440 meters) in the east. Mount Igikpak (Papiġuq) at 8,570 feet (2,667 meters) is the highest point in northwestern Alaska. (Basic information on routes through the Schwatka Mountains was obtained from Cleveland 1989; Cleveland 1970b; Douglas 1989; Sun 1970; Tickett 1970.)

The Schwatka range is cut by a number of north–south passes that link the upper and headwaters sections of the Noatak drainage on the north with the upper Kobuk River valley on the south. The valleys on the southern side of the divide originate in high, steep head walls, and they are deeply incised, glacier carved, and steep walled. The upper portions of the valleys south of the head walls are noted for rockfall danger in late spring and summer and for avalanches in winter and spring (Map 20).

30. Akillik Pass: This route ascended the Redstone River to its middle reaches, took a branch flowing in from the west, and crossed the divide (1,900 feet [580 meters]) to the head of the Cutler. From there it descended the Cutler to the Noatak. The pass is too steep for satisfactory sled travel, and there is also considerable danger from avalanches along the way. Consequently, the route was rarely used in winter. It was used quite often in summer, however, by hunters traveling north on foot.
31. Apkugaagruq Pass: A second route went up the Redstone to another western tributary, ascended it, and crossed the divide (1,400 feet [425 meters]) to the Cutler. This route is longer than route 30 but is also safer. This pass can be traversed fairly easily in winter.
32. Ivishak Pass: The third route from the Redstone followed almost the same course as route 31 but swung a bit to the north and crossed the divide (1,500 feet [460 meters]) to the Cutler via Ivishak (Ivisaaq) Pass. This route was a satisfactory trail in both winter and summer, but in summer Akillik Pass (route 30) was preferred because it was a more direct route (see also Stoney 1900:812).

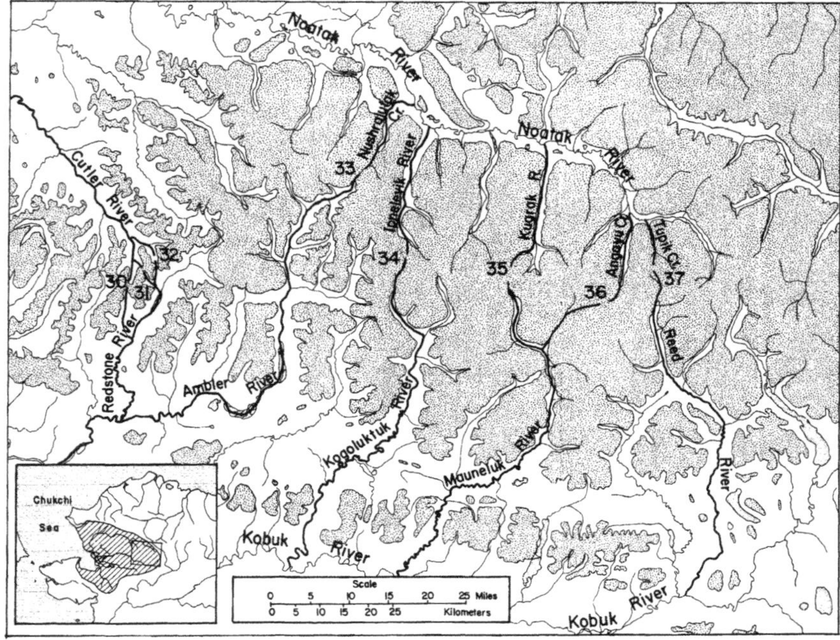

20. Major travel routes through the Schwatka Mountains.

33. Natmaqtuġiaq Pass: This route ascended the Ambler River to its head and crossed Nakmaktuak (Natmaktuġiaq) Pass (2,450 feet [745 meters]) to Nushralutak (Naqsraġluktuaq) Creek, which it descended to the Noatak. On the Kobuk side this pass is very steep, often full of deep drifts and overflow, and subject to avalanches. Even under good conditions it was often necessary for winter travelers to unload their sleds and backpack the contents over the pass. In summer, however, when a large percentage of the men from the middle portion of the Kobuk went on foot to hunt on the upper Noatak, this was the most heavily utilized route between the two rivers (see also Stoney 1900:567–569).
34. Shishakshinovik (Sisiup Sisiñġuvik) Pass: This route went up the Kogoluktuk (Quġluqtuq) River's western branch and crossed the pass (3,050 feet [930 meters]) to the upper portion of the Ipnelivik River and thence to the Noatak. Although the trail was passable in winter, there was substantial danger from avalanches. Accordingly, the route was reserved primarily for summer travel (see also Mendenhall 1902:26; Smith 1913:32).
35. Avġun Pass: This route went up the Mauneluk (Maniiḷaq) River to Ivik

Creek, which it followed to its head. Then it crossed Danger Pass (3,300 feet [1,005 meters]) to the west branch of the Kugrak River, descending it to the Noatak. This route was dangerous in winter because of avalanches and was primarily a route for hunters from the Kobuk heading north for summer hunting on the upper Noatak.

36. Aŋuniatliġatchiaq Pass: This second route from the Mauneluk River ascended its eastern branch and then crossed a very steep pass (4,050 feet [1,235 meters]) south of Mount Chitiok to the head of the western branch of Angayu Creek, which it descended to the Noatak. This pass could be used in winter, although it was dangerous to do so; it was primarily a summer trail.

37. Aŋiliġaaġiaq Pass: This route ascended the Reed River to its head and crossed the divide at Angiaak (Aŋiliġaaġiaq) Pass (3,650 feet [1,110 meters]) to Tupik Creek, which it descended to the Noatak. Like most of the routes listed in this section, this one traversed spectacular mountains, in this case the highest in the Schwatka group. The trail was difficult but passable by sled. During the winter it was the main route between the upper Kobuk and the Noatak headwaters. In summer it provided the primary return route for Kobuk men who had spent the summer hunting along the upper Noatak. They walked over the pass, built a raft when they reached the forested upper reaches of the Reed, and floated down to rejoin their families on the Kobuk with their summer's harvest of caribou hides, dried meat, and fat (see also Foote 1965a:map 20; Mendenhall 1902:26; Smith 1913:32).

Endicott Mountains

The Endicott Mountains form the central portion of the Brooks Range. The group consists of high and impressively rugged peaks and ridges ranging in altitude from about 4,900 feet (1,495 meters) in the west to nearly 7,500 feet (2,290 meters) in the east. These are separated from one another by relatively wide valleys, which make for both north–south and east–west travel that is surprisingly easy for such rugged country (Map 21). (Basic information on routes through the Endicott Mountains was obtained from Coffin 1970; D. Greist 1970; Paneak 1970; Sun 1970; Tickett 1970; Walker 1969b.)

38–39. Midas Creek–Nigu River: From the Noatak headwaters the best route to the North Slope lay up Midas Creek to where it divides into two branches. Someone heading north toward the Colville River took the middle fork (route 38), while someone heading east took the east fork (route 39). It could be used year-round (see also Smith 1913:32; Stoney 1900:570).

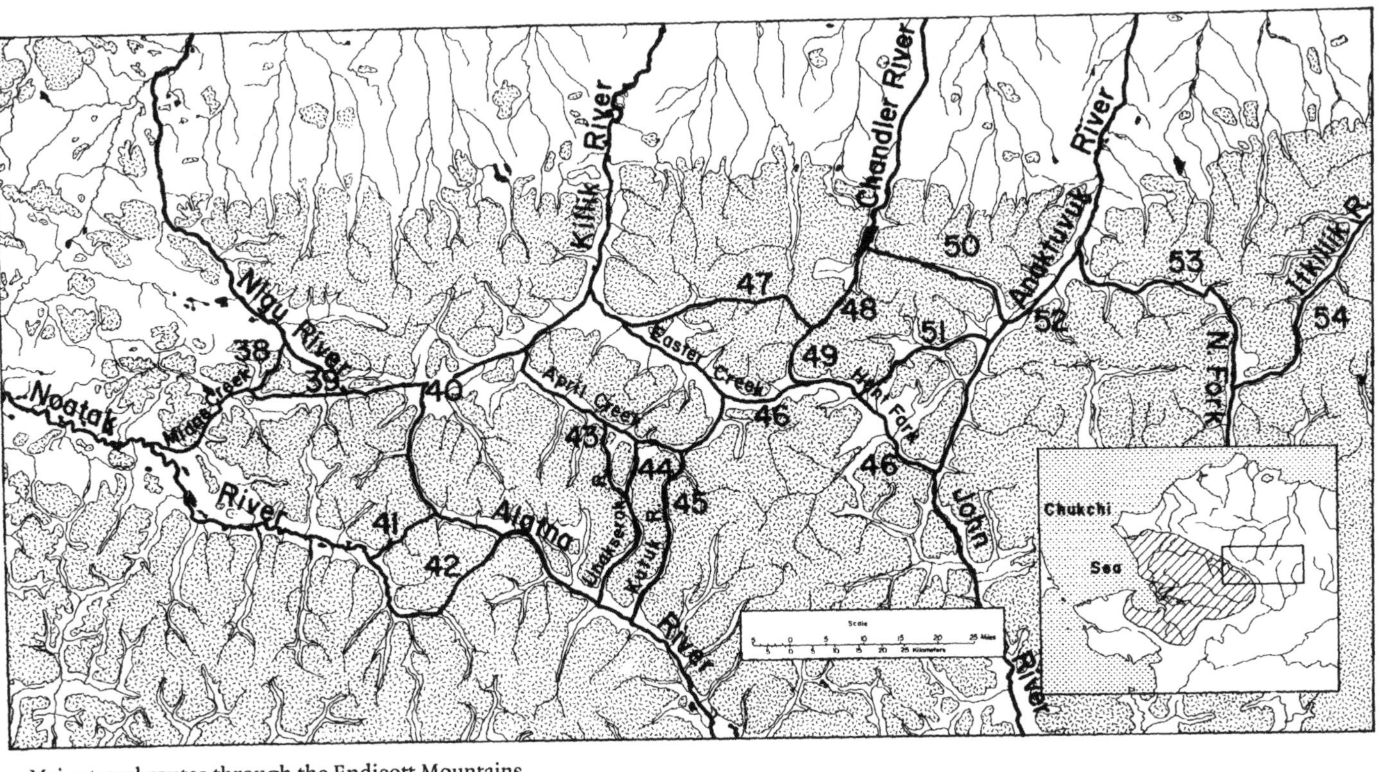

21. Major travel routes through the Endicott Mountains.

40. This is not really a route but a junction (ca. 3,000 feet [915 meters]) of routes going both north–south and east–west. It is an open, level area where the headwaters of the Nigu, Alatna, and Killik Rivers are only a few miles apart.
41. Portage Creek: The main route between the Noatak headwaters and the Alatna lay up Portage Creek (Ivisaaqtiğnilik) to its head, over the divide (3,100 feet [945 meters]), and down a short slope to the Alatna. It is an easy place to cross, and the wind is not particularly bad. The trail was used year-round (see also Smith 1913:32; Smith and Mertie 1930:35).
42. Gull Pass: This route connects the upper Alatna River with the Noatak River headwaters via Lucky Six Creek. The pass (3,500 feet [1,070 meters]) between the two drainages is steep and narrow.

43–45. Alatna River–Arctic Slope: There were three routes used by people traveling eastward from the upper Alatna River to the Arctic Slope, depending on just where in the latter region they originated (or were headed).

1. Route 43 extended from the upper Alatna up Unakserak Creek (Unaqsiaram Kuugauraŋa) to the forks. From there it angled left up Survey Creek to Survey Pass (3,300 feet [1,005 meters]) and thence down April Creek to the Killik River.
2. Route 44 extended from the upper reaches of the Alatna up Unakserak Creek. At the fork one had the choice of going west through Survey Pass (3,300 feet [1,005 meters]) to April Creek and down to the Killik or east to the head of the Unakserak, July Creek, and points farther east.
3. Route 45 led from the upper Alatna up Kutuk Creek (Tuutam Kuugauraŋa) to July Creek and then up the east branch of July Creek to its head and across the divide (2,700 feet [825 meters]) to Easter Creek (see also Foote 1965a:map 20; Smith and Mertie 1930:35; Stoney 1900:574–575).

46. Easter Creek–Hunt Fork: This route led from the head of Easter Creek across an easily traversed pass (3,100 feet [945 meters]) to upper Agiak Creek and down the latter to the Hunt Fork of the John River.
47. Killik River–Agiak Creek: The route led from the forks of the Killik up lower Easter Creek and then to Suluak Creek and across the relatively level headwaters area (3,300 feet [1,005 meters]) of the Okokmilaga (Uquqminilraa) River to Agiak Creek, where it connected with route 48 (see also Stoney 1900:575).
48. Agiak Lake–Chandler Lake: There is a level pass (3,130 feet [948

meters]) between Agiak Lake and Amiloyak Lake at the head of the Chandler River. From the latter Chandler Lake is just a few miles downstream.

49. John River–Agiak Lake: From Agiak Lake there is a relatively narrow but low pass to the head of Ekokpuk Creek, which is a tributary of the John River.

50. Chandler Lake–Anaktuvuk Pass: From Chandler Lake one ascended a small westerly flowing stream that connects over a narrow pass to the head of Kollutarak (Qalutaġiaq) Creek. From there the route led down the Kollutarak to the John River and up the latter to Anaktuvuk Pass.

51. Hunt Fork head–John River head: From Hunt Fork one ascended Loon Creek to its head and then crossed a short divide to the watershed of Ekokpuk (Ikiakpak) Creek and descended it to the John River.

52. Anaktuvuk Pass: Anaktuvuk Pass connects the northward-flowing Anaktuvuk River with the southward-flowing John River. The summit is only 2,200 feet (670 meters) in altitude and is about 2 miles (3 kilometers) wide. It is easily traversed in both summer and winter, although strong northerly winds are a frequent hindrance, especially in winter (see also Foote 1965a:map 20; Smith and Mertie 1930:35).

53. Anaktuvuk River–North Fork of the Koyukuk: This route ascended the Anaktuvuk to Grayling Creek and then went up the latter to its head. It then crossed Ernie Pass to Ernie Creek, which it descended to the Koyukuk.

54. North Fork of the Koyukuk–Itkillik River: The head of the North Fork of the Koyukuk River and the head of the Itkillik River are separated by just a few hundred yards. The two valleys are relatively wide, and the watershed can be crossed without difficulty.

De Long Mountains

The De Long Mountains lie on the north side of the Noatak River valley and separate it from several drainages on the Arctic Slope; they constitute the northwesternmost extension of the Brooks Range as a whole. These mountains are not as formidable a topographic barrier to travel as the Schwatka Mountains, but they are high and rugged enough to restrict one's choice of useful travel routes. The most difficult routes were in the central portion, where the peaks are in the neighborhood of 3,900–4,900 feet (1,200–1,500 meters) above sea level. The easiest routes were on the west. In all areas but particularly toward the east the major difficulty for travelers was strong winds flowing through the mountain passes from the high pressure climatic zone of the Arctic Slope to the comparatively lower pressure zone of the Noatak River valley (Map 22). (Basic information on routes through the De Long Mountains was obtained from Ashby 1970; Howarth 1969; McClellan 1970; and T. Mitchell 1969.)

55. Kivalina River–Kukpowruk River: This route began on the middle portion of the Kivalina River and crossed over a break in the hills to the Kukpuk River, which curves well to the south at this point. From here travelers ascended the Kukpuk to its upper reaches and crossed over to the Kukpowruk (Kuukpauġruq) via a pass some 800 feet (549 meters) above sea level. This route is easily traveled in both summer and winter (see also Smith and Mertie 1930:35).
56. Wulik River–Kukpowruk River: This was an easy trail from the Kivalina and lower Noatak regions to the Arctic Slope, making a shortcut across the base of the peninsula that terminates at Point Hope. The route simply ascended the main branch of the Wulik (Ualliik) to its head, crossed the divide (1,400 feet [425 meters]) to the head of the Kukpowruk, and descended the latter to the coast.
57. Noatak River–Kukpowruk River: Coming from the lower Noatak, travelers ascended the Kelly (Kuugruuraq) to Wrench Creek (Kataaq), ascended it to its head, crossed the divide (2,200 feet [670 meters]), and descended the Kukpowruk to the coast. This was regarded as an easy trail for both winter and summer travel (see also Foote 1965a:map 20).
58. Noatak River–Kokolik River: From the Noatak the route ascended the Kelly to its head, crossed Iḷuyugruaq Pass (2,000 feet [610 meters]), and descended the Kokolik (Qaqalik). There was no avalanche danger on this route, but it was steep enough for people to want to cross in pairs for purposes of mutual assistance.
59. Noatak River–Utukok River: Travelers coming from the Noatak ascended the incorrectly named Kugururok (it should be the Kuugruaq) to its upper reaches, turned up Cairn Creek, crossed Nachralik (Naksrualuk) Pass (2,200 feet [670 meters]) to Tupik Creek, and descended to the Utukok. The last few hundred yards on the south side of the pass are smooth and relatively steep and hence challenging to traverse. The danger is not particularly great, however. The route was frequently used in the late spring (see also Smith and Mertie 1930:35; Solecki 1951:55).

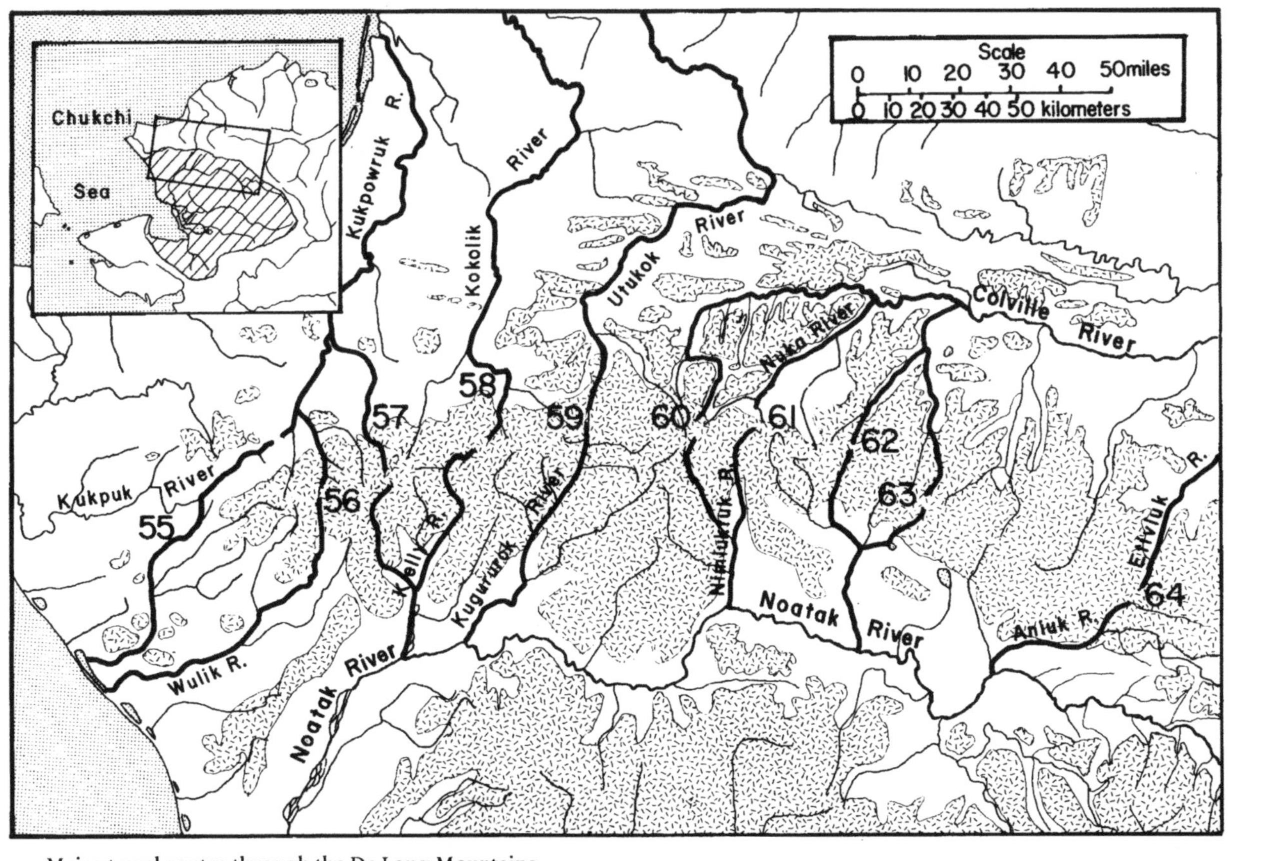

22. Major travel routes through the De Long Mountains.

60. Nimiuktuk River–Arctic Slope: Coming from the Noatak, one ascended the Nimiuktuk River and followed a tributary, Seagull Creek, to the northwest. Before reaching the head of Seagull Creek the route crossed north to the head of another branch of the Nimiuktuk and then crossed the Continental Divide (2,600 feet [790 meters]) to Putkuruk Creek (Patkuraq). From there one could go west to Driftwood Creek and down the Utukok (Utuqqaq) or east down the Putkuruk to the Nuka (Nitka) River and on to the Colville. Most people heading east took route 61, however. This route was used in all seasons (see also Smith and Mertie 1930:35).
61. Nimiuktuk River–Arctic Slope: This route led up the Nimiuktuk and then up Ignisirok Creek to the head of its eastern branch. From there it crossed Natiġnaq Qauġiaq Pass (2,400 feet [730 meters]) to the head of Chertchip Creek. From there it descended the Nuka River (Patkuram Kuuŋa) to the Colville.
62. Anisak River–Colville River: The route began at the Noatak and ascended the Anisak River to Setting Sun Creek. It continued to the head of the latter, crossed the Continental Divide (2,300 feet [730 meters]) to the head of Jubilee Creek, and descended it to the Kiligwa (Kiligvana) and subsequently the Colville. Although this route could be taken at any season, it was often dangerous in winter because of strong northerly winds.
63. Desperation Lake–Colville River: From Desperation Lake one ascended Uivaksak Creek to its head, crossed a relatively level divide (2,600 feet [790 meters]) to the head of the Kiligwa River, and descended it to the Colville. Again, winds were the main problem along this route in winter.
64. Howard Pass (Itivlik): The route from the Noatak ascended the Aniuk (Anigaaq) River to its head and crossed the pass to the Etivlik (Itivlik) River, which it descended to the Colville. The pass is low (1,700 feet [518 meters]) and wide, with low local relief. It is also one of the coldest places in northwestern Alaska due to the constant high winds that roar through it. Much of the time the wind is so strong that travel is impossible; there is no shelter in the pass itself. The windchill can be so severe as to freeze to death caribou caught there by a winter storm; after every bad blow the Eskimos used to go into the pass to look for well-preserved caribou carcasses. In summer and fall the wind reportedly sometimes gets so strong that it blows the water out of the shallow lakes in the pass. In winter the procedure for crossing Howard Pass was to ascend the Aniuk River to its upper reaches, wait for a calm period, then travel as fast as possible over the hard-packed snow through the pass and down the other side. The wind apparently diminishes considerably on the north as one

descends to lower elevations. Because of the gentle slope and the few local topographic impediments to sled travel, the Eskimos used to portage umiat between river systems via Howard Pass in the spring (see also Foote 1965a:map 20; Smith and Mertie 1930:35; Spencer 1959:10).

Arctic Slope

To the north of the Brooks Range lies the Arctic Slope. The zone consists of two distinct provinces, the northern foothills of the Brooks Range to the south and the Arctic Coastal Plain on the north (Gryc 1958). The foothills, comprised primarily of long, east–west trending ridges and wide valleys, made for relatively good travel at any time of year. The ridges are not particularly difficult to cross, but some specific routes were used much more frequently than others, and they are listed here. (Basic information on routes through the northern foothills was obtained from L. Greist 1970.)

On the Arctic Coastal Plain, just to the north of the foothills, summer travel was restricted largely to boat travel along the many rivers, the land being covered with muskeg and hence very difficult to traverse on foot. In winter, with the ground and lakes frozen, one can travel from any point to any other in almost a straight line. One's course of travel was influenced more by weather, very local topography, and snow conditions on the ground rather than by major topographic features. Accordingly, no overland routes are listed for the coastal plain (Map 23).

65. Utukok River–Kokolik: This route left the Utukok near the mouth of Driftwood Creek and led west to the head of Iliguruk Creek, just to the north of Ilinguorak Ridge. From there it descended the short distance to the Kokolik.
66. Driftwood Creek–Colville River: This route began at the Utukok River on the west, extended eastward up Driftwood Creek, and led either directly to the upper Colville or else eastward along the ridges north of Noluck Lake to the Nuka River, which it descended to the Colville. This route was easily traversed in both summer and winter.
67. Carbon Creek–Colville River: Starting on the Utukok some distance below route 48, this route ascended Carbon Creek to its head. From there it led across the divide to Awuna River (Saugvialak), descending it to the Colville. This was an easily traveled route in summer and winter. Boats were often portaged between river systems via this route in the spring, just before breakup (see also Ostermann and Holtved 1952:30).

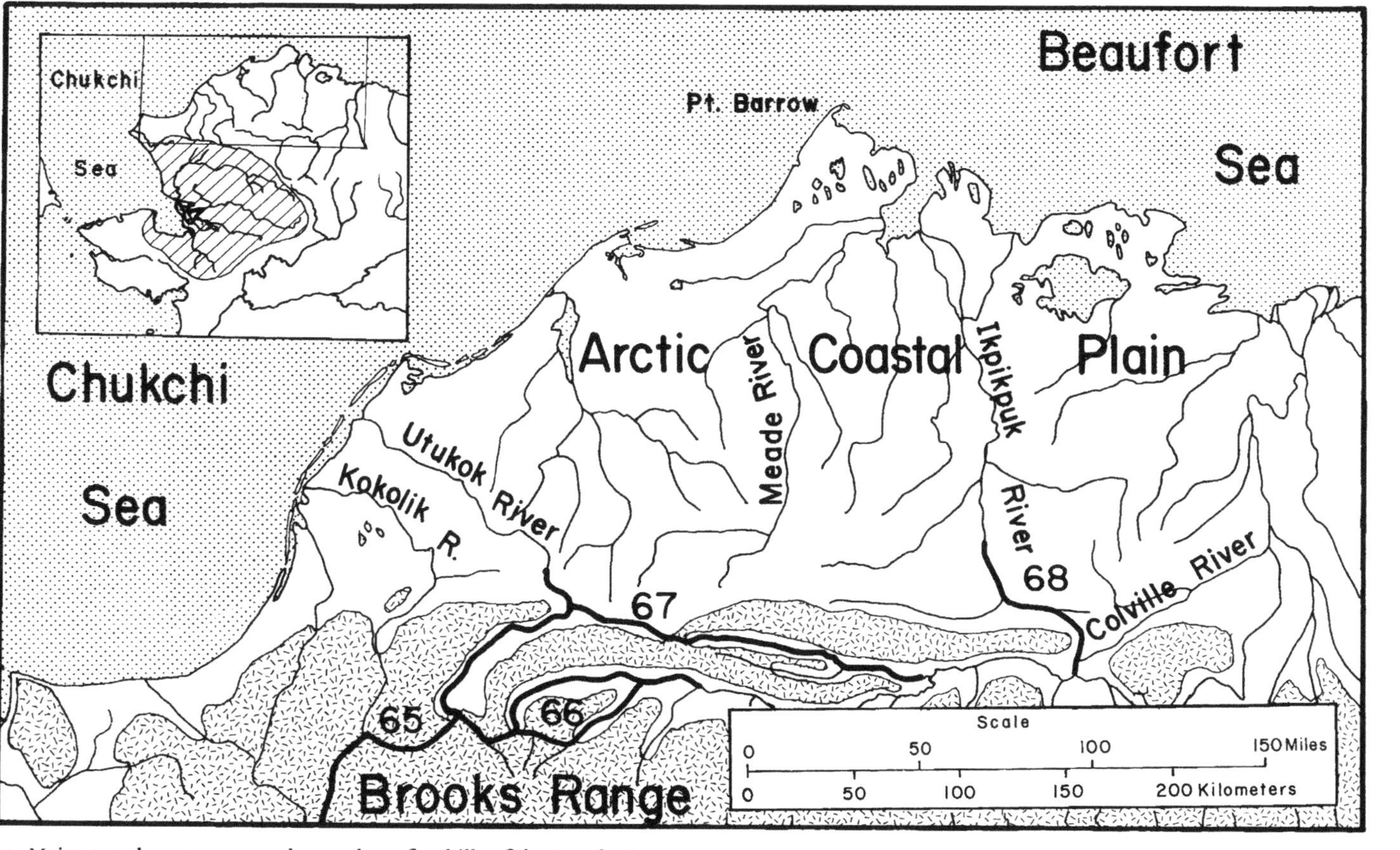

23. Major travel routes across the northern foothills of the Brooks Range.

68. Colville River–Ikpikpuk River: This route connected the upper portion of the Colville (Kaŋianik) to the Ikpikpuk (Ikpikpak) River, which flows directly north from the foothills to a point not far from Barrow. The route began on the Colville at Kakviuyat Bend, headed north over Angoyakvik (Aŋuyaaġvik) Pass (899 feet [274 meters]) to September Creek, and thence went down to the Ikpikpuk (see also Foote 1965a:map 20; Stoney 1900:816, 817).

Notes

1. Introduction

1. Structured as in patterned, as opposed to random or ad hoc.
2. A world *social* system as opposed to the more general global physical and biological systems, which, of course, are much older. See Chase-Dunn and Hall 2000:88. Frank and Gills (2000:18), among others, object to this comprehensive use of the phrase "world system."
3. A reasonable alternative, "global system," has already been adopted by natural scientists to signify the earth as a single ecosystem.
4. For more on centralization see Levy 1966:16.
5. "Nation" equals "society," the latter as defined by Levy (1952, 1966:20–21).
6. If this were a comparative analysis, I would prefer the phrase "joint family," which means a family that includes two or more related married couples (Kolenda 1968:346; Owens 1971:225).
7. These statements are phrased in the past tense because the climate has warmed significantly during the past 40 years or so. It was apparently notably colder during the early 19th century than it was in the 1960s.
8. This discussion is phrased in the past tense because many of the animal populations of the region have undergone important changes over the past 200 years.
9. Moose, which are now common in the region, were not present at all during the 19th century. Musk oxen may have been present in small numbers during the early 19th century, but if so, they were hunted to extinction. They were reintroduced in the 1960s.
10. Technically, this epidemic was reported only for Point Hope, Icy Cape, Barrow, and Point Barrow, all of which are north of the NANA Region (Simpson 1852–54:entries for May 25, 1853, January 12, 1854).
11. The traditional Native name of the nation whose territory was centered on Point Barrow was lost. We are indebted to Kashevarov for supplying us with the missing information. Unfortunately, no one I have interviewed on the subject knows what the precise referent of "Kaklig-" is, nor does anyone know how the word should be spelled in the modern orthography.
12. I have not heard "Kullyulik" spoken and hence do not know how it should be rendered in the standard Iñupiaq orthography.
13. However, just before the explorers reached Icy Cape they saw a "large native summer camp" on the mainland on the other side of a large lagoon from the beach they were following (VanStone 1977:48).

14. In this definition I take the term "singular" to mean "exceptional" or "extraordinary" and "environment" to include both social and physical phenomena.
15. There were also nonresidential marriages, in which the rate of endogamy was much lower (Burch 1975a:10–11, 47, 66–67, 75–76).
16. The offspring of an international marriage presumably became members of the nation in which they were raised, but I have no definite information on this point.
17. This posed an interesting dilemma for the murderer. On the one hand, if news got out about who the murderer was, a blood feud ensued. On the other hand, *not* to confess it to at least one other person carried the risk of angering certain spirits, who would then avenge the murder themselves. Most people preferred to deal with empirical adversaries.
18. There are some exceptions to this, however. For example, a persistent troublemaker was often killed by members of his own family.
19. This description is a composite of information acquired from Hall 1975b:40; Jones 1984; Clinton Swan 1984. See also Spencer 1959:39.
20. In the NANA Region the suffix is pronounced *-miit* in many villages, but *-miut* is used practically everywhere else in the Inuit language area and is considered the "standard" form.
21. Ray (1977:79) claims that these paddles were from Bering Strait, but Choris (1822) states specifically that they were used "par les habitants du golfe de Kotzebue." For another illustration of this custom but with much smaller boats see the paddles illustrated in Cantwell 1889a:pl. opposite 61.
22. See Burch 1998a for detailed accounts of societal dissolution in the primary study area.
23. The first part of this discussion recapitulates, almost verbatim, one in Burch (1998a:309–310).
24. Stanner's definition actually states that the estate is "the traditionally recognized locus ('country,' 'home,' 'ground,' 'dreaming place') of some kind of patrilineal descent group forming the core or nucleus of the territorial group" (1965:2). Here I have generalized it beyond the Australian context for which it was first developed and also strengthened it to include the element of ownership.
25. I substituted the word "borders" for Ray's word "boundaries" to make the passage consistent with the terminology used here. Ray's "tribe" is equivalent to my "nation."
26. One possible exception is the border between the Kiitaaġmiut and Siiḷviim Kaŋianiġmiut, where the features of the landscape are so subdued that only very subtle landmarks would have served to mark a border.
27. For consistency I replaced their word "territory" with "estate" in this passage. See also Burch 1981:62; Ray 1967:373.
28. The men had to conduct the caribou hunt then because it was the time of year when the hides were most suitable for use in clothing.
29. Point Hope informants were in complete agreement with informants from other districts on this matter.

30. Then they buried him, and the place where they did so was called Qutliq (Chukotkan) (McClellan 1970). Subsequently, the event was memorialized in the name of a nearby body of water, Kotlik (Qutliq) Lagoon. In an earlier publication (Burch 1988b:231) I erroneously stated that an entire *party* of Chukchi had been annihilated here.
31. Nelson (1899:330) was told that anyone from Alaska who somehow ended up on the Asiatic coast was killed on sight.
32. "Beringia" includes the floors of the Bering and Chukchi Seas, which have been terrestrial landscapes from time to time but which were inundated during the period of present concern.
33. My source on the Bering Strait perspective is Bogojavlensky 1969:15.
34. The primary published sources on the ethnography of the Arctic Slope are Burch 1981; Gubser 1965; Larsen and Rainey 1948; Murdoch 1892; Rainey 1947; Ray 1885; Simpson 1875; Spencer 1959; Wells and Kelly 1890. The particular view of Siḷaḷiñaġmiut societies presented here is based largely on my own research, however.
35. Qaŋmaliġmiut was also the general term used in northern Alaska to refer collectively to the Mackenzie River delta Inuit of northwestern Canada, which frequently confuses the uninformed. Native speakers know which group is the referent by the context.
36. Map 8 and Table 3 are based upon the following sources: Bogoras 1904–9:28–32; Burch 1998b; Burgess 1974:57–63; A. Clark 1981:583; Kennicott 1862–63; Krupnik 1983, 1993:30, 1996a, 1996b; Krupnik and Chlenov n.d., 1982; McKennan 1981:564; Ray 1967, 1984:286; Shinkwin and Pete 1984:97–98; VanStone and Goddard 1981.
37. The primary documentary sources on the structure of Iñupiaq societies in Bering Strait and Sakmaliaġruq are Bogojavlensky 1969; Heinrich 1955; Nelson 1877–81, 1899; Ray 1963, 1964, 1967, 1975b:103–120. I have also done some research in Nome, Wales, and Shishmaref.
38. I am grateful to Igor Krupnik for helping me understand what is known about the history, ethnic divisions, demography, and social organization of the peoples of Chukotka.
39. According to Krupnik 1996a, Qutlich is a loanword from the Chaplinski Yup'ik word for Chukchi.
40. Kaplan (1996) pointed out to me that the grammatically correct version of this would have to have been something like Qutlich Nunaŋich.
41. The sources on which I based the Asiatic portion of the map include Bogoras 1904–9:28–32; Krupnik 1983, 1993:30, 1996a, 1996b; Krupnik and Chlenov n.d.
42. The main source on the Nuvuqaghhmiit is Krupnik and Chlenov n.d.:chap. 5. See also Chlenov 1973; de Reuse 1994:308–310; Krupnik 1993:esp. 29–34, 53–54, 83–84, 196–199; Schweitzer and Golovko 1995:51.
43. The population estimate was made by Krech (1978:100).
44. The primary source on the Koyukuk River Koyukon is Annette McFadyen Clark

(1974, 1975, 1981). Her Ph.D. thesis was written under her maiden name (McFadyen 1995) but published under her married name (Clark 1996).

45. Sources on the lower Koyukon: A. Clark 1974, 1975, 1981, 1996; Loyens 1966; McFadyen 1995; Michael 1967.

2. Hostile Relations

1. When Simpson (1843:155) approached the summer camp at Barrow he could "see the men, armed with bows and arrows, conceal themselves" behind mounds that had been pushed up by ice, but his party was not threatened after he communicated his peaceful intentions. He was fortunate to be there just when the population of the settlement was at its low point for the year.
2. If Kashevarov had approached the Kivalina district from the south, it would have appeared as though he was returning from the Sisualik trade fair. An approach from the north in late August was completely anomalous from the Kivalliñiġmiut point of view and therefore a threat.
3. For other eyewitness accounts of Iñupiaq aggressiveness, in addition to those excerpted in the text, see Beechey 1831, vol. 1:426–427, vol. 2:555–559; Kotzebue 1821, vol. 1:204–205; Pullen 1979:59; Simpson 1852–54:entry for May 1, 1854.
4. While several Maritime Chukchi took up pastoralism during this period, a fair number of Reindeer Chukchi seem to have turned to fishing when some kind of calamity struck their herd.
5. Sources for the population estimates: for the Tikiġaġmiut see Burch 1981:14; for the Kiŋikmiut see Burch 1980:295.
6. For an example of assimilation see Burch et al. 1999.
7. I am indebted to Lawrence Kaplan for the gloss of this Iñupiaq term.
8. For information on the distribution of settlements in the other estates in the NANA Region see Burch 1998a.
9. I heard of very few cases where the men went to the women's country.
10. For additional information on and illustrations of bows and arrows from northwestern Alaska see Murdoch 1892:195–207; Nelson 1899:155, 157; VanStone 1976a:12–13, 77, 78, 1980:28, 100; Varjola 1990:294.
11. For further discussion and photographs of bows, arrows, and related equipment collected by Beechey see Bockstoce 1977:20–24, 27–33.
12. If the truth were known, the Natives probably had a whole lexicon of terms for different types of arrows and arrow points.
13. Peard put the distance at 40 yards (37 meters) (Gough 1973:169).
14. Throwing boards apparently were not used to hurl spears in combat.
15. For information on and illustrations of the lances acquired by the Beechey expedition see Bockstoce 1977:46–48.
16. Brower (n.d.:672) also claimed that he sent the best war club he ever found to the American Museum of Natural History in New York.
17. In 1853 a man at Point Barrow owned armor made from small plates of steel (Simpson 1852–54:entry for October 16, 1853). Chukchi and Asiatic Eskimos wore much more complex armor (Burch 1988b:227; VanStone 1983) than Iñupiat did.

18. In the Yukon–Kuskokwim delta of southwestern Alaska Yup'ik war parties often traveled by kayak. That was not true anywhere within the scope of the present study.
19. MacLaren (1991) has argued that, based on Hearne's journal, certain parts of the published account of the massacre were added by editors after Hearne's death. This particular passage is not included in the journal excerpt published by MacLaren (1991:30–32), but it seems like something the author might recall and add later when drafting the book. It does not strike me as exciting enough for the editors to have invented.
20. My sources on *iññuqutit* were the following: Adams 1986; G. Adams 1965; R. Adams 1965; Ballott 1970a; Barr 1970; Cleveland 1989; Cleveland 1965a; J. Foster 1970; Glover 1970c; A. Hawley 1965b, 1976a, 1976b, 1980; B. Hawley 1964a, 1964b, 1984; S. Hawley 1964; Ingstad 1954:108; Jensen 1970c, 1970d; Jensen and Jensen 1980; Keats 1970c, 1970e; Lee 1970; McClellan 1970; Morris 1970; T. Sage 1964, 1965; Skin 1970; Stalker 1964, 1970, 1986; Charlotte Swan 1964a, 1964b; Clinton Swan 1964, 1965; Martha Swan 1965c, 1970, 1984; Swan and Swan 1965; Milton Swan 1965; O. Swan 1964; Thomas 1970. The spelling of the terms *iññuqun*, *iññuqutit*, and *iññuququrat* represents the dialect of the NANA Region specifically. On the Arctic Slope these words have a single *-ñ-* (Kaplan 1997).
21. Very little has been written about *iññuqutit*. However, see Anderson et al. 1998:104; Dayton 1981:17.
22. "Putting away" meant placing several dozen whole fish inside a circular framework of willow branches (known as a "nest") and leaving them to freeze. In this case, several nests had to be constructed.
23. Some years later, however, I read Ingstad's comment that "the Indians have from old times been accustomed to signal to one another by whistling or by imitating the calls of birds" (1954:108).
24. Thus, he may have been an assimilated "upper Kobuk Koyukon" (Burch et al. 1999).
25. The Iñupiat were expert trackers. See Bockstoce 1988, vol. 2:357–358.
26. My primary sources on international violence, including both surprise attacks and battles, were the following: Cleveland 1965b, 1970a, 1970b; D. Foster 1970; J. Foster 1970; Gallahorn 1970b; Glover 1970a, 1970b; Edna Hunnicutt 1960a, 1970; Jensen 1970a, 1970b, 1970c, 1970d; Keats 1970b, 1970c; McClellan 1970, 1987; Paneak 1970; Smith 1970; Swan 1970.
27. Sheehan (1997:153–154) describes a prehistoric example that seems to fit this pattern and notes that sea mammal oil used in lamps and food had saturated the qargi floor. When the burning material dropped through the skylight touched the floor, fire would have quickly engulfed the building.
28. The historic name means "place where people fell into the water," which commemorates the event described here. Its previous name has been forgotten.
29. I obtained versions from David Adams (1986) and John Stalker (1986). Others were obtained by the United States Department of the Interior, Bureau of Indian Affairs

(n.d.) from Harold Downey, Ned Howarth, Kenneth Ashby, and Floyd M. Wesley Sr. Both Don Foote (Edna Hunnicutt 1960a) and Edwin S. Hall Jr. (1975b:97–100) recorded from Edna Hunnicutt a version rather different from the one presented here.

30. Other versions were obtained from Lester Gallahorn (1970b), Elwood Hunnicutt (1970, 1983), and Charlie Jensen (1970c).

31. This event took place during the lifetime of Elwood Hunnicutt's grandfather. Hunnicutt was born in 1904, which suggests that this may have occurred after the study period was over.

32. This narrative is a composite of information acquired from David Frankson (1980), Charlie Jensen (1970d), and Froelich Rainey (1947:240). Rainey got his information from Sam Uyaġaq Rock (1940).

33. This was the encounter at Tikiġaġmiut on the Arctic coast. See Appendix 1 and Map 11, location number 3.

34. This version of the story is a composite of accounts compiled by Bergsland 1987:344–349; Curtis 1930:205; Hennigh 1972:100; Lucier 1958:109–111; Swan 1965a. Bergsland's account, which was obtained by Helge Ingstad from Elijah Kakinya, differs considerably from the others with regard to the location of the events in this story. Primary reliance here was placed on Lucier's version, which was obtained from Jenny Aluniq Mitchell in 1952.

35. This version of the story is a composite of accounts obtained from Hall 1975b:388; Lucier 1954:229; NANA Cultural Heritage Project 1975b, 1975d; Savok 1986; Sunno 1951b.

36. According to Rasmussen (Ostermann and Holtved 1952:67), the man's name was Kivale.

37. In one account there was a trench rather than a stockade; in another it was a sod house whose roof had apparently caved in.

38. According to Rasmussen (Ostermann and Holtved 1952:676), this man's name was Harlarardlak.

39. This version of the story is a composite of accounts obtained from Curtis 1970; Gallahorn 1970a, 1970b; Jensen and Jensen 1980; Lucier n.d.a, 1958:109; Mendenhall, Sampson, and Tennant 1989:65–71; Ostermann and Holtved 1952:67ff. The most divergent version is Lucier 1958.

40. That the Iñupiat involved in this series of confrontations were in fact Kaŋiġmiut (Buckland River people) was confirmed by John Simpson (1850), who, on January 9, 1850, met a woman who was afraid of Europeans because "she was acquainted with a girl belonging to the Buckland river tribe whose father had been shot in the skirmish with the Blossom party."

41. Except for a few insertions the quotations here are all from Beechey's (1831, vol. 2:280–286) report of the expedition. Other versions of these events are contained in Belcher 1825–27; Gough 1973:234–241; Wolfe n.d.:199–203. For a summary that includes quotes from all of these sources see Bockstoce 1977:126–132.

42. The arrows were fired at a distance of 130 paces (Gough 1973:239).

43. The ravine was only 5 or 6 yards (5 meters) away (Gough 1973:239).
44. These songs apparently could not be sung too often or they lost their power, so one had to exercise some discipline in their use.
45. David Libbey (2000) claims that this photograph shows skeletal material that had been gathered under church supervision for a Christian burial but cannot recall the source of his information. In any event, except for its large size, the pile of bones is just what I would have expected to see on a former battlefield on the basis of my informants' accounts of similar phenomena they had observed as children. It is *not* what I would expect to see of bones specifically collected for a Christian burial.
46. Murdoch (1892:139) noted that men were tattooed as a mark of distinction in whaling. He said nothing about warfare, but his observations were made well after warfare had ceased on the Arctic Slope.
47. For an idea of how important taboos were in Iñupiaq life generally see Cantwell 1889b:82; Hooper 1881:24–25; Ostermann and Holtved 1952:36, 117, 118, 120, 124–126; Rainey 1947:274; Stefansson 1914b:126–128, 282, 284, 316–317, 320, 347, 365, 1951:410–413; Stoney 1900:569, 569–570, 814–815, 837, 838–839; Wells and Kelly 1890:24; Woolfe 1893:139, 140, 141, 147–148.
48. Most of their information is from districts well south of the study region, where the Natives used tactics somewhat different from those described here.
49. Actually, it was probably the depopulation caused by the smallpox rather than Russian influence that halted or reduced warfare in this region.
50. Shields were used as defensive devices by warriors traveling by kayak, but assault by kayakers was a tactic used primarily in the Yukon–Kuskokwim delta, south of the region of interest here.
51. Roger Dayton was a Koyukon elder whose life history was recorded and published in 1981 by the Yukon–Koyukuk school district.
52. Just which Koyukon were engaged in this encounter was not recorded.
53. The information on Gwich'in weapons was obtained from McKennan 1965:36–37; Osgood 1936:86–87; Slobodin 1960:81–82.
54. This discussion is based on Bogoras 1901:80–82, 1904–9:682–698; Forsyth 1992:145–151; Krupnik and Chlenov n.d.:chap. 5, 31–34. In interpreting this material I have benefited greatly from discussions with Igor Krupnik. See also Silook 1976:10–13.
55. Daurkin was a Chukchi working for the Russians (Pierce 1990:110–111).
56. Clerke took over command of Cook's expedition after Cook was killed in Hawaii.
57. It took a full day to cross Bering Strait (Golder 1971:152). Daurkin (Masterson and Brower 1948:65) said it took him that long just to get to Big Diomede in the middle of Bering Strait, but he started from some distance to the south. See also Stefansson 1914b:331.
58. Popov was a Cossack and an associate of Dezhnev who was sent in 1711 "in a futile attempt to persuade the Chukchi on the Chukotskiy Peninsula to submit to Russian rule" (Fisher 1981:110).

59. This is the only reference I have ever seen or heard of the use of poison-tipped weapons in northern Beringia.
60. The others were Chagnon 1968a, 1968b; Turney-High 1949; Vayda 1960, 1968. The list was actually titled "attributes of primitive warfare" because that is the phrase others had used. It makes much more sense to me now to think of it as attributes of warfare among small-scale societies.
61. The fact that the names of the participants in many of the stories were not recorded is probably more of a failure on my part to seek the relevant information than it is a sign of their antiquity.
62. Rasmussen (Ostermann and Holtved 1952:19) also stated that Charles Brower heard about "two big battles between Eskimos and Indians" in the 1880s. Whether those battles actually occurred in the 1880s and whether they took place within the study region were not recorded.
63. This account was obtained from Cleveland 1970b and Foote 1966a:story 9. The assignment of the parties to the Akuniġmiut and upper Kobuk Koyukon nations is based on internal evidence. Several anomalies make these identifications uncertain, however.
64. The account in Hall 1975b:303–304 has been published. The accounts given to me by Amos Hawley (1965c) and Walter Kowunna (1970) have not.

3. Friendly Relations

1. Here Ray uses "territory" in my sense of "estate."
2. People making this motion are also depicted on Smyth's sketch of Point Barrow, also in 1826 (Beechey 1831, vol. 1:425).
3. The grammatical and typing errors in this passage are in the original.
4. Again, errors appear in the original.
5. This possibility did not apply to Kashevarov, who was apparently regarded as being some kind of Native in most cases.
6. For an outline of how men became wealthy in traditional Northwest Alaska see Burch 1975a:205–221.
7. Iḷḷuġiik were cross-cousins, but Spencer (1959:172–177) apparently did not know that.
8. I described this relationship in an earlier paper (Burch 1970a), but I have learned much more about it since then. Another author who paid special attention to it is Robert Spencer (1959:167–172). See also Giddings 1961:148–149; Gubser 1965:32, 133, 160–161, 179; Pospisil 1964:408, 427; VanStone 1962:92–93.
9. "Boundary" in the specific sense used in this volume. Theoretically, kin relationships might have been the most numerous, since kinship ties carry forward from one generation to the next, ad infinitum. In fact, after about two generations most of the ones existing in principle were very inactive in fact.
10. The word is made up as follows: *niiviq* = "partner"; *-gi-* = "relationship"; *-ik* = "dual."
11. I include both consanguines and affines under the general heading of "kin."

12. Others have made the same finding. See, for example, Lucier 1997:286; Northwest Iñupiat Elders Conference 1976:76–07a, 9; Rainey 1940.
13. The Koyukon term for trading partnership is *neelghok'elaayhkkaa*. Many of the Koyukon relationships with Iñupiat fell under the heading of *hebeghok'elaayh*, which is usually translated as "special friend" (Jones 1991; see also Solomon 1981:49).
14. They might, for example, be forced to do menial work for an umialik while being fed scraps and dressed in tattered furs.
15. In northwestern Alaska today this term is usually rendered in English as "half-brother" or "half-sister." This is not a technically correct translation, but there is no direct English-language equivalent of qataŋun.
16. The major exception to this statement was when a man had to take a long trip and his wife was unable to accompany him for some reason. He might exchange her temporarily for another man's wife who could.
17. See also Clark and Clark 1976:202 and Lucier n.d.a for comarriage-type relations between Koyukon and Iñupiat.
18. This is a bit of an overstatement, since there are indeed hazards involved in travel over freshwater ice in northwestern Alaska. Frozen rivers in many areas are frequently flooded with water bursting up through cracks ("overflow"), while in others a rapid current prevents a thick buildup of ice. On the ocean wind and ocean currents move ice around, causing it to break apart and/or pile up, particularly but not necessarily around points of land.
19. This section is adapted from Burch 1975b. It is based on personal observation and the following sources: Brower n.d.:148; Cantwell 1889b:85; Douglas 1976; Giddings 1961:144–145; Gubser 1965:289–291; Murdoch 1892:344–360; Nelson 1899:205–211; Ray 1885:28; Seemann 1853:56–57; Spencer 1959:465–469; Stoney 1900:564–566, 568; Woolfe 1893:149.
20. Nelson (1899:205–206) includes a relatively detailed description of basket sled construction.
21. Seemann (1853, vol. 2:56–57) says a basket sled could carry 500–700 pounds (225–315 kilograms). Temperature significantly affects the friction of different types of material being drawn across the snow surface.
22. According to Schweitzer and Golovko (1995:39), the main season for international boat travel in Bering Strait was July and August, although it began in June and continued until late September or early October.
23. Sources on umiaq construction, use, and characteristics: Beechey 1831, vol. 1:346, 389–390, 404–405, 418, 439; Bockstoce 1988, vol. 2:431, 452; Hooper 1884:102; Kaplan 1988:19–22; Kingston 1996; Kotzebue 1821, vol. 1:199, 202, 204, 226, 232; Murdoch 1892:335; Nelson 1899:216–218; Seemann 1853, vol. 2:55; Simpson 1843:148; Snaith 1997; Stefansson 1944:37, 1951:106; Stoney n.d.:160–162; Thornton 1931:125–126; Trollope 1855:875; and personal observation.
24. For descriptions of river travel by umiaq see Stoney 1900:818, 836–837.
25. Trollope (1855:875) gave roughly the same dimensions for the boats at Wales.

26. Foote (1965a:227) calculated that traveling umiat contained an average of 6.99 (= 7) people per boat plus an unspecified amount of equipment and other goods.
27. Sources on messenger feasts: Attla and Attla 1991; Ballott 1970a; Barr 1970; Bockstoce 1988, vol. 1:128, 141–142; Brower n.d.:553; Burns 1952; Cleveland 1970a, 1970b; Curtis 1930:146–147; Curtis 1970; Dall 1870:154–157; Fair 2001; D. Foster 1970; J. Foster 1970; Gallahorn 1969, 1970a; Gallahorn 1952; Glover 1970b; Hawkes 1913:1, 1914:40–41; Hopson 1978:90–93; Howard 1952; Edna Hunnicutt 1960b; Jacobsen 1884:285; Jensen 1970a, 1970e; Keats 1970f; Lucier n.d.a, n.d.b, 1952; Luther 1960a, 1960b; McClellan 1970; Mitchell 1970; Monroe 1960; Morris 1970; Murdoch 1892:365, 373; Nelson 1899:358; Ostermann and Holtved 1952:103–112; Ray and Blaker 1967:34–36, 45–46; Ray 1885:41; Sampson 1970; Senungetuk and Tiulana 1987:11; Simpson 1875:262; Smith 1970; Spencer 1959: 210–228; Stefansson 1951:87–88; Sunno 1951d, 1951e; Swan 1970; Thomas 1970; Vestal 1970; Wells and Kelly 1890:24–25.
28. This is the term used in the NANA Region. On the North Slope it is *kivgiq*.
29. In most parts of the Iñupiaq-language sector of northwestern Alaska a messenger feast was the major feast of the year. In the Yup'ik sector, however, it was just one among many and not necessarily the most important (Hawkes 1914; Nelson 1899:357–393).
30. Sources on the conduct of messenger feasts: Alġaqsruutit 1983; Attla and Attla 1991; Booth 1960; Cleveland 1970b; Curtis 1930:173–177, 213–214; Curtis 1970; Fair 2001; D. Foster 1970; Gallahorn 1969; Gallahorn 1952; Giddings 1956:37–38, 43–46, 1961:24–28, 52–60, 151–153; Glover 1970b; Hall 1975b:18–19, 259–262; Howard 1952; Edna Hunnicutt 1960a:33–35; Kakaruk 1983:141–149; Killigivuk 1961; Kisautaq and Kean 1981:559–591; Lucier 1952; Luther 1960a:59–65; Monroe 1960:88–90; NANA Cultural Heritage Project 1975b; Northwest Iñupiat Elders Conference 1983:83–31A; Oquilluk 1973:149–166; Samms 1899–1900:entries for November 27–28, 1899; Smith 1970; Sunno 1951d, 1951e, 1951f, 1951g; Vestal 1970.
31. For the Arctic Slope see Murdoch 1892:373–375; Ostermann and Holtved 1952: 103–111; Ray 1885:41–42; Spencer 1959:210–218. For the Norton Sound area see Dall 1870:152–154; Hawkes 1913, 1914:40–41; Nelson 1899:361–363.
32. For the uninitiated it should be noted that a snow-covered landscape north of the tree line can be fairly bright under starlight, and visibility can be several miles under a full moon.
33. On the North Slope the term was apparently *kaŋuġaqtuġniq* or *kaŋuġaqtuaniq* (Elavgak 1980).
34. Spencer (1959:199) unaccountably refers to the Sisualik fair as taking place at a locality called Kiŋaliq.
35. According to my informants, the shoals are much more extensive than the United States Geological Survey topographic maps indicate. Not knowing the channel, I once ran aground here in a small boat, got out, and, wearing hip boots, walked for some distance when I was a good 5–6 miles (8–9.5 kilometers) offshore.

36. The soundings on Beechey's chart indicate that the barge did not approach to within less than about 4 miles (6.5 kilometers) of Sisualik on the southeast and perhaps 20 miles (30 kilometers) on the west. Even on the Baldwin Peninsula side of the opening to Hotham Inlet the party was met by 14 umiat full of armed men (Beechey 1831, vol. 1:351–352).
37. Sources on the Sisualik fair schedule: Beechey 1831, vol. 1:390–391, 441; Cantwell 1887:25, 51, 1889a:70, 71, 72; Foote 1959–61:box 3, folder 2, 33–34; Healy 1887:13; Hooper 1881:44, 1884:39–40, 78; McLenegan 1887:73, 74; Nelson 1899:261; Samms 1897–98, 1899–1900, 1901–2; Simpson 1875:236; VanStone 1977:58–59; White 1889:entry for August 22, 1889. I am fairly certain that people stayed longer after Western traders began to frequent the fair, particularly after it was moved from Sheshalik to where the modern town of Kotzebue now stands.
38. Spencer (1959:198) claims that people from the Kuk River near modern Wainwright, who would have been Silaliñaġmiut, regularly attended the Kotzebue fair. This is a mistake.
39. The identification of Ilaviñiq as a Nuataaġmiu is based on comments in Stefansson 1914b:320, 341, 345.
40. By Ilaviñiq's time the upper Kobuk Koyukon had been assimilated by the Iñupiat, and at least some of them had become regular participants in the fair. During the first half of the 19th century they would have been only occasional visitors.
41. See Hooper 1884:102; VanStone 1977:20, 53, 58. Foote's (1965a:227) calculations yielded an average of just under seven people per boat, but he included some dubious figures from Barrow. If they are excluded, his average rises to 11 people per boat, exactly the average of my maximum and minimum assumptions.
42. The people were accompanied by several hundred dogs (Cantwell 1889a:72).
43. According to Gal (1997), these people were not seen at the "Cape Blossom" of the United States Geological Survey maps but at the headland at June Creek, just south of the modern town of Kotzebue.
44. Hooper (1881:26) said a "large number" in his report, but Nelson (1899:231), who accompanied him the following year, said that Hooper had told him it was around 1,200. In his report on the 1881 voyage, Hooper said that there were "perhaps a thousand people at Cape Blossom" (1884:102), but he must have been referring to the year before. Nelson's diary (1877–81, notebook 12:entry for July 15, 1881) says that there was only one tent at Cape Blossom in 1881.
45. Stoney's survey shows the "native trading station" at Sisualik and a "native fishing station" on the "Kotzebue peninsula" (1883). In 1884, however, Cantwell (1889b:77) reported that the people had rendezvoused on the spit projecting into Kotzebue Sound from the south side of Hotham Inlet, which has to mean the Kotzebue peninsula. In the United States Revenue Marine (Healy 1887:end map) report for the following year, Cantwell's map locates the "native trading station" on Kotzebue peninsula, where it remained in subsequent years.
46. For the arrangement of camps after the fair was moved to the Kotzebue peninsula see Burch 1998a:217.

47. Sources on fair activities: Anderson 1974–75:69–70; E. Atoruk 1989; Barr 1970; Bockstoce 1988, vol. 1:305–307; Gallahorn 1970a, 1970b; Glover 1970c; Healy 1889:16; Hooper 1881:26, 28, 1884:39, 102; Elwood Hunnicutt 1970; Jensen 1970e; Keats 1970e; Kisautaq and Kean 1981:619–621; Nelson 1877–81, journal 12:entry for July 16, 1881; Rainey 1947:267–268; Simpson 1875:236; Vestal 1970; Woolfe 1893:137.
48. Ridicule, teasing, and practical joking were acceptable only between cross-cousins and very good friends. Even in my time the comment "he can talk to me any old way" marked a relationship that was unusual because ridicule and joking were considered acceptable.
49. In the early years the rule against bearing weapons seems to have been temporarily abrogated when Iñupiat confronted Europeans.
50. The experience of W. L. Howard, from Stoney's expedition, on the Arctic coast is a concrete example of the constraints imposed on troublemakers at these peaceful gatherings (Stoney 1900:821).
51. The Russians forbade the sale of firearms to Natives while the Russians "owned" Alaska.
52. The man I think was this Samaruraq was an umialik judged to be about 35 years old in February 1853, when, with 2 beautiful wives, he visited the *Plover* at Point Barrow (Simpson 1852–54:entry for February 7, 1853). If so, he is also the man referred to in Chapter 2 who wore armor all the time because he feared revenge for a murder he committed. Whether or not that identification is correct, the man who is featured in this story was killed by Kivalliñiġmiut assassins during the summer of 1881.
53. I strongly suspect that Samaruraq's qataŋun was older than he was. His brother, Kataliña, who did not offer comment, was not in a position to do so because he was younger.
54. Sources on the Niġliq fair: Bockstoce 1988, vol. 1:79, 230, 237–239, vol. 2: 408, 410; Elavgak 1978; Hopson 1978:93–94; Itaałuk 1980b, 1981b, 1981c, 1982b, 1982c, 1982d, 1982e, 1982f; Kisautaq and Kean 1981:142–143, 591–599, 608–611, 617–620; Larsen 1958:577–578; Maguire 1857:448–449, 456–457; Morry n.d.; North Slope Borough, Commission on History and Culture 1980:156–157; Ostermann and Holtved 1952:30–31, 139–140; Ray 1885:39; Simpson 1875:236, 264–265; Spencer 1959:198; Stefansson 1914a:10, 1914b:9; Woolfe 1893:137–138.
55. Why the Ikpikpagmiut did not participate in this fair is a mystery to me.
56. By the early 1900s the number of people involved in this fair had declined to just a few dozen (Stefansson 1914b:209).
57. Excellent descriptions of their traveling procedures are contained in Bockstoce 1988, vol. 1:237–238; Simpson 1875:264–265.
58. Sources on the Niġliq fair: Ahkivgak 1980; Ekolook 1980; Elavgak 1978; Hopson 1978:90–94; Irving 1953; Itaałuk 1981a, 1981c; Kisautaq and Kean 1981:595–598; Samuel Kunuknana 1980:156–157; Nashanik 1980; Numnik 1978; Ostermann and Holtved 1952:30–31; Spencer 1959:199–207; Woolfe 1893:137–138.

59. For the location of Pigniq see Bockstoce 1988, vol. 1:84, where it is spelled "Pergniak." See also Schneider, Pedersen, and Libbey 1980:198–208.
60. The place reference is in Kisautaq and Kean 1981:622–624. Its location is shown in Bodfish 1991:32.
61. In 1881 Nelson (1899:231) saw 9 umiat containing about 100 Tikiġaġmiut who were apparently headed for this fair. Warren Neakok, whose grandparents were from Point Hope, said that they used to attend this event every summer (Neakok and Neakok 1984). Other sources include Aġviqsiiña 1940:60; Foote and Williamson 1966:1045; Quwana 1940; Rock 1940; Woolfe 1893:137.
62. Gubser (1965:344) states that this event took place in the Nigu River valley, which was certainly one of the possibilities. Joe Sampson (1970) told me that his former father-in-law, an old Nuataaġmiu, used to talk about a katŋut at the mouth of Makpik Creek in the upper Noatak basin.
63. Sources on the Barter Island fair: Bockstoce 1988, vol. 1: 216–217, 238; Collinson 1889:320–321; Franklin 1828:130–131, 146–147, 149; Gubser 1965:49; Maguire 1857:449–450; McKennan 1965:25; Schneider 1976:290–291; Simpson 1875:236, 265–268; Simpson 1843:118–119; Stefansson 1914a:10, 1914b:186–187, 195; Woolfe 1893:138.
64. Sources on the Nuklukayet fair: A. Clark 1981:595–596; Dall 1870:93, 198; Michael 1967:167–168; Whymper 1868:210, 230, 1869a:176, 1869b:236–240. Turck and Turck (1992) describe trading posts that were located here (or nearby) *after* the period of interest in this book.
65. Actually, the participants are said to have been more specifically from the Ayasaaġiaaġmiut settlement of Aziaq, which was located on Sledge Island, a short distance off the coast from where Nome now stands. In my judgment that settlement was much too small for its inhabitants to have done all the trading with which they have been credited.
66. Here niuviq- is a verb stem rather than a noun.
67. Spencer (1959:205–206) gives a more extended account of trading at the Nigliq fair.
68. In 1822 Khromchenko (VanStone 1973:84–85) made a remark almost identical to this one.
69. All typographical errors in this passage are retained from the original.
70. The Nuataaġmiut (upper Noatak) and Utuqqaġmiut (Utukok River), whose estates were a considerable distance inland, spent at least a month on the coast every year hunting seals or beluga.
71. In 1996 the combined population of the western Arctic, Teshekpuk, and central Arctic herds was estimated to be nearly half a million animals, which probably approximates the number of caribou in northwestern Alaska in good years during the early 19th century. The projected annual harvest of 120,000 based on Spencer's numbers would have been nearly a quarter of the total population. In 1995–96 the estimated harvest from these herds was 20,341 animals (Alaska 1996:57).
72. Again, part of Spencer's problem may have been the fact that his analysis focused

on the situation in the 1880s and 1890s, after the western Arctic caribou herd had crashed. After 1890 the inland–coastal distinction was much more sharply drawn than it had been previously, particularly on the Arctic Slope.

73. The importance of fish in interior northwestern Alaska is almost always overlooked by anthropologists except for those who have worked in the Selawik and Kobuk River valleys. This is amazing to me, since practically all of the fall–winter sites I ever heard about on the upper Noatak River, the Colville River, the rivers in the Endicott Mountains, and the rivers on the Arctic Coastal Plain were located where they were because of the fishing.

74. Sources on the Eskimo–Athapaskan trade: Allen 1887:102; Anderson 1974–75:67–71; Andrews and Koutsky 1979; Ballott 1970a; Bockstoce 1988, vol. 1:126, 156; Clark 1970, 1974:205–253, 1977, 1981:595; Clark and Clark 1976; Curtis 1930:214, 227; Dall 1870:143–144; Engelhard 1992:40; Hadley and Sunno 1951; Huntington 1984; Huntington 1993:16; Lee 1970; Michael 1967:100–102, 152, 153; Stuck 1917:340; VanStone 1976b, 1979a; Whymper 1869b:162–163.

75. Sources on the Alaska–Chukotka trade: Bockstoce 1988, vol. 1:78; Bogoras 1901:83, 1904–9:53–60, 83–84; Curtis 1930:161; Erman 1855; Forsyth 1992:150; Fortuine 1989:265–274; Kingston 1996, 2000; Kotzebue 1821, vol. 1:211, 228, 236, 262; Lucier 1995b, 1997:333; Maguire 1857:444; Merck 1980:186; Michael 1967:101; Miller 1994:16–21; Morris 1970; Nelson 1877–81, notebook 12:July 12, 1881, 1899:228–230; Northwest Iñupiat Elders Conference 1976:76–08; Sauer 1802:255; Schweitzer and Golovko 1995:39–41; Simon 1998:76–86; Stefansson 1914b:331; Thornton 1931:33, 46, 120; VanStone 1977:47; Whymper 1869b:137–138; Wrangell 1980:30–33.

76. After the caribou herds of northwestern Alaska began their dramatic decline during the late 1870s, the market for Asiatic reindeer hides increased dramatically until well after domesticated reindeer were introduced there in the 1890s.

77. The Anyui fair was not the only outlet for Russian goods among the Chukchi during the late 18th and early 19th centuries, but it was far and away the most important one with regard to the trade across Bering Strait (Antropova and Kuznetsova 1964:803–804; Burch 1988b:236; Erman 1855; Ray 1975b:97–102; Wrangell 1980:30). Cochrane (1825, vol. 1:311–318) has written an interesting account of this fair as he observed it in 1822.

78. Sources on Native–Westerner trade: Arndt 1990, 1992, 1996; Beechey 1831, vol. 1:343–345, 352, 394, 395, 397, 408–409, 456, 352, vol. 2:265, 306; Bockstoce 1988, vol. 1:128; Kashevarov 1994; Kotzebue 1821, vol. 1:209–210, 262; Krause and Krause 1882:30; Merck 1980:192; Michael 1967:100–103; Ray 1975a, 1975b:97–102, 1983:34; Sarychev 1806–7, vol. 2:44, 46; Sauer 1802:245–246; Stefansson 1914b:390; VanStone 1959, 1979b:53–58.

79. Most of the "Malemiut" who visited Saint Michael and the shores of Norton Sound during the 1840s were apparently Iñupiaq speakers from the western and southern parts of the Seward Peninsula (Arndt 1986a, 1986b; Netsvetov 1984). Some may have been Kaŋiġmiut from the Buckland district, however.

80. According to Russian colleagues, Chukotka is not considered part of Siberia, which is farther west.
81. Aniliukhtakpak was located just where the letter N, designating the route between the Yukon and Kuskokwim Rivers, touches the Yukon River on Map 13.
82. Simpson acquired most of his information while stationed at Point Barrow. See his journal entries (Simpson 1852–54) for February 10, 27, May 25, June 22, 24, and November 8, 10, 14, 17 for the original data.
83. Simpson's text was first published in 1855 on the basis of what he had learned in various parts of northwestern Alaska between 1848 and 1854. For an even more comprehensive overview of the system, more specifically as it was toward the end of the 19th century, see Stefansson 1914a.
84. Ray used English names, whereas I am using the Native forms.
85. Ray (1967:384) includes the Imaqłit in this alliance, but both Nelson (1899:330) and Weyer (1962:157) indicate that they were enemies of the Kiŋikmiut during this period.
86. My own sources confirmed the former existence of this alliance.
87. The Kuuvaum Kaŋiaġmiut were probably well along in the assimilation process by this time.
88. Lucier (1997:276) notes that allies crossed one another's estates via established routes, to which I would add that they also did so at established times of year.

4. Conclusions

1. Most of these examples were described in Chapter 2 and involved people returning home from the Sisualik trade fair.
2. A few Russian traders may have visited Kotzebue Sound before Kotzebue did.
3. Sheehan (1997:33, 45, 48–49) uses identical logic but places the inception of war in northwestern Alaska at a later date than I do.
4. The most recent summary of information relevant to this issue was written by Heather Pringle (1997). For earlier summaries of early iron distribution and use see McCartney 1988; McCartney and Mack 1973. For copper see Franklin et al. 1981:93–101. Other pertinent sources include A. Clark 1996:21; Collins 1932:107–108; Larsen and Rainey 1948:83–84, 254; Levin and Sergeyev 1964; Okladnikov 1963; Rainey 1971:15, 26–27. Friesen (1995:81–92) describes the precontact world system near the northeastern border of what I label in this book the North Pacific Interaction Sphere.
5. The soapstone trade with the Canadian Inuit that was fairly important during the early 19th century apparently did not develop until perhaps the 16th or 17th century. This fact does not affect my thesis on the antiquity of international trade because the Inuit living near the soapstone deposits did not begin to mine soapstone until the 15th century (Morrison 1987, 1991a:241).
6. Conceivably, this coal could have been brought by Thule migrants.
7. Many authors (e.g., Ackerman 1984:108–109; Ford 1959:151–156; Giddings 1952:61–63; Hall 1978; Rudenko 1961:172) maintain that the evidence of dog traction dates only from the early 17th century. Hickey (1979:427) says that the archaeologi-

cal evidence from Kotzebue indicates a ninefold increase in "sleds, dog traction, and snowshoes" between 1400 and 1550. Lucier (1997:374), however, basing his opinion on the work of Helge Larsen (1982), makes what to me is a persuasive case that dog traction has been present in northwestern Alaska since at least Ipiutak times, giving it an antiquity of at least a thousand years.

8. They agree on this point with Hickey 1979. All four of us disagree with Ray 1975b:97–99.
9. For a general discussion of the tobacco trade see Ray 1975b:101–102. See also Nelson 1899:229.
10. In the selection of terms and definitions I have been influenced by the following: Chase-Dunn and Hall 1995:109, 112, 1997:271–275; Frank and Gills 1993:3; Hall 1999:4, 7; Hannerz 1989:201; Jeske 1999:216; McNeil 1993:xi; Neitzel 2000:25–26; Sanderson and Hall 1995:95–97; Wilkinson 1993:229, 239.
11. Levy's (1966) analysis of intersocietal social systems had a focus different from the one that has guided world systems analysis.
12. An ecumene is the same as a "world-system" (hyphenated) as discussed in much of the literature on world systems and as a "civilization" in the so-called civilizationist literature. I find the former term to be confusing with regard to the level of generalization of its referent and the latter to be troublesome because of the judgmental overtones associated with it.
13. A few other nations had larger total populations than the Kiŋikmiut, but their members were much more widely dispersed, which apparently limited their ability to exercise hegemony over their neighbors.
14. The Di'hąįį Gwich'in seem to have been at least as warlike as the Tikiġaġmiut.
15. Conceivably, the Tikiġaġmiut were on good terms with the Silaliñaġmiut. I mention this possibility because no one has told me otherwise and because, when Kashevarov traveled along the coast in 1838, the Silaliñaġmiut did not mention the Tikiġaġmiut as being their enemies.
16. The subsistence base of the Tikiġaġmiut was different enough from that of the others as to make this a plausible scenario.
17. In northern North America these areas were often located north of the latitudinal tree line. People whose estates were located immediately south of the tree line ventured north onto the tundra in summer to hunt caribou.
18. These assertions are based on my own research, of which only a general account has been published to date (Burch 1995).
19. Correll (1976) has done a neat job of showing how these variations in precision were reflected in the place-names.
20. "Carrying capacity," as defined by Chase-Dunn and Hall, is "the population any natural environment can support within a specific region with a given production technology" (1997:271).
21. It changed in respects other than complexity, however.
22. For the distinction between simple and complex chiefdoms see Anderson 1994:8, 9, 13–14; Johnson and Earle 1987:207, 225.

23. For an example of an accident with major demographic implications see Burch 1998a:203–204, 375–380.
24. See Redmond 1998b:69, 70, 95, 97 for a discussion of how this actually worked in parts of South America.
25. For the Northwest Coast see Boyd 1990:135; Mitchell and Donald 1988:309–312. For the Wintu of north-central California see DuBois 1935:6–9, 28–29.
26. There is a huge literature on the people of this region to which I cannot possibly do justice here; see Suttles 1990. Accounts of particular relevance to the present work are the following: Donald 1997:1–8, 17–18, 301–310; Donald and Mitchell 1994; Mitchell 1983a, 1983b; Mitchell and Donald 2001. The "tribes" of these authors were "societies" as defined here.
27. This brief analysis is based on the basic ethnography by Cora DuBois (1935), the reconstruction by Chase-Dunn and Mann (1998), and summaries prepared by Chase-Dunn and Hall (1997:121–148) and Lapena (1978). It is presented using the concepts employed in this book.
28. This population figure is from Chase-Dunn and Hall 1997:126 and Chase-Dunn and Mann 1998:79; the number of societies figure is from Lapena 1978:324. According to Lapena (1978:325, table 1), the "precontact" population was 14,250, more than 2.5 times the estimate of Chase-Dunn and his coauthors. I have accepted their figure because it is based on a more recent analysis of the demographic and historical data.
29. This figure was calculated using the aboriginal population figures for the Wakashan epidemic area published by Boyd (1999:264) in the column headed "Boyd 1996," divided by the 79 "local groups" noted by Donald and Mitchell (1994:96).
30. Questions about coresident endogamy focus on the chances of finding a suitable mate given particular marriage rules and populations of various sizes (see, e.g., Wobst 1974, 1976). My concern here, however, is with the degree of biological (genetic) isolation of a given population.
31. Binford (2001:373–374) employs the term "packing" to refer to increasing *population* density. I employ the term to refer to increasing *estate* density. The two do not necessarily go together.
32. The nine Wintu estates encompassed an area of about 1,850 square miles (4,810 square kilometers). The packing figure was calculated by dividing one SRU by 1,850 square miles to get the extrapolation ratio (26.98), then multiplying that times the number of societies (9). This yielded a result of 242.82 societies per SRU.
33. I am equating Heinz's "band" with my "local family" and his "band nexus" with my "society." See Barnard 1992 for general information on the Bushmen and related peoples.
34. See Lee (1972c:350–359) for an excellent summary of Bushman band (i.e., local family) structure.

References Cited

Ackerman, Robert E.

1962 Culture contact in the Bering Sea: Birnirk–Punuk period. *In* Prehistoric cultural relations between the Arctic and temperate zones of North America. John M. Campbell, ed. Pp. 27–34. Technical Paper no. 11. Montreal: Arctic Institute of North America.

1984 Prehistory of the Asian Eskimo zone. *In* Arctic. David Damas, ed. Vol. 5, Handbook of North American Indians. William C. Sturtevant, gen. ed. Pp. 106–118. Washington DC: Smithsonian Institution Press.

Adams, David Iñuqtaq

1970 Personal oral communication to the author, Kotzebue AK, March 2.

1986 Personal oral communication to the author, Noatak AK, February 25.

Adams, Edward

1850–51 Journal kept ashore, from October 12, 1850, to July 3, 1851, on the expedition in search of Sir John Franklin on H.M.S. "Enterprise" under the command of Richard Collinson. Manuscript no. 1115. Archives of the Scott Polar Research Institute, Cambridge, England.

Adams, Gladys

1965 Personal oral communication to the author, Kivalina AK, June 11.

Adams, Ruth

1965 Personal oral communication to the author, Kivalina AK, September 10.

Agnasagga, Samuel

1984 Coastal sites in the Point Lay area. Traditional land use inventory of the North Slope Borough, tape no. 20. Interview by David Libbey, Wainwright AK, July 20. Transcript in possession of the author.

Ahkivgak, Otis

1980 Trading out east. Personal oral communication to Emily Wilson, October 3. Transcript in possession of the author, courtesy of David Libbey.

Aġviqsiiña, Frank

1940 Frank's story. Froelich G. Rainey Collection. Archives, Alaska and Polar Regions Department, Rasmuson Library, University of Alaska Fairbanks.

Alaska

1996 Caribou update. Alaska 62(9):57.

Aldrich, Herbert L.

1889 Arctic Alaska and Siberia, or, eight months with the Arctic whalemen. Chicago: Rand McNally.

Alġaqsruutit

1983 Messenger feast. Alġaqsruutit: Words of wisdom from your elders, September, 1983. Kotzebue AK: Mauneluk.

Allen, Henry T.

1887 Report of an expedition to the Copper, Tanana and Koyukuk Rivers, in the Territory of Alaska, in the year 1885. Washington DC: Government Printing Office.

Alunik, Ishmael, Eddie D. Kolausok, and David Morrison

2003 Across time and tundra: The Inuvialuit of the western Arctic. Vancouver: Raincoast Books; Seattle: University of Washington Press; Gatineau: Canadian Museum of Civilization.

Ames, Kenneth M., and Herbert D. G. Maschner

1999 Peoples of the Northwest Coast: Their archaeology and prehistory. London: Thames and Hudson.

Anderson, David G.

1994 The Savannah River chiefdoms: Political change in the late prehistoric Southeast. Tuscaloosa: University of Alabama Press.

Anderson, Douglas D.

1970 Athapaskans in the Kobuk Arctic woodlands, Alaska? Canadian Archaeological Association Bulletin 2:3–12.

1974–75 Trade networks among the Selawik Eskimos, northwestern Alaska, during the late 19th and early 20th centuries. Folk 16–17:63–72.

1984 Prehistory of North Alaska. *In* Arctic. David Damas, ed. Vol. 5, Handbook of North American Indians. William C. Sturtevant, gen. ed. Pp. 80–93. Washington DC: Smithsonian Institution Press.

Anderson, Douglas D., Wanni W. Anderson, Ray Bane, Richard K. Nelson, and Nita Sheldon Towarak

1998 *Kuuvaŋmiut* subsistence: Traditional Eskimo life in the latter twentieth century. Washington DC: National Park Service.

Anderson, Douglas D., and Robert Gal

1991 An archaeological survey at the mouth of the Pah River, northwestern Alaska: Draft preliminary report, state of Alaska field archaeology permit 91-09. On file at the Department of Anthropology, Brown University.

Andrews, Elizabeth F.

1977 Report on the cultural resources of the Doyon region, central Alaska. 2 vols. Occasional Paper no. 5. Anthropology and Historic Preservation Section, Cooperative Park Studies Unit, University of Alaska Fairbanks.

Andrews, Elizabeth, and Kathryn Koutsky

1979 Ethnohistory of the Kaltag Portage, west central Alaska. *In* Proceedings: First conference on scientific research in the national parks, New Orleans, November 9–12, 1976. Robert M. Linn, ed. Pp. 921–994. Washington DC: National Park Service, Transactions and Proceedings Series no. 5.

Antropova, V. V., and V. G. Kuznetsova

1964 The Chukchi. *In* The peoples of Siberia. M. G. Levin and L. P. Potapov, eds. Pp. 799–835. Chicago: University of Chicago Press.

Arndt, Katherine L.

1986a Composition of Russian-American Company personnel in the Saint Michael area, 1843–1867: Preliminary findings. Paper presented at the Russian American symposium, Alaska Anthropological Association 13th Annual Meeting, Fairbanks.

1986b Personal written communication to the author, June 24.

1990 Russian-American Company trade on the middle Yukon River, 1839–1867. *In* Russia in North America: Proceedings of the 2nd International Conference on Russian America, Sitka AK, August 19–22, 1987. Richard A. Pierce, ed. Pp. 180–192. Kingston ON: Limestone Press.

1992 Tapping the trade of the middle Yukon. *In* Bering and Chirikov: The American voyages and their impact. O. W. Frost, ed. Pp. 323–328. Anchorage: Alaska Historical Society.

1996 Dynamics of the fur trade on the middle Yukon River, Alaska, 1839 to 1868. Ann Arbor MI: UMI Dissertation Services.

Arundale, Wendy H., and William S. Schneider

1987 Quliaqtuat Iñupiat Nunaniññiñ: The report of the Chipp–Ikpikpuk River and upper Meade River oral history project. On file at the North Slope Borough, Commission on Iñupiat History, Language and Culture, Barrow, Alaska.

Arutiunov, Serghei A., and William W. Fitzhugh

1988 Prehistory of Siberia and the Bering Sea. *In* Crossroads of continents: Cultures of Siberia and Alaska. William Fitzhugh and Aron Crowell, eds. Pp. 117–129. Washington DC: Smithsonian Institution Press.

Ashby, Wilson Titqiaq

1970 Personal oral communication to the author, Kotzebue AK, May 12.

Atoruk, Effie Taapsuk

1989 Personal oral communication to the author, Kiana AK, March 1.

Atoruk, Peter Aaquuraq

1989 Personal oral communication to the author, Kiana AK, March 1.

Attla, Catherine Nodoyedee'onh, and Steven Denaa'ek'oogheełtune' Attla

1991 Personal oral communication to the author, Fairbanks, March 16.

Attungana, Patrick Kimmiałuk

1980 Personal oral communication to the author, Point Hope AK, October 16.

Ballott, Walter Mannik

1970a Personal oral communication to the author, Selawik AK, March 9.

1970b Personal oral communication to the author, Selawik AK, March 11.

Bandi, Hans-Georg

1995 Siberian Eskimos as whalers and warriors. *In* Hunting the largest animals: Native whaling in the western Arctic and Subarctic. Allen P. McCartney, ed. Pp. 165–183. Edmonton: Canadian Circumpolar Institute. Studies in Whaling no. 3; Occasional Publication no. 36. Edmonton: Canadian Circumpolar Institute.

Barnard, Alan

1992 Hunters and herders of southern Africa: A comparative ethnography of the Khoisan peoples. Cambridge: Cambridge University Press.

Barnett, H. G.

1938 The nature of the potlatch. American Anthropologist 40(3):349–358.

Barr, Emily Qimmikpiauraq

1970 Personal oral communication to the author, Kotzebue AK, April 23.

Beckerman, Stephen, and Roberto Lizarralde

1995 State–tribal warfare and male-biased casualties among the Barí. Current Anthropology 36(3):497–500.

Beechey, Frederick William

1831 Narrative of a voyage to the Pacific and Bering's Strait to co-operate with the polar expeditions; performed in His Majesty's Ship "Blossom" . . . in the years 1825, 26, 27, 28. 2 vols. London: Colburn and Bently.

Belcher, Edward

1825–27 Private journal, remarks, etc., H.M. Ship "Blossom" on discovery during the years 1825, 6, 7, . . . and continuation of private journal. Manuscript no. 1044/.1. Archives of the Scott Polar Research Institute, Cambridge, England.

Bergsland, Knut, ed.

1987 Nunamiut unipkaaŋich [Nunamiut stories]. Collected by Helge Ingstad with the help of Homer Mekiana. Knut Bergsland, trans. and ed., with the help of Ronald W. Senungituk and Justus Mekiana. Barrow AK: North Slope Borough, Commission on Iñupiat History, Language and Culture.

Berkh, Vasilii N.

1983 Captain–Lieutenants Vasil'ev and Shishmarev, 1819. *In* Ethnohistory in the Arctic: The Bering Strait Eskimo. Rhea Josephson, trans. Dorothy Jean Ray, ed. Pp. 15–24. Kingston ON: Limestone Press.

Berndt, Ronald M.

1959 The concept of "the tribe" in the western desert of Australia. Oceania 30:81–107.

Bertholf, Ellsworth Price

1899a Report of Second Lieut. E. P. Bertholf, R.C.S., Point Hope, Alaska, July 15, 1898. *In* United States Treasury Department, Report of the cruise of the U.S. Revenue Cutter "Bear" and the overland expedition for the relief of the whalers in the Arctic Ocean from November 27, 1897, to September 13, 1898. Pp. 18–27. Washington DC: Government Printing Office.

1899b Report of Lieutenant Bertholf, September 1, 1898. *In* United States Treasury Department, Report of the cruise of the U.S. Revenue Cutter "Bear" and the overland expedition for the relief of the whalers in the Arctic Ocean from November 27, 1897, to September 13, 1898. Pp. 103–114. Washington DC: Government Printing Office.

Binford, Lewis R.

2001 Constructing frames of reference: An analytical method for archaeological theory building using ethnographic and environmental data sets. Berkeley: University of California Press.

Black, Lydia T.

2004 Russians in Alaska, 1732–1867. Fairbanks: University of Alaska Press.

Bockstoce, John R.

1977 Eskimos of Northwest Alaska in the early nineteenth century, based on the Beechey and Belcher collections and records compiled during the voyage of H.M.S. "Blossom" to northwest Alaska in 1826 and 1827. Oxford: University of Oxford. Pitt Rivers Museum Monograph Series no. 1.

1985 The search for Sir John Franklin in Alaska. *In* The Franklin era in Canadian Arctic history, 1845–1859. Patricia D. Sutherland, ed. Pp. 93–113. Ottawa: National Museum of Man. Archaeological Survey of Canada Paper no. 131.

1986 Whales, ice and men: The history of whaling in the western Arctic. Seattle: University of Washington Press.

n.d. The opening of the maritime fur trade at Bering Strait. Transactions of the American Philosophical Society. In press.

Bockstoce, John R., ed.

1988 The journal of Rochefort Maguire, 1852–1854: Two years at Point Barrow, Alaska, aboard H.M.S. "Plover" in the search for Sir John Franklin. 2 vols. London: Hakluyt Society.

Bodenhorn, Barbara A.

1989 "The animals come to me, they know I share": Iñupiaq kinship, changing economic relations, and enduring world views on Alaska's North Slope. Ph.D. dissertation, Department of Social Anthropology, University of Cambridge.

Bodfish, Waldo Kusiq

1984 Coastal sites in the Point Lay area. Traditional land use inventory of the North Slope Borough, tape no. 18. Interview by David Libbey, Wainwright AK, August 20. Transcript in possession of the author.

1991 Kusiq: An Eskimo life history from the Arctic coast of Alaska. William Schneider, comp. and ed. in collaboration with Leona Kisautaq Okakok and James Mumigana Nageak. Fairbanks: University of Alaska Press. Oral Biography Series no. 2.

Bogojavlensky, Sergei

1969 Imaangmiut Eskimo careers: Skinboats in Bering Strait. Ph.D. dissertation, Department of Social Relations, Harvard University.

Bogoras, Waldemar G.

1901 The Chukchi of northeastern Asia. American Anthropologist 3(1):80–108.

1904–9 The Chukchee: Part 1, material culture; part 2, religion; part 3, social organization. Memoirs of the American Museum of Natural History, vol. 11.

Booth, Ezra Kumak

1960 Notes from an interview by Don Foote, Noatak AK, February 11. Don Charles Foote Papers, box 3, folder 1. Archives, Alaska and Polar Regions Department, Rasmuson Library, University of Alaska Fairbanks.

Boyd, Robert T.

1990 Demographic history, 1774–1874. *In* Northwest Coast. Wayne Suttles, ed.

Vol. 7, Handbook of North American Indians. William C. Sturtevant, gen. ed. Pp. 135–148. Washington DC: Smithsonian Institution Press.

1999 The coming of the spirit of pestilence: Introduced infectious diseases and population decline among Northwest Coast Indians, 1774–1874. Seattle: University of Washington Press.

Bronshtein, Mikhail M., and Kirill A. Dneprovsky

2002 The northeastern Chukchi peninsula during the Birnirk and early Punuk periods. In Archaeology in the Bering Strait region: Research on two continents. Don E. Dumond and Richard L. Bland, eds. Pp. 153–166. University of Oregon Anthropological Paper 59.

Brooks, Alfred Hulse

1901 A reconnaissance of the Cape Nome and adjacent gold-fields of Seward peninsula, Alaska, 1900. In Reconnaissances in the Cape Nome and Norton Bay regions, Alaska, 1900, by A. H. Brooks et al. Pp. 1–180. Washington DC: Government Printing Office.

1953 Blazing Alaska's trails. Washington DC: University of Alaska and the Arctic Institute of North America.

Brower, Charles David

n.d. The northernmost American: An autobiography. Manuscript, Stefansson Collection, Dartmouth College Library, Hanover NH.

Brown, Anthony Cave

1975 Bodyguard of lies. New York: Harper and Row.

Burch, Ernest S., Jr.

1970a The Eskimo trading partnership in North Alaska: A study in balanced reciprocity. Anthropological Papers of the University of Alaska 15(1):49–80.

1970b Marriage and divorce among the North Alaskan Eskimos. In Divorce and after: An analysis of the emotional and social problems of divorce. Paul Bohannan, ed. Pp. 152–181. Garden City NY: Doubleday.

1974 Eskimo warfare in northwest Alaska. Anthropological Papers of the University of Alaska 16(2):1–14.

1975a Eskimo kinsmen: Changing family relationships in northwest Alaska. St. Paul MN: West Publishing. American Ethnological Society Monograph no. 59.

1975b Inter-regional transportation in traditional northwest Alaska. Anthropological Papers of the University of Alaska 17(2):1–11.

1976 Overland travel routes in northwest Alaska. Anthropological Papers of the University of Alaska 18(1):1–10.

1979 Indians and Eskimos in North Alaska, 1816–1977: A study in changing ethnic relations. Arctic Anthropology 16(2):123–151.

1980 Traditional Eskimo societies in northwest Alaska. Senri Ethnological Studies 4:253–304.

1981 The traditional Eskimo hunters of Point Hope AK: 1800–1875. Barrow AK: North Slope Borough.

1988a Modes of exchange in northwest Alaska. In Hunters and gatherers 2: Property, power and ideology. Tim Ingold, David Riches, and James Woodburn, eds. Pp. 95–109. New York: Berg.

1988b War and trade. In Crossroads of continents: Cultures of Siberia and Alaska. William W. Fitzhugh and Aron Crowell, eds. Pp. 227–240. Washington DC: Smithsonian Institution Press.

1990 The cultural and natural heritage of northwest Alaska. Vol. 1, Geology. Kotzebue AK: NANA Museum of the Arctic.

1991 From skeptic to believer: The making of an oral historian. Alaska History 6(1):1–16.

1994 Rationality and resource use among hunters. In Circumpolar religion and ecology: An anthropology of the north. Takashi Irimoto and Takako Yamada, eds. Pp. 163–185. Tokyo: University of Tokyo Press.

1995 The Caribou Inuit. In Native peoples: The Canadian experience, 2nd ed. R. Bruce Morrison and C. Roderick Wilson, eds. Pp. 115–142. Toronto: Oxford University Press.

1998a The Iñupiaq Eskimo nations of northwest Alaska. Fairbanks: University of Alaska Press.

1998b Boundaries and borders in early contact north-central Alaska. Arctic Anthropology 35(2):19–48.

1998c The cultural and natural heritage of northwest Alaska. Vol. 7, International affairs. Prepared for NANA Museum of the Arctic, Kotzebue, and the National Park Service, Anchorage.

Burch, Ernest S., Jr., and Thomas C. Correll

1972 Alliance and conflict: Inter-regional relations in North Alaska. In Alliance in Eskimo society: Proceedings of the American Ethnological Society, 1971, supplement. D. L. Guemple, ed. Pp. 17–39. Seattle: University of Washington Press.

Burch, Ernest S., Jr., Eliza Jones, Hannah P. Loon, and Lawrence D. Kaplan

1999 The ethnogenesis of the Kuuvaum Kaŋiaġmiut. Ethnohistory 46(2):291–327.

Burch, Ernest S., Jr., and Craig W. Mishler

1995 The Di'hąįį Gwich'in: Mystery people of northern Alaska. Arctic Anthropology 32(1):147–172.

Burgess, Stephen M.

1974 The St. Lawrence islanders of Northwest Cape: Patterns of resource utilization. Ann Arbor MI: University Microfilms.

Burns, Frank

1952 Napaaaktomyut messenger feast. Personal oral communication to Charles Lucier, June. Charles Lucier Collection, box 3, folder 15. Archives, Alaska and Polar Regions Department, Rasmuson Library, University of Alaska Fairbanks.

Butlin, Noel G.

1983 Our original aggression: Aboriginal populations of southeastern Australia, 1788–1850. Sydney: Allen and Unwin.

Caldwell, Joseph

1964 Interaction spheres in prehistory. Hopewellian Studies 12(6):133–156.

Campbell, John M.

1998 North Alaska chronicle: Notes from the end of time: The Simon Paneak drawings. Santa Fe: Museum of New Mexico Press.

Campbell, Judy

2002 Invisible invaders: Smallpox and other diseases in Aboriginal Australia, 1780–1880. Carlton South, Victoria: Melbourne University Press.

Cantwell, John C.

1887 A narrative account of the exploration of the Kowak River, Alaska, under the direction of Captain Michael A. Healy. *In* Report of the cruise of the Revenue Marine steamer "Corwin" in the Arctic Ocean in the year 1885, by M. A. Healy. Pp. 21–52. Washington DC: Government Printing Office.

1889a A narrative account of the exploration of the Kowak River, Alaska. *In* Report of the cruise of the Revenue Marine steamer "Corwin" in the Arctic Ocean in the year 1884, by M. A. Healy. Pp. 47–74. Washington DC: Government Printing Office.

1889b Exploration of the Kowak River, Alaska, 1884: Ethnological notes. *In* Report of the cruise of the Revenue Marine steamer "Corwin" in the Arctic Ocean in the year 1884, by M. A. Healy. Pp. 75–98. Washington DC: Government Printing Office.

Carneiro, Robert L.

1970 A theory of the origin of the state. Science 168:733–738.

1978 Political expansion as an expression of the principle of competitive exclusion. *In* Origins of the state: The anthropology of political evolution. Ronald Cohen and Elman R. Service, eds. Pp. 205–223. Philadelphia: Institute for the Study of Human Issues.

1981 The chiefdom: Precursor of the state. *In* The transition to statehood in the new world. Grant D. Jones and Robert R. Kautz, eds. Pp. 37–79. Cambridge: Cambridge University Press.

1988 The circumscription theory. American Behavioral Scientist 31(4):497–511.

1998 What happened at the flashpoint? Conjectures on chiefdom formation at the very moment of conception. *In* Chiefdoms and chieftaincy in the Americas. Elsa M. Redmond, ed. Pp. 18–42. Gainesville: University Press of Florida.

2002 Was the chiefdom a congelation of ideas? Social Evolution and History 1(1):80–100.

Cashdan, Elizabeth

1983 Territoriality among human foragers: Ecological models and an application to four Bushman groups. Current Anthropology 24(1):47–66.

1984 G//ana territorial organization. Human Ecology 12(4):443–463.

Chagnon, Napoleon

1968a Yanomamö: The fierce people. New York: Holt, Rinehart and Winston.

1968b Yanomamö social organization and warfare. *In* War: The anthropology of armed conflict and aggression. M. Fried, M. Harris, and R. Murphy, eds. Pp. 109–158. New York: Natural History Press.

Chamisso, Adelbert von

1986a A voyage around the world with the Romanzov exploring expedition in the years 1815–1818 in the brig "Rurik," Captain Otto von Kotzebue. Henry Kratz, trans. and ed. Honolulu: University of Hawaii Press.

1986b The Alaska diary of Adelbert von Chamisso, naturalist on the Kotzebue voyage, 1815–1818. Robert Fortuine, trans. Anchorage: Cook Inlet Historical Society.

Chase-Dunn, Christopher, and Thomas D. Hall

1995 Cross-world-system comparisons: Similarities and differences. *In* Civilizations and world systems: Studying world-historical change. Stephen K. Sanderson, ed. Pp. 109–135. Walnut Creek CA: AltaMira Press.

1997 Rise and demise: Comparing world-systems. Boulder CO: Westview Press.

2000 Comparing world-systems to explain social evolution. *In* World system history: The science of long-term change. Robert A. Denemark, Jonathan Friedman, Barry K. Gills, and George Modelski, eds. Pp. 85–111. London: Routledge.

Chase-Dunn, Christopher, and Kelly M. Mann

1998 The Wintu and their neighbors: A very small world-system in northern California. Tucson: University of Arizona Press.

Chernenko, M. B.

1957 [The voyages of Ivan Kobelev, Kazak Sotnik, to Chukotka; land and sea voyage to Alaska in 1779 and 1789.] Letopis' Severa 2:121–141.

Chernow, Barbara A., and George A. Vallasi, eds.

1993 The Columbia encyclopedia, 5th ed. New York: Columbia University Press.

Chlenov, Michael

1973 Distinctive features of the social organization of the Asiatic Eskimos. Paper presented at the Ninth International Congress of Anthropological and Ethnological Sciences, August–September 1973, Chicago.

Choris, Ludovik

1822 Voyage pittoresque autour du monde, avec des portraits de sauvages d'Amérique, d'Asie, d'Afrique, et des les du Grand Ocean; des paysages, des vues maritimes, et pleusiers objets d'histoire naturelle; accompagné de descriptions par M. Le Baron Cuvier, et M. A. de Chamisso, et d'observations sur les crânes humains par M. le Docteur Gall. Paris: Firmin Didot.

Claessen, Henri J. M.

2002 Was the state inevitable? Social Evolution and History 1(1):101–117.

Clark, Annette McFadyen

1970 The Athabaskan–Eskimo interface. Canadian Archaeological Association Bulletin 2:13–23.

1974 Koyukuk River culture. Ottawa: National Museum of Man. Canadian Ethnology Service Paper no. 18.

1975 Upper Koyukuk River Koyukon Athapaskan social culture: An overview. *In*

Proceedings: Northern Athapaskan Conference, 1971, vol. 1. A. McF. Clark, ed. Pp. 146–180. Ottawa: National Museum of Man. Canadian Ethnology Service Paper no. 27.

1977 Trade at the cross roads. *In* Problems in the prehistory of the North American Subarctic: The Athapaskan question. J. W. Helmer, S. Van Dyke, and F. J. Kense, eds. Pp. 130–134. Calgary: University of Calgary Archaeological Association.

1981 Koyukon. *In* Subarctic. June Helm, ed. Vol. 6, Handbook of North American Indians. William G. Sturtevant, gen. ed. Pp. 582–601. Washington DC: Smithsonian Institution Press.

1996 Who lived in this house? A study of Koyukuk River semisubterranean houses. Hull QC: Canadian Museum of Civilization. Archaeological Survey of Canada Paper no. 153.

Clark, Annette McFadyen, and Donald W. Clark

1976 Koyukuk Indian–Kobuk Eskimo interaction. *In* Contributions to anthropology: The interior peoples of northern Alaska. Edwin S. Hall Jr., ed. Pp. 193–220. Ottawa: National Museum of Man. Archaeological Survey of Canada Paper no. 49.

Clark, Donald W.

1981 Prehistory of the western Subarctic. *In* Subarctic. June Helm, ed. Vol. 6, Handbook of North American Indians. William C. Sturtevant, gen. ed. Pp. 107–129. Washington DC: Smithsonian Institution Press.

Cleveland, Mark Uluatchiaq

1989 Personal oral communication to the author, Ambler AK, February 23.

Cleveland, Robert Nasruk

1965a The early days. Interview by Don Charles Foote. Typescript no. H88-2D-1. Kotzebue: NANA Elders Council Collection.

1965b Tumitchiałuk. Interview by Don Charles Foote. Typescript no. H88-2D-1. Kotzebue: NANA Elders Council Collection.

1965c Kititiraarvaat: Warfare between the Noatak and Kobuk River people. Interview by Don Charles Foote, July 24. Don Charles Foote Papers, box 8, folder 1. Archives, Alaska and Polar Regions Department, Rasmuson Library, University of Alaska Fairbanks.

1970a Personal oral communication to the author, Shungnak AK, January 28.

1970b Personal oral communication to the author, Shungnak AK, January 29.

1970c Personal oral communication to the author, Shungnak AK, January 30.

Cochrane, John Dundas

1825 Narrative of a pedestrian journey through Russia and Siberian Tartary, from the frontiers of China to the frozen sea and Kamchatka. 3rd ed. 2 vols. London: Charles Knight.

Coffin, Issak Irauraq

1970 Personal oral communication to the author, Noorvik AK, April 1.

Collins, Henry Bascom

1929 The ancient Eskimo culture of northwestern Alaska. *In* Explorations and field-work of the Smithsonian Institution in 1928. Pp. 141–150. Washington DC: Smithsonian Institution.

1931 Ancient culture of St. Lawrence Island, Alaska. *In* Explorations and field-work of the Smithsonian Institution in 1930. Pp. 135–144. Washington DC: Smithsonian Institution.

1932 Archeological investigations in northern Alaska. *In* Explorations and field-work of the Smithsonian Institution in 1931. Pp. 103–112. Washington DC: Smithsonian Institution.

1933 Archeological investigations at Point Barrow, Alaska. *In* Explorations and field-work of the Smithsonian Institution in 1932. Pp. 45–48. Washington DC: Smithsonian Institution.

1934 Archaeology of the Bering Sea region. *In* Proceedings of the Fifth Pacific Science Congress, 1933, vol. 4. Pp. 2825–2839. Toronto.

1937a Archaeological excavations at Bering Strait. *In* Explorations and field work of the Smithsonian Institution in 1936. Pp. 63–68. Washington DC: Smithsonian Institution.

1937b Archaeology of St. Lawrence Island, Alaska. Washington: Smithsonian Miscellaneous Collections, vol. 96, no. 1.

1964 The Arctic and Subarctic. *In* Prehistoric man in the New World. Jesse D. Jennings and Edward Norbeck, eds. Pp. 85–114. Chicago: University of Chicago Press.

Collinson, Richard

1889 Journal of H.M.S. "Enterprise" on the expedition in search of Sir John Franklin's ships by Bering Strait, 1850–55. London: Sampson, Low, Marsten, Searle and Rivington.

Commack, Louie Aquppak, Sr.

1970 Personal oral communication to the author, Noorvik AK, March 30.

Cook, James, and James King

1784 A voyage to the Pacific Ocean, vols. 2 and 3. London: Strahan.

Correll, Thomas C.

1971 Personal oral communication to the author, February 21, Winnipeg MB.

1972 Ungalaqlingmiut: A study in language and society. Ph.D. dissertation, University of Minnesota, Minneapolis.

1976 Language and location in traditional Inuit societies. *In* Supporting studies. Vol. 2, Inuit land use and occupancy project. Milton M. R. Freeman, ed. Pp. 173–179. Ottawa: Supply and Services Canada.

Crosby, Alfred W.

1997 The measure of reality: Quantification and Western society, 1250–1600. Cambridge: Cambridge University Press.

Crowell, Aron L.

1997 Archaeology and the capitalist world system: A study from Russian America. New York: Plenum Press.

Csonka, Yvon

2000 Personal oral communication to the author, Fairbanks AK, March 22.

Curtis, Edward C.

1930 The North American Indian, vol. 20. New York: Privately printed.

Curtis, Mary Aullaqsruaq

1970 Personal oral communication to the author, Kotzebue AK, April 24.

Dall, William Healy

1870 Alaska and its resources. Boston: Lee and Shepard.

1898 Travels on the Yukon and in the Yukon Territory. *In* The Yukon Territory. Pp. 1–242. London: Downey and Company.

Dayton, Roger

1981 Roger Dayton—Koyukuk: A biography. Blaine WA: Hancock House.

de Laguna, Frederica

1947 The prehistory of northern North America as seen from the Yukon. Memoirs of the Society for American Archaeology 3, Menasha WI.

Denemark, Robert A., Jonathan Friedman, Barry K. Gills, and George Modelski

2000 An introduction to world system history: Toward a social science of long term change. *In* World system history: The science of long-term change. Robert A. Denemark, Jonathan Friedman, Barry K. Gills, and George Modelski, eds. Pp. xv–xxii. London: Routledge.

de Reuse, Willem Joseph

1994 Siberian Yupik Eskimo: The language and its contacts with Chukchi. Salt Lake City: University of Utah Press.

Dives, Ququk

1940 Dive's [*sic*] story, as told to Froelich G. Rainey, Point Hope, Alaska. Archives, Alaska and Polar Regions Department, Rasmuson Library, University of Alaska Fairbanks.

Divin, Vasilii A.

1993 The great Russian navigator, A. I. Chirkov. Raymond H. Fisher, trans. Fairbanks: University of Alaska Press.

Dixon, R. M. W.

1976 Tribes, languages and other boundaries in northeast Queensland. *In* Tribes and boundaries in Australia. Nicolas Peterson, ed. Pp. 207–238. Canberra: Australian Institute of Aboriginal Studies.

Dmytryshyn, Basil, E. A. P. Crownhart-Vaughan, and Thomas Vaughan, trans. and eds.

1985 Russia's conquest of Siberia, 1558–1700: A documentary record. Vol. 1, To Siberia and Russian America: Three centuries of Russian eastward expansion, 1558–1867. Portland OR: Western Imprints. North Pacific Studies Series 9.

1988 Russian penetration of the North Pacific Ocean: A documentary record, 1700–1797. Vol. 2, To Siberia and Russian America: Three centuries of Russian eastward expansion, 1558–1867. Portland OR: Historical Society Press.

Dolgikh, B. O.

1972 The formation of the modern peoples of the Soviet North. Arctic Anthropology 9(1):17–26.

Donald, Leland

1997 Aboriginal slavery on the Northwest Coast of North America. Berkeley: University of California Press.

1999 Personal written communication to the author, December 15.

2000 Patterns of war and peace among complex hunter-gatherers: The case of the Northwest Coast of North America. *In* Hunters and gatherers in the modern world: Conflict, resistance, and self-determination. Peter P. Schweitzer, Megan Biesele, and Robert K. Hitchcock, eds. Pp. 164–179. New York: Berghahn.

2002 Personal written communication to the author, December 6.

Donald, Leland, and Donald H. Mitchell

1994 Nature and culture on the Northwest Coast of North America: The case of the Wakashan salmon resources. *In* Key issues in hunter-gatherer research. Ernest S. Burch Jr. and Linda J. Ellanna, eds. Pp. 95–117. Providence RI: Berg.

Donan, Hastings, and Thomas M. Wilson

1999 Borders: Frontiers of identity, nation, and state. Oxford: Berg.

Doty, William F.

1900 The Eskimo on St. Lawrence Island, Alaska. *In* Ninth annual report on introduction of domestic reindeer into Alaska, by Sheldon Jackson. Pp. 186–223. Washington DC: Government Printing Office.

Douglas, Arthur Siḷaigaq, Sr.

1976 Old way of traveling. Typescript no. H88-2A-10. Kotzebue: NANA Elders Council Collection.

1989 Personal oral communication to the author, Ambler AK, February 24, 1989.

Douglas, Tommy Paaniikaliaq

1986 Personal oral communication to the author, Kivalina AK, February 23.

Drucker, Philip

1967 The potlatch. *In* Tribal and peasant economies. George Dalton, ed. Pp. 481–493. Garden City NY: Natural History Press.

DuBois, Cora

1935 Wintu ethnography. *In* University of California publications in American archaeology and ethnology, vol. 36. Pp. 1–148. Berkeley: University of California Press.

Dumond, Don E.

2001 The archaeology of eastern Beringia: Some contrasts and connections. Arctic Anthropology 38(2):196–205.

2002 Words in closing. *In* Archaeology in the Bering Strait region: Research on two continents. Don E. Dumond and Richard L. Bland, eds. Pp. 345–357. University of Oregon Anthropological Paper 59.

Dunnigan, James, and Albert A. Nofi

1990 Dirty little secrets: Military information you're not supposed to know. New York: William Morrow.

Earle, Timothy

1987 Chiefdoms in archaeological and ethnohistorical perspective. Annual Review of Anthropology 16:279–308.

1991 The evolution of chiefdoms. *In* Chiefdoms: Power, economy, and ideology. Timothy Earle, ed. Pp. 1–15. Cambridge: Cambridge University Press.

[Edington, Arlo Channing, and Carmen Ballen Edington]

1930 Tundra: Romance and adventure on Alaskan trails, as told by former deputy United States Marshall Hansen to the Edingtons. New York: Century Co.

Ekolook, Etta Aġnigalauraq

1980 Traditional trade in the mid-Beaufort region. Interview by Leona Okakok, Barrow AK, September 26. Transcript in possession of the author, courtesy of David Libbey.

Ekowana, Roxy

1978 Interview by Ernest Kignak, Barrow AK, July 25, recorded by David Libbey. Transcript in possession of the author.

Elavgak, Freda Iḷġutchiaq

1978 Trade fair at Niglik. Interview by David Libbey, Barrow AK, January 19. Transcript in possession of the author, courtesy of David Libbey.

1980 Interview by Emily Wilson, Barrow [?] AK, October 2. Transcript in possession of the author, courtesy of David Libbey.

Eliyak

1931 The Oppownie (old) Eskimo and his customs, as told by Eliyak (Pechuk) and Oolooaharuk (Charley Wood) to Ira S. Purkeypile. Typescript appended to Bulletin of the N.W. District, United States Department of the Interior, Office of Indian Affairs, Alaska Division, October 28 [Kotzebue AK]. Laurel Bland Collection, box 30, folder 38. Archives, Alaska and Polar Regions Department, Rasmuson Library, University of Alaska Fairbanks.

Ember, Carol R.

1978 Myths about hunter-gatherers. Ethnology 17(4):439–448.

Ember, Carol R., and Melvin Ember

1992 Resource unpredictability, mistrust, and war. Journal of Conflict Resolution 36(2):242–262.

1994 War, socialization, and interpersonal violence: A cross-cultural study. Journal of Conflict Resolution 38(4):620–646.

1997 Violence in the ethnographic record: Results of cross-cultural research on war and aggression. *In* Troubled times: Violence and warfare in the past. Debra L. Martin and David W. Frayer, eds. Pp. 1–20. Langhorne PA: Gordon and Breach.

Engelhard, Michael

1992 Koyukon Athabaskan occupancy and land use on the upper Kobuk and Koyukuk Rivers. M.A. thesis, Department of Anthropology, University of Alaska Fairbanks.

Ericklook, Bessie Paniġłuk

1977 Nuiqsut area. Traditional land use inventory of the North Slope. Interview by

Frank Long Jr. Barrow AK: North Slope Borough, Commission on History, Culture and Language. Transcript in possession of the author.

Erman, [Georg] Adolf

1855 Der handel der Tschuktschen mit den Russen und den Inselbewhohnern des nordöstlichen oceans. Archiv für wissenschaftliche Kunde von Russland 14:202–211.

Esquimaux

1866–67 Newspaper published at Port Clarence, Russian America, and Plover Bay, Siberia. John J. Harrington, ed. San Francisco: Turnbull and Smith.

Evok, John Ivaak

1970 Personal oral communication to the author, Kotzebue AK, April 7.

Fair, Susan W.

1998 Documentation of toponyms and site information along the Saniq Coast and in Bering Land Bridge National Preserve. Final report to the Department of the Interior, National Park Service, and the Shishmaref IRA Village Council. Copy in possession of the author.

2001 The Inupiaq Eskimo messenger feast: Celebration, demise, and possibility. Journal of American Folklore 113(450):464–494.

Ferguson, R. Brian

1984 A reexamination of the causes of Northwest Coast warfare. *In* Warfare, culture, and environment. R. Brian Ferguson, ed. Pp. 267–328. Orlando FL: Academic Press.

Ferguson, R. Brian, and Neil L. Whitehead

1992 The violent edge of empire. *In* War in the tribal zone: Expanding states and indigenous warfare. Pp. 1–30. Santa Fe NM: School of American Research Press.

Fienup-Riordan, Ann

1984 Regional groupings on the Yukon–Kuskokwim delta. Études/Inuit/Studies 8(supplementary issue):63–93.

1990 Yupik warfare and the myth of the peaceful Eskimo. *In* Eskimo essays: Yupik lives and how we see them, by Ann Fienup-Riordan. Pp. 146–166. New Brunswick NJ: Rutgers University Press.

1994 Eskimo war and peace. *In* Anthropology of the North Pacific rim. William W. Fitzhugh and Valerie Chaussonnet, eds. Pp. 321–335. Washington DC: Smithsonian Institution Press.

Fisher, Raymond H.

1981 The voyage of Semen Dezhnev in 1648. Cambridge: Hakluyt Society.

Fitzhugh, William W., and Valerie Chaussonnet, eds.

1994 Anthropology of the North Pacific rim. Washington DC: Smithsonian Institution Press.

Fitzhugh, William W., and Aron Crowell, eds.

1988 Crossroads of continents: Cultures of Siberia and Alaska. Washington DC: Smithsonian Institution Press.

Fitzwater, Marlin

1995 Call the briefing! Reagan and Bush, Sam and Helen: A decade with presidents and the press. New York: Times Books.

Foote, Don Charles

1959–61 Field notes from northwestern Alaska. Don Charles Foote Collection, boxes 3 and 4, Archives, Alaska and Polar Regions Department, Rasmuson Library, University of Alaska Fairbanks.

1965a Exploration and resource utilization in northwestern Arctic Alaska before 1855. Ph.D. dissertation, Department of Geography, McGill University.

1965b Field notes from Shungnak, Alaska. Don Charles Foote Collection, box 8, folders 1 and 2. Archives, Alaska and Polar Regions Department, Rasmuson Library, University of Alaska Fairbanks.

1966a Human geographical studies in northwestern Alaska: The Point Hope and upper Kobuk River projects, 1965. Appendix C, Eskimo stories and songs of the upper Kobuk River. Manuscript. Copy in the Archives, Alaska and Polar Regions Department, Rasmuson Library, University of Alaska Fairbanks.

1966b Human geographical studies in northwest Arctic Alaska. The upper Kobuk River project: Final report. Department of Geography, McGill University.

Foote, Don Charles, and H. Anthony Williamson

1966 A human geographical study. *In* Environment of the Cape Thompson region, Alaska. Norman J. Wilimovsky and John N. Wolfe, eds. Pp. 1041–1111. Oak Ridge TN: United States Atomic Energy Commission.

Ford, James A.

1959 Eskimo prehistory in the vicinity of Point Barrow, Alaska. Anthropological Papers of the American Museum of Natural History 47(1):1–272.

Forsyth, James

1992 A history of the peoples of Siberia: Russia's north Asian colony, 1581–1990. Cambridge: Cambridge University Press.

Fortescue, Michael, Steven Jacobson, and Lawrence Kaplan

1994 Comparative Eskimo dictionary with Aleut cognates. Fairbanks: Alaska Native Language Center, University of Alaska Fairbanks.

Fortuine, Robert

1989 Chills and fever: Health and disease in the early history of Alaska. Fairbanks: University of Alaska Press.

Foster, Daniel Kunaŋnaaluk

1970 Personal oral communication to the author, Noorvik AK, March 31.

Foster, Johnnie Tuuyuq

1970 Personal oral communication to the author, Selawik AK, March 11.

Frank, Andre Gunder, and Barry K. Gills

1993 The 5,000-year world system. *In* The world system: Five hundred years or five thousand? Andre Gunder Frank and Barry K. Gills, eds. Pp. 3–55. London: Routledge.

2000 The five thousand year world system in theory and praxis. *In* World system history: The science of long-term change. Robert A. Denemark, Jonathan Friedman, Barry K. Gills, and George Modelski, eds. Pp. 3–23. London: Routledge.

Franklin, John

1828 Narrative of a second expedition to the shores of the polar sea in the years 1825, 1826, and 1827. London: J. Murray.

Franklin, U. M., E. Badone, R. Gotthardt, and B. Yorga

1981 An examination of prehistoric copper technology and copper sources in western Arctic and Subarctic North America. Archaeological Survey of Canada Paper no. 101. Ottawa: National Museum of Man.

Frankson, David Umigluk

1980 Personal oral communication to the author, Point Hope AK, October 16.

Friesen, T. Max

1995 "Periphery" as centre: Long-term patterns of intersocietal interaction on Herschel Island, northern Yukon Territory. Ph.D. dissertation, Department of Anthropology, University of Toronto.

Gal, Robert

1997 Personal written communication to the author, February 18.

Gallahorn, Lester Qaluraq

1969 Personal communication to the author, Kotzebue AK, December 29.

1970a Personal oral communication to the author, Kotzebue AK, January 8.

1970b Personal oral communication to the author, Kotzebue AK, April 21.

Gallahorn, Ralph Aŋnuyaq

1952 Napaaqtuġmiut (and Kotzebue?) inviting-in feast or "eagle-wolf dance." Charles Lucier private collection, consolidated field notes, North Kotzebue Sound, 1950–52. Copy in possession of the author.

Garber, Clark McKinley

1975 [1940] Stories and legends of the Bering Strait Eskimos. New York: AMS Press.

Geary, Lulu Tuttugruk

1976 Before modern medicine. *In* Timimun mamirrutit [Eskimo folk medicine], by Minnie Gray, Bertha Sheldon, Arthur Douglas Sr., Mamie Beaver, and Lulu Geary. Kotzebue: Mauneluk Cultural Heritage Program.

Geist, Otto W., and Froelich G. Rainey

1936 Archaeological excavations at Kukulik, St. Lawrence Island AK: Preliminary report. Miscellaneous Publications of the University of Alaska, vol. 2. Washington DC: Government Printing Office.

Gerlach, Craig, and Edwin S. Hall Jr.

1988 The later prehistory of northern Alaska: The view from Tukuto Lake. *In* The late prehistoric development of Alaska's Native people. Robert D. Shaw, Roger K. Harritt and Don E. Dumond, eds. Pp. 107–135. Aurora Monograph Series no. 4. Anchorage: Alaska Anthropological Association.

Gerlach, Craig, and Owen K. Mason

1992 Calibrated radiocarbon dates and cultural interaction in the western Arctic. Arctic Anthropology 29(1):54–81.

Giddings, James Louis, Jr.

1952 The Arctic Woodland Culture of the Kobuk River. University of Pennsylvania Museum Monographs.

1956 Forest Eskimos: An ethnographic sketch of Kobuk River people in the 1880s. University Museum Bulletin 20(2):1–55.

1961 Kobuk River people. College: University of Alaska Press.

1965 A long record of Eskimos and Indians at the forest edge. *In* Context and meaning in cultural anthropology. Melford E. Spiro, ed. Pp. 189–205. New York: Free Press.

Glover, Frank Kutvak

1970a Personal oral communication to the author, Kotzebue AK, February 16.

1970b Personal oral communication to the author, Kotzebue AK, April 6.

1970c Personal oral communication to the author, Kotzebue AK, January 9.

Goldenberg, L. A.

1983 Geodesist Gvozdev was here in 1732: Eighteenth century cartographic traditions in the representation of the discoveries in Bering Strait. W. Barr, trans. Polar Geography and Geology 7(3):214–223.

1990 Goldenberg's Gvozdev: The Russian discovery of Alaska in 1732. James L. Smith, ed. Anchorage: White Stone Press.

Golder, Frank Alfred

1968 [1922, 1925] Bering's voyages. 2 vols. New York: Octagon Books.

1971 [1914] Russian expansion on the Pacific, 1641–1859 . . . New York: Paragon Book Reprint.

Goldfrank, Walter L.

2000 Paradigm regained? The rules of Wallerstein's world-system method. Journal of World-Systems Research 6(2):150–195.

Gough, Barry M., ed.

1973 To the Pacific and Arctic with Beechey: The journal of Lieutenant George Peard of H.M.S. "Blossom," 1825–1828. London: Hakluyt Society.

Gray, Minnie Aliitchak

1976 Body healers. *In* Timimun mamirrutit [Eskimo folk medicine], by Minnie Gray, Bertha Sheldon, Arthur Douglas Sr., Mamie Beaver, and Lulu Geary. Kotzebue: Mauneluk Cultural Heritage Program.

Great Britain, Parliament, House of Commons

1850 Narrative of the proceedings of Captain Kellett, of Her Majesty's Ship "Herald," and Commander Moore and Lieutenant Pullen, of Her Majesty's Ship "Plover," through Behring's Straits, and towards the mouth of the Mackenzie River. In Sessional Papers. Accounts and Papers, vol. 35, no. 107, pp. 9–44.

1854a Orders to, and proceedings of, Commander Henry Trollope, Her Majesty's discovery ship "Rattlesnake." In Sessional Papers. Accounts and Papers, vol. 42, no. 1725, pt. 11, pp. 147–156.

1854b Report of the proceedings of Her Majesty's discovery ship "Plover," Commander Rochefort Maguire. In Sessional Papers. Accounts and Papers, vol. 42, no. 1725, pt. 13, pp. 160–186.

Green, Paul Aġniq

1969 Personal oral communication to the author, Kotzebue AK, December 18.

Greist, David Nasaġniq

1970 Personal oral communication to the author, Kotzebue AK, March 20.

Greist, Levi Qaġġauluk

1970 Personal oral communication to the author, Barrow AK, May 12.

Griffin, Dennis

1996 A culture in transition: A history of acculturation and settlement near the mouth of the Yukon River, Alaska. Arctic Anthropology 33(1):98–115.

Grinnell, Joseph

1901 Gold hunting in Alaska. Elizabeth Grinnell, ed. Chicago: David Cook Publishing.

Gryc, George

1958 Arctic slope. *In* Landscapes of Alaska: Their geologic evolution. Howel Williams, ed. Pp. 119–127. Berkeley: University of California Press.

Gubser, Nicholas J.

1965 The Nunamiut Eskimos: Hunters of caribou. New Haven CT: Yale University Press.

Hadley, John Aulaġiaq

1951 Elevated carved animal figure in front of Selawik house. Charles Lucier Collection, box 3, folder 10. JH-SEL-1, January 31. Archives, Alaska and Polar Regions Department, Rasmuson Library, University of Alaska Fairbanks.

1960 An Eskimo journey (1897). Grace N. Lucier, trans. Charles Lucier, ed. Privately printed. Copy in possession of the author.

Hadley, John Aulaġiaq, and Andrew Sannu Sunno

1951 Buckland Eskimo–Koyukuk Indian relations. Undated personal oral communication to Charles Lucier. Charles Lucier private collection, JH,AS-KAN-9.

Hall, Edwin S., Jr.

1970 The late prehistoric/early historic Eskimo of interior northern Alaska: An ethnoarcheological approach? Anthropological Papers of the University of Alaska 15(1):1–11.

1975a Kutchin Athapaskan/Nunamiut Eskimo conflict. Alaska Journal 5(4):248–252.

1975b The Eskimo storyteller: Folktales from Noatak, Alaska. Knoxville: University of Tennessee Press.

1978 Technological change in northern Alaska. *In* Archaeological essays in honor of Irving B. Rouse, by Robert C. Dunnell and Edwin S. Hall Jr. Pp. 209–229. The Hague: Mouton Publishers.

1984 Interior North Alaska Eskimo. *In* Arctic. David Damas, ed. Vol. 5, Handbook of North American Indians. William C. Sturtevant, gen. ed. Pp. 338–346. Washington DC: Smithsonian Institution Press.

Hall, Thomas D.

1999 World-systems and evolution: An appraisal. *In* World-systems theory in practice: Leadership, production, and exchange. P. Nick Kardulias, ed. Pp. 1–23. New York: Rowman and Littlefield.

Hannerz, Ulf

1989 Culture between center and periphery: Toward a macroanthropology. Ethnos 54:200–206.

Harris, Albert Yaiyuk

1952 War at Segoruitch: A spirit kills a hunter. Personal oral communication to Charles Lucier, Sheshalik AK, July 28. Charles Lucier Collection, box 3, folder 14. Archives, Alaska and Polar Regions Department, Rasmuson Library, University of Alaska Fairbanks.

Harrison, Alfred H.

1908 In search of a polar continent, 1905–07. London: E. Arnold.

Hawkes, Ernest William

1913 The "inviting-in" feast of the Alaskan Eskimo. Canada Department of Mines, Geological Survey Memoir 45, Anthropological Series no. 3. Ottawa: Government Printing Bureau.

1914 The dance festivals of the Alaskan Eskimo. University of Pennsylvania Anthropological Publications 6(2):3–41.

Hawley, Amos Apuġiña, Sr.

1964a Personal oral communication to the author, Kivalina AK, August 17.

1964b Personal oral communication to the author, Kivalina AK, August 27.

1965a Personal oral communication to the author, Kivalina AK, July 6.

1965b Personal oral communication to the author, Kivalina AK, August 7.

1965c Personal oral communication to the author, Kivalina AK, August 11.

1967 Personal oral communication to the author, Kivalina AK, November 24.

1973 Personal oral communication to the author, Kivalina AK, June 5.

1976a Personal oral communication to the author, Kivalina AK, April 10.

1976b Personal oral communication to the author, Kivalina AK, August 26.

1980 Personal oral communication to the author, Kivalina AK, October 12.

Hawley, Bob Tuvaaksraq, Sr.

1964a Personal oral communication to the author, Kivalina AK, August 31.

1964b Personal oral communication to the author, Kivalina AK, October 4.

1967 Personal oral communication to the author, Kivalina AK, November 22.

1970 Personal oral communication to the author, Kivalina AK, February 11.

1984 Personal oral communication to the author, Kivalina AK, May 5.

Hawley, Sarah Nigiaġvik

1964 Personal oral communication to D. M. Burch, Kivalina AK, October 9. Transcript in possession of the author.

Hayden, Brian

1995 Pathways to power: Principles for creating socioeconomic inequalities. *In* Foundations to social inequality. T. Douglas Price and Gary M. Feinman, eds. Pp. 15–86. New York: Plenum Press.

Headland, Thomas N., and Lawrence A. Reid

1989 Holocene foragers and interethnic trade: A critique of the myth of isolated independent hunter-gatherers. *In* Between bands and states. Susan A. Gregg, ed. Pp. 333–340. Carbondale: Southern Illinois University Press.

Healy, Michael A.

1887 Report of the cruise of the Steamer "Corwin." *In* Report of the cruise of the Revenue Steamer "Corwin" in the Arctic Ocean, 1885, by M. A. Healy. Pp. 5–20. Washington DC: Government Printing Office.

1889 Report of the cruise of the Revenue Steamer "Corwin" in the Arctic Ocean in the year 1884. Washington DC: Government Printing Office.

Hearne, Samuel

1795 A journey from Prince of Wales's fort in Hudson's Bay to the Northern Ocean . . . London: Strachan and Cadell.

Heinrich, Albert C.

1955 An outline of the kinship system of the Bering Straits Eskimos. M.A. thesis, Department of Education, University of Alaska.

1963 Eskimo type kinship and Eskimo kinship: An evaluation and a provisional model for presenting data pertaining to Inupiaq kinship systems. Ann Arbor MI: University Microfilms.

Heinz, H. J.

1972 Territoriality among the Bushmen in general and the !Ko in particular. Anthropos 67:405–416.

1979 The nexus complex among the !xo Bushmen of Botswana. Anthropos 74(3–4):465–480.

Helm, June

1965 Bilaterality in the socio-territorial organization of the Arctic drainage Dene. Ethnology 4(4):361–385.

1968 The nature of Dogrib socio-territorial groups. *In* Man the hunter. Richard B. Lee and Irven DeVore, eds. Pp. 118–125. Chicago: Aldine Publishing.

Hennigh, Lawrence

1972 You have to be a good lawyer to be an Eskimo. *In* Alliance in Eskimo society: Proceedings of the American Ethnological Society, 1971, supplement. Lee Guemple, ed. Pp. 89–109. Seattle: University of Washington Press.

1983 North Alaskan Eskimo alliance structure. Arctic Anthropology 20(1):23–32.

Hickey, Clifford G.

1979 The historic Beringian trade network: Its nature and origins. *In* Thule Eskimo culture: An anthropological retrospective. Allen P. McCartney, ed. Pp. 411–434. Ottawa: National Museum of Man. Archaeological Survey of Canada Paper no. 88.

Hobson, W. R.

1855 Journal of the proceedings of Mr. W. R. Hobson (mate) and party under his charge, whilst travelling from Port Clarence to Chamisso Island, and returning to the ship, between February 9 and March 27, 1854 (inclusive). *In* Great Britain,

Parliament, House of Commons. Sessional Papers. Accounts and Papers, 1854–55, vol. 35, no. 1898, pp. 884–898.

Holm, Gustav Frederik

1914 Ethnological sketch of the Angmagsalik Eskimo. *In* The Ammassalik Eskimo: Contributions to the ethnology of the East Greenland natives, pt. 1, no. 1. William C. Thalbitzer, ed. Meddelelser om Grønland 39:1–147.

Holmes, Richard

2001 Redcoat: The British soldier in the age of horse and musket. London: Harper Collins.

Hooper, Calvin Leighton

1881 Report of the cruise of the U.S. Revenue Steamer "Corwin" in the Arctic Ocean . . . 1880. Washington DC: Government Printing Office.

1884 Report of the cruise of the U.S. Revenue Steamer "Thomas Corwin" in the Arctic Ocean, 1881. Washington DC: Government Printing Office.

Hooper, William Hulme

1853 Ten months among the tents of the Tuski, with incidents of an Arctic boat expedition in search of Sir John Franklin . . . London: J. Murray.

Hopkins, David M.

1959 Cenozoic history of the Bering land bridge (Alaska). Science 129:1519–1528.

1996 The concept of Beringia. *In* American beginnings: The prehistory and palaeoecology of Beringia. Frederick Hadleigh West, ed. Pp. xvii–xxi. Chicago: University of Chicago Press.

Hopkins, David M., J. V. Matthews Jr., C. E. Schweger, and S. B. Young, eds.

1982 Paleoecology of Beringia. New York: Academic Press.

Hopkins, J. P., and David M. Hopkins

1958 Seward Peninsula. *In* Landscapes of Alaska: Their geologic evolution. Howel Williams, ed. Pp. 104–110. Berkeley: University of California Press.

Hopson, Flossie, trans. and ed.

1978 North Slope Elders Conference, May 22–26. Manuscript on file at North Slope Borough, Commission on History and Culture, Barrow AK.

Howard, Mary Akuliaq

1952 Napaktoktuok messenger feast, circa 1893. Personal oral communication to Charles Lucier, Sheshalik AK, July 2. Charles Lucier Collection, box 3, folder 14. Archives, Alaska and Polar Regions Department, Rasmuson Library, University of Alaska Fairbanks.

Howarth, Abraham Qitchuk

1969 Personal oral communication to the author, Kotzebue AK, December 18.

Howay, F. W.

1973 A list of trading vessels in the maritime fur trade, 1785–1825. Richard A. Pierce, ed. Kingston ON: Limestone Press.

Howitt, A. W., and L. Fison

1885 On the Deme and the horde. Journal of the Royal Anthropological Institute of Great Britain and Ireland 14:142–169.

Hrdlička, Aleš

1930 Anthropological survey of Alaska. In Bureau of American Ethnology 46th annual report, 1928–1929. Pp. 19–374. Washington DC: Government Printing Office.

Hudson's Bay Company Archives, Winnipeg MB

1840–41 Peels River post journal. B.157/a/1.

1847–48 Fort Yukon post journal. B.240/a/1.

1850–51 Fort Yukon post journal. B.240/a/4.

Hultén, Eric

1937 Outline of the history of Arctic and boreal biota during the Quaternary period. Stockholm: Bokforlagsaktiebolaget Thule.

Hunnicutt, Edna Iragauraq

1960a Personal oral communication to Don Foote, Noatak AK, February 9. Don Charles Foote Papers, box 3, folder 2. Archives, Alaska and Polar Regions Department, Rasmuson Library, University of Alaska Fairbanks.

1960b Notes from an interview by Don Foote, Noatak AK, February 12. Don Charles Foote Papers, box 3, folder 2. Archives, Alaska and Polar Regions Department, Rasmuson Library, University of Alaska Fairbanks.

1970 Personal oral communication to the author, Kivalina AK, February 10.

Hunnicutt, Elsie Siaksruk

1989 Personal oral communication to the author, Kiana AK, March 1.

Hunnicutt, Elwood Uyaan

1970 Personal oral communication the author, Kotzebue AK, March 26.

1983 Raid on Kotzebue. Typescript no. 83–31A. Kotzebue: NANA Elders Council Collection.

Hunnicutt, Susie Igauna

1970 Personal oral communication to the author, Kotzebue AK, January 6.

Huntington, Jimmy

1984 Trading on the edge of nowhere. Alaska Geographic 8(3):63.

Huntington, Sidney

1993 Shadows on the Koyukuk: An Alaskan native's life along the river, as told to Jim Reardon. Anchorage: Alaska Northwest Books.

Ingstad, Helge Marcus

1954 Nunamiut: Among Alaska's inland Eskimos. London: Allen and Unwin.

Irving, William

1950 Field notes from Anaktuvuk Pass and Killik River. Originals in possession of Edwin S. Hall Jr., Brockport NY.

1953 Letter to Robert F. Spencer, October 30. Original in possession of the author.

Isbister, A. K.

1845 Some account of Peel River, North America. Journal of the Royal Geographic Society 15:335–336.

Itaałuk, Arctic John

1980a Ulumiut and Indians. Interview by Grant Spearman and Louisa M. Riley,

Anaktuvuk Pass, November 20. Typescript, Ulumiut tape 12. Simon Paneak Memorial Museum, Anaktuvuk Pass AK.

1980b Ulumiut territories. Interview by Grant Spearman and Louisa M. Riley, Anaktuvuk Pass, November 18. Typescript, Ulumiut tape 7. Simon Paneak Memorial Museum, Anaktuvuk Pass AK.

1981a Nigliq activities. Interview by Grant Spearman and Louisa M. Riley, Anaktuvuk Pass, November 16. Typescript, Ulumiut tape 7. Simon Paneak Memorial Museum, Anaktuvuk Pass AK.

1981b Ulumiut series. Interview by Grant Spearman and Louisa M. Riley, Anaktuvuk Pass. Typescript, Ulumiut tape 4. Simon Paneak Memorial Museum, Anaktuvuk Pass AK.

1981c Niglik trading. Interview by Grant Spearman and Louisa M. Riley, Anaktuvuk Pass. Typescript, Ulumiut tape 5. Simon Paneak Memorial Museum, Anaktuvuk Pass AK.

1982a Dietrich River hunting area, graves, Indian contact, places of supernatural power, fishing holes. Interview by Grant Spearman and Louisa M. Riley, Anaktuvuk Pass, June 7. Typescript, Ulumiut tape 30. Simon Paneak Memorial Museum, Anaktuvuk Pass AK.

1982b Chandler Lake: Fight with Indians; Ulu valley and Itkillik River fishing areas; marmot colonies. Interview by Grant Spearman and Louisa M. Riley, Anaktuvuk Pass, June 8. Typescript, Ulumiut tape 32. Simon Paneak Memorial Museum, Anaktuvuk Pass AK.

1982c Niglik physical layout; games; subsistence and arrival of traders. Interview by Grant Spearman and Louisa M. Riley, Anaktuvuk Pass, November 26. Typescript, Ulumiut tape 56. Simon Paneak Memorial Museum, Anaktuvuk Pass AK.

1982d Niglik subsistence; games; food preparation and sharing. Interview by Grant Spearman and Louisa M. Riley, Anaktuvuk Pass, November 26. Typescript, Ulumiut tape 57. Simon Paneak Memorial Museum, Anaktuvuk Pass AK.

1982e Niglik trade and camp structure; karigi; dancing; women's roles. Interview by Grant Spearman and Louisa M. Riley, Anaktuvuk Pass, November 27. Typescript, Ulumiut tape 58. Simon Paneak Memorial Museum, Anaktuvuk Pass AK.

1982f Siqtukuich men's house; trade items and partnerships; games, and women's work. Interview by Grant Spearman and Louisa M. Riley, Anaktuvuk Pass, November 27. Typescript, Ulumiut tape 59. Simon Paneak Memorial Museum, Anaktuvuk Pass AK.

Ivashintsov, N. A.

1980 Russian round-the-world voyages, 1803–1849, with a summary of later voyages to 1867. Glynn R. Barratt, trans. Kingston ON: Limestone Press.

Ivie, Pamela, and Bill Schneider

1988 Land use values through time in the Wainwright area. North Slope Borough and the Anthropology and Historic Preservation Section, Cooperative Park Studies Unit, University of Alaska Fairbanks.

Jackson, Percy Uula

1989 Personal oral communication to the author, Kiana AK, March 1.

Jacobsen, Johan Adrian

1884 Captain Jacobsen's reise an der Nordwestküste Amerikas, 1881–1883. A. Woldt, ed. Leipzig: M. Spohr.

1977 Alaskan voyage, 1881–1883: An expedition to the Northwest Coast of America, from the German text of Adrian Woldt. Erna Gunther, trans. Chicago: University of Chicago Press.

Jans, Nick

1996 A place beyond: Finding a home in Arctic Alaska. Anchorage: Alaska Northwest Books.

Jarvis, D. H.

1899 Report of First Lieut. D. H. Jarvis, July 10, 1898. In United States Treasury Department, Report of the cruise of the U.S. Revenue Steamer "Bear" and the overland expedition for the relief of the whalers in the Arctic Ocean from November 27, 1897, to September 13, 1898. Pp. 29–103. Washington DC: Government Printing Office.

Jenness, Diamond

1924 Eskimo folk-lore: Myths and traditions from northern Alaska, the Mackenzie delta, and Coronation Gulf. In Report of the Canadian Arctic expedition, 1913–18, vol. 13, pt. A. Ottawa: King's Printer.

1928 Archaeological investigations in Bering Strait, 1926. In Annual report for 1926. Pp. 71–80. National Museum of Canada Bulletin no. 50.

1946 Material culture of the Copper Eskimo. Report of the Canadian Arctic expedition 1913–18. Southern party—1913–16, vol. 16. Ottawa: King's Printer.

Jenness, Stuart E.

1990 Diamond Jenness's archaeological investigations on Barter Island, Alaska. Polar Record 26(157):91–102.

Jenness, Stuart E., ed.

1991 Arctic odyssey: The diary of Diamond Jenness, ethnologist with the Canadian Arctic expedition, in northern Alaska and Canada, 1913–1916. Hull QC: Canadian Museum of Civilization.

Jensen, Charlie Saġġaaluraq

1970a Personal oral communication to the author, Kotzebue AK, February 19.

1970b Personal oral communication to the author, Kotzebue AK, March 5.

1970c Personal oral communication to the author, Kotzebue AK, April 9.

1970d Personal oral communication to the author, Kotzebue AK, May 20.

1970e Personal oral communication to the author, Kotzebue AK, May 22.

Jensen, Charlie Saġġaaluraq, and Lucy Ayagiaq Jensen

1980 Personal oral communication to the author, Kotzebue AK, October 8.

Jeske, Robert J.

1999 World-systems theory, core–periphery interactions, and elite economic exchange in Mississippian societies. In World-systems theory in practice: Leadership, production, and exchange. P. Nick Kardulias, ed. Pp. 203–221. Lanham MD: Rowman and Littlefield.

Joe, Martha

1987 Martha Joe, Nulato: A biography. Interview by Yvonne Yarber and Curt Madison. Fairbanks: Spirit Mountain Press. Yukon–Koyukuk School District of Alaska Biography Series.

Johnshoy, J. Walter

1944 Apauruk in Alaska: Social pioneering among the Eskimos. Philadelphia: Dorrance and Company.

Johnson, Allen W., and Timothy Earle

1987 The evolution of human societies: From foraging group to agrarian state. Stanford CA: Stanford University Press.

Johnson, Sam, comp.

n.d. Reports concerning various roads and trails, 1904–1957. In Roads and trails reports collection 1904–1957. Archives, Alaska and Polar Regions Department, Rasmuson Library, University of Alaska Fairbanks.

Jones, Eliza Neełteloyeenełno

1991 Personal oral communication to the author, Fairbanks AK, March 12.

Jones, Jack

1984 Personal oral communication to the author, Noatak AK, May 2.

Kakaruk, John A.

1983 Drumbeat of time. Charles Lucier, ed. Manuscript copy in possession of the author.

Kalkreuth, Wolfgang, and Patricia D. Sutherland

1998 The archaeology and petrology of coal artifacts from a Thule settlement on Axel Heiberg Island, Arctic Canada. Arctic 51(4):345–349.

Kaplan, Lawrence D.

1984 Inupiaq and the schools: A handbook for teachers. Juneau: Alaska Department of Education, Bilingual/Bicultural Education Programs.

1996 Personal written communication to the author, June 11.

1997 Personal written communication to the author, September 10.

2001 Iñupiaq identity and Iñupiaq language: Does one entail the other? Études/Inuit/Studies 25(1–2):249–257.

Kaplan, Lawrence D., comp. and ed.

1988 Ugiuvangmiut quliapyuit [King Island tales]: Eskimo history and legends from Bering Strait. Margaret Seeganna and Gertrude Analoak, trans. Fairbanks: University of Alaska, Alaska Native Language Center.

Kashevarov, Aleksandr F.

1994 Early information about conditions and activities at Redoubt Sv. Mikhail. In Notes on Russian America, parts 2–5: Kad'iak, Unalashka, Atkha, the Pribylovs, by Kiril T. Khlebnikov. Introduction and commentaries by R. G. Liapunova and S. G. Fedorova, comps. Marina Ramsay, trans. Richard Pierce, ed. Pp. 328–342. Kingston ON: Limestone Press.

Kaufman, Daniel

2002 Redating the social revolution: The case for the Middle Paleolithic. Journal of Anthropological Research 58(4):477–492.

Keats, Della Puyuk

1970a Personal oral communication to the author, Kotzebue AK, January 2.

1970b Personal oral communication to the author, Kotzebue AK, January 7.

1970c Personal oral communication to the author, Kotzebue AK, January 14.

1970d Personal oral communication to the author, Kotzebue AK, April 8.

1970e Personal oral communication to the author, Kotzebue AK, April 22.

1970f Personal oral communication to the author, Kotzebue AK, May 6.

Keeley, Lawrence

1996 War before civilization: The myth of the peaceful savage. Oxford: Oxford University Press.

Kelly, Robert L.

1995 The foraging spectrum: Diversity in hunter-gatherer lifeways. Washington DC: Smithsonian Institution Press.

Kennicott, Robert

1862–63 Tribes of the Kutchin Indians of lower Mackenzie and Youkon region. Handwritten manuscript, no. 203-b. National Anthropological Archives, National Museum of Natural History, Smithsonian Institution, Washington DC.

Kialook, Frank Qitchaun

1970 Personal oral communication to the author, Deering AK, April 15.

Kiana, Martha

1969 Personal oral communication to the author, Kotzebue AK, December 31.

Killigivuk, Jimmy Asatchaq

1960a Notes from an interview by Don Foote, Point Hope AK, January 18. Don Charles Foote Papers, box 5, folder 6. Archives, Alaska and Polar Regions Department, Rasmuson Library, University of Alaska Fairbanks.

1960b Notes from an interview by Don Foote, Point Hope AK, January 19. Don Charles Foote Papers, box 5, folder 6. Archives, Alaska and Polar Regions Department, Rasmuson Library, University of Alaska Fairbanks.

1961 Notes from an interview by Don Foote, Point Hope AK, January 19. Don Charles Foote Papers, box 5, folder 6. Archives, Alaska and Polar Regions Department, Rasmuson Library, University of Alaska Fairbanks.

Kimber, Richard G.

1988 Smallpox in central Australia: Evidence for epidemics and postulations about the impact. Australian Archeology 27:63–68.

1990 Hunter-gatherer demography: The recent past in central Australia. *In* Hunter-gatherer demography: Past and present. Betty Meehan and Neville White, eds. Pp. 160–170. Oceania Monograph 39. Sydney: University of Sydney.

Kingston, Deanna

1996 Ugiuvangmiut-middle-men in the Bering Strait trade network. Manuscript. Copy in possession of the author.

1999 Returning: Twentieth century performances of the King Island wolf dance. Ann Arbor MI: UMI Dissertation Services.

2000 Siberian songs and Siberian kin: Indirect assertions of King Islander dominance in the Bering Strait region. Arctic Anthropology 37(2):38–51.

Kirchner, Scott

1983 Andrew Skin, Sr.: Eskimo doctor. Alaska Medicine 24(6):101–105.

Kisautaq-Leona Okakok and Gary Kean

1981 Puiguitkaat: The 1978 elders conference. Kisautaq-Leona Okakok, trans. Barrow AK: North Slope Borough, Commission on History and Culture.

Kiyutelluk, Morris

1976 Statements of significance for 14(h)(1) historic and cemetery sites in the Shishmaref area. On file at the Bering Straits Native Corporation, Shishmaref AK.

Kolenda, Pauline M.

1968 Religion, caste, and family structure: A comparative study of the Indian "joint" family. *In* Structure and change in Indian society. Milton Singer and Bernard S. Cohn, eds. Pp. 339–396. New York: Wenner-Gren Foundation for Anthropological Research.

Kotzebue, Otto von

1967 [1821] A voyage of discovery into the South Sea and Beering's Straits, for the purpose of exploring a north-east passage, undertaken in the years 1815–18. 3 vols. Amsterdam NY: N. Israel.

Koutsky, Kathryn

1976 Handwritten notes from Wales AK, June 4. Kathryn Koutsky Cohen Papers, box 1, folder 10. Archives, Alaska and Polar Regions Department, Rasmuson Library, University of Alaska Fairbanks.

1981a Early days on Norton Sound and Bering Strait: An overview of historic sites in the BSNC region. Vol. 1, The Shishmaref area. Occasional Paper no. 29. Anthropology and Historic Preservation Section, Cooperative Park Studies Unit, University of Alaska Fairbanks.

1981b Early days on Norton Sound and Bering Strait: An overview of historic sites in the BSNC region. Vol. 2, The Wales area. Occasional Paper no. 29. Anthropology and Historic Preservation Section, Cooperative Park Studies Unit, University of Alaska Fairbanks.

1981c Early days on Norton Sound and Bering Strait: An overview of historic sites in the BSNC region. Vol. 3, The Port Clarence and Kauwerak areas. Occasional Paper no. 29. Anthropology and Historic Preservation Section, Cooperative Park Studies Unit, University of Alaska Fairbanks.

1981d Early days on Norton Sound and Bering Strait: An overview of historic sites in the BSNC region. Vol. 4, The Nome, Fish River and Golovin areas. Occasional Paper no. 29. Anthropology and Historic Preservation Section, Cooperative Park Studies Unit, University of Alaska Fairbanks.

1981e Early days on Norton Sound and Bering Strait: An overview of historic sites in the BSNC region. Vol. 5, The Koyuk area. Occasional Paper no. 29. Anthropology and Historic Preservation Section, Cooperative Park Studies Unit, University of Alaska Fairbanks.

1981f Early days on Norton Sound and Bering Strait: An overview of historic sites in the BSNC region. Vol. 6, The Shaktoolik area. Occasional Paper no. 29. Anthropology and Historic Preservation Section, Cooperative Park Studies Unit, University of Alaska Fairbanks.

1982a Early days on Norton Sound and Bering Strait: An overview of historic sites in the BSNC region. Vol. 7, The Unalakleet area. Occasional Paper no. 29. Anthropology and Historic Preservation Section, Cooperative Park Studies Unit, University of Alaska Fairbanks.

1982b Early days on Norton Sound and Bering Strait: An overview of historic sites in the BSNC region. Vol. 8, The St. Michael and Stebbens area. Occasional Paper no. 29. Anthropology and Historic Preservation Section, Cooperative Park Studies Unit, University of Alaska Fairbanks.

Kowalewski, Stephen A.

1996 Clout, corn, copper, core–periphery, culture area. *In* Pre-Columbian world systems. Peter N. Peregrine and Gary M. Feinman, eds. Pp. 27–37. Madison WI: Prehistory Press.

Kowunna, Walter Sigliuna

1970 Personal oral communication to the author, Kotzebue AK, March 24.

1980 Personal oral communication to the author, Kotzebue AK, October 9.

Koyama, Shuzo, and David Hurst Thomas, eds.

1981 Affluent foragers: Pacific coasts east and west. Senri Ethnological Studies 9, Osaka.

Krause, Aurel, and Arthur Krause

1882 Die expedition der Bremer geographische Gesellschaft nach der Tschuktschen-Halbinsel: Sommer 1881. I. Deutsche geographische Blätter 1(5):1–35.

Krauss, Michael E.

1993 The earliest recorded Alaskan Eskimo word. Manuscript on file at the Alaska Native Language Center, University of Alaska Fairbanks.

Krech, Shepard, III

1978 On the aboriginal population of the Kutchin. Arctic Anthropology 15(1):89–104.

Krupnik, Igor I.

1983 Early settlements and the demographic history of Asian Eskimos of southeastern Chukotka (including St. Lawrence Island). *In* Cultures of the Bering Sea region: Papers from an international symposium. Henry N. Michael and James W. VanStone, eds. Pp. 84–101. New York: International Research and Exchanges Board for the American Council of Learned Societies and the Academy of Sciences of the USSR.

1993 Arctic adaptations: Native whalers and reindeer herders of northern Russia. Expanded English ed. Marcia Levenson, trans. and ed. Hanover NH: University Press of New England.

1994 "Siberians" in Alaska: The Siberian Eskimo contribution to Alaskan population recoveries, 1880–1940. Études/Inuit/Studies 18(1–2):49–80.

1996a Personal oral communication to the author, Washington DC, July 17.

1996b Personal oral communication to the author, Washington DC, October 10.

1997 Personal oral communication to the author, North Bethesda MD, January 17.

Krupnik, Igor, and Mikhail Chlenov

n.d. Survival in contact: Asiatic Eskimo transitions, 1900–1990. Manuscript on file at the Arctic Studies Center, Smithsonian Institution, Washington DC.

1982 Personal oral communications to the author, Moscow, February 27, March 1, and March 8.

1997 Personal oral communication to the author, North Bethesda MD, January 17.

Kunuknana, Samuel

1980 [Mid–Beaufort Sea area]. *In* Qiñiqtuagaksrat utuqqanaaat Iñuuniaġniŋisiqun: The traditional land use inventory for the mid–Beaufort Sea, vol. 1, by the North Slope Borough, Commission on History and Culture. Pp. 153–159. Barrow AK: North Slope Borough, Commission on History and Culture.

Kunuknana, Sarah

1977 Interview with David Libbey, Colville River delta, August 17. Transcript in possession of the author.

Kunz, Michael L.

1977 Athapaskan/Eskimo interfaces in the central Brooks Range, Alaska. *In* Problems in the prehistory of the North American Subarctic: The Athapaskan question. J. W. Helmer, S. Van Dyke, and F. J. Kense, eds. Pp. 135–144. Calgary: University of Calgary Archaeological Association.

Kunz, Michael L., comp.

1991 Cultural resource survey and inventory: Gates of the Arctic National Park and Preserve, Alaska. Research/Resources Management Report AR-18. Anchorage: National Park Service–Alaska Region.

Kunz, Michael L., and Richard E. Reanier

1994 Paleoindians in Beringia: Evidence from Arctic Alaska. Science 263(5,147): 660–662.

Kurtz, James

1984 The bow and arrow wars; warfare between the Yukon and coastal Eskimos: The Magagmyut, warriors of the coast. Manuscript on file at the United States Bureau of Indian Affairs, ANCSA Office, Anchorage.

Lantis, Margaret

1947 Alaskan Eskimo ceremonialism. Seattle: University of Washington Press.

Lantzeff, George W., and Richard A. Pierce

1973 Eastward to empire: Exploration and conquest on the Russian open frontier, to 1750. Montreal: McGill–Queen's University Press.

Lapena, Frank R.

1978 Wintu. *In* California. Robert F. Heizer, ed. Vol. 8, Handbook of North American Indians. William C. Sturtevant, gen. ed. Pp. 324–340. Washington DC: Smithsonian Institution Press.

Larsen, Helge

1958 Material culture of the Nunamiut and its relation to other forms of Eskimo culture in northern Alaska: Proceedings of the 32nd International Congress of Americanists, 1956. Pp. 574–582. Copenhagen.

1982 Eskimo and Indian means of transport, their relationships and distribution. *In* The hunters: Their culture and way of life. Åke Hultkrantz and Ørnulf Vorren, eds. Pp. 113–118. Troms• Museum skrifter 18. Troms•: Universitetsforlaget.

Larsen, Helge, and Froelich Rainey

1948 Ipiutak and the Arctic whale hunting culture. Anthropological Papers of the American Museum of Natural History 42:44–50.

Leacock, Eleanor

1969 The Montagnais–Naskapi band. *In* Contributions to anthropology: Band societies. David Damas, ed. Pp. 1–17. National Museums of Canada Bulletin 228, Ottawa.

Lee, Charlie Qiñuġana

1970 Personal oral communication to the author, Shungnak AK, January 29.

Lee, Richard B.

1972a The !Kung Bushmen of Botswana. *In* Hunters and gatherers today. Marco G. Bicchieri, ed. Pp. 327–368. New York: Holt, Rinehart and Winston.

1972b !Kung spatial organization: An ecological and historical perspective. *In* Kalahari hunter-gatherers. Richard B. Lee and Irven DeVore, eds. Pp. 73–97. Cambridge MA: Harvard University Press.

1972c The !Kung Bushmen of Botswana. *In* Hunters and gatherers today: A socio-economic study of eleven such cultures in the twentieth century. Marco G. Bicchieri, ed. Pp. 327–368. New York: Holt, Rinehart and Winston.

Lee, Richard B., A. Pilling, and L. R. Hiatt

1968 Territorial boundaries. *In* Man the hunter. Richard B. Lee and Irven DeVore, eds. Pp. 156–157. Chicago: Aldine Publishing.

Lenski, Gerhard, Jean Lenski, and Patrick Nolan

1991 Human societies: An introduction to macrosociology, 6th ed. New York: McGraw-Hill.

Lesser, Alexander

1961 Social fields and the evolution of society. Southwestern Journal of Anthropology 17(1):40–48.

Levin, Maksim G., and Dorian A. Sergeyev

1964 The penetration of iron into the Arctic: The first find of an iron implement in a site of the Old Bering Sea culture. *In* The archaeology and geomorphology of northern Asia: Selected works. Henry N. Michael, ed. Pp. 319–326. Anthropology of the North, Translations from Russian Sources no. 5. Toronto: University of Toronto Press for the Arctic Institute of North America.

Levy, Marion J., Jr.

1952 The structure of society. Princeton NJ: Princeton University Press.

1966 Modernization and the structure of societies: A setting for international affairs. Princeton NJ: Princeton University Press.

Lewis, Martin W.

1991 Elusive societies: A regional-cartographic approach to the study of human relatedness. Annals of the Association of American Geographers 81(4):605–626.

Libbey, David

2000 Personal oral communication to the author, Anchorage, March 24.

Loyens, William J.

1966 The changing culture of the Nulato Koyukon Indians. Ann Arbor MI: University Microfilms.

Lucier, Charles V.

n.d.a Buckland field notes. Charles Lucier Collection, box 3, folder 4. Archives, Alaska and Polar Regions Department, Rasmuson Library, University of Alaska Fairbanks.

n.d.b Messenger feast, Napaktomiut. Charles Lucier Collection, box 3, folder 14. Archives, Alaska and Polar Regions Department, Rasmuson Library, University of Alaska Fairbanks.

n.d.c Buckland messenger feast—miscellaneous. Charles Lucier Collection, box 3, folder 4. Archives, Alaska and Polar Regions Department, Rasmuson Library, University of Alaska Fairbanks.

1952 Nuataaġmiut messenger feast: Consolidated notes from interviews with Jenny Aluniq Mitchell and Mark Misigaq Mitchell. Charles Lucier private collection. Transcript in possession of the author.

1954 Buckland Eskimo myths. Anthropological Papers of the University of Alaska 2(2):215–233.

1958 Noatagmiut Eskimo myths. Anthropological Papers of the University of Alaska 6(2):89–117.

1987 Personal written communication to the author, October 21.

1995a Personal written communication to the author, November 10.

1995b Personal written communication to the author, November 11.

1997 Detailed critique of a draft of "The cultural and natural heritage of northwest Alaska." Vol. 7, International affairs. Copy in possession of the author.

Lucier, Charles V., James W. VanStone, and Della Keats

1971 Medical practices and human anatomical knowledge among the Noatak Eskimos. Ethnology 10(3):251–264.

Luther, Carl Avigauraq

1960a Notes from an interview by Don Foote, Noatak AK, February 16. Don Charles Foote Papers, box 3, folder 1. Archives, Alaska and Polar Regions Department, Rasmuson Library, University of Alaska Fairbanks.

1960b Notes from an interview by Don Charles Foote, Noatak AK, February 18. Don Charles Foote Papers, box 3, folder 2. Archives, Alaska and Polar Regions Department, Rasmuson Library, University of Alaska Fairbanks.

MacDonald, George F.

1984 The epic of Nekt. *In* The Tsmimshian: Images of the past, view for the present. Margaret Sequin, ed. Pp. 65–81. Vancouver: University of British Columbia Press.

MacLaren, Ian S.

1991 Samuel Hearne's accounts of the massacre at Bloody Fall, 17 July 1771. ARIEL: Review of International English Literature 22(1):25–51.

Maguire, Rochefort

1857 Narrative of Captain Maguire, wintering at Point Barrow. In The discovery of the north-west passage by H.M.S. "Investigator" . . . appendix 2, pp. 409–463, 2nd ed. Sherard Osborn, ed. London: Longman, Brown, Green, Longmans and Roberts.

Malaurie, Jean

1974 Raids et esclavage dan les sociétés autochtones du Détroit de Behring. Inter-Nord 13–14:129–155.

Malinowski, Bronislaw

1941 An anthropological analysis of war. American Journal of Sociology 46(4): 521–550.

Maschner, Herbert D. G.

1997 The evolution of Northwest Coast warfare. In Troubled times: Violence and warfare in the past. D. Martin and D. Frayer, eds. Pp. 267–302. Langhorne PA: Gordon and Breach.

2000 Catastrophic change and regional interaction: The southern Bering Sea in a dynamic world system. In Identities and cultural contacts in the Arctic: Proceedings from a Conference at the Danish National Museum, Copenhagen, November 30 to December 2, 1999. Martin Appelt, Joel Berglund, and Hans Christian Gull•v, eds. Pp. 252–265. Publication no. 8. Copenhagen: Danish Polar Center.

Maschner, Herbert D. G., and Katherine L. Reedy-Maschner

1998 Raid, retreat, defend (repeat): The archaeology and ethnohistory of warfare on the North Pacific rim. Journal of Anthropological Archaeology 17(1):19–51.

Mason, Owen K.

1998 The contest between the Ipiutak, old Bering Sea, and Birnirk polities and the origin of whaling during the first millennium A.D. along Bering Strait. Journal of Anthropological Archaeology 17:240–325.

2000 Archaeological Rorschach in delineating Ipiutak, Punuk and Birnirk in NW Alaska: Masters, slaves or partners in trade? In Identities and cultural contacts in the Arctic: Proceedings from a Conference at the Danish National Museum, Copenhagen, November 30 to December 2, 1999. Martin Appelt, Joel Berglund, and Hans Christian Gull•v, eds. Pp. 229–251. Publication no. 8. Copenhagen: Danish Polar Center.

2003 Uivvaq heritage project. Field season 2002. Final report. Report to Aqlaq/CONAM, JV no. 2, in fulfillment of contract no. 2103-004, Cape Lisburne Clean Sweep Remedial Action. Anchorage: Geoarch Alaska.

Masterson, James R., and Helen Brower

1948 Bering's successors, 1745–1780: Contributions of Peter Simon Pallas to the history of Russian exploration toward Alaska. Seattle: University of Washington Press.

McCarthy, F. D.

1939a "Trade" in Aboriginal Australia, and "trade" relationships with Torres Strait, New Guinea and Malaya. Oceania 9(4):405–438.

1939b "Trade" in Aboriginal Australia, and "trade" relationships with Torres Strait, New Guinea and Malaya. Oceania 10(1):80–104.

1939c "Trade" in Aboriginal Australia, and "trade" relationships with Torres Strait, New Guinea and Malaya. Oceania 10(2):171–195.

McCartney, Allen P.

1988 Late prehistoric metal use in the New World Arctic. *In* The late prehistoric development of Alaska's Native people. Robert D. Shaw, Roger K. Harritt, and Don E. Dumond, eds. Pp. 57–79. Aurora Monograph Series 4. Anchorage: Alaska Anthropological Association.

McCartney, Allen P., and D. J. Mack

1973 Iron utilization by Thule Eskimos of central Canada. American Antiquity 38(3):328–339.

McClellan, Albert Nalikkałuk

1970 Personal oral communication to the author, Kotzebue AK, April 10.

1987 Personal oral communication to the author, Kotzebue AK, February 28.

McDonald, Robert

1862–1913 The journals of Reverend Robert McDonald. MSS 0195, 0196. Transcripts on file at the Yukon Archives, Whitehorse YT.

McElwaine, Eugene

1901 The truth about Alaska, the golden land of the midnight sun. Chicago: Regan Printing House.

McFadyen, Annette

1995 Who lived in this house? An ethnoarchaeologic study of Koyukuk River semisubterranean house construction, contents, and disposition of faunal remains. Ann Arbor MI: UMI Dissertation Services.

McGhee, Robert

1974 Beluga hunters: An archaeological reconstruction of the history and culture of the Mackenzie Delta Kittegaryumiut. St. John's: Memorial University of Newfoundland.

1976 West Alaskan influences in Mackenzie Eskimo culture. *In* Contributions to anthropology: The interior peoples of northern Alaska. Edwin S. Hall Jr., ed. Pp. 177–192. Archaeological Survey of Canada Paper no. 49. Ottawa: National Museum of Man.

McKennan, Robert A.

1933 Ethnographic field notes: Chandalar River region legends about war and shamans. McKennan Collection Series 2. Archives, Alaska and Polar Regions Department, Rasmuson Library, University of Alaska Fairbanks.

1965 The Chandalar Kutchin. Technical Paper no. 17. Montreal: Arctic Institute of North America.

1981 Tanana. *In* Subarctic. June Helm, ed. Vol. 6, Handbook of North American

Indians. William C. Sturtevant, gen. ed. Pp. 562–581. Washington DC: Smithsonian Institution Press.

McLenegan, S. B.

1887 Exploration of the Noatak River, Alaska. *In* Report of the cruise of the Revenue Marine Steamer "Corwin" in the Arctic Ocean, 1885, by M. A. Healy. Pp. 53–80. Washington DC: Government Printing Office.

McNeil, William H.

1993 Foreword. *In* The world system: Five hundred years or five thousand? Andre Gunder Frank and Barry K. Gills, eds. Pp. vii–xiii. London: Routledge.

Mendenhall, Hannah, Ruthie Sampson, and Edward Tennant, eds.

1989 Lore of the Iñupiat: The elders speak, vol. 1. Kotzebue: Northwest Arctic Borough School District.

Mendenhall, Walter C.

1901 A reconnaissance in the Norton Bay region, Alaska, in 1900. *In* Reconnaissances in the Cape Nome and Norton Bay regions, Alaska, 1900, by A. H. Brooks et al. Pp. 181–218. Washington DC: Government Printing Office.

1902 Reconnaissance from Fort Hamelin to Kotzebue Sound, Alaska, by way of Dall, Kanuti and Kowak Rivers. United States Geological Survey. Professional Paper no. 10.

Merck, Carl Heinrich

1980 Siberia and northwestern America 1788–1792: The journal of Carl Heinrich Merck, naturalist with the Russian scientific expedition led by Captains Joseph Billings and Gavril Sarychev. Richard A. Pierce, ed. Kingston ON: Limestone Press.

Meredith, Robyn

1999 Dollar makes Canada a land of the spree. New York Times, August 1, 1999, sec. 3:1, 11.

Michael, Henry N., ed.

1967 Lieutenant Zagoskin's travels in Russian America, 1842–1844. Anthropology of the North, Translations from Russian Sources no. 7. Toronto: University of Toronto Press for the Arctic Institute of North America.

Miertsching, Johann August

1967 Frozen ships: The Arctic diary of Johann Miertsching, 1850–1854. L. H. Neatby, trans. Toronto: Macmillan of Canada.

Miller, Polly G.

1994 Early contact glass trade beads in Alaska. Altamonte Springs FL: Bead Society of Central Florida.

Mills, Ethel Niiqsik

1960 Notes from an interview by Don Charles Foote, Noatak AK, February 17. Don Charles Foote Papers, box 3, folder 1. Archives, Alaska and Polar Regions Department, Rasmuson Library, University of Alaska Fairbanks.

Mishler, Craig, ed.

1995 Neerihiinjìk: We traveled from place to place. Johnny Sarah Hàa Googwandak: The Gwich'in stories of Johnny and Sarah Frank. Fairbanks: Alaska Native Language Center.

Mitchell, Donald H.

1983a Seasonal settlements, village aggregations, and political autonomy on the central Northwest Coast. *In* The development of political organization in Native North America. Elizabeth Tooker, ed. Pp. 97–107. Washington DC: American Ethnological Society.

1983b Tribes and chiefdoms of the Northwest Coast: The Tsimshian case. *In* The evolution of maritime cultures on the Northeast and Northwest Coasts of America. Ronald J. Nash, ed. Pp. 57–63. Burnaby BC: Simon Fraser University.

1984 Predatory warfare, social status, and the North Pacific slave trade. Ethnology 23(1):38–48.

Mitchell, Donald, and Leland Donald

1988 Archaeology and the study of Northwest Coast economies. *In* Prehistoric economies of the Pacific Northwest Coast. Barry L. Isaac, ed. Pp. 293–351. Greenwich CT: JAI Press.

2001 Sharing resources on the North Pacific coast of North America: The case of the eulachon fishery. Anthropologica 43:19–35.

Mitchell, Thomas Uqsruġaaluk

1969 Personal oral communication to the author, Kotzebue AK, December 20.

1970 Personal oral communication to the author, Kotzebue AK, May 5.

Monroe, Paul Palaŋan

1960 Notes from an interview by Don Charles Foote, Noatak AK, February 18. Don Charles Foote Papers, box 3, folder 1. Archives, Alaska and Polar Regions Department, Rasmuson Library, University of Alaska Fairbanks.

Morlan, Richard E.

1997 Beringia. Beringian Research Notes no. 9. Whitehorse YT: Yukon Beringia Interpretive Center.

Morris, Thomas Aniqsuaq

1970 Personal oral communication to the author, Deering AK, April 16.

Morrison, David

1987 Thule and historic copper use in the Copper Inuit area. American Antiquity 52(1):3–12.

1991a The Copper Inuit soapstone trade. Arctic 44(3):239–246.

1991b The Diamond Jenness collections from Bering Strait. Archaeological Survey of Canada, Mercury Series Paper no. 144. Hull QC: Canadian Museum of Civilization.

Morry, Billy

n.d. Move from mountains to coast; life on the coast, and trade at Nigliq. Interview with David Libbey. Transcript in possession of the author.

Moss, Madonna L.

1992 Relationships between maritime cultures of southern Alaska: Rethinking culture area boundaries. Arctic Anthropology 29(2):5–17.

Moss, Madonna L., and Jon M. Erlandson

1992 Forts, refuge rocks, and defensive sites: The antiquity of warfare along the North Pacific coast of North America. Arctic Anthropology 29(2):73–90.

Murdoch, John

1892 Ethnological results of the Point Barrow expedition. Ninth Annual Report of the Bureau of Ethnology, 1887–88. Washington DC: Government Printing Office.

1988 Ethnological results of the Point Barrow expedition. Classics of Anthropology Series Reprint no. 6. Washington DC: Smithsonian Institution Press.

Murray, Alexander Hunter

1910 Journal of the Yukon, 1847–48. I. J. Burpee, ed. Publications of the Canadian Archives no. 4, Ottawa.

NANA Cultural Heritage Project

1975a Cemetery sites and historical places, Ambler: Draft report. Copy in possession of the author.

1975b Cemetery sites and historical places, Buckland: Draft report. Copy in possession of the author.

1975c Cemetery sites and historical places, Deering: Draft report. Copy in possession of the author.

1975d Cemetery sites and historical places, Selawik: Draft report. Copy in possession of the author.

Nashanik, Henry Nasaġniq

1980 Trade and life out east. Personal oral communication to Emily Wilson and Leona Okakok, Barrow AK, October 3. Transcript in possession of the author, courtesy of David Libbey.

Nasugluk

1940 Nasugluk and Nasugruk in the form of a duet. Froelich G. Rainey Collection. Archives, Alaska and Polar Regions Department, Rasmuson Library, University of Alaska Fairbanks.

National Film Board of Canada

1976 Between friends/Entre amis. Toronto: McClelland and Stewart.

Nayokpuk, Walter

1999 Personal oral communication to the author, Shishmaref AK, March 4.

Neakok, Arthur Taqtu, and Dorcas Neakok

1984 Coastal sites in the Point Lay area. Interview by David Libbey and Edwin S. Hall Jr., Point Lay AK, July 12, tape 3. Transcript in possession of the author.

Neakok, Arthur Taqtu, and Ida Suksran Numnik

1978 Field trip to Nuvuk. Interview by David Libbey at Niksiuraq AK. August 11. Transcript in possession of the author, courtesy of David Libbey.

Neitzel, Jill E.

2000 What is a regional system? Issues of scale and interaction in the prehistoric Southwest. *In* The archaeology of regional interaction: Religion, warfare, and exchange across the American Southwest and beyond: Proceedings of the 1996 Southwest Symposium. Michelle Hegmon, ed. Pp. 25–40. Boulder: University Press of Colorado.

Nelson, Edward William

1877–81 Alaska journals, April 12, 1877, to October 20, 1881. Archives of the United States National Museum, Smithsonian Institution.

1899 The Eskimo about Bering Strait. *In* Eighteenth annual report of the Bureau of American Ethnology, 1896–97, pt. 1, pp. 3–518. Washington DC: Government Printing Office.

Nelson, Edward William, and F. W. True

1887 Mammals of northern Alaska. *In* Report upon natural history collections made in Alaska between the years 1877 and 1881, by E. W. Nelson. Pp. 227–293. Washington DC: United States Army Signal Service.

Netsvetov, Iakov

1984 The journals of Iakov Netsvetov: The Yukon years, 1845–1863. Introduction and supplementary material by Lydia T. Black, trans. Richard A. Pierce, ed. Kingston ON: Limestone Press.

North Slope Borough, Commission on History and Culture

1977 Traditional land use inventory, Anaktuvuk Pass. Manuscript on file at the North Slope Borough, Barrow AK.

1980 Qiñiqtuagaksrat utuqqanaaat Iñuuniaġniŋisiqun: The traditional land use inventory for the mid–Beaufort Sea, vol. 1. Barrow AK: North Slope Borough, Commission on History and Culture.

North Slope Borough, Planning Commission and Historical Commission

1976a Traditional land use inventory, national petroleum reserve in Alaska: Teshekpuk Lake and Nuiqsut area. Barrow AK: North Slope Borough, Planning Commission and Historical Commission.

1976b Traditional land use inventory, national petroleum reserve in Alaska: Wainwright area. Barrow AK: North Slope Borough, Planning Commission and Historical Commission.

Northwest Arctic Television Center

n.d. Inupiaq Heritage Series, videotape 7. Kotzebue: Northwest Arctic Television Center.

Northwest Iñupiat Elders Conference

1976 Transcripts of elders conferences held in various locations in 1976. On file at Northwest Arctic Borough School District, Kotzebue.

1983 Transcripts of elders conferences held in Deering in 1983. On file at Northwest Arctic Borough School District, Kotzebue.

Numnik, Ida

1978 Trade fair at Nirlik. Handwritten manuscript dated January 19. Copy in possession of the author, courtesy of David Libbey.

Oberg, Kalervo

1973 The social economy of the Tlingit Indians. Seattle: University of Washington Press.

Okladnikov, A. P.

1963 The introduction of iron in the Sovjet Arctic and Far East. Folk 5:249–258.

O'Leary, Matthew

1995a Geography and chronology of central Yupiit warrior traditions. Paper presented at the Annual Meeting of the Alaska Anthropological Association, Anchorage.

1995b Annotated place-name map of the Seward Peninsula and Norton Sound regions. On file at the United States Bureau of Indian Affairs, ANCSA Office, Anchorage.

Oquilluk, William A.

1973 People of Kauwerak: Legends of the northern Eskimo. Anchorage: Alaska Methodist University.

Orth, Donald J.

1967 Dictionary of Alaska place names. United States Geological Survey. Professional Paper 567.

Osgood, Cornelius

1936 Contributions to the ethnography of the Kutchin. New Haven CT: Yale University.

1937 The ethnography of the Tanaina. New Haven CT: Yale University.

1958 Ingalik social culture. New Haven CT: Yale University.

Ostermann, Hother, ed.

1942 The Mackenzie Eskimos, after Knud Rasmussen's posthumous notes. *In* Report of the fifth Thule expedition 1921–24, vol. 10, no. 2. Copenhagen: Gyldendal.

Ostermann, Hother, and Erik Holtved, eds.

1952 The Alaska Eskimos, as described in the posthumous notes of Dr. Knud Rasmussen. *In* Report of the fifth Thule expedition 1921–24, vol. 10, no. 3. Copenhagen: Gyldendal.

Oswalt, Wendell H.

1963 Mission of change in Alaska: Eskimos and Moravians on the Kuskokwim. San Marino CA: Huntington Library.

Owens, Raymond

1971 Industrialization and the Indian joint family. Ethnology 10(2):223–250.

Paneak, Simon Panniaq

1970 Personal oral communication to the author, Anaktuvuk Pass, April 28.

1971a Indian and Kobuk disputes; hunting trips. Doris Duke Foundation Oral History Archive 314, tape 842. University of New Mexico, General Library, Albuquerque.

1971b Oral narratives. Doris Duke Foundation Oral History Archive 314, tape 843. University of New Mexico, General Library, Albuquerque.

Peregrine, Peter N.

1996 Introduction: World-systems theory and archaeology. *In* Pre-Columbian world-systems. Peter N. Peregrine and Gary M. Feinman, eds. Pp. 1–10. Madison WI: Prehistory Press.

Petersen, Robert

1984 East Greenland before 1950. *In* Arctic. David Damas, ed. Vol. 5, Handbook of

North American Indians. William C. Sturtevant, gen. ed. Pp. 622–639. Washington DC: Smithsonian Institution Press.

Peterson, Nicolas

1976 The natural and cultural areas of Aboriginal Australia: A preliminary analysis of population groupings with adaptive significance. *In* Tribes and boundaries in Australia. Nicolas Peterson, ed. Pp. 50–71. Canberra: Australian Institute of Aboriginal Studies.

Phebus, George, Jr.

1972 Alaskan Eskimo life in the 1890s as sketched by Native artists. Washington DC: Smithsonian Institution Press.

Pierce, Richard A.

1990 Russian America: A biographical dictionary. Kingston ON: Limestone Press.

Pospisil, Leopold

1964 Law and societal structure among the Nunamiut Eskimo. *In* Explorations in cultural anthropology: Essays in honor of George Peter Murdock. Ward H. Goodenough, ed. Pp. 395–431. New York: McGraw-Hill.

Pratt, Kenneth L.

1984 Classification of Eskimo groupings in the Yukon–Kuskokwim region: A critical analysis. Études/Inuit/Studies 8(supplementary issue):45–61.

Prentiss, William C., and Ian Kuijt

2004 Introduction: The archaeology of the Plateau region of northwestern North America—Approaches to the evolution of complex hunter-gatherers. *In* Complex hunter-gatherers: Evolution and organization of prehistoric communities on the Plateau of northwestern North America. William C. Prentiss and Ian Kuijt, eds. Pp. vii–xvii. Salt Lake City: University of Utah Press.

Price, T. Douglas, and James A. Brown, eds.

1985 Prehistoric hunter-gatherers: The emergence of cultural complexity. Orlando FL: Academic Press.

Pringle, Heather

1997 New respect for metal's role in ancient Arctic cultures. Science 277(5,327): 766–767.

Pullen, H. E.

1979 The Pullen expedition in search of Sir John Franklin . . . Toronto: Arctic History Press.

Quwana

1940 Kuwana's story, as told to Froelich G. Rainey, Point Hope, Alaska. Froelich G. Rainey Collection. Archives, Alaska and Polar Regions Department, Rasmuson Library, University of Alaska Fairbanks.

Raboff, Adeline Peter

1999 Preliminary study of the western Gwich'in bands. American Indian Culture and Research Journal 23(2):1–25.

2001 *Iñuksuk*: Northern Koyukon, Gwich'in and lower Tanana, 1800–1901. Fairbanks: Alaska Native Knowledge Network.

Radcliffe-Brown, A. R.

1952 Structure and function in primitive society. London: Cohen and West.

Rainey, Froelich G.

1940 Partners: Field notes, Point Hope, Alaska. Original in possession of John Bockstoce; copy in possession of the author.

1947 The whale hunters of Tigara. Anthropological Papers of the American Museum of Natural History, vol. 41, pt. 2.

1971 The Ipiutak culture: Excavations at Point Hope, Alaska. Addison-Wesley Modular Publications in Anthropology, no. 8.

Rasmussen, Knud Johan Victor

1933 Across Arctic America: Narrative of the fifth Thule expedition. New York: G. P. Putnam's Sons.

Ray, Dorothy Jean

1963 The Eskimo and the land: Ownership and utilization. In Science in Alaska: Proceedings of the Thirteenth Alaska Science Conference, 1962. Pp. 19–27. Juneau.

1964 Nineteenth century settlements and settlement patterns in Bering Strait. Arctic Anthropology 2(2):61–94.

1967 Land tenure and polity of the Bering Strait Eskimos. Journal of the West 6(3):371–394.

1975a Early maritime trade with the Eskimo of Bering Strait and the introduction of firearms. Arctic Anthropology 12(1):1–9.

1975b The Eskimos of Bering Strait, 1650–1898. Seattle: University of Washington Press.

1977 Eskimo art: Tradition and innovation in North Alaska. Seattle: University of Washington Press.

1983 Ethnohistory in the Arctic: The Bering Strait Eskimo. R. A. Pierce, ed. Kingston ON: Limestone Press.

1984 Bering Strait Eskimo. *In* Arctic. David Damas, ed. Vol. 5, Handbook of North American Indians. William C. Sturtevant, gen. ed. Pp. 285–302. Washington DC: Smithsonian Institution Press.

Ray, Dorothy Jean, ed.

1966 The Eskimo of St. Michael and vicinity as related by H.M.W. Edmonds. Anthropological Papers of the University of Alaska 13(2):1–143.

Ray, Dorothy Jean, and Alfred A. Blaker

1967 Eskimo masks: Art and ceremony. Seattle: University of Washington Press.

Ray, Patrick Henry

1883 Work at Point Barrow, Alaska. *In* Work of the Signal Service in the Arctic regions. Signal Service Notes no. 5. Washington DC: Office of the Chief Signal Officer.

1885 Report of the international polar expedition to Point Barrow, Alaska. Washington DC: Government Printing Office.

Reanier, Richard E.

1995 The antiquity of Paleoindian materials in northern Alaska. Arctic Anthropology 32(1):31–50.

Redmond, Elsa M.

1998a The dynamics of chieftaincy and the development of chiefdoms. *In* Chiefdoms and chieftaincy in the Americas. Elsa M. Redmond, ed. Pp. 1–17. Gainesville: University Press of Florida.

1998b In war and peace: Alternative paths to centralized leadership. *In* Chiefdoms and chieftaincy in the Americas. Elsa M. Redmond, ed. Pp. 68–103. Gainesville: University Press of Florida.

Reinhardt, Gregory A.

2000 Personal oral and written communications, Fairbanks AK, March 24.

Reinhardt, Gregory A., and Albert A. Dekin Jr.

n.d. House structure and interior features. *In* Excavation of a prehistoric catastrophe: A preserved household from the Utqiaġvik village, Barrow, Alaska, by Daniel F. Cassedy, A. A. Dekin Jr., J. N. Kilmarx, R. R. Newell, C. R. Polglase, G. C. Reinhardt, and B. L. Turcy. Pp. 38–112. Barrow AK: North Slope Borough, Commission on Iñupiat History, Language and Culture.

Rigsby, Bruce, and Peter Sutton

1980–82 Speech communities in Aboriginal Australia. Anthropological Forum 5(1):8–23.

Rock, Sam Uyaġaq

1940 Sam's story. Froelich G. Rainey Collection. Archives, Alaska and Polar Regions Department, Rasmuson Library, University of Alaska Fairbanks.

Rogers, Edward S.

1965 Leadership among the Indians of eastern Subarctic Canada. Anthropologica n.s.(2):263–284.

1969 Band organization among the Indians of eastern Subarctic Canada. *In* Contributions to anthropology: Band societies. David Damas, ed. Pp. 21–50. National Museum of Canada Bulletin 228.

Ross, Anna Frances

1958 The Eskimo community-house. M.A. thesis, Department of Anthropology, Stanford University, Stanford CA.

Rosse, Irving C.

1883 Medical and anthropological notes on Alaska. *In* U.S. Revenue Service cruise of the Revenue-Steamer "Corwin" in Alaska and the N.W. Arctic Ocean in 1881, pp. 5–53. Washington DC: James Anglim.

Rudenko, S. I.

1961 The ancient culture of the Bering Sea and the Eskimo problem. Paul Tolstoy, trans. Anthropology of the North, Translations from Russian Sources no. 1. Toronto: University of Toronto Press for the Arctic Institute of North America.

Saario, Doris J.

1959 Progress report: Human ecology investigations, Kivalina, Alaska. Typescript report in possession of the author.

Sage, Mildred Kaguna

1965 Personal communication to the author, Kivalina AK, May 20.

Sage, Tommy Aġnagauraq

1964 Personal oral communication to the author, Kivalina AK, August 11.

1965 Personal oral communication to the author, Kivalina AK, August 25.

Sahlins, Marshall

1963 Poor man, rich man, big man, chief: Political types in Melanesia and Polynesia. Comparative Studies in Society and History 5(3):285–303.

Samms, Carrie

1897–98 Journal of Carrie Samms, June 9, 1887, through June 30, 1898. Archives, California Yearly Meeting of Friends Church, Whittier CA.

1899–1900 Friends Mission diary kept by Carrie Samms, July 1, 1899, through July 1, 1900. Archives, California Yearly Meeting of Friends Church, Whittier CA.

1901–2 Diary of Friends Mission from July 1, 1901, to July 3, 1902. Archives, California Yearly Meeting of Friends Church, Whittier CA.

Sampson, Joe Pukuluk

1970 Personal oral communication to the author, Noorvik AK, March 31.

Sanderson, Stephen K., and Thomas D. Hall

1995 Introduction [to pt. 2, World system approaches to world-historical change]. *In* Civilizations and world systems: Studying world-historical change. Stephen K. Sanderson, ed. Pp. 95–108. Walnut Creek CA: AltaMira Press.

Sarychev, Gavril A.

1806–7 Account of a voyage of discovery to the northeast of Siberia, the frozen ocean and the northeast sea. 2 vols. London: Richard Phillips.

Sauer, Martin

1802 An account of a geographical and astronomical expedition to the northern parts of Russia . . . in the years 1785 etc. to 1794. London: T. Cadell.

Savok, James Putuuqti, Sr.

1986 Personal oral communication to the author, Buckland AK, February 19.

Schneider, William S.

1976 Beaver AK: The story of a multi-ethnic community. Ann Arbor MI: University Microfilms.

1980 Written personal communication to the author, October 14.

Schneider, William, Sverre Pedersen, and David Libbey

1980 The Barrow–Atqasuk report: A study of land use values through time. Occasional Paper no. 24. North Slope Borough and the Anthropology and Historic Preservation Section, Cooperative Park Studies Unit, University of Alaska Fairbanks.

Schweitzer, Peter

1993 *Yanrakynnot*—history and ethnosocial trends of a Chukchi village. *In* Sibérie III: Questions sibériennes. Pp. 129–147. Paris.

Schweitzer, Peter P., and Evgeny Golovko

1995 Contacts across Bering Strait, as seen from Nevuqaq. *In* Traveling between continents, phase one: Report prepared for the United States National Park Service, Alaska Regional Office.

1997 Remembering and forgetting warfare: The cultural construction of external conflict in the Bering Strait area. Paper presented at the 96th Annual Meeting of the American Anthropological Association, Washington DC, December 19–23.

Seemann, Berthold Carl

1853 Narrative of the voyage of H.M.S. "Herald" during the years 1845–51 . . . in search of Sir John Franklin. 2 vols. London: Reeve and Company.

Senungetuk, Vivian, and Paul Tiulana

1987 A place for winter: Paul Tiulana's story. Anchorage: CIRI Foundation.

Service, Elman

1962 Primitive social organization. New York: Random House.

1968 War and our contemporary ancestors. *In* War: The anthropology of armed conflict and aggression. Morton Fried, M. Harris, and R. Murphy, eds. Pp. 160–167. New York: Natural History Press.

1975 Origins of the state and civilization: The process of cultural evolution. New York: W. W. Norton.

Shannon, Thomas R.

1996 An introduction to the world-system perspective. Boulder CO: Westview Press.

Sheehan, Glenn W.

1995 Whaling surplus, trade, war, and the integration of prehistoric northern and northwestern Alaska economies, A.D. 1200–1826. *In* Hunting the largest animals: Native whaling in the western Arctic and Subarctic. Allen P. McCartney, ed. Pp. 185–206. Studies in Whaling no. 3; Occasional Publication no. 36. Edmonton: Canadian Circumpolar Institute.

1997 In the belly of the whale: Trade and war in Eskimo society. Aurora Monograph Series 6. Anchorage: Alaska Anthropological Association.

Sheppard, William L.

1983 Continuity and change in Norton Sound: Historic sites and their contexts. Anthropology and Historic Preservation Section, Cooperative Park Studies Unit, University of Alaska Fairbanks.

Shinkwin, Anne, and Mary Pete

1984 Yup'ik Eskimo societies: A case study. Études/Inuit/Studies 8(supplementary issue):95–112.

Silberbauer, George B.

1995 Personal written communication to the author, July 4.

Silook, Roger S.

1976 *Seevookuk*: Stories the old people told on St. Lawrence Island. Anchorage: Privately printed.

Sim, Francis M., and David Smallen

1972 Defining system boundaries. Paper presented at the Annual Meeting of the Canadian Sociology and Anthropology Association, Montreal, May 31.

Simon, James J. K.

1998 Twentieth century Iñupiaq Eskimo reindeer herding on northern Seward Peninsula, Alaska. Ann Arbor MI: UMI Dissertation Services.

Simpson, John

1850 Journal of a journey from Chamisso Island to Spafarief Bay, January 9–12, 1850. John Simpson Papers, box 3, Eskimo files, accounts of voyages, general, September 1849–March 1854. Rare Book, Manuscript, and Special Collections Library, Duke University.

1852–54 Point Barrow Journal, 1852–1854. John Simpson Papers, box 5, accounts of voyages, oversized, 1851–54. Rare Book, Manuscript, and Special Collections Library, Duke University.

1855 Observations on the western Esquimaux and the country they inhabit; from notes taken during two years at Point Barrow, by Mr. John Simpson, Surgeon, R.N., Her Majesty's Discovery Ship "Plover." In Great Britain, Parliament, House of Commons. Sessional Papers. Accounts and Papers 1854–55, vol. 35, no. 1898, pp. 917–942.

1875 Observations on the western Eskimo and the country they inhabit. *In* A selection of papers on Arctic geography and ethnology, reprinted and presented to the Arctic expedition of 1875. Pp. 233–275. London: Royal Geographical Society.

Simpson, Thomas

1843 Narrative of the discoveries on the north coast of America: Effected by the officers of the Hudson's Bay Company during the years 1836–39. London: R. Bentley.

Skin, Ray

1970 Personal oral communication to the author, Selawik AK, March 10.

Slobodin, Richard

1960 Eastern Kutchin warfare. Anthropologica n.s. 2(1):76–94.

1981 Kutchin. *In* Subarctic. June Helm, ed. Vol. 6, Handbook of North American Indians. William G. Sturtevant, gen. ed. Pp. 514–532. Washington DC: Smithsonian Institution Press.

Smith, Charlie Nalikkałuk

1970 Personal oral communication to the author, Selawik AK, January 17.

Smith, Derek G.

1984 Mackenzie Delta Eskimo. *In* Arctic. David Damas, ed. Vol. 5, Handbook of North American Indians. William C. Sturtevant, gen. ed. Pp. 347–358. Washington DC: Smithsonian Institution Press.

Smith, Elijah Everett

1873 Vocabulary of the Malemute, Kotzebue. Manuscript on file at the Bureau of American Ethnology Library, Smithsonian Institution, Washington DC.

Smith, Philip Sidney

1913 The Noatak–Kobuk region of Alaska. United States Geological Survey Bulletin 536. Washington DC: Government Printing Office.

Smith, Philip S., and J. B. Mertie

1930 Geology and mineral resources of Northwestern Alaska. United States Geological Survey Bulletin 815. Washington DC: Government Printing Office.

Snaith, Skip

1997 Umiak: An illustrated guide. Eastbound WA: Walrose and Hyde.

Sokonik, Joe

1918 The story of *Kai-ya-yuh-tua-look*. Eskimo 2(5).

Solecki, Ralph S.

1951 Archaeology and ecology of the Arctic Slope of Alaska. *In* Annual report of the Board of Regents of the Smithsonian Institution for 1950. Pp. 469–495. Washington DC: Government Printing Office.

Solomon, Madeline

1981 Madeline Solomon-Koyukuk: A biography. Blaine WA: Hancock House.

Sours, Lena Suuyuk

1987 Personal oral communication to the author, Kotzebue AK, February 26.

Spencer, Robert Francis

1952 Field notes from Barrow AK. Originals in possession of the author.

1959 The North Alaskan Eskimo: A study in ecology and society. Bureau of American Ethnology Bulletin no. 171. Washington DC: Government Printing Office.

1984 North Alaska coast Eskimo. *In* Arctic. David Damas, ed. Vol. 5, Handbook of North American Indians. William C. Sturtevant, gen. ed. Pp. 320–337. Washington DC: Smithsonian Institution Press.

Stalker, John Pamiiqtaq

1964 Personal oral communication to the author, Kivalina AK, September 26.

1970 Personal oral communication to the author, Shungnak AK, January 27.

1986 Personal oral communication to the author, Noatak AK, February 25.

Stanford, Dennis J.

1976 The Walakpa site AK: Its place in the Birnirk and Thule cultures. Washington DC: Smithsonian Institution Press.

Stanner, W. E. H.

1965 Aboriginal territorial organization: Estate, range, domain, and regime. Oceania 36(1):1–26.

Stefansson, Vilhjalmur

1909 Northern Alaska in winter. American Geographical Society Bulletin 41(10): 601–610.

1914a Prehistoric and present commerce among the Arctic coast Eskimo. Geological Survey of Canada, Museum Bulletin no. 6.

1914b The Stefansson–Anderson Arctic expedition of the American Museum: Preliminary ethnological report. Anthropological Papers of the American Museum of Natural History, vol. 14, pt. 1.

1933 Introduction, to the anthropometry of the Western and Copper Eskimos, based on data of Vilhjalmur Stefansson by Carl C. Seltzer. Human Biology 5(3): 313–370.

1944 The friendly Arctic: The story of five years in the polar regions. New ed. with new material. New York: Macmillan.

1951 My life with the Eskimo. New York: Macmillan.

Stiner, Mary C., Natalie D. Munro, and Todd A. Surovell

2000 The tortoise and the hare: Small-game use, the broad-spectrum revolution, and Paleolithic demography (with CA comment). Current Anthropology 41(1): 39–73.

Stiner, Mary C., Natalie D. Munro, Todd A. Surovell, Eitan Tchernov, and Ofer Bar-Yosef

1999 Paleolithic population growth pulses evidenced by small animal exploitation. Science 283(5,399):190–194.

Stoney, George Morse

n.d. Report of the "northern Alaska exploring expedition, April 13, 1884–November 9, 1886." Ms. no. 2925. National Anthropological Archives, Smithsonian Institution, Washington DC.

1883 Survey of Hotham Inlet and the Kobuk delta: Letters received by the Revenue Cutter Service, 1867–1914. H37, vol. 40, 1883. Records of the Coast Guard, Record Group 26. National Archives, Washington DC. (Also on microcopy 641, roll 1, frames 640–641.)

1900 Naval explorations in Alaska. United States Naval Institute Proceedings, September and December 1899, 91:533–584, 92:799–849.

Stuck, Hudson

1914 Ten thousand miles with a dog sled. New York: Charles Scribner's Sons.

1917 Voyages on the Yukon and its tributaries. New York: Charles Scribner's Sons.

1920 A winter circuit of our Arctic coast. New York: Charles Scribner's Sons.

Sun, Joe Immałuuraq

1970 Personal oral communication to the author, Shungnak AK, February 28.

1985 My life and other stories. Susie Sun, trans. David Libbey, comp. Kotzebue: NANA Museum of the Arctic.

Sunno, Andrew Sannu

1951a Aŋuiaktuq: War. Personal oral communication to Charles Lucier. Charles Lucier private collection, AS-KAN-23. Transcript in possession of the author.

1951b Before the Buckland messenger feast. Charles Lucier Collection, box 3, folder 4. Archives, Alaska and Polar Regions Department, Rasmuson Library, University of Alaska Fairbanks.

1951c A cycle of games and contests following the gift exchange at the messenger feast, Buckland. Charles Lucier Collection, box 3, folder 4. Archives, Alaska and Polar Regions Department, Rasmuson Library, University of Alaska Fairbanks.

1951d Indians live at Igloo Point. Personal oral communication to Charles Lucier. Charles Lucier private collection, AS-KAN-60. Transcript in possession of the author.

1951e Iñuktat: Place of the dead. Personal oral communication to Charles Lucier. Charles Lucier private collection, AS-KAN-61. Transcript in possession of the author.

1951f Kivyiksuat: Messenger feast at Buckland. Personal oral communication to Charles Lucier. Charles Lucier private collection, AS-KAN-11. Transcript in possession of the author.

1951g Trading songs. Personal oral communication to Charles Lucier. Charles Lucier private collection, AS-KAN-77. Transcript in possession of the author.

Suttles, Wayne

1990 Introduction. *In* Northwest Coast. Wayne Suttles, ed. Vol. 7, Handbook of North American Indians. William C. Sturtevant, gen. ed. Pp. 1–15. Washington DC: Smithsonian Institution Press.

Sutton, Peter

1991 Language in Aboriginal Australia: Social dialects in a geographic idiom. *In* Language in Australia. Suzanne Romaine, ed. Pp. 49–66. Cambridge: Cambridge University Press.

Swan, Charlotte Saviugan

1964a Personal oral communication to the author, Kivalina AK, October 5.

1964b Personal oral communication to the author, Kivalina AK, October 8.

Swan, Clinton Iŋnitchiaq

1964 Personal oral communication to the author, Kivalina AK, July 23.

1965 Personal oral communication to the author, Kivalina AK, August 15.

1983 Personal oral communication to the author, Kivalina AK, June 14.

1984 Personal oral communication to the author, Kivalina AK, March 7.

1989 The old woman and her fire power. *In* Lore of the Iñupiat: The elders speak, vol. 1. Hannah Mendenhall, Ruthie Sampson, and Edward Tennant, eds. Pp. 112–115. Kotzebue: Northwest Arctic Borough School District.

Swan, Martha Nunamiu

1965a Personal oral communication to the author, Kivalina AK, June 5.

1965b Personal oral communication to the author, Kivalina AK, August 18.

1965c Personal oral communication to the author, Kivalina AK, August 27.

1970 Personal oral communication to the author, Kivalina AK, February 10.

1984 Personal oral communication to the author, Kivalina AK, May 5.

Swan, Martha Nunamiu, and Milton Niaqualuk Swan

1965 Personal oral communication to the author, Kivalina AK, August 27.

Swan, Milton Niaqualuk

1965 Personal oral communication to the author, Kivalina AK, August 27.

Swan, Oscar Kiñugana

1964 Personal oral communication to the author, Kivalina AK, October 4.

Terrell, John Edward

1998 30,000 years of culture contact in the southwest Pacific. *In* Studies in culture contact: Interaction, culture change, and archaeology. James G. Cusick, ed. Pp. 191–219. Occasional Paper no. 25. Carbondale: Center for Archaeological Investigations, Southern Illinois University.

Testart, Alain

1982 The significance of food storage among hunter-gatherers: Residence patterns, population densities, and social inequalities. Current Anthropology 23(5): 523–304.

Thalbitzer, William Carl

1914 Ethnographical collections from east Greenland (Angmagsalik and Nualik) made by G. Holm, G. Amdrup, and J. Petersen, described by W. Thalbitzer. The Ammassalik Eskimo, pt. 1, no. 7. Meddelelser om Grønland 39:319–755.

Thomas, Susie Siqvaun

1970 Personal oral communication to the author, Deering AK, April 15.

Thornton, Harrison R.

1931 Among the Eskimos of Wales, Alaska, 1890–93. Neda S. Thornton and William M. Thornton, eds. Baltimore MD: Johns Hopkins Press.

Tickett, Herman Aumaałuuraq

1969 Personal oral communication to the author, Kotzebue AK, December 31.

1970 Personal oral communication to the author, Kotzebue AK, May 8.

Tobuk, Frank

1981 Arcticers attack Sickrik in winter. Alaska Geographic 8(3):61–62.

Townsend, Joan B.

1983 Firearms against Native arms: A study in comparative efficiencies with an Alaskan example. Arctic Anthropology 20(2):1–33.

Trollope, Henry

1855 Journal kept by Commander Henry Trollope during a trip from H.M. Sloop "Rattlesnake" in Port Clarence to King-A-Ghee, a village four or five miles round Cape Prince of Wales, January 9, 1854–January 27, 1854. In Great Britain, Parliament, House of Commons. Sessional Papers. Accounts and Papers, 1854–55, vol. 35, no. 1898, pp. 868–879.

Tuckfield, Bob Qipmiuraq, and Christopher Tiŋuk Tingook

1960 Notes from an interview by Don Foote, Point Hope, Alaska, February 1, 1960. In Don Charles Foote Papers, box 5, folder 6. Archives, Alaska and Polar Regions Department, Rasmuson Library, University of Alaska Fairbanks.

Turck, Thomas J., and Diane L. Lehman Turck

1992 Trading posts along the Yukon River: Noochuloghoyet trading post in historical context. Arctic 45(1):51–61.

Turney-High, H.

1949 Primitive war: Its practice and concepts. Columbia: University of South Carolina Press.

Ungarook, Andy

1952 Personal oral communication to Robert F. Spencer, Barrow, Alaska, September 4, 1952. Field notes of Robert F. Spencer, Barrow, Alaska. Notebook 2. Pp. 88–88d. Original notes in the possession of the author.

United States Department of the Interior, Bureau of Indian Affairs

n.d. Report of investigation for Allutunittuq, NANA Regional Corporation. BLC F-22300. Bureau of Indian Affairs, ANCSA Office, Anchorage.

1987a Interview of Paul Stanley by Debra Corbett and Lisa Hutchinson, Selawik AK, June 18. Mary Savok, interpreter. Transcript 87NAN15. Bureau of Indian Affairs, ANCSA Office 14(h)1 Program, Anchorage.

1987b Interview of Minnie Gray, Mark Cleveland, and Clara Lee by Robert Drozda and David Staley, Ambler AK, July 11. Transcript 87NAN31. Bureau of Indian Affairs, ANCSA Office, 14(h)1 Program, Anchorage.

1987c Interview of Harold Downey, John Stalker, and Kenneth Ashby by Robert Drozda, Noatak AK, August 11. Rick Ashby, interpreter. Transcript 87NAN46. Bureau of Indian Affairs, ANCSA Office, 14(h)1 Program, Anchorage.

1988 Report of investigation for Pastuliarraq, Calista Corporation. BLM AA-10071, BLM AA10391. Bureau of Indian Affairs, ANCSA Office, Anchorage.

1991 Report of investigation for Millitaavik, Bering Straits Native Corporation. BLM F-22006. Bureau of Indian Affairs, ANCSA Office, Anchorage.

1995 Report of investigation for Qaġriuġvik, Bering Straits Native Corporation. BLM F-21974. Bureau of Indian Affairs, ANCSA Office, Anchorage.

1996 Report of investigation for Pingu, Bering Straits Native Corporation. BLM F-21963. Bureau of Indian Affairs, ANCSA Office, Anchorage.

Usher, Peter

1971 The Canadian western Arctic: A century of change. Anthropologica 8(1–2):169–183.

1976 Fur trade posts of the Northwest Territories, 1870–1970. *In* Supporting studies. Vol. 2 of Inuit land use and occupancy project. Milton M. R. Freeman, ed. Pp. 153–168. Ottawa: Supply and Services Canada.

VanStone, James W.

1959 Russian exploration in interior Alaska: An extract from the journal of Andrei Glazunov. Pacific Northwest Quarterly 50(2):37–47.

1960 An early nineteenth century artist in Alaska: Louis Choris and the first Kotzebue expedition. Pacific Northwest Quarterly 51(5):145–158.

1962 Notes on nineteenth century trade in the Kotzebue Sound area, Alaska. Arctic Anthropology 1(1):126–128.

1976a The Bruce collection of Eskimo material culture from Port Clarence, Alaska. Fieldiana: Anthropology 67.

1976b The Yukon River Ingalik: Subsistence, the fur trade, and a changing resource base. Ethnohistory 23(3):198–212. (Published in 1978.)

1979a Athapaskan–Eskimo relations in west-central Alaska: An ethnohistorical perspective. Arctic Anthropology 16(2):152–159.

1979b Ingalik contact ecology: An ethnohistory of the lower-middle Yukon, 1790–1935. Fieldiana: Anthropology 71.

1980 The Bruce collection of Eskimo material culture from Kotzebue Sound, Alaska. Fieldiana: Anthropology n.s. 1.

1983 Protective hide body armor of the historic Chukchi and Siberian Eskimos. Études/Inuit/Studies 7(2):3–24.

1984 Exploration and contact history of western Alaska. *In* Arctic. David Damas, ed. Vol. 5, Handbook of North American Indians. William J. Sturtevant, gen. ed. Pp. 149–160. Washington DC: Smithsonian Institution Press.

VanStone, James W., ed.

1973 V. S. Khromchenko's coastal explorations in southwestern Alaska, 1822. David H. Kraus, trans. Fieldiana: Anthropology 64.

1977 A. F. Kashevarov's coastal explorations in northwest Alaska, 1838. David H. Kraus, trans. Fieldiana: Anthropology 69.

1988 Russian exploration in southwest Alaska: The travel journals of Petr Korsakovskiy (1818) and Ivan Ya. Vasilev (1829). David H. Kraus, trans. Fairbanks: University of Alaska Press.

VanStone, James W., and Ives Goddard

1981 Territorial groups of west-central Alaska before 1898. *In* Subarctic. June Helm, ed. Vol. 6, Handbook of North American Indians. William G. Sturtevant, gen. ed. Pp. 556–561. Washington DC: Smithsonian Institution Press.

Van Valin, William B.

1944 Eskimoland speaks. Caldwell ID: Caxton Printers.

Varjola, Pirjo, with contributions by Julia P. Averkieva and Roza G. Liapunova

1990 The Etholén collection: The ethnographic Alaskan collection of Adolf Etholén and his contemporaries in the National Museum of Finland. Helsinki: National Board of Antiquities of Finland.

Vayda, Andrew

1960 Maori warfare. Maori Monographs no. 2. Wellington: Polynesian Society.

1967 Pomo trade feasts. *In* Tribal and peasant economies. George Dalton, ed. Pp. 494–500. Garden City NY: Natural History Press.

1968 Hypotheses about functions of war. *In* War: The anthropology of armed conflict and aggression. M. Fried, M. Harris, and R. Murphy, eds. Pp. 85–91. Garden City NY: Natural History Press.

Vestal, Leonard Putuuraq

1969 Personal oral communication to the author, Kotzebue AK, December 31.

1970 Personal oral communication to the author, Kotzebue AK, May 4.

Walker, Nelson

1969a Personal oral communication to the author, Kotzebue AK, October 27.

1969b Personal oral communication to the author, Kotzebue AK, December 11.

Wallerstein, Immanuel

1974a The rise and future demise of the world capitalist system: Concepts for comparative analysis. Comparative Studies in Society and History 16(4):387–415.

1974b The modern world system: Capitalist agriculture and the origins of European world-economy in the sixteenth century. New York: Academic Press.

Wells, Roger, and John W. Kelly

1890 English–Eskimo and Eskimo–English vocabularies, preceded by ethnographical memoranda concerning the Arctic Eskimos in Alaska and Siberia. Bureau of Education Circular of Information no. 2. Washington DC: Government Printing Office.

Weyer, Edward M., Jr.

1928 Field notes of the Stoll–McCracken expedition. Department of Anthropology Archives, American Museum of Natural History, New York.

1962 The Eskimos: Their environment and folkways. Hamden CT: Archon Books.

Weyiouanna, Alex Nuusi

1999 Personal oral communication to the author, Shishmaref AK, March 5.

White, James T.

1889 Diary, "Bear" cruise, 1889. Gary Stein, transcriber. James T. White Papers. Archives, University of Alaska Anchorage.

Whymper, Frederick

1868 A journey from Norton Sound, Bering Sea, to Fort Yukon. Journal of the Royal Geographical Society 38:219–237.

1869a Russian America, or "Alaska": The Natives of the Youkon River and adjacent country. Transactions of the Ethnological Society of London 7:167–185.

1869b Travel and adventure in the territory of Alaska. New York: Harper and Bros.

Widmer, Randolph J.

1988 The evolution of the Calusa, a nonagricultural chiefdom on the southwest Florida coast. Tuscaloosa: University of Alabama Press.

Wiessner, Polly

1983 Style and social information in Kalahari San projectile points. American Antiquity 48(2):253–276.

Wilkinson, David

1993 Civilizations, cores, world economies, and oikumenes. *In* The world system: Five hundred years or five thousand? Andre Gunder Frank and Barry K. Gills, eds. Pp. 221–246. London: Routledge.

Williams, Nancy M.

1982 A boundary is to cross: Observations on Yolngu boundaries and permission. *In* Resource Managers: North American and Australian hunter-gatherers. Nancy M. Williams and Eugene S. Hunn, eds. Pp. 131–153. Boulder CO: Westview Press.

Williams, Susie Helohoołtunh

1991 Personal oral communication to the author, Fairbanks AK, March 14.

Wobst, H. Martin

1974 Boundary conditions for Paleolithic social systems: A simulation approach. American Antiquity 39:147–148.

1976 Locational relationships in Paleolithic society. Journal of Human Evolution 5(1):49–58.

Wolf, Eric R.

1982 Europe and the people without history. Berkeley: University of California Press.

Wolfe, James

n.d. Journal of a voyage on discovery in the Pacific and Beering's Straits on board H.M.S. "Blossom," Capt. F. W. Beechey. Manuscript, Beinecke Rare Book and Manuscript Library, Yale University, New Haven CT.

Wood, Charley Ulugaaġruk

1931 The Oppownie (old) Eskimo and his customs, as told by Eliyak (Pechuk) and Oolooaharuk (Charley Wood) to Ira S. Purkeypile, Selawik AK. Transcript appended to Bulletin of the Northwest District, United States Department of the Interior, Office of Indian Affairs, Alaska Division, October 28 (Kotzebue). Laurel Bland Collection, box 30, folder 38. Archives, Alaska and Polar Regions Department, Rasmuson Library, University of Alaska Fairbanks.

Woodburn, James

1980 Hunters and gatherers today and reconstruction of the past. *In* Soviet and Western anthropology. Ernest Gellner, ed. Pp. 95–117. New York: Columbia University Press.

1982 Egalitarian societies. Man 17(3):431–451.

Woodbury, Anthony C.

1984 Eskimo and Aleut languages. In Arctic. David Damas, ed. Vol. 5, Handbook of North American Indians. William C. Sturtevant, gen. ed. Pp. 49–63. Washington DC: Smithsonian Institution Press.

Woolfe, Henry D.

1893 The seventh or Arctic district. *In* Report on the population and resources of Alaska: Eleventh census of the United States, 1890, by Robert Porter. Pp. 129–152. Washington DC: Government Printing Office.

Wrangell, Ferdinand P. von

1980 Russian America: Statistical and ethnographic information. Mary Sadouski, trans. Richard A. Pierce, ed. Kingston ON: Limestone Press.

Wright, John Qaniqsiruaq

1969 Personal oral communication to the author, Kotzebue AK, December 10.

Wright, Miranda

1995a Joys and conflicts of being a native anthropologist. Northern Review 14(summer):59–63.

1995b The last great Indian war (Nulato 1951). M.A. thesis, University of Alaska Fairbanks.

Znamenski, Andrei A.

1999 "Vague sense of belonging to the Russian Empire": The Reindeer Chukchi's status in nineteenth century northeastern Siberia. Arctic Anthropology 36(1–2):19–36.

Index

Page numbers in italics indicate illustrations.

www.ingramcontent.com/pod-product-compliance
Ingram Content Group UK Ltd.
Pitfield, Milton Keynes, MK11 3LW, UK
UKHW041907060225
454777UK00001B/119